EPIDEMIC ORIENTALISM

EPIDEMIC ORIENTALISM

*Race, Capital, and the Governance
of Infectious Disease*

ALEXANDRE I. R. WHITE

STANFORD UNIVERSITY PRESS
Stanford, California

STANFORD UNIVERSITY PRESS
Stanford, California

Printed in the United States of America on acid-free, archival-quality paper

Library of Congress Cataloging-in-Publication Data

Names: White, Alexandre Ilani Rein, author.
Title: Epidemic orientalism : race, capital, and the governance of
    infectious disease / Alexandre I.R. White.
Description: Stanford, California : Stanford University Press, 2023. |
    Includes bibliographical references and index.
Identifiers: LCCN 2022015695 (print) | LCCN 2022015696 (ebook) |
    ISBN 9781503630260 (cloth) | ISBN 9781503634121 (paperback) |
    ISBN 9781503634138 (ebook)
Subjects: LCSH: Epidemics—Prevention—International cooperation—History.
    | Communicable diseases—Prevention—International cooperation—History. |
    Imperialism—Health aspects—History. | Racism—Health aspects—History. |
    Public health—Political aspects—History.
Classification: LCC RA643 .W385 2023 (print) | LCC RA643 (ebook) |
    DDC 614.409—dc23/eng/20220628
LC record available at https://lccn.loc.gov/2022015695
LC ebook record available at https://lccn.loc.gov/2022015696

Cover design: Jason Anscomb

Cover art: Boris Artzybasheff, *World Map of the Major Tropical Diseases*,
David Rumsey Historical Map Collection.

Typeset by Newgen in 10.5/15 Minion Pro

For Erica Jawin

CONTENTS

Preface   ix

Acknowledgments   xv

Introduction   1

1   Epidemic Orientalism   53

2   The International Sanitary Conventions at   90
    a Colonial Scale

3   Epidemics Under the WHO   128

4   The Battle to Police Disease   171

5   Epidemics, Power, and the Global Management   198
    of Disease Risk

6   Pricing Pandemics   227

    Conclusion   249

    Notes   253
    Index   295

PREFACE

On January 30, 2020, the Danish newspaper *Jyllands-Posten*, infamous for publishing deeply insensitive cartoons of the prophet Muhammad in 2005, published a satirical image of the Chinese flag with the characteristic yellow stars replaced by the recognizable image of a coronavirus. Depictions in the Belgian, Dutch, and Mexican press have also produced similar images, but with the international symbol for biohazard.

Epidemics reflect the political, social, and economic circumstances in which they emerge. Within the responses to a seemingly natural event lie the lenses through which medical actors, public health officials, and political and economic authorities perceive and assess the threat of infectious disease. Far before the events of this book, epidemics were blamed upon those most marginalized in society. In response to the Black Death in the fourteenth century and in addition to a host of other anti-Semitic prejudices, many Jews were burned at the stake, expelled from European cities or forced to convert to Christianity.[1] While this work itself touches on some of the disease controls that centered upon racial and xenophobic anxieties in the early period of European colonization in the fifteenth and sixteenth centuries, it was in the nineteenth century that understandings of contagion and disease spread came to be viewed through a wider prism of medical knowledge, global politics, and economic risks that have augmented the perceptions of how epidemic threat is understood globally and how epidemic responses are carried out.

In writing this book I hope to show the continuities and shifts within the history of international infectious disease control and the legacies of nineteenth-century practices of disease control that in some forms persist to this day. The deeply racial, xenophobic anxieties around infectious disease, motivated by concerns of disease spreading to the West, continue to animate responses and affect global health priorities in the present. This particular European- and Western-centric perspective is still evident in the distasteful cartoons discussed earlier.

COVID-19 has done more than merely expose the underlying xenophobia and racism evident in the history of international infectious disease control. It has also exposed the ways in which these histories have built a durable myth of the West's supremacy over infectious disease and its relative invulnerability to these pathogens. This myth has been exposed and operates very much to the detriment of the inhabitants of the West.

The eradication of smallpox, the mostly successful eradication of polio, and the development of vaccines against childhood diseases like measles, mumps, and rubella have made these formerly devastating illnesses a lingering concern only if anti-vaccination discourses take hold in the West's cosmopolitan centers. By the 1970s and especially after the eradication of smallpox, there was optimism that the era of infectious disease was over for humanity. The merciless pandemic of HIV/AIDS shattered this belief, though after tens of millions of lives have been lost, HIV/AIDS has become a chronic disease that can be controlled and managed in pharmaceutical and bureaucratic ways. Access to treatments continue to differ drastically by geography, access to resources, and social inequalities.

Prior to 2020, biomedical and technical optimism had led to the somewhat comfortable acceptance among leaders, many (though not all) health actors, and the general public in Europe and North America that major epidemics or pandemics, especially of novel diseases, are rare or unlikely to occur at home in as devastating a fashion as they can in the rest of the world—or at the very least, the dynamics will be different.[2] A triumphalist reading of the history of twentieth-century public health in the West could read as (to paraphrase Sylvia Wynter) a history of "securing the well-being of the Western bourgeois conception of man."[3] Dr. Peter Piot, the discoverer of the Ebola virus suggested that he "would happily sit next to an Ebola Suffer on the Tube [London underground system]" in an effort to calm concerns and stigma around the threat of Ebola arriving from West Africa to the United Kingdom.[4] His statement suggested that citizens need not be frightened of the disease because the dynamics of contagion and the health systems in the United Kingdom made it very unlikely that the epidemic dynamics that had occurred in Liberia, Guinea, and Sierra Leone could occur in Britain.

Piot's statement suggested that the crisis the world was witnessing playing out via news outlets, on social media, and on our phones and televisions would not occur "over here." The scenes of doctors dressed in what looked like space suits with limited access to personal protective equipment,[5] overworked and at high risk for contracting the disease themselves, were widely publicized as a ghastly reminder of the limited capacities of African health systems to care for their populations.[6]

In places far away from the epicenter of the epidemic, much of the world watched as victims of Ebola virus disease died lonely deaths far away from their loved ones, to be buried under intense sanitary controls without formal ceremonies carried out by their families. The prolonged epidemic was blamed on "West African cultural practices," widespread ignorance of science, mistrust in doctors, and a host of other banal actions that outside of an epidemic were barely scrutinized but under the harsh gaze of illness had now been pathologized as the markers of backwards people and unhealthy behavior.[7] Social distancing, isolation, quarantine, and curfews were seen as the scrambling practices of a bygone epidemic order, wholly alien from the sanitized spaces of modern hospitals and the cosmopolitan streets of US and European urban metropoles.[8] These tropes of chaos, horror, and cultural incommensurability with modern medicine harken back to early twenty-first-century discussions about South African presidents Thabo Mbeki and Jacob Zuma's HIV/AIDS denialism[9] and claims that the disease could be prevented by showering.[10]

COVID-19, an acronym for Coronavirus Disease 2019—a term less evocative of place than Ebola virus disease, Zika virus, or Middle East Respiratory Syndrome and less rooted in time than bubonic plague, cholera, or yellow fever—is a modern pandemic that has shattered the myth that the West had transcended the era of pandemic vulnerability or that it was *sufficiently civilized* to respond to such threats better than the rest of the world.

In New York City (the global epicenter of the pandemic for some time), victims of COVID-19 died alone without family beside them in some of the most technically advanced hospitals, their doctors rationing personal protective equipment as they fight an epidemic threatening to cripple the health system. In March 2020, at a moment of reflection, former president Trump considered the horror of the spectacle he was witnessing:

> I've been watching that for the last week on television body bags all over in hallways. . . . I have been watching them bring in trailer trucks, freezer trucks—they are freezer trucks because they can't handle the bodies, there are so many of them. This is essentially in my community in Queens— Queens, New York. I have seen things I've never seen before. I mean, I've seen them, but I've seen them on television in faraway lands.[11]

The United States, when this comment was made, was on its way to becoming the global epicenter of the ongoing COVID-19 pandemic. This realization highlighted an uncomfortable and important myth of our current moment, that epidemics are forces that those in the West are *to be protected from* and witness play out on the news in reports *from far away*. While the pandemic has ravaged much of the Western world, its effects on the United States look to be the gravest. Donald Trump publicly endorsed unproven drugs for COVID-19 treatment, such as the malaria medication hydroxychloroquine, and rejected lifesaving practices such as wearing masks.[12] In a statement that echoed Mbeki's HIV/AIDS denialism and the treatment suggestions of his health department, President Trump mused that exposure to light and the ingestion or injection of disinfectants into a patient's body might cure the disease.[13] Former UK prime minister Boris Johnson, before falling ill to the disease himself, suggested that the British people could develop herd immunity from COVID-19 such that formal social distancing measures would be unnecessary, against nearly all information from public health experts. Likewise, as President Trump contracted the disease after exposure at his own political events, he continued to preach the necessity of Americans to trust in technological solutions to the pandemic and reject proven public health responses. Despite a change in leadership under President Biden, effective public health measures such as wearing masks remain the subject of deep political debate in the United States. The levels of mortality from this pandemic have not been seen in the United States for decades, while the effects of racism and class inequalities continue to elevate that death toll. Meanwhile many nations outside of the mythological container known as the West have weathered the storm, in spite of lack of access to a reliable delivery of vaccines, through steady and at times compassionate public health controls rooted in limiting spread of disease. The United States, United Kingdom, and others assumed that keeping disease out would protect and offset the troubles within, but COVID-19 has exposed more starkly the weakness of supposedly vaunted public health systems that in fact were understaffed, underfunded, and ill equipped to manage a disaster of this scale.

All the while, the United States has continued to blame China for spreading the disease and the WHO for operating in China's interests rather than those of the United States. Much of the justification for this claim lay in what has been described as the failures of what were once a little-known set of regulations, the International Health Regulations. Former President Trump's attempts to remove the United States from the World Health Organization and spreading of xenophobic and racist tropes regarding the origins of the disease highlight a foundational guiding ideology of international infectious disease control: that the systems in place to control epidemics must protect the West and its interests from the epidemic risks posed by the rest of the world.

This perspective has been central to the International Health Regulations and prior international infectious disease regulations since they were first developed in the nineteenth century, and it is ever-present today in the responses to COVID-19. The marker of the supremacy of Western civilization over the rest of the world has historically been the absence of infectious epidemics of the scale seen recently in West Africa and the Democratic Republic of Congo caused by Ebola virus disease and Zika virus microcephaly in South and Central America. Effective infectious disease control and the absence of epidemics are markers of modernity and Enlightenment ideals. They prop up the myth of inherent European and North American superiority. COVID-19 has shattered this myth, although the negative effects of such a myth are very visible in the responses to this pandemic. How did the world of international infectious disease control come to center its objectives *in protecting the West from the rest*?

ACKNOWLEDGMENTS

This book began many years ago as I was examining two epidemic episodes separated by over one hundred years. While writing an article on British colonial responses to bubonic plague in 1901 Cape Town, an epidemic that led to the first racially segregated urban township in South Africa, I was haunted by the parallels to some of the violent responses occurring in Monrovia, Liberia, in response to the epidemic or Ebola virus disease there. I became fascinated by the similar dynamics occurring at two very different moments. This curiosity led to what would ultimately be this book.

I want to thank all of the interviewees who gave their time and insights to this project for sharing how they approach the challenges of infectious disease control. They say that public health work is thankless, because no one notices you when you succeed and everyone blames you when you fail. Now, more than ever, we see how difficult this task is. I hope that this book highlights that individuals struggle against inequitable structures but that this is often a losing battle against deeply entrenched inequities. Thank you for all of your work. This work would not have been possible without the brilliant archivists at the archives of the Western Cape, the Wellcome Library, the British National Archives at Kew, the British Library, the League of Nations archives, and the archives and library of the World Health Organization. Thank you for all of your help, support, and patience as I sifted through your materials. The research for this book was only possible with the funding support of the Boston University Department of Sociology Morris Fund, the Boston University Graduate Research Abroad Funding grant, and the Pardee Center for the Study of the Longer-Term Future, as well as funding support from Johns Hopkins University and School of Medicine. I am also indebted to seminars and conferences with the Yale University Department of Sociology; Brown University Department of Sociology; University of Virginia Department of Sociology; University of California, Berkeley; University of Chicago; and Johns Hopkins University Department of Anthropology, as well as the numerous American Sociological Association annual conferences and Social Science History Association conferences where I presented draft excerpts of this book. I am indebted beyond words to the generous and generative comments from the anonymous reviewers of this book. My deepest thanks to Marcela Maxfield for your decision to support my work as editor at Stanford University Press. My deepest thanks also to Sunna Juhn for her aid with the project and Tere Mullin who provided the index for this book.

No book can truly be said to be produced by a single author. I hope that those mentioned in these acknowledgements will recognize their fingerprints and thoughts throughout this work. This book is so much better for their kind and patient engagement, and all faults that remain with this text are most certainly my own. This work could not have been possible without the immense support I have received from all of my advisors. At Amherst College, John Drabinski and Jeffrey Ferguson taught me that maybe I could be a producer of knowledge and not solely a recipient of it. At the London School of Economics, Paul Gilroy taught me to be patient with my thoughts and became my model for crafting powerful and humanistic work. This work would not have been possible to any extent without the deep and continued engagement of Julian Go, who pushed me in new scholarly directions and teaches me how to speak to the world of sociologists, who perhaps didn't want to listen, and how to shape fields. The advising and friendship of these people have shaped me greatly.

No one makes it through graduate school without the communities we build together. Daryl Carr, Pamela Devan, Emily Bryant, Reya Farber, and I came to Boston University together and sailed through so many of the joys, sorrows, and struggles of grad school together. They had to listen to me talk about epidemics far before such things were part of our universal experience. Without you all, I would not be anywhere near where I am. Jonathan Shaffer and Kelsey Harris also taught me how to mentor and think about how to teach and be there for others in this world of higher education. Thank you for being there for me, as I hope you know I am for you. I am so proud to count you as my friends.

I am deeply indebted to the colleagues I have made since coming to Johns Hopkins. Randall Packard has always been the sort of historian of medicine I wanted to be, and to receive his input on my work has been an immeasurable blessing. I am so grateful for the support of Graham Mooney, Mary Fissell, Nathaniel Comfort, Marta Hanson, Gianna Pomatta, Marian Robbins, Maggie Cogswell, and Carolyn Sufrin. Without you all I would not be at this university, and with you it has become a true home. The Department of Sociology and in particular Beverly Silver, Ho-Fung Hung, Christy Thornton, Stuart Schrader, Lingxin Hao, Rina Agarwala, Michael Levien, Ryan Calder, and Joel Andreas have mentored me so immensely and have provided incredible support for this work. I am so grateful to count you as colleagues. The support, guidance, and friendship of Robbie Shilliam, Jeremy Greene, Elizabeth O'Brien, Yulia Frumer, Loren Ludwig, Ahmed Ragab, Soha Bayoumi, and Minkah Makalani have made this a far stronger book than it ever could have been.

I have been so immensely blessed to have the support of friends and mentors like Isaac Arial Reed, Jonathan Wyrtzen, Ruha Benjamin, and Claire Decoteau, who have all pushed me in my insights, offered me their friendship, and supported my work. I am so deeply honored to count you as my friends. The inspiration I gain from you is incalculable. I admire your scholarship and your ethical and political orientations to your practice as academics.

In so many ways I would not be happy, healthy, or capable of anything close to the thinking required in this book without my closest cadre of intellectual collaborators. It has been a great pleasure to collaborate, scheme, and organize with Julia Bates, Omri Tubi, Heidi Nicholls, Katrina Quisumbing King, Marcelo Bohrt, and Tina Park. I hope the world of academia is a bit more hospitable a place for us because of one another. I will forever be indebted to Zophia Edwards, Trish Ward, Jake Watson, Meghan Tinsley, and Ricarda Hammer, who have taught me what it is to build community and care for one another in this work.

My students have been a massive inspiration as well as a very patient audience for some of the more half-baked aspects of this work. It has been a real honor to think with you. I want to especially thank Durgesh Solanki,

Vincenza Mazzeo, Ayah Nurridin, Jessica Hester, and Pyar Seth for your kind engagement with my work and for letting me learn from you. I want to also thank Mina Richard, Carolina Andrada, Erin Jones, Peggy-ita Obeng Nyarkoh, Gwyneth Wei, Wingel Xue, Ashley Chen, and Earl Goldsborough III, for their engagement and brilliant insights into both my own work and their own.

Finally I want to thank my friends and family who have sustained me and given so much so that I can be doing what I love. All my work is bearable because of Nikhil, Trinity, Bethany, Kyle, and Diane, who bring constant joy to my life. My friends Emily Joseph, Teddy Blank, Nicole Cabrera, Zach Cherry, Jason Han, Ashfin Islam, Ireen Ahmed, J. N. Gallant, Jessica Gallant, Will Kenney, David Crane, Liz Dang, Mark Knapp, Ben Dunmore, Chris McConkey, Trevor Wikstrom, and Charles Diamond, who have known me both before and during this process, will always keep me humble, and for that I am so grateful. Know that a large part of this book is because of you. I want to thank my parents-in-law Wendy and Ron and my aunts, uncles, and cousins for being the people that I try to do this work for and strive to emulate. I wish to especially thank my parents. My father who taught me that thought, reading, and concern are all important aspects of human existence, and that care, kindness, and dignity are integral to it. So much of this work was possible because of the many long conversations my mother and I shared about the themes, theories, and minutiae of this work. This book owes everything to your presence and for being a continued source of guidance. Lastly, nothing about any of this, from my decision to pursue a PhD to the life we have to the book this is would have been possible without the love, companionship, and partnership of Erica Jawin. From college to world travel through to COVID-19 isolation and working from home, we have done it all together, and this book is a small token dedicated to our dedication to one another.

INTRODUCTION

I spread the whole earth out as a map before me. On no one spot of its
surface could I put my finger and say, here is safety. In the south, the
disease, virulent and immedicable, had nearly annihilated the race of
man; storm and inundation, poisonous winds and blights, filled up the
measure of suffering. In the north it was worse—the lesser population
gradually declined, and famine and plague kept watch on the survivors,
who, helpless and feeble, were ready to fall an easy prey into their
hands. I contracted my view to England. The over-grown metropolis,
the great heart of mighty Britain was pulseless. Commerce had ceased.
All resort for ambition or pleasure was cut off—the streets were grass-
grown—the houses empty—the few, that from necessity remained,
already seemed branded with the taint of inevitable pestilence. In the
larger manufacturing towns the same tragedy was acted on a smaller, yet
disastrous scale.[1]

WHEN MARY WOLLSTONECRAFT SHELLEY was writing her mas-
terpiece of gothic science fiction, *The Last Man* (1826), she probably would
have been aware of the cholera pandemic spreading across India and South-
east Asia.[2] In her book, which envisions a global pandemic plague eradicating the human race in 2094, Shelley locates the seed of the disease's spread
in the expansion and conquest of the British Empire eastward. As an over-
confident empire conquers Constantinople, it unleashes the plague, which
had laid low the city after traveling from Asia into Egypt and ultimately
to present-day Turkey, on a hapless and unsuspecting Western Europe.[3]
The juxtaposition of colonial exploitation, trade, and conquest echoed in
the siege of Constantinople and this opening quotation encapsulates the
uneasy and destabilizing realities made possible by European imperial invasion around the world. In the nineteenth century, diseases previously
unseen in Europe for some time began to spread back from the colonial
dominions taken by force.

Shelley's vision is of a dying world, in particular a dying Europe and a
dying Britain, "pulseless" from physical death from disease, and the collapse

of an imperial economic world system that had ceased to be. The paired phenomena of pandemic catastrophe and the subsequent economic plague crept from the furthest outposts of British colonial dominion back through Europe and ultimately to the metropoles of Britain itself.

Shelley, as her character narrates, "spread the whole earth out as a map," but like all prescient science fiction, she may well have been ahead of her time. She lays out a fictive geography of relations of political and social power as told through disease. Her narrator begins with an eye cast to the south, the origin point of the plague where it is virulent and untreatable. Moving northward, the disease ravages lands nearer to home before focusing ultimately on Britain. Writing in 1826, Shelley could not have known with any certainty that the way of seeing and dividing the world that her character lays out would become the dominant frame through which disease threat would be understood in global politics for the next two centuries. Shelley sketches simply and in fiction several aspects of what I call *Epidemic Orientalism*,[4] a way of apprehending and recognizing infectious disease threat that is based on the ways that the West has come to see itself in relation to the rest of the world.

The ongoing global pandemic of COVID-19 has laid bare the politics of global relations at work at the heart of pandemic governance. It is much clearer now that an epidemic, far from signifying solely a biological threat to life, is also an economic and political phenomenon that produces cascading and conjoined effects—including xenophobia, nationalist fervor, racial oppression (and the exposure of the health effects of racism in starkly violent disparities), and economic power struggles. In the earliest stages of this COVID-19 pandemic, the West and especially the United States and the United Kingdom failed to respond to the pandemic, with a mixture of what could be called willful negligence, insufficient capacity, and heartless neglect as millions succumbed to the disease. Presently (as of February 2022), as novel variants of SARS-CoV-2 continue to spread, our ongoing moment of mass vaccination has also laid bare the global inequalities in political and economic power. Many nations, whose public health responses to the virus had hitherto been more effective than those of Western nations, now face an uneasy moment where access to vaccines and therapeutics, a potentially sustainable route to controlling this disease, is mediated by the whims and greed of European and American pharmaceutical companies.

To see epidemics only through a single register is to misunderstand the complex landscapes of meaning[5] in which an epidemic operates and exists. This book is concerned with a central question: What forces have governed and continue to govern global responses to epidemic threats? After this research and after examining the practices, tactics of regulation, scientific discoveries, and geopolitical transformations over the last two centuries, it has become clear to me (as I hope it will be clear to you soon) that in order to answer this question, it is not sufficient solely to examine the practices by which governments, international organizations, public health actors, and diplomats have attempted to control infectious disease spread. Instead we must unearth and interpret the discourses that motivate and constrain the possible material responses to global pandemic threats. In short, rather than a study of the practice of infectious disease control, this book sets out to explain the terrain upon which epidemic threats are understood in geopolitical terms and subsequently how the practices by which they are managed are rationalized. This is not a study of subnational or humanitarian-agency-based work in the domain of global health. This book analyzes the dynamics of infectious disease control as organized through regulations, treaties, and agreements between states, development organizations, and, previously, empires. When I employ the term *international infectious disease control*, I refer to these supranational dynamics of political, economic, and health relations. This project is therefore both historical and epistemological in its approach. I contend that it is largely impossible to understand how and why international infectious disease responses and diseases themselves are understood and acted on without examining the discourses that have allowed epidemics to be the objects of regulation, control, and management at a global level. At the same time this argument is specific: this book focuses on the International Sanitary Conventions and the International Health Regulations, which have been maintained since the nineteenth century as the only structures to this point governing the threat of infectious disease carried by humans across borders.

Argument: The Persistent Durability
of the International Disease Regulatory Logics

Since 1851, the international spread of infectious disease has been a focus of international coordination and concern. Over thirty years before the Prime Meridian Conference, which established the standard twenty-four-hour day beginning and ending in Greenwich, United Kingdom,[6] the major empires of Europe and the Ottoman Empire convened the first International Sanitary Conferences to establish a global sanitary order. These early sanitary conferences did not set out to establish global health regulations for the objective of the effective provision of healthcare for all. These first conferences and conventions aimed to produce standard agreements for the effective control of disease without hindering global trade. From 1851 to 1938, fourteen conferences were held to standardize international regulations for the establishment of quarantine and sanitary management. These regulations prioritized the management of three primary diseases: plague, cholera, and yellow fever. These particular diseases are notable as they reflect specific diseases that were seen in the nineteenth century to exist and spread outside of the boundaries of Europe and had the capacity, if global spread occurred, to lead to mass death and political and economic challenges to European trade, traffic, and peoples. In 1892 the first International Sanitary Conventions were adopted, codifying the first regulations for the prevention of the international spread of infectious disease with a mission to maximize the protection from disease with minimum effect on trade and traffic.[7] In 1907 the Office International d'Hygiène Publique (OIHP) took over the authority of the International Sanitary Conventions and the responsibility for maintaining this multilateral treaty between the signatory empires and nations to it. In 1948, the responsibility for the management of international infectious disease threats transferred to the World Health Organization (WHO).[8]

Until the establishment of the WHO, the responsibility for the management of international disease threats was the domain of individual nation-states or regional health bodies operating in adherence to international treaty. There was no separate global regulatory body or facilitator for disease

TABLE 1: Diseases Prioritized by International Sanitary Regulations and International Health Regulations. Source: Made by author.

Regulations	Dates of operation	Governing body	Notifiable diseases	Agents responsible for operation
International Sanitary Conventions	1859–1938	Coalition of European and North American Nations and Empires; Office International d'Hygiène Publique after 1926	Plague (bubonic/pneumonic); cholera; yellow fever	Colonial representatives and diplomats; doctors and medical experts; colonial administrators who implemented policy
International Sanitary Regulations	1952–1969	World Health Organization	Plague (bubonic/pneumonic); cholera; yellow fever; typhus; relapsing fever; smallpox	World Health Assembly member states; WHO
International Health Regulations	1969–2005	World Health Organization	Plague (bubonic/pneumonic); cholera; yellow fever	World Health Assembly member states; WHO
International Health Regulations (2005)	2005–present	World Health Organization	Notification based on contextually derived factors and severity of outbreak	World Health Assembly member states; WHO; Global Alert and Response network; Emergency Committee Members tasked with assessing threat of outbreaks

Sources: Norman Howard-Jones, *The Scientific Background of the International Sanitary Conferences, 1851–1938* (Geneva: World Health Organization, 1975), http://apps.who.int//iris/handle/10665/62873; E. Mayor et al., International Sanitary Convention, Signed at Venice, March 18, 1897; Special Committee established by the third World Health Assembly to consider the Draft International Sanitary Regulations, "Draft International Sanitary Regulations: Proposal for the Machinery to Review the Functioning of the International Sanitary Regulations and the Settlement of Disputes Arising Therefrom Presented by Dr Raja, Delegate for India," 1951, https://apps.who.int/iris/handle/10665/100844; S. Smith, "International Sanitary Conference," *Journal of Social Science* 32 (November 1, 1894): 92–111; Geo M. Sternberg, "The International Sanitary Conference at Rome," *Science* 6, no. 131 (August 7, 1885): 101–3, https://doi.org/10.1126/science.ns-6.131.101; P. G. Stock, "The International Sanitary Convention of 1944," *Proceedings of the Royal Society of Medicine* 38, no. 7 (May 1945): 309–16; World Health Organization, ed., *International Health Regulations (2005)* (Geneva: WHO, 2008).

management. Even after the creation of the WHO, the primary focus of international health regulations until 2005 was the three diseases (plague, cholera, and yellow fever) outlined by the first International Sanitary Conventions of the late nineteenth and early twentieth centuries.[9] The International Sanitary Conventions were reformed and renamed under the WHO to the International Sanitary Regulations in 1951 and ultimately renamed the International Health Regulations in 1969, with the same motto: the maximum protection from infectious disease with the minimum effect to trade and traffic.

The most recent instantiation of the International Health Regulations was ratified in 2005 (IHR [2005]) with a broad mandate, greatly expanding the domain of the prior regulations to any potential health threat capable of travelling across international borders. It also established policies and standard practices by which to monitor and surveil all outbreaks of disease and assess the risk of disease spread. Through its acceptance, the 194 signatory nations of the World Health Assembly—the governing body of the WHO—acceded to maintaining an international minimum standard for disease control and surveillance.[10] The WHO today has the responsibility for assessing the relative threats of disease to the global community and ultimately decides whether any outbreak constitutes a Public Health Emergency of International Concern (PHEIC, pronounced *P-Heic*). Not only did the transition to the IHR (2005) usher in an organizational transformation in how international health threats are confronted on a global scale, but this transition signified a shift in how international disease threats are conceptualized, diagnosed, and managed. In pivoting from a focus on particular diseases capable of international spread, the WHO and its member nations turned its attention to *any* emergent or reemerging disease capable of presenting an international threat to public health, trade, and traffic.[11] While the shift to the IHR (2005) was seen by many to finally be a break from the anachronistic focus on the three diseases of nineteenth-century concern in Europe,[12] criticisms of its prejudices persist. Many epidemics appear to meet the threat level of a PHEIC by their own definition yet do not receive the final designation. While variation exists between diseases, it is clear that there is no one factor that serves as justification for the distinction of a PHEIC. Many international organizations and actors continue to criticize the deployment of the PHEIC designation and the application of the IHR (2005) as operating in the interests of Western health concerns rather than global health writ large. In particular, the declaration of PHEIC is seen to occur too slowly such that the epidemic cannot be effectively contained or only to occur once an epidemic is capable of affecting the Western world and interests.[13] While the IHR (2005) is expressly designed to evaluate the epidemiological context of an outbreak as well as the pathologies of a disease in order to determine threat, the contextual nature of these determinations highlights the vital importance of interpretation in assessing a PHEIC. These priorities would seem to run counter to a geopolitical moment whose polarity is shifting more and more away from any concentrated national or regional powers in Europe and North America toward China, India, Brazil, South Africa, and a host of global nongovernmental organizations (NGOs) such as the Bill and Melinda Gates Foundation.

The empirical puzzle borne out of this is twofold: Why, despite massive shifts in political and economic power, transformations in geopolitics, shifts in demographics, and the emergence of new and ever-changing institutions in the world of international health, did most of the same priorities for infectious disease control regulations persist from the nineteenth century to the early twenty-first century? How do we understand the ideological and political priorities of this particular area of international public health? This puzzle is both historical and particular to the domain of international infectious disease regulation operating through the International Sanitary Conventions of the past and International Health Regulations of the present. What can explain this persistent Eurocentric and Western-centric gaze on infectious disease regulation?

Epidemics are governed differently in the global sphere from all other health threats. The persistence of infectious diseases that can travel across borders presents a challenge to state sovereignty over healthcare. Since the passage of the International Health Regulations of 2005, the monitoring of and responses to infectious disease operate in a domain of international cooperation and universal standards defined by the WHO and the World Health Assembly. The IHR (2005) maintains the international legal significance of a treaty and requires "that all nations adhere to minimum standards for disease prevention and surveillance, the mandatory notification to the

WHO of all disease outbreaks that potentially threaten international spread, allow the WHO to investigate and declare public health emergencies of international concern, issue formal recommendations and permit the WHO to accept surveillance information from nonstate sources."[14] The IHR (2005) also permits the WHO to suggest the limitation of trade and transit in the interest of global health.

Despite operating as the only regulations to manage the spread of infectious disease among humans over international borders, these regulations have failed to attend to some of the most urgent threats to world health. The International Sanitary Conventions of the early twentieth century for both regulatory and scientific reasons provided no systems by which to control the influenza pandemic of 1918–1919,[15] and the International Health Regulations of 1969 failed to comprehensively address the emergent HIV/AIDS pandemic in the 1980s and 1990s. Even more recently during both the ongoing COVID-19 pandemic and the earlier epidemics of Ebola virus disease in West Africa, the International Health Regulations and WHO were roundly criticized for their actions. In 2016, to accommodate for significant funding failures in the West African Ebola response, the World Bank announced the development of the first-ever Pandemic Emergency Financing Facility to prevent the worst humanitarian and economic effects of epidemic emergencies. The creation of this facility introduced a variety of new assumptions into the management of infectious disease.

Unlike other areas of international and global health such as projects of disease eradication in the mid-twentieth century or even the anti-HIV/AIDS projects led by large entities such as UNAIDS, PEPVFAR, or the Global Fund, all of which seek some sort of equity in global health outcomes, the domain of infectious disease regulation has retained significant uniformity in its vision. The IHR's mandate is the same today as it was in the nineteenth century during the earliest International Sanitary Conferences. Similarly the Pandemic Emergency Financing Facility exists primarily as a market instrument to ensure disease control. Where many other domains of the WHO's operations and other global health actors have moved to humanitarian-centered approaches to "health for all," the realm of epidemic infectious disease control marches to a different beat.

Global Health and the Politics of Knowledge

Acute, fast-spreading epidemics of infectious disease have historically not been the domain of or included within the critical phenomena of social analysis. Perhaps this is because they often occur so quickly and seem to dissipate before sustained ethnographic or critical inquiry is possible.[16] Certainly, the epidemics that resist control and containment for long periods such as the HIV/AIDS pandemic have produced the most investigation and have reshaped social thought in numerous ways.[17] The most sustained research into what I call *acute epidemics*, such as the recent epidemics of Ebola virus disease in West Africa and the Democratic Republic of Congo, Zika virus, or yellow fever, most often arise in the fuzzy domain of global health research that focuses, by and large, on the concerns and health problems occurring in the developing world. This focus leaves spaces like Europe and North America outside the realm of direct analysis save for migrant populations and the international organizations[18] and geopolitical entities involved in health policy making. Whether intentional or not, much of the thought produced within the domain of global health about infectious disease, by its focus on the "developing world," perhaps would overassume the differences in dynamics shaping epidemic responses and crises based on this distinction between "West and rest."[19] This distinction has been buttressed to varying degrees by scientific discourse.

The early twentieth century in Europe and North America witnessed what is perceived as an epidemiological transition in the dynamics of disease risk and causes of mortality. Important scientific contributions to understandings of germ theory, contagion, and the isolation of pathogens made infectious disease something that could be controlled. The development of sanitation systems in much of Europe and North America in the late nineteenth and early twentieth centuries shrank the prevalence of food- and water-borne diseases in urban areas, making cities a more salubrious environment than rural areas.[20] The development of understanding of mammalian and insect vectors of disease brought scourges such as bubonic plague, yellow fever, and malaria into novel domains of control, especially in the West where effective eradication campaigns against them were waged. At the same time, so much of this knowledge as well as treatment practices emerged out of colonial sites and from non-Western knowledge systems, or through violent experimentation on non-Europeans.[21] Policy and public health measures in the twentieth century in much of Europe and North America shifted toward questions of chronic disease and issues of social medicine and population health.[22] International health actors such as the Rockefeller Foundation, colonial medical officers, and a host of intermediaries in the late nineteenth and early twentieth centuries spread a gospel of Western medical superiority to the colonies controlled by European and North American powers.[23] Western medicine spread across the world, with Western colonization as an exemplar of European and American modernity and the superiority of Western civilization, while at the same moment turning colonial dominions into laboratories for experimentation and extraction.[24] Sanitation and hygiene became signifiers, especially to Western eyes, of the cultural superiority of a salubrious *West* against a potential pestilential *rest* of the world.[25] This has at times led to the production of racist medical science,[26] as well as the application of xenophobic and racially organized systems of disease surveillance, exclusion, and control.[27]

To bear witness uncritically to the history of global public health in the West is to participate in an exercise in myth making. It is to take part in believing that through biomedical intervention, sanitary development, and international controls, the West is able to separate itself from the parts of the world suffering from infectious diseases and is thus superior in its civilization. The elimination of many disease threats over the course of the nineteenth and twentieth centuries are some of the most powerful signifiers of Western modernity's capacity for progress through scientific mythological rationality and bureaucratization. The construction of this vision of modernity built from epidemic control obscures the ways in which it is scaffolded on histories of colonialism, racism, and global political organization that have maintained effective systems of disease control privileging the geographies of Europe and North America, and the economic interests they rely on to maintain political power in the world.

This book examines through the histories of infectious disease regulations how Western and Eurocentric discourses are produced and reproduced through disease control and why these discourses have shaped the formation of disease control systems. This work also explores how particular *discourses* have remained durable while *practices* of control have changed. While many debates have been had and won that have demonstrated the Western-centric nature of international health and the power dynamics within global health responses,[28] I argue that not only does the history of international infectious disease control reflect the desires of imperial European and post–World War II Western nations but also that they were actually critical to realizing a stable vision of the modern "West." As much as infectious disease control has been a project of protectionism, it has also been a project of defining difference for the purpose of control. This vision of the modern West exists by constructing a veil of difference between West and rest, with disease, differentials of political and economic power, and race operating as signifiers of difference. In short, these regulations have been critical for producing the image by which the West sees itself in contrast to the other parts of the world, as a space that must be protected from the diseases emergent from the rest of the world.

This introduction serves as a broad outline of this book, explaining the main argument and the layout of chapters. It also provides a framework for encountering and understanding infectious disease, epidemics, and the international responses to them within the geopolitical, scientific, and sociological imaginaries in which they are embedded—namely, colonial and imperial dynamics of economic and political relation and domination and of knowledge production.

Epidemics at the Level of Discourse

How does a disease event become an epidemic? The question at first may lead us in an epidemiological direction, which would have us attempting to calculate the reproduction rate or infectivity of a disease, rates of transmission, severity of illness, and so on, in order to understand the threat in terms of spread and lives lost. This approach would apply techniques, policies, scientific knowledge, and practices of public health developed through medical and social scientific research, supported by national and international organizations such as the US Centers for Disease Control and Prevention and the WHO to respond to the natural phenomenon of disease emergence. Thus one mode of analysis may examine the practices and policies put in place to assess how an epidemic emerges and how a threat is defined through policy and best practices. This analysis may provide us with an understanding of why certain strategies were taken, why certain calculations were made, and how an epidemic is defined given a particular ecosystem of policies. However, which systems of knowledges, relations of power, and practices of bureaucratic rationalization were organized to constitute an accepted, *naturalized* understanding of an epidemic that allows for the creation of policies to control its spread? What are the governing logics of international infectious disease control? What sorts of symbolic, political, economic, and social relations are assumed, or made real and legible, in the management of infectious disease? And how do these affect the construction of and responses to epidemic emergencies? To answer these questions, we must dive deeper than the analysis of policy action and outcomes to understand what systems form the basis of thinkable action on a subject, at the level of discursive formation. Which forms of knowledge need to be produced in order for a disease to become an object that can be controlled by human action in international space? What sorts of policies and regimes of sovereignty are rationalized so that epidemics can become manageable events? What sorts of relations of power prioritize certain responses to epidemics and not others? Which populations become the object of surveillance and scrutiny? Who are perceived as victims or vectors?

Situating International Infectious Disease Control within Research on Global Health

Analyses of the geopolitics of infectious disease control have generally bifurcated the periods of the latter twentieth and twenty-first centuries from international activities prior to World War II. This research has been composed of institutional histories that have explored how organizations like the WHO[29] and other entities[30] have operated as health actors among a constellation of particular political and global dynamics in relation to state actors and NGOs. Significant research has also contributed greatly to our understanding of how certain global health priorities have developed. Some of the most notable campaigns in global health over the last seventy years have been in the area of disease eradication. Histories of these projects have demonstrated how the complex intertangling of geopolitical priorities, medical knowledge, and technical and chemical strategies combined in variably effective campaigns to wipe out infectious disease.[31] Historical analysis prior to World War II reflects a periodization separate from much of the postwar transformations of international politics. Some writers such as Randall Packard and Neel Ahuja[32] have written histories that comprise both the nineteenth-century developments of colonial and tropical medicine and the early development of international health through a variety of pre–World War II organizations such as the League of Nations Health Organization[33] (LNHO) and the Office of International Public Hygiene (OIHP). However, there is a tendency to view these earlier periods as analytically, ideologically, and politically distinct from our current era.

Much analysis on the politics of epidemic response has engaged in a critical examination of the phenomenon of biosecurity.[34] Biosecurity as a practice of global health has been described as a confluence of national security concerns for both infectious disease and bioweapons, reflecting national risks to health from the natural world. The history of this approach can largely be read through the fall of the Cold War; the emergence and reemergence of infectious disease threats such as HIV/AIDS, Ebola virus disease, and others; and notable biological attacks like the 1995 Tokyo subway sarin gas attack and the 2001 anthrax attacks in the United States. Scholarship on biosecurity has been incredibly important for understanding the developments in global health tied to national security over the last thirty years. Biosecurity analyses have drawn on the theories of risk developed by Ulrich Beck[35] and explored the rising phenomenon of complex technical and systems approaches to managing biosecurity hazards.[36] This research would suggest that the approaches to the disease threats of the present are marked by a fundamentally new approach to the control of disease, emergent out of a post–Cold War world. Others such as Neel Ahuja have traced the US imperial histories of disease control, especially in the Pacific, to the emergence of contemporary biosecurity practices.[37] Ahuja's work has intimately traced the links between settler colonialism, racism, and American biosecurity systems, demonstrating the lingering and durable logics of nineteenth-century racism and colonialism still at work in American empire today.

This book aims to analytically engage with the histories of international health in a different but complementary way. The International Sanitary Conventions and the International Health Regulations today exist somewhat out of time and out of step with these dominant framings of the histories and logics of international health. While the 1990s reflected a period when the WHO was seeing health interventions and standards of health more broadly through economic lenses,[38] understanding ideas of health and illness through concepts like disability-adjusted life years that quantified infirmity in terms of labor lost, in the middle of the nineteenth century, the major nations and empires of Europe were already appraising disease risk in terms of threat to trade and traffic. Similarly, international coordination of infectious disease regulations has persisted through, at times complemented, and pre-dated disease eradication strategies. Simultaneously while comprehensive disease surveillance, tracing, and tracking may appear as wholly contemporary phenomena, these practices and approaches, including the use of biometric data and surveillance, can be traced back to international and colonial infectious disease responses of the late nineteenth and early twentieth centuries and linked to the International Sanitary Conventions.[39] While the WHO was shifting to prioritize health for all and universal primary healthcare in the 1970s and 1980s, led primarily by nonaligned states and non-Western nations, the International Health Regulations remained focused on the same disease priorities of the nineteenth century and maintained their commitment to the maximum protection from infectious disease with the minimum effect to trade and traffic. The history of these conventions and regulations, the oldest continuous regulations and only health treaty devoted to the control of infectious disease among humans,[40] has operated as a missing link in the world of international health, often anachronistic, either foreshadowing future health strategies or conserving old ideologies. Theorist Ann Stoler has demonstrated how colonial reason—ways of seeing the world rooted in systems of colonial and imperial dynamics of power and sovereignty—can remain as operable modes of thought, ordering knowledge production and forms of governing long after the formal structures of empire and colony have disappeared.[41] It is not the argument of this book that the logics and practices of disease control are exactly the same today as they were in the nineteenth century, but rather that particular discourses have remained stubbornly durable throughout the last two centuries and have produced varying forms of epidemic response practice as a result.

International Infectious Disease Control as a Discursive Project

This book takes as its primary focus the history of the International Sanitary Conventions of the past, the International Health Regulations of today, and the recent global health strategies that have emerged since the West African Ebola epidemic, the Pandemic Emergency Financing Facility of the World Bank. The goal of this book is not to write a history of these regulations over time. Rather, it is to examine how the dominant discourses surrounding the space of infectious disease control have produced knowledge and practice toward epidemic threats and how these knowledges and practices have structured the appraisal of disease threat and responses to epidemics. In examining the histories of these regulations and strategies, we can see the interplay between scientific knowledge and various forms of political and economic power. These regulations reflect not merely banal forms of trade and travel protections from infectious disease but also a landscape onto which systems of relations among states, empires, and peoples are mapped and global economic and political orders are rationalized into infectious disease controls. Moments of reform and regulatory creation, as well as the drafters of these regulations, expose debates and struggles over how diseases, those carrying them, and those at risk from disease should be managed globally. The final forms that these regulations have taken presuppose particular dynamics of power, forms of sovereignty, and political and economic rationalities that augment and orient their ultimate structure. These regulations are in fact landscapes onto which the drafters of these documents sought to map global relations of power and order the world. We can learn a great deal from the format of these regulations and how their framers conceive of epidemic spread, what sorts of regulations are and can be imposed to prevent the spread of disease, and what species of power are mobilized onto which spaces and bodies to prevent it. The need to protect colonial and global trade around the world has rationalized systems of surveillance and the production of controls understood through political and economic equations relating capitalism and racial and ethnic difference to disease. Beyond the epidemiology and scientific understanding of disease, I have become fascinated with the ways that successive generations of framers of infectious disease regulations have justified the need for infectious disease controls in part by producing or reproducing a vision of the Western world apart from a diseased rest.

In order to understand the histories of international infectious disease control, the epidemic responses of the past, and the pandemic responses of the present, one must understand the ways in which the regulations and practices of disease control are located within wider projects of Western modernity. At the core of this is a recognition of the fundamental relationship between Western modernity and colonialism.[42] While Western visions of modernity are described as a progressive pursuit to emancipation, this modernity was only made manifest through the domination and colonization of much of the world. These systems of colonial domination produced racial subjects, created categories of difference that separated the colonized and colonizer, and also, (and perhaps most critically) allowed for the categorization of colonial difference to also produce a vision of Western humanity. The relationship between modernity and colonialism elevates the superiority of Western civilization through the machinations of colonialism and on the backs of the colonized.[43] The project of modernity therefore is predicated on the colonization of the world and subordination of it. While forms of systemic oppression and physical domination may have existed through colonial rule, in our current era after most formal colonialism, the repression and controls over ways of seeing the world are still dominated by a certain coloniality of knowledge that recognizes the voices and ways of seeing in the West against epistemologies in the rest of the world.

These regulations and systems of disease control are therefore embedded within wider knowledge regimes that precede the production of these policies. It is these knowledge regimes, namely, conceptions of Western visions of modernity rooted in the capitalist and colonial exploitation of power, that augment and shape the nature of international policy on disease control. Infectious disease regulations—the International Sanitary Conventions of the past and the International Health Regulations and Pandemic Emergency Financing Facility of the present—far from being neutral vessels of asocial scientific and technocratic rationalities, rather presuppose and envision world systems of trade and human mobility that define populations and regions for control and/or protection from infectious disease. Embedded within these regulations are rationalities that position Europe and more broadly the West as the sites that must be protected from the infectious threats of the rest of the world. As we will see, before global regulations controlling infectious disease can be produced, a fictive vision of the world must be imagined, in this case out of the imperial imaginaries of the nineteenth century. I call this particular vision of the world that orders and structures international epidemic regulations and controls *epidemic Orientalism.*

Epidemic Orientalism

To understand the political terrain of infectious disease control in both the present and over the last 175 years, we must recognize and account for the "limitations on thought or action"[44] imposed by this discourse operating on epidemics. Over the next many years much ink will be rightly poured onto the pages of books and articles attempting to explain how and why particular policy approaches to COVID-19 could perhaps have prevented the disaster we have all as a planet been living through and suffering with to varying degrees of severity. Epidemics generally and COVID-19 in particular are not purely natural objects existing outside of signifying systems of meaning, but rather are located within a discursive formation that organizes how they are discussed, responded to, and ultimately governed. I do not wish to argue that the discourse of epidemic Orientalism can explain causally all responses and governing approaches to epidemics. Rather, it is a mode of thought, meaning system, representational schema, and rationalization that is imposed on any moment when an international epidemic threat is thought to emerge.

I propose the reinterpretation of Edward Said's concept of Oriental-ism to define *epidemic Orientalism*—that particularly durable discursive formation—the discourse and viewpoint, rooted in Europe's engagements with the rest of the world as colonizer, through which Europe and later the West recognized itself in relation to the world it was colonizing (the non-European and the colonized) and the disease threats they posed. This concept (as I will show) develops not only through Said but also through interventions made by Stuart Hall, Michel Foucault, Sylvia Wynter, and others. Epidemic Orientalism describes a dominant discursive frame in infectious disease control that motivated the rise of international infectious disease regulation and has persisted in certain forms since the International Sanitary Confer-ences to the present and to which all the actors in this work (from Chapter 2 onward) seem to respond. As a discourse it operates through, is built from, and is implicated in ideologies of European and Western exceptionalism, colonialism, and racial capitalism. Epidemic Orientalism takes as its root the ontological separation between West and rest, colonized and colonizer, and the attendant racializing processes that obliterate any subjectivity of the other beyond their relation to the West.[45] Epidemic Orientalism emerged out of the encounters between Europeans and non-Europeans in colonial zones in the eighteenth and nineteenth centuries after the threats of the diseases of colonial sites to European economic and political interests and bodies were made visible through colonial endeavors. As diseases encountered by Europeans for the first time began to spread in new colonies and return to Europe, the continent began to relocate its understanding of itself relative to the rest of the world and the disease threats within it, repositioning the colonial world as a locus of disease threat from which the colonizer and empire needed to be protected. Importantly, this is not an argument about how European modernity was structured through the exclusion of the rest of the world from modernity. Quite the opposite, in fact. Epidemic Orien-talism as a theory suggests that through particular understandings of the rest of the world in relationship to itself, Europe and later the broader West could construct an image of itself in opposition to the rest of the world, as perceived through the threat of disease, while still locating the wider world as a site of exploitation, extraction, and knowledge creation.

Epidemic Orientalism is the discursive frame that describes how the world of infectious disease control has been and continues in no small part to be organized. The effect of epidemic Orientalism is to produce a way of engaging and organizing the object of international epidemic, as understood through international regulations, for the purpose of control. As a discourse this produces several effects that organize knowledge around the field of infectious disease control while also determining practice and policy.

Discourses are central for representing the world—they produce knowledge through language.[46] They formally determine the ways of talking about a subject, defining the boundaries and possibilities for practice and thought on it. Epidemic Orientalism organizes the possibilities for disease control within a frame that situates the West, understood broadly as the site that requires protection from epidemic threat, and much of the rest of the world, namely, Asia, the Middle East, and Africa, as the sources of perpetual potential epidemic threat. Epidemic Orientalism allows for the "classification, as well as categorization of difference" that both reify the distinctions between the *modern West* and rest of the world and subsequently make the distinction operable as a structure of thought.[47] Epidemic Orientalism therefore represents a mode through which epidemic knowledge has been produced and thought about. Disease risk, understood as a biological, political, and economic force affecting trade and wealth accumulation in Europe, signifies superiority or inferiority relative to the modern world. The map of the world can therefore be read not only according to national, imperial, or geographical boundaries but also as spaces of disease threat and vulnerability relative to the Western world.

Second, this has an attendant effect on subject formation. Those peoples and populations understood in relation to disease and the relative threats they present, both as vectors and victims, can be organized accordingly. This always intertwines the discourse within logics and rationalizations of racial and ethnic superiority derived from Western epistemes. The people in places reflective of disease risk to Europe are subsequently read into an epidemic Orientalist equation that appraises their existence relative to disease threats to the West on top of dehumanizing schemas of racism. Epidemic threat or the presence of epidemics themselves provide justification, a dog whistle that marks the unbridgeable gap between white bourgeois humanity from all others. Thus disease threat comes to signify further difference from Western subjects that overlie onto or reproduce systems of racial difference, dynamics of colonial exploitation, and economic subjectivities already present.

Third, this epidemic Orientalism as a discursive frame classifies and categorizes difference along these fictive geographies while also establishing a teleological model of comparison and evaluation. All that exists in the West is modern, biomedical, and sufficiently advanced as to not breed epidemics; all that is outside must therefore attempt to progress to the level of the West. This staircase concept[48] of modern sanitary progress seats the Western world at the top level with a vision of the rest of the world needing to climb the flight in the same manner laid out by the West. This intersects with visions of racial difference rooted in tropes of cultural and civilizational inferiority and signified as innate incompatibility with the Western world.

The history of international infectious disease control is the history of a variety of ontological and epistemological orientations toward the phenomena of epidemics. Before diseases were isolated to their pathogenic causes or formally understood as biological phenomena, epidemic diseases were already an object of forms of political control and knowledge production for the purposes of control. Medieval quarantine ordinances date back to the twelfth century. Isolation and expulsion of the sick within a society date back even earlier. However, in the nineteenth century, still before the formal and widespread acceptance of germ theory or concepts of contagion, epidemics were becoming the object of international coordination and control.

While the importance and efficacy of the International Sanitary Conventions and later International Health Regulations have been much debated,[49] they were and remain the only international regulations policing disease spread in humans. I argue that the international infectious disease control and explicitly epidemic disease control organized primarily through the International Sanitary Conventions and later International Health Regulations have and continue to operate under a certain discursive formation that organizes how epidemics are discussed, appraised for risk, and managed.

Epidemic Orientalism provides the field of infectious disease control with a system of representing epidemic threat in a particular relation to a certain vision of division of the world. Epidemic Orientalism operates as discourse that gives meaning to epidemics and subsequently determines certain courses of action in response to them. To explain the concept, I will begin by discussing how I am employing the terms *discourse* and *Orientalism* before explaining in greater detail the dynamics by which epidemic Orientalism exists and operates as discourse.

Edward Said refers to the power-knowledge relation at work in the operation of colonialism (with a particular focus on Asia) as *Orientalism*. Orientalism is the discourse that motivated and mobilized the practices by which the world colonized by European empires could be managed, dominated, and understood, creating the idea of the Orient in opposition to the Occident, the site of European civilization.

> Therefore as much as the West itself, the Orient is an idea that has a history and a tradition of thought, imagery and vocabulary that have given it reality and presence in and for the West. The two geographical entities thus support and to an extent reflect each other.[50]

Orientalism, is in short "the Western style for dominating, restructuring, and having authority over the Orient" rooted in the practice of claiming an understanding and thereby the authority to control it.[51] Orientalism represents chiefly a colonizing worldview rooted in a perspective of Western superiority that allows for distinctions and divisions to be drawn and claimed between the Occident and Oriental cultures, peoples, and spaces. It is through the process of creating the Orient as an ontologically distinct alter-space, separate from the West, that Orientalism establishes its power over colonial space. By claiming the power to name, define, and construct a vision of the Orient, the Orientalist can define its spaces and peoples for the purposes of colonialism and recognizing modernity's others. Said argues that without an understanding of the discourse of Orientalism, it is impossible to comprehend the systems of domination through which colonialism operates. Locating the theoretical roots of Orientalism in Gramsci's concept of hegemony, Said recognizes the relationship between the Orient and Occident, the colony and colonizer, as a relationship of power and of domination,[52] which operates as a mode of "holding down" the Oriental world, rendering it stable and legible only through the discourse itself.

Said's analysis of Orientalism (as well as much anti- and postcolonial theory) has come under significant critique for being too reductive in its theorizing of power.[53] Homi Bhabha, Henry Louis Gates, and others have reflected on the reductive binary constitutions of power between the colonized and colonizer.[54] In many ways their analyses and critiques have expanded Said's own concept of Orientalism by highlighting the ways in which colonized people consistently resist colonial forms of power and subordination at the same time colonial power attempts to incorporate and structure itself around, against, and in relation to that resistance.[55] Abdul JanMohamed and Benita Parry have also further highlighted the materiality of colonial power that exists outside of the text and in the wider scope of colonial violence, military power, and colonial governance within Said's work.[56] While much of *Orientalism* is devoted to textual analysis, these analyses exist within the domain of colonial power that, through violence, can impose a certain reading of the world while also negating the perspectives of the colonized. Resituating our understanding of the theoretical lessons of *Orientalism* provides us with an important sociological account of how dynamics of colonial knowledge are critical to the larger project of governance and produce power in themselves.

Said sketches out both the dynamics of power made possible through Orientalism and the power and force located *within* the signification of colonized and colonizer as binary forces. As JanMohamed writes of this Manichean allegory, the binarism itself derives benefits for the colonial system of governance:

> The fetishizing strategy and the allegorical mechanism not only permit a rapid exchange of denigrating images which can be used to maintain a sense of moral difference; they also allow the writer to transform social and historical dissimilarities into universal, metaphysical differences. If . . . African natives can be collapsed into African animals and mystified still further as some magical essence of the continent, then clearly there can be no meeting ground, no identity, between the social, historical creatures of Europe and the metaphysical alterity of the Calibans and Ariels of Africa.

If the differences between the Europeans and the natives are so vast, then
clearly, as I stated earlier, the process of civilizing the natives can continue
indefinitely.[57]

Colonial constructions of colonizer and colonized thereby make colonialism possible and enactable as a project of violent governance through
their maintenance of the differences between these two subject positions.
As JanMohamed also writes, by overdetermining the colonized other and
fixing them as infantile or backward, this relation between colonized and
colonizer allows the conqueror to feel vindicated and morally secure as
the superior actor engaging with someone lesser than. The system of relations in turn confers the benefit of valorizing colonial practice even as it
violently subjugates. The colonizer represents the makers of modern civilization, while the colonized is always already requiring civilization. The
subject formation and dynamics of colonial rule elaborated by Said, Fanon,
and others then gives us insight into not only the power dynamics made
possible by forms of colonial knowledge production but also the phenomenological power of colonial epistemology. As Frantz Fanon describes, this
is both a dehumanizing process and a racializing one, ascribing novel subjectivities defined for and by the colonizer, locating inalienable difference
on the basis of skin, hair, bone, culture, or other markers of innate difference and thereby inferiority.[58] It is not solely the practice of producing colonial knowledge that serves systems of colonial power but the logics of that
practice that also weave oppressive potentialities into the very fabric of that
knowledge.

Orientalism demonstrates how ideas operating at the level of discourse
produce and reproduce material effects through the employment of this
discourse in the practices of governance, control, the application of scientific
knowledge, and oppression, and shape the conditions for action within the
domain of international infectious disease control. Orientalism as it operates
at a discursive level, patterning all levels of interaction between colonized
and colonizer, resolves the bifurcation between science and the natural world
as it assumes these constructions to be subsumed within the larger discursive frame. As such, epidemic Orientalism is always already structuring the

activities and application of medical knowledge, as the discourse emergent in the nineteenth century largely preceded the formulation of that scientific knowledge which it served. It is the commonsense logic that structures how diseases are perceived relative to the concerns of the dominant group.

In employing Orientalism as my point of theoretical departure, I am keenly sensitive to what Said himself thought of "travelling theory."[59] Said most specifically develops his concept of Orientalism from colonial knowledges derived in the Middle East and North Africa. I intend to stretch this definition. My theory of epidemic Orientalism, while drawing extensively on the work of Said, departs insofar as I seek to resituate my theoretical formulation within this different landscape of disease control emerging in the nineteenth century that, while geographically wedded in large part to anxieties in the Indian Ocean, also produces a global vision of disease threat from sites within Europe and "near Asia." This is not an attempt to universalize the theory but rather to locate it within landscapes of relation that are produced both by epidemiological concern, trade and political economic anxieties, and racist and xenophobic logics. These in turn interrelate and structure racialized logics of disease response. In this work I suggest that epidemic Orientalism refers not solely to the relationships between imperial metropoles and colonial peripheries in Asia but also many parts of Africa and at times South America. While Said is at his most detailed when he discusses the particularities of the formations that constitute the Orient through the knowledge projects of European imperial incursion in the East, namely, visions of decay, archaic civilizations steeped in mystery, and emasculated men, epidemic Orientalism diverges by examining how disease and its emergence constitutes new ways of creating difference between the West and much of the rest of the world. I am most indebted to Said's theory when considering how Orientalism, beyond defining an Eastern world for the purposes of colonial control, also reflected back a stable vision of Europe as distinct from it. This element—how Orientalism reifies supremacist visions of Western knowledge and civilization—is of critical importance for understanding how epidemic Orientalism is able to produce a mythological vision of a sanitary Western world in need of protection from an unsanitary other. The International Sanitary Conferences, in attempting to produce globally sanctioned regulations for the control of infectious diseases, also produced a global *vision of division*, separating the world between those requiring epidemic controls to halt the spread of disease from afar, and those upon which controls could be implemented for the benefit of the other group.

In addressing these epistemological questions of historical and social scientific thought, it is critical to recenter a conversation about racism, xenophobia. and colonialism within the history of the rise of both the International Sanitary Conferences and Conventions and concomitantly the present International Health Regulations (which sprang directly from the International Sanitary Conventions) and infectious disease controls. Doing so demonstrates the ways in which infectious disease and the emergence of epidemics within certain geographies come to signify and be signified as markers of racial difference. While the economic and political dynamics of empire have in many ways expired, particular modes of thought and knowledge systems endure and transform.

The present-day and historical systems of infectious disease control, the logics of which have and continue to prioritize infectious threats very much from a geographically grounded position in the Northern and Western Hemispheres, are rooted in a persistent and adaptive engagement with how Europe and the West more colloquially have historically constructed race and wielded racism and xenophobia from the first colonial moments of encounter, through settler colonial action, and in the aftermath and decline of formal empires. How systems of governance and control rooted in racist organizing structures interact with shifting practices of international health operations speaks to the durability of these forms beyond the epochal shifts that are often erased by optimistic evangelists for postmodern progress or rediscovered by critical scholars who see the current moment of global health as wholly novel. Racism, Orientalism, and colonial exploitation, mobilized through imperial economic concerns, were central to the rise of international health and persist in the logics of infectious disease control today. Adopting a scholarly approach that grounds our analysis in these moments highlights the role of these logics as the frameworks for our contemporary world.

In writing this book I am not the first to suggest that infectious disease regulations of the past have been a vehicle for ascribing difference geographically, racially, ethnically, and nationally.[60] This work pushes beyond the confines of the earliest International Sanitary Conferences to argue that the ghosts of colonialism are not specters of the past but the intellectual grandparents of our current period. Infectious disease control remains a project bound up with the production of subjects for control and regulation rooted in beliefs of Western exceptionalism.

This argument fits within existing academic discourses surrounding histories of colonial medicine and the ways that scientific and medical knowledge crafted novel subjects under colonialism. As such it benefits greatly from the work of Valeska Huber, Meghan Vaughan, Alison Bashford, David Arnold, Warwick Anderson, Neel Ahuja, Julie Livingstone, Nükhet Varlik, and many others. In building from this wealth of scholarship, I examine how these dynamics of subject formation and the interplay between disease, risk, racism, xenophobia, and political and economic expediencies affect the field of health globally and have done so for the last two centuries.

Epidemic Orientalism and Biopolitics

Any time one considers forms of power operating on bodies, the constitution of subjects, or the formation of populations on to which forms of power are imposed in various ways, we tend to read this in terms of Foucault's concepts of discipline and biopower. I don't wish to add to the chorus of critique of Foucault's approaches. This book, while considering these practices and strategies of power, departs from Foucauldian analyses. Foucault's genealogies of systems of power flow through an explicitly Eurocentric and one could say Franco-centric historical narrative. Foucault understands the body as the site of power relations and disciplinary institutions as locations for the production of subjects: the prison, the school, the military, and others.[61] Foucault's genealogy of power from punishment and the negation of bodies and people through torture and execution to the production of productive, docile subjects and populations provides us with a very effective mode for understanding modern forms of power. However, this genealogy has been noted for recognizing these developments to have occurred almost exclusively within the container of Europe without recognition of the role of the world beyond as affecting these shifts in power on the body.[62] While Foucault's conceptualization of biopower considers relations within a modern state between an individual and sovereign power, he largely leaves unaddressed differential forms of power, supranational institutions, or the constitution of subjects in ways that do not privilege an individuated neoliberal actor. Foucault's biopolitics, while not ignoring racism as a central component of biopower, does develop its genealogy through Britain and France, which limits his recognition of a variety of other traditions of subject formation and thinking on the way power is visited on the body. Postcolonial and anticolonial thinkers have long produced their own conceptions of racialized and colonial subject relations that consider how power is visited on bodies, how populations are produced, and how knowledges operate in the service of controlling life.[63] While Achille Mbembe connects these distinct threads in his paper and book on necropolitics,[64] in most biopolitical analyses we ignore these other genealogies of power derived from colonial conquest, slavery, and imperialism.[65] One of the most significant lessons taken from Mbembe's examination of necropower is that the colony represents the site where sovereignty consists fundamentally in the exercise of a power outside the law (*ab legibus solutus*) and where "peace" is more likely to take on the face of a "war without end."[66] Within colonial sites the role of sovereign power is not to manage the lives and biological outcomes of citizens but rather the to navigate land and territories for conquest inhabited by those who, through "the racial denial of any common bond,"[67] can exist outside the boundaries and protections of sovereign law. Thus, in contrast to Foucault's analysis of biopolitics as power "to make live and let die,"[68] in the colonial space, where colonized and colonial populations are marked by racial difference that determines entry into the body politic, for those operating as agents of colonial power the right to kill or let die is not bound to rule of law. This genealogy of necropower thereby draws from a different history for understanding the imposition of power over biological processes and life.

This is very important for considering how to appraise the history of colonial medicine and the healing power of biomedicine in colonial sites. A simplistic argument would suggest either that all biomedicine operating in colonial space, or all systems of public health, reflect a violent and purely coercive endeavor. Mbembe provides us a useful lens in order to complicate this narrative. It is not that all biomedical interventions into the lives of those in colonial spaces are inherently harmful or salvational, but rather that since the colonial space operates outside of the rules and laws of the metropole, we have to not solely see biomedicine as an agent of colonialism but as operating outside of the parameters that it does in Europe. This should recast our perspectives of how we see both notions of colonial resistance and how this shifts our understandings of medicine and power outside of Europe.

Employing a purely Foucauldian genealogy of biopower to understand the histories and discursive formations of international infectious disease control, by limiting our genealogical understanding of it to the inner workings of Europe, would make two critical errors. The first would be to presuppose that Europe is or has ever been a static object defined by the national boundaries imposed on the continent. The second would be to suggest that we can read the history of international infectious disease control solely through European actors, Europe, or the West. The former would lead us to a crisis whereby we would have to accept that there is such a thing as Europe (or the West) that exists and is not an invention of and for itself, to stand in opposition to that which is not Europe (and the West). This would then ignore the cosmologies of power at work in producing a stable version of themselves that perpetuates a vision of superiority and civilizational hierarchy. The latter error would then miss how the privileging of European actors as the only agents of historical production ignores those outside of it as political forces themselves and further reproduces a fetishistic obsession with the world-historical force of a thing called Europe (and the West) that can be set apart from the rest of the world. To confront these potential pitfalls in intellectual practice, drawing on Edward Said, epidemic Orientalism as a theory to explain the history of international infectious disease control takes the production of a superior mythic West as its starting point for considering the relationships between power and knowledge that shape action on disease threats.

A final departure from the biopolitical mode lies in the understandings of the role of medicine and biomedicine, in particular in the practice of infectious disease control. This book seeks to complicate a flat reading of power operating on the body as being purely coercive and operating only in the interests of power. The complexity of epidemic response highlights a critically productive tension between the justifiable need to manage and control populations for the purpose of limiting contagion and ensuring health, and how those systems of control through intent or neglect define who is deserving of health protections and who can be sacrificed or allowed to die. Systems of lockdown, quarantine, and disease control that apply equally and equitably across an entire population are a different beast from those that would seek to impose particular forms of control on racialized or marginalized populations or withhold care from certain groups in order to privilege others. This book takes seriously the modes of public health provision that fundamentally provide care and support in equitable and effective ways while troubling the histories of violence, oppression, and the limits of discourses in allowing for equitable care.

Epidemics, Modernity, and the Signification of Difference

We find that while the threat of epidemic spread is ostensibly the concern at stake in the history of international disease control, the perception of epidemic threat has at times been mediated by a host of wider factors. The ultimate forms these regulations controlling infectious disease would take over time are embedded within existing concerns for global economic flows and trade, new or hastening forms of mobility, and a need to control population movement through the remote management of bodies and geographies. These concerns have historically been especially focused on European colonies in the Indian Ocean and postcolonial spaces worldwide. In short, the framers of the International Sanitary Conventions and the International Health Regulations of the present have been uniquely concerned with imposing and maintaining a particular system of relation on the world and maintaining that order in opposition to the threat of certain infectious diseases that may upset that order. Unlike so many international agreements or regulations that emerged out of a post–World War II global order that reflected a new and different internationalism, one in many ways led by nations outside of Europe and North America,[69] the perspectives guiding the regulations themselves have remained remarkably durable in the face of a tumultuous twentieth century with a unique legacy rooted in an era in which global relations were shaped by imperial actors but now exist in a postimperial geopolitical present.

We can see this influence in the fictive geographies of disease at work in statements made across time by numerous key health actors involved in drafting these regulations. It is no coincidence that in the 175-year history of internationally coordinated infectious disease control, we can find almost identical justifications for systems of epidemic disease management.

From *La Défense de l'Europe Contre Le Choléra*, by Adrian Proust (1892):

It [cholera] extends into the Far East, in the Gulf Bengal, Burma, Indo-China, the treaties of China, Korea, Japan, and all the coast of the seas of China, as far as Wladivostock. In recent years, it has been raging in Iraq-Arabia, Mesopotamia, Persia, Syria, Arabia (Mecca) and Africa (Massawa). The economic transformations that are on the entire surface of the African continent, will further aggravate the danger. So the question of the defense of Europe against the cholera always stands with a pressing interest and a fearful actuality. The aim of our efforts is to intercept all direct communication between the contaminated provenances of the Far East on one side; Egypt, the Mediterranean and Europe, on the other.[70]

From an excerpt from the minutes of the committee on international quarantine tasked with amending the International Sanitary Regulations (1951):

Therefore when the Additional regulations come into force, it is possible that the countries or areas which fall into the yellow-fever endemic zone may not be declared as infected local areas, or may subsequently be declared as free from infection after a period of three months has elapsed. . . . The periods now prescribed for determining freedom from yellow-fever infection are too short. . . . The information provided in this publication indicates that, year after year, yellow fever is a constant and continuous problem in various parts of Latin America. Secondly the possibility of a person getting out of a jungle area, leaving by plane and arriving at an airport in a receptive area within the incubation period, has always to be borne in mind.[71]

From noted microbiologist, Nobel laureate, and key framer of US and International epidemic policy Joshua Lederberg in 1988:

> The increasing density of human habitations as well as inventions such as the subway and the jet airplane that mix populations all add to the risks of spread of infection. Paradoxically, improvements in sanitation and vaccination sometimes make us the more vulnerable because they leave the larger human herd more innocent of microbial experience. . . . The opening of wild lands to human occupation has exposed people unaccustomed to viruses. . . . Such research should be done on a broad international scale to both share the progress made in advanced countries and amplify the opportunities for fieldwork at the earliest appearance of outbreaks in the most afflicted areas. No matter how selfish our motives, we can no longer be indifferent to the suffering of others. The microbe that felled one child in a distant continent yesterday can reach yours today and seed a global pandemic tomorrow. "Never send to know for whom the bell tolls; it tolls for thee."[72]

These three quotations were each uttered in response to the reform or failures of the International Sanitary Conventions or International Health Regulations. In these three statements we find the markers of epidemic Orientalism: the geographic representation of the world through relations of disease threat to the West, the interpolation of innate difference and inferiority signified by disease, and the production of a teleological vision of disease control that elevates the West above all others. The coalescence of these three elements forms the justification for international infectious disease control. These quotations reflect a haunting continuity in the modes of thought and perceptions of disease threat. In each, the deadliest threats emerge from the *darkest* parts of the world—the lands beyond Europe, the *jungles*, the distant continent—and reflect an immediate threat to an a priori defined Western perspective. By contrasting much of the rest of the world as threat, the West remains an untroubled site of disease. The presence of infectious disease threats to the West therefore reflects a lack, an innate problem of civilization, both of the lands and people from which they emerge. Disease becomes that marker of inferiority. Each of these quotes seeks to prevent the spread of disease in a manner consistent with keeping particular forms of relation *as they have always been*. In crafting these visions of the world as seen through the risk of disease to the West, epidemics operate as a signifier[73] of inferiority and differences, rendering the spaces where epidemic threats to the West emerge and the people residing in them as inferior and requiring of surveillance, scrutiny, and control.

In the first quote from Adrien Proust, a noted physician who was the representative of France to numerous International Sanitary Conventions, he depicts Europe as beset from all sides by the threat of pestilence. The colonies of Europe reflect the possibility for great economic exploitation but also great risk. The world and its inhabitants become framed in terms of victim and threat, constructing novel boundaries of difference that reify the European and Western world as distinct. The objective then must be both the maintenance of colonial economic relations and the establishment of a sanitary boundary between Europe and the sites of European colonies. In the second, a quote from the Government of Ceylon in 1956, this same preoccupation is presented though updated to accommodate the looming threat of pandemic disaster through swift air travel. The threat is the lone traveler "getting out of a *jungle area*" afflicted with yellow fever, capable of devastating colonized Asia. In this language the markers of racial and civilizational difference are evident. Jungles are not Western forests and modern humans do not inhabit jungles—the innuendo is clear. This time the problem is not only the foreign, dangerous environment but the capacity of those living there to travel to a space that the author implies that they should not. The concern for this person is not their disease so long as it stays within the jungle area but rather how by their own agency they can travel to a place where they and their disease do not belong.

Finally in a quote from noted microbiologist and Nobel laureate Joshua Lederberg, despite his humanistic calls to not close ourselves off to human suffering, the specter of the distant microbe that felled a child coming to the shores of America haunts his vision of the future. Once again the risk is not so much the disease in its place of origin but rather for the mixing of populations that comes about through increased global relations and conviviality. Without being explicit in its racial language as seen in the first two quotes, the invocation of *wild lands*, the *mixing of populations*, and the distinctions made between *advanced countries* and *afflicted areas* exposes a racial/ethnic schema of difference reflecting all too clearly that these diseases are not an endemic problem to the West but emerge from the spaces beyond. Moreover, these discussions are not nationalistic in their scope but rather civilizational, regional, and hemispheric. The problem of epidemics for Lederberg, the representative of Ceylon, and Adrien Proust are not problems for single nations to confront but *all advanced nations* and civilizations. Epidemics represent the lingering risk at the center of global connectedness—the microbe is not the problem, but rather its capacity to travel westward. Lederberg also raises the teleological superiority of the West. While sanitation and hygiene leave the Western world vulnerable, it is simultaneously the responsibility of the West, for its own sake, to raise up the rest of the world to the hygienic superiority of itself, for the sake of the herd.

These three quotes set up a particular vision and division of the world that persists across the time periods considered in this work, that the epidemics that most threaten the globe are ones that emerge in the distant lands of what was once colonial exploitation, now perhaps politely described as the "developing world," and travel to lands unspoiled by such pestilence, almost always reflexively Europe and North America. In these moments we see a whole idealized geography of the world mapped out before us. For to understand how disease control operates, it is not sufficient to understand the biology of our most pressing threats; we must also understand the assumptions of those assessing these threats.

The terrain upon which disease threat is seen must be viewed through the eyes of those with their feet firmly planted not at the site of epidemic occurrence but in the distant places where these epidemics may one day reach. These quotations are a window into a landscape of relations onto which epidemiological and medical knowledge are mapped with the omnipresent but unstated purpose of recognizing epidemic threat, foremost as that which threatens a vision of the world that divides *West from rest*.

The Racial Perspectivism of Epidemic Orientalism

We see critically in each quote a vision of the political-economic neces-
sities of Western power systems. But our interpretation cannot end with
political economy. Each quotation justifies its position through the constitution of those other to the Western world, the epidemic-resistant world
in need of protection, thus exposing the racial and xenophobic contract
at the core of epidemic Orientalism.[74] Global economic gain necessitates
trade and traffic, but the necessity of economic flows is perceived to produce physical and civilizational vulnerabilities as assumed white Western
bodies are exposed to the world and bodies of others. Semiotically the
author of each statement recognizes this tension and thus categorizes the
populations of the world according to those at risk and those who pose
a threat. The diseases that will fell the world never come from within but
rather from without, and this subsequently invites a certain calculus to define who is worthy of participating in Western modernity and by extension
salvation from epidemics, and thus who is to be excluded and isolated. The
specter of disease becomes a mode by which, whether indirectly or not,
sovereign claims can be suggested over populations ruled outside of the
Western imperial or postimperial metropoles in order to protect the health
and political and economic interests of those within. As we will see in further chapters (Chapters 2 and 3 in particular), the manner in which these
remote sovereign decisions about the lives of others are meted out too often
align along the racial, caste, or xenophobic orders already in existence at
the sites of epidemic. Thus at its core, epidemic Orientalism reflects the
role of racism as both central to the mechanisms at work within the modern world and its successful operation as being contingent on the mobilization of racial regimes to confront disease threats from afar. Global capital
concerns informing local responses to epidemics do not fully explain epidemic responses on the ground. In the early period of the International
Sanitary Conferences when imperial concerns broadly dominated the domain of international health, global epidemic threats were represented as
a problem emerging from the lands beyond Europe. Colonial knowledge
of the disease threats at the geographic peripheries of empire and later the

knowledge of their ability to travel "home" mobilized the sanitary conferences. While this established an East/West distinction between victim and vector of disease, as we will see in Chapter 2 and in the prior quotations, the control of disease at the site of epidemic assumed that white supremacist racial orders in colonial settings would be mobilized not only to protect the human and economic vitality of empire but also divide populations and conquer disease (see Chapter 3). Thus rather than racist epidemic response responding solely to the economic threats of epidemic, local concerns of racial mixing, residential segregation, eugenics, and racial decline intersect and complicate epidemic responses far from imperial metropolitan halls of power. As we see in the further chapters that explore the world after the end of most formal empires, the quandary of how to maintain sanitary controls without the power and force of remote sovereignty and its attendant racial governance becomes a prominent preoccupation of later framers of international health regulations. The scaffolding of epidemic Orientalism and international epidemic control on practices of localized racial governance continue to be evident and at times foundational in the ideologies of infectious disease control today. Thus epidemic Orientalism was first organized around colonial anthropological and medical knowledge of the sites and peoples within colonial environments, and of the imminent political and economic threats disease posed to imperial power, but it also implicitly relied on colonial systems of racial control in order to quell epidemics and protect both global economic flows and the Orientalist divisions critical to the vision of European modernity.

In the combined 130-year history of the International Sanitary Conventions and the International Health Regulations and the 171 years since the first International Sanitary Conferences, these regulations and other global epidemic response mechanisms like the Pandemic Emergency Financing Facility have engaged in a project of more than solely infectious disease control. While also prioritizing those diseases and epidemics that can threaten global economic orders, they have engaged in a project of *signification and meaning making* that have advocated interventions around the world in the interests of Europe and North America as well as those variably incorporated into mythologies of the West such as Japan and Singapore. The creation of these regulations was not only a matter of seeking to protect Europe and North America from external disease threats but also an act of authoring Eurocentric visions of modernity *into* being. The process and practice of regulating infectious diseases are doubly a process of mapping geographies of modernity. This occurs in a dialectic form—raising up Western or European spaces and peoples as hygienically and civilizationally superior in contrast to those at the sites of epidemic outbreak. This double move locates the West as the space that requires protecting from the savage rest of the world, ensuring a Eurocentric or Western gaze permeates and orients how international disease control operates under these regulatory systems. Disease regulations and the debates around them have been central vehicles through which the terrains of modernity are contested and mapped. From the International Sanitary Conventions of the past to the International Health Regulations of today, in attempting to rationalize natural phenomena of epidemics and bring them to heel through global regulations, regulators and their spokespersons have also prefigured Europe and later North America as the sites needing protection from infectious threats, thereby imposing this viewpoint on the rest of the world. The mapping of the modern world through perspectives and vectors of disease in turn also maps designations of *modern* and *non-modern* onto those perceived as the potential victims of epidemics and those persons perceived as the carriers of disease, respectively. These fictive geographies created through these regulations highlight the Eurocentric histories of epidemic controls that historically have prioritized the management of epidemics capable of spreading to Europe and North America from the rest of the world and not in the opposite direction, or epidemics that threaten to affect prevalent structures of global systems of trade. The encoding of this Eurocentric perspective through global disease regulations thus perpetuates the myths of modernity that locate Europe and those of European descent as the only agents of progress, who must be protected at times at the expense of the rest of the world. The history of epidemic responses in modernity is also the history of colonialism, colonial violence, and their residual debris in the postcolonial moment. As the West grapples with its own previously inconceivable susceptibility to pandemic threats during this ongoing pandemic of COVID-19, we can see how these myths produce very real monsters of its own creation.

This book begins with an exploration of how the epidemic frontiers around Europe and in the colonies of European empires presented Europeans with a novel existential threat and terrain upon which they could conceive of spaces and peoples different from themselves and from which they required protection. This early formation of Modern Europeanness as distinct in form from the rest of the world (and also in important ways different from the Persian and Ottoman Empires) in bio-/epidemiological terms allowed for the formation of the first international health regime, the International Sanitary Conferences and Conventions, which dictated the first regulations for the management of disease around the world. These regulations paired economic and trade concerns with the threat of infectious disease, inextricably linking global capital with the perceptions of infectious disease threat emanating in large part from the areas surrounding the Indian Ocean. From here we will examine how the imperial concerns of the International Sanitary Conventions transformed and endured in the postwar period marked by the formation of international organizations such as the World Health Organization. Finally we will explore the constructions of epidemic threats in the present at both the World Health Organization and World Bank, denaturalizing the financial and geopolitical rationalities of both organizations to see how our commonsense beliefs of disease threat are modulated by a series of wider political and economic concerns.

I do not seek to exclude the epidemiological or public health rationales for action that demonstrate the epidemic consequences of disease. This work seeks to ascertain how political, racist, economic, and social concerns have shaped perceptions and responses to disease threats. This in turn helps to explain how these forces augment understandings of threat and the hidden roles of regulations. Many scholars of the current moment of disease control—what can be broadly termed the era of *biosecurity*—have sought to examine the novelty of our contemporary era, making what amount to detours around history to describe what is original about the phenomena of the present.[75] The rise of the social scientific study of global health is largely located in the periods after World War II contemporaneously with the emergence of large international organizations.[76] Within certain areas of health research, the term *international health*, designating an earlier era of colonial health interventions and state-state engagement, contrasts with the more transnational global health approach premised on tenets of health equity.[77] In fetishizing the technological or political transformations after World War II or more immediately after the ideological changes that rose from the aftermath of the events of September 11, 2001, our optics have conformed to what the historian, sociologist, and scholar of Cultural Studies Paul Gilroy has termed "the radical or even catastrophic nature of the break between contemporary conditions and the epoch of modernism."[78] The explanatory force and purchase of such periodization can often oversell the radical shifts in world-historical eras when confronted with some of modernity and empire's most durable and adaptive of concepts, such as race and racism. What is precisely important is how ideas wrought in the furnaces of empire and modernity remain durable once the formal epochs of both have seemed to wane. I wish to examine how these ideas become intertwined with postcolonial modes of thought. The aim is not to establish a bifurcation between imperial and postimperial eras but rather to show how systems of thought transform, disappear, shift, and endure.

The Others of Modernity—The Problem of Colonial Knowledge and the Enlightenment

Histories of empire and science have shown that travel writings,[79] natural science depictions,[80] and medical treatises[81] effectively *produced* the rest of the world for European readerships and for their consumption. Naturalist and later scientific writings in particular from 1492 until the late nineteenth century became a way for Europeans to conceptualize the rest of the world on their terms, dialectically construct colonial subjects in opposition from their colonizing selves,[82] conceive of racial categories, and develop methods of colonial governance based on these constructions. In turn observations of the natural world merged with the motivations, interests, and concerns for European populations in colonial spaces. Colonialism provided the knowledges of far-off lands from which to construct the concept of the modern (European) self and its history in opposition to the unmodern masses of the rest of the world. Colonialism is therefore not only a mode of rule but a way of seeing and creating subjects for rule in other domains. It is in effect an act of world making through which social relations are constructed for the purposes of domination.[83] Sylvia Wynter reminds us that within the construction of a European vision of modernity, there is always a system of exclusion at work. To legitimize European knowledge systems as the only rational form of thought, those operating outside of them must be *negatively represented* as outside the rational and the modern.[84] Modernity as a project can be read as one that secures the superiority of the Western bourgeois conception of the human[85] and the welfare and well-being of those inducted into modernity as such.

Immanent critiques of modernity's exclusions have attempted to attack the central dialectic rooted in its Eurocentrism that the world peripheral to Europe is immature. Postcolonial thinkers have endeavored to demonstrate that the notion of tradition as the anterior stage to modernity is a mode of rendering the colonized world as savage and lacking civilization.[86] Partha Chatterjee has critiqued the civilized tenets of a European notion of modernity in order to draw out that which was beneficial and superior in tradition. However, such critiques often reinforce this binary between tradition and modernity, leading not so much to an effective critique of modernity but rather a turn toward an ossified and romanticized concept of non-European traditions.[87] The issue of the binary between tradition and modernity is not merely an academic issue relegated to theory but one that has produced extreme consequences. Sociologist Claire Decoteau has demonstrated how the discourses of modernity, tradition, and colonialism informed Thabo Mbeki's HIV/AIDS denialism and formulated the discursive space upon which battles over HIV/AIDS policy in South Africa was conceived. In framing his avowed commitment to an anticolonial "African" set of solutions to the problem of HIV/AIDS, Mbeki positioned local health practices as traditional and oppositional to the colonialist reason of biomedicine when neither were in fact incommensurate with one another. Debates over biomedicine or indigenous healing practices were fought over this binary of tradition and modernity when in actual fact there was little to prevent both being incorporated into

South Africa's HIV/AIDS response. These debates cost hundreds of thousands of lives.[88]

In examining modernity as a central ordering concept of contemporary times, many have rightfully criticized the empirical and theoretical presuppositions of modernity's roots in Europe. Paul Gilroy, examining the role of the Atlantic in the formulation of the modern world, demonstrates how modernity, far from being shaped entirely by Europeans, was and is continuously constructed out of the ideas and experiences of those seen on the periphery of modernity, namely, those of African descent.[89]

Argentine philosopher Enrique Dussel coined the term "myths of modernity" to capture both the savagery and the occlusions at the heart of the concept of modernity as writ through Kant, Hegel, Weber, Habermas, and others. Dussel lays out a series of myths that lie at the center of modernity's promise and its mission, the first being the origin of modernity in Europe. The mapping of the rest of the world in a Kantian state of immaturity against a Europe situated in modernity locates Europe and the European as the most developed and superior civilization. Dussel argues that this particular myth

> obliges it, in the form of a categorical imperative, as it were, to "develop" (civilize, uplift, educate) the more primitive, barbarous, underdeveloped civilizations. The path of such development should be that followed by Europe in its own development out of antiquity and the Middle Ages. Where the barbarian or the primitive opposes the civilizing process, the praxis of modernity must, in the last instance, have recourse to the violence necessary to remove the obstacles to modernization. This violence, which produces, in many different ways, victims, takes on an almost ritualistic character: the civilizing hero invests his victims (the colonized, the slave, the woman, the ecological destruction of the earth, etc.) with the character of being participants in a process of redemptive sacrifice. From the point of view of modernity, the barbarian or primitive is in a state of guilt (for, among other things, opposing the civilizing process). This allows modernity to present itself not only as innocent but also as a force that will emancipate or redeem its victims from their guilt. Given this "civilizing" and redemptive character of modernity, the suffering and sacrifices (the costs) of modernization

imposed on "immature" peoples, enslaved races, the "weaker" sex et cetera, are inevitable and necessary.

In Dussel's understanding of the myth of modernity's origins in Europe, we find the dynamic force that this myth carries in particular to mobilize violent and colonizing practices and impose European will on those perceived outside the world of the modern, transforming this barbarity into a necessary and inevitable product of the progress of modernity. Dussel here captures the critical force and power of Enlightenment philosophy and modernity's conceptualizations. The fundamental belief in the unreason of the rest of the world reconfigures the violences carried out in the name of modernity as progress toward freedom. Modernity therefore for Dussel is dialectically constituted out of the Eurocentric myth of its own origins and the supposition that those outside of the geographically bounded space of modernity (the West) remain in a state of immaturity and savagery. Therefore modernity as a concept rests on this dialectic relationship that for modernity to exist it must therefore have its other in nonmodernity. Thinking through modernity in such a way prescribes the conflation of Europe with modernity and realizes the historical production of modernity to one entirely endogenous to Europe or expandable broadly to the West.[90] This, as has been highlighted by many, erases the production of modernity in Europe out of the exploitation and conquest of much of the rest of the world through colonialism and enslavement, as evidenced by the work of Walter Rodney and others[91] while supporting beliefs that modernity could arise solely from cultural and philosophical transformations that are the products exclusively of a clearly defined and discrete European world.

International Disease Control, Empire, and Modernity

In these critiques, the lurking violences at the essence of modernity as a concept emerge. By extension these critiques expose the limitations of its emancipatory project to reimagine radical freedom, self-consciousness, and self-determination. Still some would seek to recuperate the project of modernity for its idealistic ends while iterating on that which would make it a violent force for subjugation (seemingly antithetical to its lofty ideals).[92]

While the above critiques leveled from all sides toward what would now appear to be a rather naïve project rooted in violence, the notion of thinking through modernity as a project rather than a concept or epoch is one that I suggest is worthy of interrogation for novel approaches to understanding the power of modernity in the current setting. Thinking modernity as a concept, as a static object marked by the dynamics we have already discussed, fails to recognize that modernity is also a project always already in the process of becoming. Modernity progressively marches toward its objective of radical freedom. It has arrived, and it is also *modernizing* all at once.

It is in this particular knowledge project into which international disease regulations and policies both reproduce and require certain myths of modernity in order to rationalize the world and the diseases within it. At the same time these regulations have the effect of producing and reproducing modernity as a form, justifying its existence through the creation of modern subjects against nonmodern others. As the philosopher V. Y. Mudimbe has shown, the signification of modernity against that which and those who are considered not modern or reflecting some form of primordial, ahistorical traditionalism is the basis for the dialectical formations of subjects on a trajectory from the savage to the modern.[93] The practice of creating and imagining a universal vision of history, of time and agency, is the marker of modernity.[94]

Unlike some more orthodox postmodern readings of this history or a purely social constructivist approach, the meanings of diseases are not made purely in the domain of human perception but rather the power and dynamics of epidemics as physical phenomena themselves serve as sites on and through which to make meaning and subjects of others. Within the colonial dynamics of power and in the arena of geopolitics, scientific knowledge, beyond defining the human as apart from the natural, is also employed for the delineation of modern humans from those considered outside of modernity—*modernity's others*. To return to Wynter once more, the domain of international infectious disease control has been maintained as a project to secure the well-being of Western bourgeois man and its conception of those who matter in modernity.[95] Scientific knowledge becomes complicit in this action. This occurs not only through racist sciences such as eugenics but also in passing judgement of culture and behavior through a scientific lens. In this regard the presence of disease becomes the basis of defining human worth.

As we will encounter in Chapters 2 and 3, debates through the International Sanitary Conferences to the production of the first international sanitary conventions hinged not solely on scientific knowledge of disease, which by contemporary terms was still in its infancy in its biomedical understandings, but also on the appropriate means to understand global disease spread as a phenomenon and as something that could be controlled. As Weber and others have shown us, bringing the natural world to heel through regulation, rationalization, and bureaucracy is a central element of modernity. The question of how to control the seemingly irrational movements of diseases that do not obey human order was the central one of concern. That the rise of international infectious disease control grew out of systems of colonial relation is no surprise. Several scholars have conducted significant research on the role of colonial relations to the rise of the International Sanitary Conferences.[96] How can you control the spread of disease without the ability to police and control remote populations, flows of travel and trade, ports, sea lanes, and other sites of transit? And what scripts and orders will be applied in order to police these populations? Remote sovereignty is and has been a critical concern to all international regulations on infectious disease, and thus the roots of these first sets of regulations within colonial systems is of critical inquiry. This requires a turn toward the political-economic force of colonialism as seen explicitly from outside of Europe.

Within the wider cosmologies of imperial knowledge productions sits the role of infectious disease control. From this period of global imperial territorial control emerges the International Sanitary Conferences and Conventions that are central to this book. The regulations for the management and control of infectious disease set out in these conventions assume from the outset the capacity to impose these controls on extraterritorial space beyond Europe and its colonies. As we will see, these conventions allowed for a paradigmatic shift in the practice of disease control away from the centuries-old methods of costly port quarantines on the borders of Europe to the enforcement of sanitary and shipping controls to the sites of colonial enterprise. The International Sanitary Conventions were themselves a technology for the application and implementation of a global transimperial order, and their creation established new patterns of colonial governance, the practice of novel forms of political control over colonized populations, and new systems of relation and subjectification brought about by concerns over disease control. The fact that these conventions persist to this day in some form means that they had to adjust to a world without empire when they were transferred to the authority of the WHO, and the problem of extraterritorial sovereignty persists as a central concern of infectious disease control today as a result.

That colonial and European imperialism was a world-historical force must be of little dispute. By the outbreak of World War I, the rise of European imperial expansion had consumed and occupied 90 percent of the world's land mass with Britain governing 20 percent of the total globe and 25 percent of its population.[97] One of the most important contributions to human knowledge in the twentieth century was the formal, intellectual, and critical examination of empires as world-historical forces that governed extraterritorially and of imperialism and colonialism as the practices and systems of that governance.[98] As stated earlier, prominent anticolonial thinkers have shown that far from purely a system of governance, the enduring power of ideas rooted in the management of empire affects social hierarchies and racial categories,[99] state formation, the production of rights,[100] as well as the roots of liberal democracy and the civil sphere[101] today.

Forms of colonialism, be they trade oriented through the establishment of ports and unequal economic relations or via settler colonialism that consists of total occupation of land and territory, produce entirely distinct patterns of relation between people, space, and environment. The process of colonial occupation mandated the creation of new borders; the instantiation of new legal systems, economic relations, and categories of people; and the transformation of sovereignty.[102] It also produced genocide, forcefully eradicating millions of indigenous peoples in the Americas, the Pacific, Asia, and Africa as well as organizing the largest violent forced movement in human history, the transatlantic slave trade.[103] Into this cauldron of new social relations were thrown the establishment of novel racial categories for the delineation of economic and social relationships relative to colonial authorities.

What makes the actions of colonization so totalizing is the transformation in worldview that it brings about for those under its yoke. Former uncolonized subjects suddenly are forced to confront a system of power in which their own personhood operates in relation to the colonized, altering power dynamics and meaning structures in all aspects of life.[104]

Source Material and Methods

The evidence in this book is taken primarily from sources drawn from several major archives within Europe: the British Library, British National Archives at Kew, and Wellcome Library, all in London; the World Health Organization Archive and the League of Nations Archive in Geneva; and the Archives of the Western Cape in South Africa. All but one of these physical archives are located in European metropoles and are almost exclusively in French or English, though some sources are also in Spanish. In addition, primary source materials available online supplement these sources. Any scholar engaging with questions of power from a place of epistemic analysis must consider the role of sources. Whose voices are driving the narrative and whose are silenced? This is not explicitly a story of resistance to systems and structures of power; it is an analysis of how such structures come to be and the struggles associated with them. However, it is a story of how those of great power attend and respond to resistances to their power as well as the anxieties they provoke. In addition, this book explores moments when different health strategies, introduced overwhelmingly by actors beyond the Western world, produced novel ways of framing health. These perspectives, while immeasurably shaping the structure of our global health field today, often failed to shift the dynamics of the International Sanitary Conventions and later regulations. The comparison and contrasting of social medicine and other health movements, especially those emerging in South and East Asia and Africa (see Chapter 4), with the durable epidemic Orientalist logics of the International Sanitary Conventions and International Health Regulations should have us reflect on the immense divergence of thought from Western visions and the possibilities for thinking otherwise, while also recognizing the durability of colonial systems of thought. The majority of the sources examined are meeting minutes, official communications between actors at international organizations, or regulatory documents. These are the stories of large bureaucracies, international officials, and major voices in the scientific community.

This is not a book meant to depict spectacular suffering or violence. The effect of the diseases in this book are awful. Similarly, some of the responses taken up in the name of health security have also produced great harm. But to depict scenes of subjection in their most violent and perhaps voyeuristic would be to overwhelm a key claim of this book: that power also lies in and can pivot in the most banal and quotidian spaces of social life. As Saidiya Hartman shows in *Scenes of Subjection*, authors' often casual call for their readers to bear witness to spectacular violence "immures us to pain by virtue of their familiarity".[105] For Jean Améry, the experience of torture at the hands of the Nazi SS reduced his existence to one of pure corporeality: he no longer existed as a subject capable of agency but as a somatic body only feeling and reacting to painful stimuli.[106] In comparing Hartman with Améry, these moments of violence either felt or depicted can generate sympathy, but the debasement of human life to such a level that all we can see is dehumanization can reduce the subjects of this violence to purely objects of pity, not complex people whose lives were rich and varied, as all are, prior to these acts of violence. These moments are as equally capable of producing a voyeuristic fascination as empathy and obscure the bureaucratic, bloodless ways in which regulations and disease controls shape the fabric of one's social existence in a manner that may be imperceptible but deeply consequential and often violent. It is important to note that many of the justifications for the development of disease control systems or international regulation emerge from a single and enduring concern over the agency of those capable of traversing the world in ways invisible to the mechanisms of global capital, disease surveillance, and international or governmental orders: the pilgrim on Hajj, the Black African in the British Cape Colony, the Dalit population in colonial India, the peoples of the Eastern Congo. Too often the spread of infectious disease has been met with a need to control the bodies of those who powerful actors see as outside the bounds of their sovereignty and outside of modernity; thus these reactions are always already in response to those resisting those forces. In these ways I hope that the voices silenced by the archive come through as the object of ever-present anxiety and concern throughout the time periods examined.

Durability and Change

At the same moment, this work and this focus on these particular sets of regulations and responses does not negate the actions of actors beyond the Global North in very powerfully shaping the field of international health. Doctors and diplomats from China, the Soviet Union/Russia, Brazil, India, Cuba, Mexico, and multitudes of others have been critical to shaping our modern global health moment. The history examined in this book reflects a remarkably durable and Eurocentric framing of infectious disease control, which has remained so despite so many efforts to shift international health dynamics away from perspectives that locate Western Europe and North America as the sole sites of historical agency or power. As we will see, epidemic Orientalism has stubbornly persisted as a discursive frame despite much movement in different directions at both the World Health Organization and earlier the League of Nations Health Organization, and more contemporaneously as the spheres of power have shifted in international health from Europe and the United States toward China, India, and other centers over the last fifty years. This is not to negate those shifts but rather to highlight the stubbornness of Eurocentric and colonial modes of thought that sediment the foundations of new political and economic orientations. Epidemic Orientalism, rather than a static object in space, is a sticky feature of international infectious disease control that has maintained even as it has been shown time and time again, especially in the last forty years, to fail to control emergent disease threats and foreclose equitable and effective responses.

Organization of This Book

This book is organized chronologically following the history of the development of international regulations for the management of infectious disease. While this provides the empirical grounding of the chapters, the book aims to describe how the discourse of epidemic Orientalism has developed, shifted, or remained durable through the almost two-hundred-year history of international cooperation in infectious disease management. As such this book seeks to examine how epidemic Orientalism has structured and restructured thought on infectious disease control and continues to persist as a powerful discursive framing in international health.

Chapter 1 explores how a globally constituted infectious disease control system could emerge in the nineteenth century by looking backward in time. How could epidemic diseases come to be a subject of regulation, let alone one of international collaboration in a time when the very concept was in its nascence? I chart the processes through which the first systems for internationally regulated infectious disease control were formed. In examining the factors that led to the first International Sanitary Conferences to the instantiations of the major conventions in the 1890s through the early twentieth century, I suggest that a new epidemic Orientalism emerged that would structure how disease threat is perceived. The major world powers of the nineteenth century constructed a system for disease control made up of sovereign nations, imperial states, and their colonial dominions that operated to replicate existing relations of trade for the purposes of capital accumulation in Europe and proliferated a certain discourse that allowed for those relations to maintain themselves in light of a pandemic threat. This structure, buoyed by an Orientalist perspective that positioned the effective and safe maintenance of trade to Europe as critical, facilitated the effective continuance of world trade from colony to metropole and within Europe. This apparatus, eventually developed by consensus both on scientific understandings of disease and on standardized modes of sanitary control through the International Sanitary Conventions, established a global disease management system for policing the spread of three diseases around the world.

In Chapter 2 I explore how central to the operation of these systems was the export of traditional forms of sanitary controls away from European ports to colonial points of departure, prompting massive disease and sanitary monitoring systems in colonial spaces. While the actors at the WHO tasked with revising the conventions would later suggest that these International Sanitary Conventions primarily provided a standardized model for defending unaffected ports from the spread of disease, this chapter shows how these regulations proliferated specific responses to the diseases covered in the conventions. These colonial systems of disease control in turn reproduced and exacerbated existing Orientalist anxieties around race and facilitated novel, repressive forms of population management to prevent economic isolation from Europe.

Chapter 3 examines how the International Sanitary Conventions transformed under the control of the WHO in the mid-twentieth century and how this affected the management and control of epidemic threat. This chapter considers the role that the international disease regulations played in the formation of the WHO. I argue that in the transformation of the International Sanitary Conventions to the International Sanitary Regulations and International Health Regulations in 1969, the WHO attempted to implement a global vision for the organization of the natural world to facilitate the sanitized transmission of goods and bodies across space. Maintaining the mission of the International Sanitary Conventions to provide maximum protection for public health with minimum restrictions to travel and trade, the International Health Regulations expanded the Orientalism of the earlier conventions from Europe to the broader West and globally. In addition the multiple sanitary conventions of the pre–World War II moment were incorporated and universalized into a single binding set of regulations. The additions to the International Sanitary Conventions in the updated regulations were novel. Rather than operating as multilateral agreements between nations and imperial actors as the sanitary conventions did prior, the member nations of the World Health Assembly formed a covenant between themselves and the WHO, directly delegating powers for upholding the regulations to the WHO. Thus, the WHO became the arbiter of the regulations and the disseminating agent of disease surveillance knowledge.

Chapter 4 examines the most recent process of revision of the International Health Regulations. This chapter asks why, despite massive transformations in the political field of international health and the rise of novel pathogens, did the International Health Regulations continue to prioritize regulation of the three diseases originally focused on in the International Sanitary Conventions. Prior to 1995, the IHRs had largely remained unchanged since the birth of the WHO in their focus on plague, yellow fever, and cholera (with a few exceptions). The revisions of the IHR beginning in 1995 and ending with the formation of the IHR (2005) transformed global responses to infectious disease outbreak drastically. In shifting from a focus on three diseases capable of international spread, the WHO and the World Health Assembly turned its attention to any emergent or reemerging disease capable of presenting an international threat to trade and traffic, thus producing massive demand for disease surveillance and control. I argue that significant challenges to the authority of the WHO in the latter half of the twentieth century and the emergence of new global health actors in the early 1990s provoked a need within the WHO to reestablish its dominance in the emergent field of global disease control. The rise of global disease surveillance systems, challenges to the WHO's airport insect controls, an outbreak of Ebola in then Zaire and the 2003 Severe Acute Respiratory Syndrome Coronavirus (SARS) epidemic greatly conditioned the move toward reform and shaped the nature of policies developed in the most recent iteration of the IHR. These determined how disease risk is constructed and responses were previously conceived. In claiming dominance in the rapidly crowded arena of global health, the WHO reproduced the epidemic Orientalism of the past through different practices of control.

Chapter 5 explores how the risk of epidemic outbreak is determined and which threats trigger international responses, through an analysis of the determination process of the World Health Organization's highest disease threat level, Public Health Emergency of International Concern. The designation mandates that the WHO and its member nations commit resources and impose extraordinary measures to combat a threat. Through interviews with health experts involved in the PHEIC assessment process, this chapter explains why certain diseases receive more attention from global health actors. In also examining the effects of the COVID-19 response by the WHO on its authority, this chapter analyzes the effects of most of the epidemic events designated as PHEICs.

The final chapter examines how epidemic threat is read through novel financial products produced by the World Bank, the PEF. On May 21, 2016, the World Bank announced the development of the first ever PEF to prevent the worst humanitarian and economic effects of epidemic emergencies. The PEF is a twofold structure: a cash window that can pay out up to $50 million to support early response to escalating epidemic crises, and a much larger insurance window that provides up to $425 million to afflicted countries, aid agencies, and NGOs to facilitate support. This novel funding strategy was designed to limit the deadly delays and false promises of country pledges to support epidemic response and provide swift funding within a matter of days. The head of derivatives and structured finance for the World Bank's Capital Markets Department, Michael Bennett, stated via Reuters that "if the pandemic emergency financing facility (PEF) had existed in 2014, some $100 million could have been mobilized as early as July." However, when faced with the 2018–2019 Ebola epidemic in the Democratic Republic of Congo. the largest set of funds, the potential $425 million, has contributed nothing to the effort to control the spread of the disease. Though the WHO declared a PHEIC in July 2019, as of September 2020 though the WHO has contributed $50 million from the PEF cash window and an additional $100 million from the World Bank's International Development Association, the largest tranches of funds have not been paid out. How does the largest funded epidemic response facility in the world, designed in the shadow of one Ebola epidemic, fail to pay out for another? Since then the PEF has only paid out in response to COVID-19, and the response was far too little and far too late.

Drawing on the work of Achille Mbembe and Baudrillard's examinations of the political economies of commodity fetishism to analyze the formulation of the PEF, I put forward a new concept to understand this expression of financial power: necrofinance, the capacity to speculate on the lives and deaths of others in order to dictate who may live and who may die. Necrofinance is the speculative logic through which economic value is conferred in life and loss in death, abstracted from the lived experience of those who perish. Central to necrofinancial systems is the reconstitution of human life at a population level into quantifiable metrics for the purposes of speculation.

Where necropolitics examines the production of a necropolitical order of things through the question of sovereignty, I expand on the concept of commodity fetishism to explore how the PEF produces novel subjects for financial speculation. This book ends with a recognition of the way in which durable historical discourses continue to shape and condition our present and the possibilities for our health responses.

EPIDEMIC ORIENTALISM

One looks at the brilliant fires of Port Said,
As the Jews looked at the Promised Land;
Because one cannot go there; it is forbidden
—It seems—by the Convention of Venice
To those in the yellow quarantine pavilion.
We will never calm our anxious desires on this shore
To provide ourselves with the obscene photos
And the excellent tobacco of Latakia . . .
Poet, one would have loved, during the short call at port
To spend an hour or two treading the soil of the Pharoahs,
Instead of listening to Miss Florence Marshall
Sing "The Belle of New York"—in the salon

EGYPT–PORT SAID—EN ROUTE

TO GABRIEL FABRE [1902]

By *Henry Jean-Marie Levet*[1]

Mid Jeddah and Aden way,
The Quarantine at Kamaran lay
The Hajis of the Indian land
Are first tried here on this sand;
If once can save his life here,
In going to Haj he has no fear.
Who does not die in ten days,
Good luck he has in all his ways.
. . . O! for the sake of quarantine,
Thy (god's) prisoners all of us have been.

A PILGRIMAGE TO MECCA [1896][2]

By *Mirza Irfan Ali Begh*

THESE TWO POEMS, WRITTEN WITHIN ten years of one another,
depict two very different visions of travel through the Red Sea. In the piece

by Levet, a French poet and diplomat, we find him writing a postcard to his friend. He laments that he cannot travel ashore from his vessel sitting at the mouth of the Suez Canal because of the Venice International Sanitary Convention of 1897. Instead of being able to walk the Egyptian streets, he is sequestered during his "short" stay at port before travelling on through the canal—a small encumbrance as a result of sanitary controls, though not a burden.

The tale told in the poem of Mirzah Irfan Ali Begh, a deputy collector from the United Provinces of British India, is a very different one.[3] Writing of an experience at the quarantine station off the coast of Yemen, Ali Begh speaks of the quarantine process required for Muslim pilgrims on hajj as an abject one of life and death. Many pilgrims starved or suffered for days during quarantines required under the International Sanitary Conventions. While wealthier pilgrims such as Ali Begh would likely have been able to travel through with relative ease after clearing quarantine requirements, for many poorer travelers, quarantine meant suffering and, in the case of illness, missing out on the entire pilgrimage or death.

In these brief poems we see two travelers sailing the same waters but with vastly different relationships to sanitary controls and power. On one side we can envision a Western European experience, devoid of the threat of disease and indignity, and on the other, a violent engagement with a sanitary order. Both situations derived from policies written out in the International Sanitary Conventions—for Levet, the International Sanitary Convention of 1897, which expanded the convention of 1894 that would have applied to Ali Begh. How did these conventions help to concretize a conception of a world in which European travel produced limited engagement with sanitary controls while Muslim pilgrims on hajj through and across the same seas were subjected to much greater scrutiny? What sorts of systems of relation were the International Sanitary Conventions and their creators imagining?

In this chapter I will explore the process and logics by which infectious disease control came to be an object of international coordination and regulation for the furtherance of European interests. European knowledge of disease threats derived from colonial expansion across the world east of the Mediterranean, across the Atlantic, and throughout Africa. Such geographical expansion honed new visions of the world, including an increased under-standing of the vulnerability of the West to disease. The Orientalist vision of infectious disease control emerged both through the arrival of diseases like cholera in Europe and through colonial encounters that formed a particular vision of the rest of the world as an epidemic risk to Europe.

Indeed the early International Sanitary Conferences prior to the final Paris Conference and Convention of 1926 were framed primarily around the anxieties of European and American interests, trade, and imperial con-cerns. An analysis of the International Sanitary Conferences demonstrates that in order for diseases to become the objects of regulation, they had to be reconceived within the context of the political systems of the day through imperial forms of sovereignty. In order for the project of disease control to be implemented internationally, sanitary practices had to be naturalized into the structures of global governance. While certain quarantines and sanitary controls existed over and above the demands of the International Sanitary Conventions, these conventions represented by the end of the nineteenth cen-tury a guiding system for managing disease threats globally. For the framers of the International Sanitary Conventions it wasn't sufficient to solely define the epidemiological characteristics of disease threats, identify their patho-gens, and interrupt transmission. The practices of control had to fit within the technologies of power available at the time. Plague, cholera, and, by the early twentieth century, yellow fever, could not be the focus for regulation unless those developing regulations could control the ports, sea lanes, and quarantine stations and have sovereignty over subjects who must then be "known" in relation to disease. In this vein, international infectious disease control in the nineteenth and early twentieth century could only be achieved within a world dominated by imperial powers. In essence, without imperial networks and remote sovereignty of people beyond your terrain, disease could not be the subject of global regulation in the nineteenth century.[4]

This chapter examines how the first international regulations for the man-agement of infectious disease came into existence and explores how and why these early International Sanitary Conventions came to focus on three diseases—plague, cholera, and yellow fever—as the threats requiring inter-national cooperation to control. Further, why, given the economic, political, and military competition between European empires and nations, the Ottoman Empire, the Persian Empire, and the United States in the nineteenth century, would they choose to produce a binding set of international regulations for the prevention of the spread of disease? The International Sanitary Conferences and Conventions that these nations and empires produced were the first significant international health agreements and some of the earliest international agreements ever to be developed. The first International Sanitary Conferences pre-dated the creation of the International Bureau for Weights and Measures by nearly twenty-five years, the first major discussions on global time zones by almost twenty years, and the first International Sanitary Convention of 1892 preceded the formal establishment of the prime meridian by eight years.[5]

The simplest answer to the questions raised in the previous paragraph lies in a purely economic explanation. The mandate of these first global agreements for the prevention of disease spread was to maximize the protection from disease with minimum effect on trade and traffic.[6] This objective might suggest that the International Sanitary Conventions were purely a sanitary trade agreement. But this is an oversimplification of their wider effect on global trade and health. Certainly plague, cholera, yellow fever, and the other later diseases also included in the conventions represented extreme threats to colonial trade and were capable of traveling via international shipping routes. However, historians have been quick to point out that diseases such as smallpox, typhus, syphilis, malaria, and dengue fever limited the movement of colonial forces across the world and limited the possibilities for colonial expansion.[7] This chapter explores the other forms of relations and dynamics that emerged from the increasing concern over the threat of disease from colonial spaces and peoples to European states and empires.

A significant period of time elapsed between the first International Sanitary Conference (1851) and the first sets of International Sanitary Conventions (1892). Prior to the first conferences and through this time, the threat of diseases returning from colonial sites to Europe, combined with the rising consensus around the contagiousness of certain diseases, constructed a radical ontology of disease threat that recognized epidemics emerging and spreading from colonial spaces and bodies that threatened the economic and political objectives of empire as more significant than those spreading from within Europe. This consolidated a European vision of disease threat that overwhelmingly focused on the three diseases most capable of threatening the terrain of Europe, its interests, and its peoples. The rise of the International Sanitary Conferences and the attendant conventions they produced were about more than the sanitary travel of goods across the world. They ushered in a new mode for how infectious disease could be managed in international space, placing the threat of significant restrictions on sites exhibiting epidemics of the three diseases under the regulations and calibrating a system of controls designed to protect Europe and the United States. But the International Sanitary Conferences also went further. In designing a system for preventing the spread of these three diseases to imperial centers, an ontological shift occurred in how European and Near-Asian countries saw themselves and others, relative to the rest of the world.[8] The new sanitized political economic order for transimperial trade ushered into being through the International Sanitary Conferences required the refashioning of subject relations, geographies, and forms of rule between the colonized and the colonizer, producing novel racial hierarchies for the purposes of economic extraction through subjugation. International Sanitary Conferences were particular sites in which Western Europe would come to define itself, not only against those outside Europe but also to refashion hierarchies between states and empires internal to the continent of Europe itself. The existence of sanitary systems and the ability to manage populations perceived as unsanitary became a powerful tool for legitimating sovereignty and power at these conferences. Thus it was a refashioning of the idea of Europe and the West from both without and within. The refashioning that emerged from these early international health conferences was an epidemic Orientalism that prioritized the control of diseases emanating from colonial sites that could threaten entry into Europe or contaminate or halt trade.

Within Europe, there were many divergences between states over how to manage infectious disease, improve sanitation, and control illness. Historian Peter Baldwin has beautifully chronicled this history in great detail.[9] While this chapter is concerned with the domain of international responses to disease, the nineteenth century saw the massive development both of science and sanitation especially in Europe.

Epidemic Orientalism to Confront an Unruly Present

Edward Said describes Orientalism as "the discipline by which the Orient was (and is) approached systematically as a topic of learning, discovery and practice."[10] In "Projects," the third section of the first chapter of *Orientalism*, Said explores how the objective of the Orientalist, crafting their expertise from direct encounter with the space of the Orient, came to serve the objectives of imperial capture. Said details how Napoleon's conquest of Egypt was a double project of acquiring knowledge of the Egyptians in order to govern and justify that conquest. Napoleon crafted his vision of Egypt not from direct encounter but rather by cultivating an archive of Orientalist texts. In short, in replacing any first-hand knowledge of Egypt that could be gleaned from a relational encounter with its peoples, Napoleon built himself a preexisting archive of knowledge that transformed Egypt into an object, from which knowledge could be recovered for inclusion into a grand narrative of Western history. Building, prior to invasion, a core understanding of travel writings and classical knowledges of Egypt, Napoleon immersed himself in understanding the Egypt of the Western gaze. Upon conquest, Napoleon established an institute operated by Egyptologists to note, report, and collect the histories and ethnographic details of the country, preserving a vision of Egypt that now existed not as foreign but as a collected and ordered piece of French Empire. The subsequent twenty-three-volume *Description de l'Egypte* sought to take the knowledges of the exotic, foreign Egypt of prior Orientalist study (which saw the land as shrouded in mystery, Eastern mysticism, Islam, and the now barbaric ruins of a once great civilization) and recover its grand history and peoples from that barbarism for the purpose of their inclusion into the West. Convinced of the radical, exotic alterity of Egypt to the French, the *Description* emptied Egypt of any definitional form it may have crafted of itself, to produce an Egypt that exists only in relation to Europe, to its objectives and as an appendage from which it could now be known, governed though force, and restored through imperial eyes. From "silent distance and alienation" Said writes, the "Orient, needed first to be known, then invaded and possessed, then re-created by scholars, soldiers, and judges who disinterred forgotten languages, histories, races and cultures in order to posit them—beyond the modern Oriental's ken—as the true classical Orient that could be used to judge and rule the modern Orient."[11] This is fundamentally how the Orientalist project of knowledge accumulation of the distant Orient comes to claim authority and power over such spaces, inserting itself into the colonial practices of rule.

Breaking down the dynamics of Orientalism further, the project of the Orientalist is one of removing all ontological resistance of the Orient to the gaze of the Orientalist. Said, in examining the practices of Orientalism, finds that every author or expert on the Orient separates and locates themselves relative to the colonial world, producing and imposing essential characteristics on the Oriental world to which they claim to speak with authority.[12] This orientation has been central to the maintenance of imperialism, even beyond the formal end of empire. Pivotal to the formation of the Orientalist outlook—the Orientalist gaze—is the repetition of discourses and practices that produce distinct ontologies of the colonized subject for the purposes of existentially disqualifying the colonized from incorporation in the colonizer's world.[13] Disease and the pairing of epidemic threat and colonial trade with these Orientalist aspects come together in the nineteenth century to render populations at the sites of epidemic origins as signifiers of the profane and as savage and enemies of the progress seen to be wrought by colonial rule. As we will see, health interventions and international sanitary conventions were justified in these terms.

At the same time, however, I will demonstrate in this chapter and the next that epidemic diseases and their meanings as signifiers of non-Western uncivilization was also a powerful force for policing the boundaries of what is and is not civilized in Europe and the West. As I will show, the eighteenth, nineteenth, and twentieth centuries exhibited moments where the colonies of European and American empires feared disease, not only for their health and economic effects, but also through the ways that their dominions would become associated in particular with Asia and the Middle East. No longer would the empires be beacons of spreading civilization and the success of the "White Man's burden,"[14] but rather reflect a pestilential premodern other.

Central to the production of empire and the systems that allow for the economic extraction of materials from colonial sites is the belief in the maintenance of the "rule of colonial difference," whereby the dominated within the colonial territory are controlled and subjugated by the colonizing forces.[15] Imperial power assumes the maintenance of a particular order of things in order to structure a subservient relationship between the colonized, who requires suppression, and colonizer, who must maintain separation from the colonized. The imposition of this difference diminishes the colonized relative to the colonizer. Orientalism, Said writes, "is a style of thought based upon an ontological and epistemological distinction made between 'the Orient' and (most of the time) 'the Occident.'"[16] The assumption of the separation of these two spaces is the defining characteristic in Said's understanding of imperial regimes.[17] The spaces between the Orient and Occident are assumed to be separate, and that separateness is thereby enforced through dynamics of power and domination that would seek to make these separations material in their effects. The difference in itself becomes a factor and justification for differing modes of control and the governing of peoples.[18] It is this ontological separation of spaces and the enforcement of that difference that, in Said's vision, produces the hierarchies that situate the colonizer as superior and the colonized as worthy of subjugation. This ontological frame positions the imperial metropole as distinct from colonial periphery and European as distinct from those they sought to colonize, while systematically occluding how these positions are actually constituted by one another.

A colonial worldliness was critical to European understandings of disease threat. As colonial expansion spread across the world and especially across the Atlantic, imperial actors in the nineteenth century realized that diseases carried by the colonized threatened to disturb the colonial order by permeating the boundary between colonizer and colonized, afflicting colonial actors while also disturbing the economic objectives of empire. While colonial spaces were often read as impenetrable, "overspread with misery,"[19] and dangerous to European conquerors, diseases came to represent an unwanted piece of the colony that could ultimately travel back to Europe. The evidence of this becomes clear in the colonial prioritization of sanitary controls for diseases emerging from colonial space, contrasting with limited attention being paid to diseases emerging from Europe. The recognition of the disease threats of colonial spaces produced in and of itself an epidemic Orientalism that recognized diseases emerging from the colony as more significant than those that were already common in Europe and spread only from colonizer to colonized. The colonized world was a space of disease threat from which the colonizer and empire needed to be protected. Simultaneously, the ability to effectively govern borders and the populations where epidemics were occurring came to represent a marker of Western civilization and superiority.

The rise of infectious diseases capable of traveling across the globe, primarily to Europe but also to a lesser extent North America[20] and throughout the Ottoman Empire, represented a threat to this "vision of division" that separated the colonized from colonizer, and metropole from colony, as ontologically and geographically separate spaces. The pace of global trade as well as the possibilities of transcolonial migration meant that the goods and the conquered peoples that maintained the wealth of empires could be vectors of diseases capable of destabilizing imperial orders. The challenge to a transimperial project of disease control was the problem of how to manage the risk of disease through the governance of people and spaces. In order to achieve the management of non-Western disease risk, the colonial world from which plague, cholera, and yellow fever would ultimately have to be understood through novel sanitary terms both locally, through the management of epidemics, and globally, through their relation to Europe. This produced divergent responses to epidemic threats in the nineteenth and early twentieth centuries, prioritizing the control of diseases threatening the lives of colonial actors such as yellow fever, plague, and cholera, while diminishing actions against diseases brought by empire such as smallpox (see Chapter 3).[21] This transformation of the European global consciousness of disease threat in the nineteenth century came to define colonial sites and the colonized as perpetual potential vectors of disease, and the colonizer as their perpetual potential victims. Disease in this period also continues to be read through economic terms, as a justification for quarantine and controls that slow the pace of trade and limit profit. The International Sanitary Conventions sought to confront this concern through the management of the "unruly" bodies and spaces that lurked beyond or between the domains of colonial control, thus making the problems of global trade manageable through the imposition of sovereign power on colonized peoples. The effective application of these regulations was made possible by the emergence of global communication via telegraph and the development of epidemiological knowledge, the isolation of the causes of illness, and contagion theories, which could trace the root of disease threats. This allowed for the formerly inward-looking quarantine methods of Europe to be made external, pushing the practices of quarantine to colonized sites.

The Rise of Epidemic Orientalism

Before the mid-nineteenth century, ad hoc and piecemeal quarantine practices at European ports marked the limits of the international sanitary order in the Western Hemisphere. The earliest sanitary trade ordinances can be traced back to 1348, in response to the threat of plague.[22] Though germ theory and contagionism would not become an accepted scientific theory until the nineteenth century, quarantine developed much earlier. The first quarantines began in the Republic of Ragusa in 1397 and allowed for any ships, their goods, and their crews suspected of carrying disease to be held at port for a period of forty days.[23] Epidemics at this time came to be conceived of as an object that required governing. Florence was notable for imposing particular restrictions of movement in and out of the generally poorer areas in which disease spread across the city during outbreaks of plague. These included the imposition of emergency powers by the duchy to require particular burial practices, the isolation of the sick, and the closure of markets. Merchants, given their significant travel and interaction with peoples around the world, quickly became associated with the spread of disease, as well as Jews, the Romany, foreigners (especially foreign Muslims), and women, among others.[24] As the scope of European colonial enterprise extended across the Atlantic from the fifteenth to the eighteenth centuries, disease controls shifted in their priorities. Smallpox, influenza, measles, diphtheria, pertussis, yellow fever, and malaria spread devastatingly from Europe and Africa to Central, North, and South America, while syphilis among the European elite was considered to be an unwanted import from their newly conquered overseas territories. For the first time, disease was becoming a concern for the maintenance of global territory, and colonial knowledge of disease became critical to imperial systems of governance at local and global scales.[25] Diseases were starting to move from seized territories back to imperial power centers. Despite the contagiousness of disease being a deeply contested theory at this time, this galvanized a concern in Europe for the origin sites of these diseases and the tactics by which to prevent them.

In *The Spirit of the Laws* (1748), the same work that would ultimately articulate the concept of separation of powers to fledgling Western democracies, Montesquieu would frame the management of diseases among the populace as the domain of sovereign authority and as justification for differential treatment of political subjects, namely, foreigners. Montesquieu drew on the history of leprosy as a basis for exclusion from the polis for the purposes of limiting the spread of syphilis, rooted in the Americas, to a previously untainted Europe. Montesquieu highlights how the prevention of disease spread to European states reflects a major responsibility of the sovereign while also associating the threat of disease with the presence of foreigners in European space. Positioning the spread of disease in grand historical terms as a perpetual battle between Europe and other, Montesquieu suggests it is the European responsibility to prevent the spread of unwanted invaders, human or biological, from entering the domains of Europe.

> We ourselves have suffered the effects of disease. The Crusades brought us leprosy; wise rulings were made that prevented it from spreading to the mass of the people. One sees in the Law of the Lombards that this disease was widespread in Italy before the Crusades and deserved the attention of legislators. Rotharis ordered that a leper driven from his house and kept in a particular spot could not make disposition of his goods, because he was presumed dead from the moment he was taken from his house. In order to prevent any communication with lepers, they were not allowed to have any possessions. I think that this disease was brought to Italy by the conquests of the Greek emperors, whose armies may have included militia

from Palestine or Egypt. . . . Two centuries ago, a disease unknown to our fathers traveled from the New World to this one and came to attack human nature at the very source of life and pleasures. Most of the important families of southern Europe were afflicted by a disease that became so common that it was no longer shameful and was merely deadly. It was the thirst for gold that perpetuated this disease; men continued their voyages to America and brought back new leaven of it each time they returned. . . . As it is in the wisdom of legislators to keep watch over the health of the citizens, it would have been very sensible to check the spread of the disease by laws made on the plan of the Mosaic laws. The plague is an evil whose ravages are even more prompt and rapid. Its principal seat is in Egypt, from which it spreads over the universe. In most of the states of Europe very good regulations have been made to prevent its entry, and in our times a remarkable means has been devised to check it; a line of troops is formed around the infected country, which prevents communication of the disease. The Turks, who have no police on these matters, see Christians in the same town escape the danger and themselves alone perish.[26]

Situating the site of disease threat externally, with syphilis in the Americas and plague from Egypt and reconstituting modern Europe, in grand historical and civilizational terms (linking legacies of Ancient Greece to the present) as the site of concern, Montesquieu advocates the establishment of separations, physical and cultural, from the ill effects of these spaces in order to maintain the purity of Europe.

As the trade in enslaved people grew from the early seventeenth century onward, smallpox spread rapidly from Europeans to indigenous or unexposed enslaved populations from Africa. The effects of this disease emanating from Europe were particularly devastating across the Americas. In the early 1560s a serious outbreak of smallpox in Brazil killed in excess of 30,000 Amerindians over a period of three to four months. While outbreaks of smallpox were exceedingly common in much of the Caribbean, South America, and Central America, quarantines were rarely employed against the disease. The disease rarely affected the colonizing population, and despite often affecting the enslaved, the demand was so great for their labor that even those who were dying or morbidly ill were still purchased at a rapid pace.[27] Though quarantines were imposed in times of frequent or severe outbreak, in general sanitation controls were lax; despite the increased pace of the slave trade in the seventeenth century, such policies were rare.[28] Inoculation against smallpox on slave vessels also lessened the effects of the disease over time as prevention improved. This medical care was given in the interests of preserving the value of human cargo at a moment when diseases greatly decreased the profitability of slavery.[29]

The dissonance between responses to smallpox, the signifier of European disease threat, and yellow fever, the signified colonial disease, demonstrates one aspect of the sanitary divisions that would form the basis of later perspectives on disease control. While smallpox, emanating from Europe, posed few major challenges to the objectives of colonialism,[30] diseases such as yellow fever disturbed the networks of trade and threatened the lives of colonial actors. Diseases that transferred from colonized to colonizer, enslaved to slaver, represented the diseases that merited coordinated responses. While smallpox rarely produced any significant quarantines or responses, yellow fever was met with aggressive quarantine across the western Atlantic. First documented in Barbados in 1647, it spread throughout North and South America within a century, prompting significant quarantine controls and killing colonizer and colonized alike.[31] Mosquitos traveling in water barrels across the Atlantic spread the disease quite quickly through port cities, appearing as far south as Brazil and in severe outbreaks as far north as New York City and Boston. Individual American colonies imposed significant quarantine measures to prevent the disease's spread, and prior to the American War of Independence the thirteen colonies had tallied roughly twenty-five major outbreaks of yellow fever.[32] Quarantine practices in the colonies became much more about enforcing and maintaining borders between the colonized and colonizer, while the spread of disease from colonizer to colonized produced no such boundaries. The colonized body, the body of the enslaved, the indigenous person, signified often an always-already disease threat that had to be confined, controlled, or quarantined to prevent contagion affecting colonial missions. The threat of disease in colonial spaces becomes at this time synonymous with the colonial encounter and the colonized "other."

Diseases from without raised concern from colonial authorities while those from within or emanating from Europe, though devastating, produced far fewer responses.

While colonial regions established quarantines against yellow fever and other diseases, European port cities sought also to mitigate the threat of foreign disease invasion. Though quarantine was the most widespread method of disease control, as the eighteenth century drew to a close, the method began to enflame international relations as European ports enforced quarantines against their colonial sites and one another. Recognizing the disease threats from their colonies and beyond Europe, focusing on limiting the spread of disease from without to within, many European nations took advantage of the protection afforded by quarantine both medically and economically. Concerns for the spread of plague and the subsequent quarantining of merchant ships from foreign nations allowed quarantining sites to delay the trading and shipment of goods, which in turn limited the profits to be made from shipping. Plague, thought to emanate from the Levant or eastern Mediterranean, arrived in France and Italy in the 1720s and prompted swift quarantine responses from Western European nations. Foreign merchants were excluded from trade on the basis of such quarantine realizing a form of strict economic protectionism benefiting European traders against their North African and Middle Eastern counterparts.[33] However, these quarantine ordinances also limited trade between Western European nations such as Britain, France, Spain, and Portugal. Portugal imposed such a significant quarantine that any vessel trading with the Levant was to be subject to quarantine in Portuguese ports if it had not passed through sufficient quarantine processes at all prior ports of call.[34] This policy especially weakened British trading in the region relative to Spain, to whom they were hostile at the time, and almost provoked a war between the three states. As plague continued to spread, further aggressive measures were placed on vessels leaving the eastern Mediterranean, providing further opportunity for trade manipulation under the auspices of sanitation. War similarly almost broke out as a result of quarantine measures between Tunisia and the Venetian Republic over quarantine and destruction of cargo. Quarantine stations adjacent to bordering territories were also used as potential staging points for foreign invasions and military facilities in case these resources were necessary.[35]

As quarantine measures continued to halt trade and invoke nationalist fervor and xenophobia, dissatisfaction grew from all parties regarding the policy. Central to the recognition of the scope of these disease threats was the origin and the apportioning of blame on the foreign agent responsible for bringing the disease, in many cases merchants. Merchants petitioned to have their ships freed from aggressive quarantine at foreign ports while sovereign nations lamented that their own exports were halted on foreign shores. Diseases emerging from colonial sites were being seen not only through the lens of physical threat but simultaneously as foreign agents carried by outsiders and warranting national responses.

Quarantine, Medical Knowledge, and the Rise of a New Paradigm

By the early nineteenth century a creeping anxiety was emerging throughout the European landmass around the threat of infectious disease from beyond its borders. While quarantine was a prominent approach to preventing disease, it was not a settled or accepted approach universally. Many anticontagionists and miasmatists argued that diseases such as cholera and plague emerged spontaneously from local environments or were not contagious. Contagionists in favor of quarantine argued that such controls prevented the spread of illness. While these positions may reflect the poles on either side of the debate, many officials and health actors across Europe found themselves and their positions on the matter somewhere in between.[36] Sanitationist approaches, most famously encapsulated by the position of Edwin Chadwick,[37] argued that rather than relying on quarantine, social uplift, sanitary system and housing improvements, and hygiene would restore natural balance and improve society and health by reducing illness. Sanitationist approaches à la Chadwick in the 1830s would not often distinguish between diseases or illnesses but would rather suggest sanitation as a panacea for all diseases affected by the imbalance and inequities within nature and society.[38] Debates over whether the emergent diseases of the nineteenth century, especially cholera, were diseases from within or without the territories of Europe would become a central component of debate throughout the century.[39]

Though quarantine, the dominant method for securing European cities against disease, afforded a modicum of protection and satisfied xenophobic anxieties about disease spread, it was the disputes that emerged from disjointed quarantine practices that provoked the need for a coordinated system of sanitary controls. Despite differences of opinion on the efficacy of quarantine versus the benefits of sanitationist responses, by the mid-nineteenth century every sovereign nation in Europe and within the Ottoman and Persian Empires had some form of quarantine law that was subject to change depending on the severity of outbreak.[40]

However, a settled understanding of disease in medical terms and a discursive frame through which to produce consensus on how to manage disease threats were still developing. While a concern for diseases arriving from beyond the borders of Europe was emerging across parts of Europe and in the colonies of empires, prioritizing the control of diseases emanating from abroad, the technologies and methods to prevent the spread of diseases were highly disputed. Particular questions regarding the causes of different diseases and their need for quarantine became paramount to their effective and fair regulation in the eyes of the European powers. A desire for a globally regulated system of disease management was growing, but such could only be possible if medical consensus on the cause of disease spread could be found and achieved. Where the efficacy of quarantine in relation to plague may have been more or less accepted, cholera and yellow fever would weaken the foundations of the method. Scientific knowledge mobilized by the diplomatic core of the European and Ottoman empires would become the language through which they would justify their sanitary controls and would become the basis of a new era of standardized disease control.

While debates over the effective strategies for disease control developed internally to European states with varying supports for quarantine and sanitary approaches that focused on local causes of disease, epidemics of cholera within British Indian dominions were disastrous. The cholera epidemic of 1817–1821 was said to be absolutely devastating if not the worst epidemic of the nineteenth century, though statistical records were not kept at the time.[41]

French estimates based on mortality rates in Bengal and among the troops of the East India Company suggested that 1.25 million people died of cholera in India each year between 1817–1831.[42] While this number was most likely a stark overexaggeration of death rates during this time, the news of this degree of death was chilling to European actors fearing that such a situation might shortly arrive on their shores.

Soon after those first reports of cholera returned from British India, Europe's fears were in no small part realized. The spread of cholera in Europe in the early nineteenth century was disastrous. Cholera outbreaks in Britain claimed more than 130,000 lives over the course of the century, while claiming 25 million lives in India where it was first discovered.[43] Across the whole of Europe, cholera would take over 1 million lives between 1829 and 1851, and over 100,000 would die in Mecca alone. Despite quarantines established across the Persian, Ottoman, and Russian Empires, cholera spread largely unabated through Asia and into Europe and across the Atlantic. Yellow fever likewise appeared in Europe for the first time in 1800.[44] As these diseases spread from their sites of origin to European space, similar disputes arose from nations over the efficacy and penalties of quarantine. One of these disputes occurred in 1843 between Austria and British-controlled Greece over the quarantining of Austrian vessels in the port of Corfu. Prince Esterhazy of Austria, in claiming punitive measures against his empire's vessels, suggested that the contagiousness of cholera was the justification Britain used for its aggressive responses.

> The Government of His Majesty the Emperor of Austria having been informed by its Consul at Corfu, of the impediments thrown in the way of the navigation in the Ionian Sea, arising from the progress of the cholera in Italy, the Undersigned has been instructed to do himself the honor of bringing to the knowledge of His Britannic Majesty's Principal Secretary of State for Foreign Affairs the following circumstances. At the time the cholera made its appearance at Venice and Trieste, the quarantine prescribed by the Government of the Ionian Islands was fixed at fourteen days, and subsequently increased to twenty-one, upon the appearance of the cholera at Ancona; . . . It follows from these numerous impediments, that the real

duration of the quarantine is generally forty-two days; and even that period is extended, in case where, through stress of weather, the unlading of vessels is delayed. Moreover, the lazaretto affording but very little room, a further delay often occurs, before the merchandize can take its turn to be admitted for the purpose of being fumigated. To the losses caused by these delays are added the expenses of the sanatory [sic] taxes, which have not been diminished, and from the circumstance of a chemical process being made use of in order to fumigate the goods, which are opened and spread for the purpose, they lose, by such means, their freshness and the appearance of being new. To such an extent are these measures prejudicial to commerce, that the captains of vessels now at Corfu, have, of their own accord, had a meeting, and handed to the Consul-General the declaration that they would prefer remaining at home without employ, rather than undertake voyages to the Ionian Islands, where the existence of the restrictions in question would infallibly occasion their ruin. The steps repeatedly taken for the purpose of inducing the Government of the Ionian Islands to lessen the severity of these measures have all failed through the apprehension of the Sanatory [sic] Inspector-General, who considers cholera as a contagious disease.[45]

As quarantining for plague and cholera were now becoming more common practice across Europe, these methods caused what many merchants and sovereign states considered to be overwhelming delays. While the diseases were significant health threats, the quarantines that they provoked incurred a double penalty.

Cholera was a terrifying disease in the eyes of Europe, causing swift death and spreading quickly across the continent, capable of taking otherwise healthy people to death's door in a matter of hours.[46] While according to Europe the plague had its source in the Levant and quarantine procedures against plague reflected this opinion, the origin of cholera remained deeply unknown and disputed within European states.[47] Further, the piecemeal and highly variable nature of quarantine regulations between ports left effective controls both weakened and complying with onerous, bespoke practices.[48]

While Britain maintained a certain broad resistance to widespread and complete quarantines, nations along the Mediterranean and France in particular expressed a commitment as a state to quarantine practices. France, however, sought to standardize and reduce the necessary levels of quarantine needed to prevent disease spread.[49] In 1834, after traveling significantly and reporting on the sanitary regulations across the Mediterranean, the secretary of the Superior Council of Health for France, wrote a report under the auspices of the minister of commerce highlighting the unnecessary challenges that emerge from the differing quarantine methods across the sea. Secretary Dupeyron suggested that an international conference be held to establish standard measures for disease control. Though France struggled to host a conference on such issues for almost twenty years, the Ottoman Empire's perspective on cholera reflected a similar impulse.[50] Ottoman regulations on plague control, given their Western trading partners' claim that plague emanated from Ottoman territories, were very strict. However, they had failed to prevent the spread of cholera.

In 1831 the Khedive of Egypt established a sanitary council governed by a committee of European diplomats to prevent the spread of disease to Europe.[51] In 1838 the Ottoman Empire established seventy-seven new public health and quarantine stations across Anatolia (much of modern-day Turkey) and in 1840 convened an international council of representatives from the United States, Germany, Greece, Austria, France, Sweden, Norway, Iran, Russia, the Netherlands, Britain, and Spain. Ultimately this would become the Ottoman Supreme Council of Health consisting of twenty-one members, including thirteen foreign members.[52] At their first meeting in 1840 codified regulations were suggested for controlling the international spread of disease. A later international meeting of the Istanbul Supreme Council of Sanitation, consisting of medical experts and diplomats from nine European states and the Ottoman Empire, pledged to improve and coordinate quarantine efforts at a conference in Vienna in 1845. These failed to produce any tangible, accepted regulations. This direct precursor to the International Sanitary Conferences solidified a demand for internationally standardized disease regulations.

The International Sanitary Conferences

Where solely nationalistic systems of control through quarantine were proving to be less desirable and fractious, a new paradigm ushered in over the course of the International Sanitary Conferences of the nineteenth century redefined the relations between Europe and the rest of the world regarding disease control. Despite ongoing disputes over the methods of sanitary control of disease, by the 1866 International Sanitary Conference the world east of the Bosporus came to be legitimized in these conferences and conventions as the sites of the most concerning diseases because of the effects that they could have on a modernizing and sanitizing Europe.

These early concerns for trade and the threat of diseases from colonial sites guided the formation of what would become the International Sanitary Conventions. The International Sanitary Conferences, which laid the groundwork for the first International Sanitary Conventions, did more than produce standard and accepted regulations. The conferences themselves served as a powerful discursive vehicle for uniting all of Europe under the same epidemic Orientalist perspective, firmly linking the threat of global epidemic disaster with diseases emanating from the sites of colonial encounter and requiring colonial containment. As new diseases such as cholera and yellow fever, not yet fully understood by medical science, emerged throughout Europe and Asia, existing measures for plague both halted trade and were ineffective at preventing the spread of these other diseases, causing significant death in Europe and the colonies of their empires. While disputes still occurred between European powers, the coalescence of a largely singular vision of a unified Western Europe around infectious disease emerged from Western European and imperial powers coming to see themselves as distinct from Eastern empires in both their management and proximity to infectious disease. This unification was further made possible through the application and practices of infectious disease controls against non-European peoples.

From this Orientalist vision, two objectives emerged for the parties that would ultimately represent the International Sanitary Conventions. The first was to prevent the spread of infectious diseases primarily to the European continent while minimizing the punitive effects of quarantine to trade and travel. This would prove to be the overarching mission of both the International Sanitary Conventions, later the International Sanitary Regulations and ultimately the present-day International Health Regulations. This first objective informed the second, which was to halt the spread of disease at the source of outbreak through containment in order to limit the possibility of diseases reaching European ports, spreading death and affecting trade. The latter objective was facilitated by two complementary technologies: the telegraph, which provided for swift global communication, and the rise of modern epidemiology, which allowed for the effective and scientific charting of the causal factors of disease and thereby disinfection and sanitation. These conferences allowed for the swift discussion and later acceptance of scientific findings on the cause and spread of disease that could be quickly diffused around the world.

But the formulation of these sanitary conventions would be anything but straightforward. It would take seven International Sanitary Conferences and over forty years before the parties involved agreed on any formal standards. The first International Sanitary Conference was convened by France in Paris in 1851. Eleven European nations and Turkey, representing the Ottoman Empire, were in attendance.[53] Each party was represented by one medical expert and one diplomat.[54] This is notable as it would mark one of the first times that medical officials would be directly involved in drafting international regulations.[55] Three diseases of colonial encounter were the focus of the first conference: plague, cholera, and yellow fever. Smallpox, as a supposedly "universal" disease in the eyes of the parties in attendance, did not merit inclusion.

These International Sanitary Conferences emerged at a critical turning point in international knowledge dissemination. Contemporary to these first conferences, the first nondiplomatic international standards were being established on matters from weights and measures and time zones as well as agreements on the elimination of the international slave trade.[56] What France initially proposed was an internationally accepted and standardized system of disease surveillance that would allow for the swift dissemination of information on outbreaks. Sanitary councils would be established at the local level, headed by directors of health. These sanitary councils would also be international in character, with envoys representing foreign nations. This drew the ire of several of the nations represented including Britain, Russia, and Austria, who were concerned that such an organization would infringe on national sovereignty. While some nations favored solely regulations, to be abided by globally, the French sought to model all sanitary systems on their own vision. This did not sit well with most members of the conference. While the infringement of national sovereignty was of paramount concern for the European delegates, they were not above requiring more stringent reforms in the Ottoman Empire to prevent the spread of plague within all of its territories.[57]

A second dispute arising from the first conference that would linger throughout the first seven conferences was the cause and mode of transmission of cholera. This would have a persistent effect on the belief of the efficacy of practices deemed to be valid to be applied against non-Europeans and especially Indians and Muslims in the Middle East and Indian ocean. The great divergence between the contagionist and anticontagionist understandings of cholera left the control of the disease off the negotiating table for several parties, including Austria who was prohibited by its government to discuss the control of any diseases but plague and yellow fever.[58] The British delegation likewise agreed that cholera was not worthy of quarantine and was only spread through filth and certain other climactic and environmental effects and therefore not worthy of quarantine. Where the Ottoman Empire was largely blamed for the spread of cholera to Europe, Ottoman envoys to the conference suggested that it was Indian pilgrims to Mecca that had spread the disease to Ottoman lands. Designating cholera as a quarantinable disease would have huge trade repercussions on British-controlled India and the empire as a whole, and this consideration affected the acquiescence of Britain to quarantine controls for much of the future conferences.[59] The British Empire had several reasons to support their position. As Javed Siddiqi has written, if cholera was demonstrated to be a contagious disease, sanitary controls on trade between India and Europe would be legitimated, costing the empire and British India immense wealth.[60]

The first sanitary conference produced no implementable or accepted convention. Despite progress made in the scientific isolation of cholera in Britain, the British delegation to the Second International Sanitary Conference of 1859 continued to argue that cholera be omitted from the diseases subject to quarantine regulations.[61] They were far from alone in this debate as several of the other parties also supported the anticontagion claim regarding cholera. However, general European consensus was emerging on the transmissibility of cholera and its transit from East to West.

These disagreements persisted through the third conference held explicitly on cholera in Constantinople in 1866. The purpose of this conference was to halt the rapid spread of cholera from incoming pilgrims from Egypt to Mecca and onward to Europe.[62] While no international regulations emerged from this conference, the European powers once again sought to impose significant measures on the Ottoman Empire while levying no measures on themselves. However, this conference boasted the first effective scientific consensus on cholera, formally establishing the reservoir of cholera to be in India, primarily emanating from the Ganges River.[63] This was to be the only major scientific outcome of the conference.

Cholera, Epidemic Orientalism, and the Muslim Other

During the 1866 Conference many aspects of an emergent Orientalist lens were solidified through discussions over potential controls of cholera. Historian Valeska Huber has written of the Constantinople conference that "the conflict between the 'Orient' and the West became more explicit."[64] Conference delegates from Western Europe devoted much time to not only rendering Muslim pilgrims as subjects of aggressive sanitary control because of the high numbers of deaths from cholera in Mecca and its ability to spread but also ascribing the cause of this to habits considered to be unsanitary and distinctly un-European in nature. In justifications for increased global controls against infectious diseases, European powers at the Constantinople conference argued that non-European peoples were fundamentally incapable of managing the sanitation of their spaces without European intervention. Moreover, European powers argued that only European intervention into non-European spaces and the lives of non-European peoples could ensure the protection of Europe.

While the British had previously believed that cholera emerges at random from spoiled earth, the formal isolation of the reservoir of cholera interpolated the disease through the Orientalist gaze as the primary disease of international concern. Of all the diseases recognized as grave threats by the International Sanitary Conferences, cholera and its threat of transmission via

the Mecca pilgrimage represented the apotheosis of the imaginative combination of disease, trade, and colonial alterity. Cholera represented a disease
emergent from within British India, spread by human vectors from South
Asia to the Middle East and Europe. In traversing the border between colonial
space and Europe in or on people, it captured the majority of the attention
of the members of the International Sanitary Conferences, and the sanitary
management of the Mecca pilgrimage would later become its own subsection
of the sanitary conventions.

The impending opening of the Suez Canal in 1869 weighed heavily on
the minds of many of the delegates from nations along the Mediterranean
as sea-borne travel between the Middle East, the Red Sea, and India would
now be far more swift. Peter Baldwin writes that the French, viewing themselves as "the outer gate of the European sea" claimed that "the nations of
Europe have a right to arrest the approach of Asiatic diseases."[65] Where it
was suggested that the nations of the North Atlantic including Britain may
naturally be protected from cholera due to the duration of travel from the
Suez Canal to the ports of Britain or north to Scandinavia, Mediterranean
Europe was distinctly vulnerable. Reports presented to the 1866 Conference
further supported what was now the near-unanimous position that cholera
emerged from India, where it was endemic.[66] This concentrated the peoples
and geographies of India and the East as the site of primary epidemic concern
drawing need for scrutiny.[67]

The anxiety around the Hajj emerged around the particular concerns of
Muslims traveling from India to the Red Sea and then on to Mecca, where
they would interact with European Muslims who would transfer cholera
back to Europe. The focus of control turned to its prevention of transfer to
Europe. The suggestion was for the Ottomans who controlled Mecca at the
time to erect massive quarantine facilities in the Red Sea. Britain maintained a
reticence in accepting that cholera was emanating from its Indian colony but
recognized that sanitary measures would need to change in India. The focus
of these reforms would be placed on the surveillance and control of cultural
practices such as the cremation and interment of bodies in the Ganges River.[68]

Debates over the causes of spread of cholera and the best means to prevent its spread to Europe became the terrain for conceptualizing difference

between East and West writ large. The responses to the threat of cholera emanating from the East and Mecca and spreading to Europe operated through particular imperial logics of control and subject formation that envisioned new forms of European imperial sovereignty over Persian and Ottoman spaces. In the debates over the control of cholera in the Arabian Peninsula and its potential spread to Europe, the ability to control disease through the management of Muslim populations, considered unruly and unsanitary in the eyes of Europe, became a condition for sovereign power over Eastern spaces.

Of particular importance to these debates were several reports and an emergency proposition that would, in the event of a cholera epidemic in and around Mecca, halt all maritime travel between Arabian ports and Egypt.[69] This would in effect leave massive groups of Muslim pilgrims essentially stranded in the Arabian desert without the supplies to support themselves for an overland trip back to their homes. While this measure was ultimately passed with massive outcry from Persian and Ottoman representatives, mercifully for those pilgrims who would have been stranded in the Arabian desert without food, water, or transportation, there was no epidemic of cholera in Mecca during that year's Hajj. During discussions over "the measures to be adopted in the East to prevent a renewed invasion of Europe by Cholera,"[70] delegates from several European nations and one delegate from Egypt[71] laid out the justifications for increased controls on non-European space, including support for the termination of marine transport to and from the Arabian Peninsula.

The committee framed the threat of cholera not only as a medical threat but an explicitly economic one, suggesting that while the first consideration is for "the desolation caused by the ravages of the disease," the next is the "disorder it [cholera] imports into social relations and business of every kind."[72] Misery increases due to not only the disease but also the economic losses incurred by the quarantines and controls imposed. This economic threat was described both in local and global and distinctly imperial terms:

> The disastrous influence of an epidemic of cholera in Europe is not limited to the countries affected; it has its natural repetition not only in those who try to secure themselves by measures of quarantine but also in those who

think proper to oppose no barrier to the scourge. These last in reality, inde-
pendently of the ravages of the disease, suffer from two causes—the force
diminution of their commercial relations with the tainted countries . . . and
from the measures taken by neighboring countries with which they of necessity have relations. Ask England, whether, last year, though she instituted
no restrictive measures herself, her commerce did not suffer from the effects of the epidemic prevailing on the Mediterranean coasts?

The disruptions to European commerce and the onerous nature of controls
were demonstrated as justifications for the imposition of controls outside
of Europe in order to protect the continent and its interests. Further, as
indicated in this quotation in discussion of England's losses, the fate of the
whole was reliant on the ability to manage populations extraterritorially.
The committee concluded that restrictive measures, imposed externally to
Europe were much "less prejudicial to commerce and international relations"[73] than the disturbances to trade and commerce produced by the invasion of cholera.

Sanitation, Sovereignty, and Power

Arguments over the rights to sovereignty and claims to modern imperial
power ran through Eurocentric beliefs about sanitation and the capacity
to effectively sanitize foreign populations. In claiming the need for more
aggressive sanitary controls against the spread of cholera to Europe, members of the same committee that argued for these increased responses also
argued that the Persian- and Ottoman-controlled spaces that formed the
buffer zone between Europe and cholera were not sufficiently governed by
those powers. In describing the threat posed to Europe from the invasion of
cholera, the committee took particular aim at the weaknesses of Persia's capacity to control the spread of cholera, asking, "Is the Persian Government
in possession of the means adapted to make the proper measures work use-
fully?"[74] The answer to this rhetorical question posed by the committee was
"It is very doubtful."[75]

Criticisms of Ottoman capacities to manage the territory in and around
the Red Sea on approach to and from the soon-to-be-opened Suez Canal were

also raised vigorously at the 1866 Conference. When the committee raised the question of who should control the quarantine stations in the Red Sea, the answer hinged on the lack of capacity of the Ottoman Empire to manage both their own and international populations travelling through their territory.

> What should be the character of this establishment? Assuming it to be capable of realization, on whom should devolve the duty of setting it up, of making it work and maintaining it? Who should have its direction? It must be remembered that we are speaking of an institution which interests all Europe; which would necessitate great expenditure in setting it up and maintaining it; and which would require a large staff of officers, and the concurrence of a considerable military and naval force to ensure the execution of the prescribed measures. Where is the territorial Power capable of taking all these duties upon itself? It certainly cannot be found upon the Arabian coast amongst the independent and hostile chiefs occupying it. Should the charge devolve as proposed in Committee, on the Ottoman Government or the Egyptian Administration? But Admitting the normal authority of the Porte in these parts is it though that it, or Egypt by delegation possesses suitable means of execution? . . . after serious and careful examination [the Committee] arrived at the conclusion that the projected institutions at the entrance of the Red Sea . . . ought to be of an international character; that it should be founded and maintained at the common charge of the Powers interested and placed under the surveillance of a mixed Board in which a Delegate of each of these Powers should sit.[76]

In the committee report, the global problem of cholera was reframed exclusively as a threat to European interests, and as such all suggestions were framed as useful only insofar as they supported European security against disease. Even Persian sanitation projects were framed as being of a benefit not foremost to those in Persia but rather as a sanitary improvement that would limit the spread of pestilence to its Western neighbors.[77]

If Europe could not rely on the Persian Empire to sanitize and modernize, then it was suggested that responsibility should be given to European powers. Moreover, the notion of modern European civilizational superiority in morality, government, and sanitation was reflected in relation to the disease control capacities of Asian geographies as informed by perspective derived from European explorers and colonial actors. While controls on the Russian borders with Turkey and Central Europe were largely praised, populations and governing forces in Asia were considered incapable of sanitary practices.[78] The peoples of the lands between the Persian Empire and China were rendered as threats requiring European civilization. Describing Great Bukharia (the areas around present-day Uzbekistan) the committee stated,

> Of all this immense extent of country,—which, if the hopes we cherish be realized, will soon be brought under the influence of European Civilization,—the latter portion, that is Bukharia, is of particular interest to our subject. . . . There, in short, an Asiatic civilization flourishes, barbarous no doubt, but very superior to that of the adjoining nomadic hordes.[79]

The rendering of the Eastern world entire through its relation to the disease threats posed to Europe culminated in the suggested interventions to be imposed outside of Europe for the benefit of its own protection. While the populations beyond Europe's borders were rendered incapable of hygiene and effective sanitary controls without European intervention, the emergency proposal brought forward by the French delegation also rendered them disposable to the interests of Europe. By forcing the closure of sea lanes to pilgrim travel, the emergence of cholera would leave potentially tens of thousands of pilgrims without food, water, or shelter in the Arabian desert or force them to cross it on foot. This grim fact was raised by the Ottoman and Persian delegations in protest. In making a plea to the humanity of the European delegations, a delegate of the Sublime Porte (Ottoman Delegation), Salih Effendi, brought an amendment to the proposal recognizing that the transportation or water supply necessary to support the stranded pilgrims would be impossible to provide and lead to massive loss of life:

> The assemblage of crowding, indefinitely prolonged in towns already compromised beyond expression would infallibly result in the creation of immense pestilential foci—not one of their inhabitants would survive for

more than a few days,—and these towns of living sentient beings would soon be transformed into necropoli. But if a murderous epidemic devastates the holy cities, if famine and thirst multiply the ravage and horrors of the Indian scourge [cholera] a hundredfold, can we believe that their populations—native or foreign—would rest passive spectators of so many calamities? Can it be thought that they would resign themselves to death as quietly as the sheep and camels slaughtered by them during the sacrificial ceremonies?[80]

At the 1866 Conference, the terms for imagining a Europe beset on all sides from the specter of disease was fully realized, and the means of enacting extraterritorial controls through imperial networks were employed in support of these aims. Existing sanitary regulations such as the British Indian Native Passengers' Act (1858), which placed additional aggressive sanitary controls and quarantine requirements on any vessel traveling to and from the Red Sea and Persian Gulf carrying greater than thirty "natives of Asia or Africa," were held up as models for sanitary controls writ large.[81] In addition, populations beyond Europe were reduced to expendable persons, worthy of sacrifice en masse for the interests of Europe and its peoples.

The policing of the sanitary authority of other powers was not exclusively limited to non-European powers. European imperial powers were also judged on their capacity to suppress disease spread from their domains as a sign of sanitary superiority. The British Empire's economic growth was affected by its responses to the debates around infectious disease and India. The threats of quarantines and economic penalties forced Britain to police its Indian and especially Indian Muslim population more aggressively over time. Between the 1866 Conference and the conferences of the 1890s that produced formal conventions, Britain was forced to shift its position in relation to quarantine and the internal controls on especially its Muslim colonial subjects in India.

As Mark Harrison has written, between 1866 and 1900 the link between cholera and India left the British metropolitan authorities and its colonial government in India in a tenuous position, especially relative to its Muslim colonial subjects from whom British Colonial forces attempted to win support in order to diminish the power of a rising Hindu middle class.[82] The

French government at the 1866 Conference explicitly advocated for stricter controls against Muslim pilgrims on Hajj and especially Indian Muslims travelling to Mecca, calling for more aggressive internal controls against British India's colonial subjects. Fearing reprisals and resistance from its Muslim inhabitants, the British Indian government resisted calls for increased controls until 1870 when sanitary controls were implemented especially on lower-class vessels and compartments of ships carrying pilgrims.[83] In the absence of the ultimate conventions of the 1890s, between 1870 and 1897 many quarantine and sanitary measures were imposed on British India especially by France. In 1882 the Ottoman Turkish government imposed sanitary passport controls and financial requirements on pilgrims on arrival to Jeddah that proved they had the funds for the return voyage.[84] Political and economic pressure on the British would eventually give way to strict controls against Muslim pilgrims and Indians more generally across the Indian subcontinent and Middle East into Eastern Europe. India's population of sixty million Muslims at the time was central to maintaining the legitimacy of the colonial project. At the core of this was also the maintenance of transit to Mecca for pilgrimage. Fearing resistance from Muslim leaders in India, the British Indian government resisted this policy. In 1882 however, a massive epidemic of cholera levied severe quarantines from several European nations and produced disruptions of trade to and from India through the Suez Canal as well as limits on the movement of British troops. While the British Indian government and British imperial authority fought to appease Muslim leaders, these and other restrictions to imperial trade as a result of quarantines imposed due to cholera would ultimately lead to the British government breaking with the British Indian government and supporting stricter controls on the Hajj at the 1894 Conference in Paris. This provoked consternation from the British Indian government as well as vocal critique from India's Muslim community that the imperial authority lacked any concern for the health of pilgrims due to the violent and unsanitary nature of quarantines.[85] As we will see in the next chapter, many of the impositions into the lives of Britain's colonial Indian population were aggressive and brutal in order to maintain trade, political, and economic relations with Europe and secure the continent from the illnesses seen to be spread from east of the Suez Canal.

Causes and Origins: The Consolidation of an Epidemic Vision

The isolation of the cholera bacillus in 1882 by Robert Koch proved to be the most major of several death blows to anticontagionist arguments. The discovery of a causative agent of cholera would prove too significant to ignore for long. By the Venice International Sanitary Conference of 1892, a convention for the control of cholera in westbound shipping in the Mediterranean was established, attempting explicitly to halt the spread of cholera from the Suez through to Europe. These regulations advised the maximum impositions that a nation or port could take in controlling disease, thereby solving the previous problems of differing quarantine practices. The scope of the danger of cholera, recognized in Orientalist terms to be a global one, was illustrated by Adrien Proust, a noted epidemiologist, doctor, and member of the French delegation.[86] In his work *The Defense of Europe Against Cholera* (1892) he sets out the risks of infectious disease explicitly in terms positioning Europe as the site of risk and the broader Eastern and African world as threat:

> It [cholera] extends into the Far East, in the Gulf Bengal, Burma, Indo-China, the treaties of China, Korea, Japan, and all the coast of the seas of China, as far as Wladivostock. In recent years, it has been raging in Iraq-Arabia, Mesopotamia, Persia, Syria, Arabia (Mecca) and Africa (Massawa). The economic transformations that are on the entire surface of the African continent, will further aggravate the danger. So the question of the defense of Europe against the cholera always stands with a pressing interest and a fearful actuality. The aim of our efforts is to intercept all direct communication between the contaminated provenances of the Far East on one side; Egypt, the Mediterranean and Europe, on the other.[87]

Reflecting on the scale of European colonialism, especially the recent division of the African continent into European colonies at the Berlin conference of 1884–1885, the world is laid out in terms relevant to Europe and its dominions with respect to disease. At the Venice conference itself, Proust argues in even more explicit terms for the focus of the conventions to be on

diseases of direct concern to Europe and makes an argument for incorpo-
rating plague into the International Sanitary Conventions as well, a move
that will occur a few years later:

> Monsieur Professor Proust reminds us of the distinction made by science
> between exotic diseases and indigenous diseases. The first are part of in-
> ternational hygiene. These are mainly cholera, yellow fever and plague. In
> Vienna in 1874, in Rome in 1885, we first treated with cholera, then yellow
> fever and plague, modifying for these two diseases the principles laid down
> for cholera. The greatest danger for Europe being that of cholera invasions,
> it is natural for the Conference to deal, above all, with this disease that
> threatens us the most. We know, however, that the plague is raging in Ye-
> men, that is to say almost at the gates of Europe. He believes it will be wise
> to think of protecting ourselves (Europe) also against the plague.[88]

These statements provide a clear depiction of the discourse of epidemic
Orientalism. Proust, in making a claim to the global threat of cholera, frames
that threat only in its proximity to Europe. He presents Europe as threatened
on all sides by cholera, with that threat only increasing through colonial exploitation in Africa and elsewhere. The protection of Europe is therefore only
possible through the control of colonized bodies and transports to Europe.
Second, the threat of the diseases stems from their ability to travel outside
of their "indigenous" regions, thus making them of importance to international health and the Sanitary Conferences more broadly. Those diseases that
remain autochthonous to their regions are not the domain of international
health.

By the Dresden Sanitary Conference of 1893, the British moved fully in
line with the contagionist view of cholera. The 1892 Convention was revised
in 1893 to include measures for notifying other nations of outbreaks and
import restrictions. Only cloth-based goods and clothing would be subject to disinfection or prohibited, and not subject to quarantine. The Ninth
Conference focused exclusively on policing the Mecca pilgrimage. By the
1894 Conference there was scientific consensus that cholera was only spread
around the world through human agency and that controls on that agency

would halt its movement. With the full force of Western scientific consensus on the cause of spread and origin of cholera, the question of how maximum disease security to Europe could be maintained while minimizing the effects to international trade could now be explored in greater detail. In the opening address to the Ninth Conference, the president of the conference and president of France, Jean Casimir-Perier, remarked:

> The modern scientific spirit has proved both its firmness and its flexibility in the course of extended efforts to combat the Asiatic pestilence by means of international agreement. . . . It is the common labor and the common honor of science and diplomacy to acquire and exercise the knowledge necessary to reconcile the customs which govern international commerce and the laws on which depends the protection of human life.[89]

With this prerogative in mind, the parties to the conference set out to add an entire section of the International Sanitary Conventions to solely resolve the threat of the spread of cholera to Europe. Scientific, economic, and political concerns had converged around a unified understanding that the most pressing threats to Europe emanate from the colonial world and the colonial encounter. Britain objected to the strict policing of Muslim pilgrims on the Hajj, suggesting that the convention would be better served to improve the state of health in the endemic regions while limiting the control of the disease at ports to a minimum.[90] This unpopular view was also held by the Ottoman delegation, who felt their sovereignty was being imposed upon.[91]

The regulations placed on the Hajj were more aggressive and invasive than previous controls, requiring both male and female passengers to be strip-searched as well as significant sanitary measures to be emplaced on all vessels carrying pilgrims. Dr. Stephen Smith, an American observer to the proceedings, suggested in his report:

> It can be stated that the pilgrim is placed under sanitary surveillance of a very rigorous character from the moment he announces his intention to go on a pilgrimage till his return home. First, he must obtain a sanitary

passport from the local authority. . . . Before the passport is issued, the intending pilgrim must prove that he has compiled with all the conditions necessary for his departure and that he has money sufficient for the voyage and to sustain his family in his absence. This passport the pilgrim must retain, and show to the sanitary authorities *en route;* and he can enter Hedjaz, the province in which Mecca is located, only on presentation of it, and on passing an examination. He is under sanitary observation while at Mecca and on his return a new passport is given him, which he must show *en route.*[92]

All pilgrims were also subject to medical inspections on boarding each vessel en route to and returning from Hajj.

Such a stringent sanitary policing of the Hajj was unique among the mass migrations of the time, highlighting the profound effect of the Orientalist vision embodied in the International Sanitary Conventions and reflecting again the unidirectional perception of disease threat from colonized to colonizer and not the other way around. No Christian pilgrimages required the same level of scrutiny nor did any large-scale movements of Europeans anywhere in the world attract similar concern. During the third plenary session of the 1894 International Sanitary Conference, Doctor Shakespeare of the American delegation, recognizing parallels to their experience with increasing migrants from Europe, put forth a proposal that the same measures should also apply to Europeans immigrating to the United States:

> I would like to add that I express here not only the opinion of the American Delegation, but also the unanimous opinion of our health authorities when I declare that these International Conferences offer the only rational means of arriving at a result when is to successfully prevent the spread of a plague like cholera. . . . I will now ask permission to touch on an important branch of the great international defense problem against cholera, which, in our opinion, has been somewhat neglected in past health conferences: I am referring to European emigration to America. Although our Government has not had the honor of being represented at the Health Conferences

of Venice and Dresden, it is no less certain that there is an intimate relationship between the public health of Europe and the sanitary health of
America. Thanks to the facilities of the transatlantic trade, huge numbers
of emigrants (more than 400,000 per year) from all corners of Europe and
even from Asia Minor arrive in American ports incessantly and spread all
over our territory, in a worrisome state of health because of their misery
or uncleanliness. The sanitation of Europe, as you understand it, is of great
interest to us, and we are far from losing interest in the course and fluctua-
tions of cholera in Europe. We have indeed the incontestable proof that this
plague has always arrived to us from Europe, either by transports of sick
emigrants or by their contaminated effects. . . . There is, in our opinion, a
great analogy between these great movements of Muslim pilgrims, who pe-
riodically threaten the health of Europe, as well as the interests of international trade, and those emigrants who are moving from Europe to America
in quantities much more important and under very favorable conditions for
the repetitive propagation of cholera. The United States Government has
agreed to participate in the discussions and conclusions of this Conference
in the hope that it will not only deal with the question of the spread of cholera by pilgrims traveling from India to Mecca, but also the very important
question of the spread of cholera by emigrants traveling from Europe to
America.[93]

After presenting his case in several pages of minutes, including the presentation of tables and dates referring to the numbers of migrants to the
United States and their nations of origin, this motion was permanently
tabled and never accepted.[94] Most nations speaking on this particular motion spoke in positive terms, embracing the possibilities for future agreements with the United States, while offering little to no suggestion that they
were willing to entertain the proposal at the time. Count Kuefstein, the senior delegate of the Austro-Hungarian Empire, was much less equivocal in
his displeasure regarding the comparison between European immigrants
and Muslims participating in the Hajj. Though not specifically mentioning
Muslims, Kuefstein remarked:

> Austria-Hungary has not, it says, emigration ports properly so called. Its emigrants often embark abroad in Hamburg, Genoa, Le Havre, etc. etc. It is therefore for the States directly concerned to formulate an opinion in the first place. Nevertheless, it seems to him that the question of emigrants has only a remote analogy with that of pilgrims, and that he does not need to dwell upon the points which distinguish them from each other.[95]

After the 1894 Convention, the International Sanitary Conventions were amended again to incorporate both plague (Venice 1897) and, more marginally, yellow fever (Paris 1912) into their controls. It would not be until the twentieth century that sanitary regulations between European nations would emerge.

Conclusion

Despite the nineteenth century being a period of great debates within European states regarding the causes of disease as well as methods of control, quarantine, sanitationism, and the decline or transformation of miasmatic theory, the space of the International Sanitary Conferences coalesced on a vision of the world that placed Europe as a virgin continent beset from the East by disease. The implementation of the International Sanitary Conventions in the latter part of the nineteenth century produced a dramatic shift in disease control globally and represent the ancestors of all future international disease regulations. The conventions set out standard regulations for the control and management of three diseases considered most concerning not only to Europe but to their international relationships and colonial dominions elsewhere. The International Sanitary Conferences united Europe's understanding of disease threat under an epidemic Orientalism that mediated the construction of disease risk and organized responses to threats accordingly.

This chapter has shown how and why the International Sanitary Conventions were ratified and the concerns from which they emerged. Global imperial expansion prompted a new threat of diseases returning to imperial centers from their colonial domains. These threats strained piecemeal quarantine systems, triggered political crises between trading nations, and risked economic and epidemiological catastrophe. Scientific knowledge of the causes of disease, merging with these wider economic and Orientalist concerns, provided the groundwork for a novel form of standardized international disease control. Europe managed to protect itself from the threat of these diseases while reestablishing their power through the shifting of aggressive sanitary responses from their shores to those of their colonies.

2 THE INTERNATIONAL SANITARY CONVENTIONS AT A COLONIAL SCALE

THE DISEASES OF CONCERN INSCRIBED in the International Sanitary Conventions, through their threat to trade that interrupted the circuitry of European empires and their ability to disturb the boundaries between Europe and the colonized world beyond the Mediterranean globally, would continue to be the dominant diseases of focus for international regulations until 2005 when the International Health Regulations were comprehensively reformed. The conventions formulated a new apparatus of disease control, whereby diseases could be monitored and controlled at a distance by telegraph and the imposition of economic penalties on any port region afflicted. The conventions also presupposed the management of disease in colonial sites predicated on technologies and forms of control located within the already-active local racial governance systems.

The effect of this was at times profound on the European and American colonies afflicted with these diseases. The emergence of these three diseases by 1912, yellow fever and especially plague and cholera, could spell ruin for colonial powers reliant on global trade. As a result they levied aggressive systems of disease control on their colonial populations. Disease further mobilized racial and ethnic anxieties about the quotidian actions of colonized subjects, which provoked massive responses in the name of sanitation. At the same time, epidemic events of the diseases incorporated into the International Sanitary Conventions also became moments for colonial powers to define themselves often through racial difference as separate from those under colonial rule. While European nations were interpreting their vulnerability to disease in civilizational difference between the East and Western Europe, similar boundaries were drawn through disease in their colonial dominions. While disease control had been a technology for establishing the rule of colonial difference and justification for racial and colonial separation in colonies across the world previously,[1] global epidemic diseases effectively linked concerns for global trade, disease, and colonial difference together.

In provoking such responses, which produced novel forms of population surveillance in regard to the ever-constant threat of economic isolation, European empires were able to remotely determine the strategies of health interventions in affected areas. European powers were able to monitor, through a practice of surveillance, the effects of plague, cholera, and yellow fever and their proximity to their ports. This chapter explores the responses to epidemics that were conditioned by the concerns for the effects of these diseases under the International Sanitary Conventions. In exploring responses to plague epidemics in British India, the Cape Colony, and American-controlled Hawaii, this chapter explores how epidemic Orientalist logics merged with local colonial and racial anxieties to produce aggressive and unequal responses to disease threat.

Orientalizing the Relations between Metropole and Colonies

The Third Plague Pandemic, which occurred between 1855 and 1960, killed over twelve million people, largely in India and China—yet only 457 deaths occurred in Europe. Though the International Sanitary Conventions only concerned plague and cholera for much of their early existence, they drastically altered the nature of disease responses at the endemic sites from which these diseases emerged. The International Sanitary Conventions were to have profound effects on the practices of disease control in colonial sites of outbreak. Where the conventions oriented global disease concerns around those threats seen as most pressing to Europe, the burden for preventing those diseases arriving on European shores shifted to the colonies of their empires. The new system of disease control imposed through the conventions established a mode of disease management that shifted the responsibility for containment from quarantine practices in Europe to the colonies. These practices produced systems of racial surveillance that positioned the colonized as the vector of disease spread who required permanent sanitary disciplining in order to protect the networks of global trade and the colonizers themselves.

While epidemic Orientalism constructed the priorities of disease threat and medical science provided the means to control these threats, the emergence of the telegraph truly allowed for a global system to operate to prevent the spread of disease to Europe. Prior to the arrival of transoceanic telegraph systems, correspondence between sites like London and India could take a year to effectively travel back and forth. Telegraph systems, connecting the world by the mid-nineteenth century, allowed for global communication that would take days rather than months. While spatial isolation from their colonies had previously required imperial actors and nations to anticipate colonial threats of all kinds and establish systems by which networks of colonial actors could manage them,[2] the telegraph provided the opportunity for near-instant dialogue and a constant surveillance of colonial activities in almost real time. The International Sanitary Conventions simultaneously provided a means and procedure by which all information would be disseminated globally. This would allow controls at European ports to be put in place to prevent the spread of disease prior to the arrival of ships from an infected location. As European ports were now able to anticipate the arrival of disease at their home ports, the responsibility for disease control could be shifted from Europe's harbor quarantines to colonial cities.

Under a unified vision of disease control operating through the same Orientalist gaze, quarantine could be shifted to colonial port cities to enforce borders between colonized and colonizer at the origin sites of outbreaks, rather than isolating European ports from one another and raising disputes. Central to this new apparatus was also a two-tiered system of intervention and surveillance whereby European powers sought to impose aggressive controls on their colonies and non-European powers while limiting the regulations imposed on one another. The system of surveillance imposed through the International Sanitary Conventions provided a way of exerting constant disciplinary pressure on suspect populations on an individual level without the need for disease to be present among them and without exerting direct power at the state level. In order to prevent outbreaks in Europe, a global monitoring project of non-European bodies had to occur. This project was supported by bureaucratic regulatory practices of exclusion that prevented access into Europe from infected ports without strict scrutiny and in-depth examination.[3] This in turn prompted overwhelming forms of control and oppression on colonized populations in the name of sanitation.

The first section of both the Paris Convention of 1894 and the Venice Convention of 1897 bound all signatory countries to alerting one another in the event of outbreaks within their borders.[4] Upon the confirmation of disease within the boundaries of the nation, the convention required all signatories to commit to a course of prophylactic public health actions including the formation of a sanitation force to inspect infected sites and conduct medical examinations, the quarantine and isolation of all infected persons, and the disinfection of all goods, foodstuffs, and clothing susceptible to plague.[5] Further, all ships outbound from afflicted ports were required to uphold strict standards of sanitation, disinfection, and quarantine on board, during the voyage, and in port.[6]

The major empires of the world and nations of Europe had successfully standardized their systems of disease control to (by and large) prevent the sort of customs and trade battles seen throughout the eighteenth and nineteenth centuries. Imperial centers sought to protect themselves by further solidifying the boundaries between them and their colonies. However, for colonial sites relying on trade for their prolonged exploitation of territory, the burdens of disease control shifted from the European quarantine zone to the Southern Hemisphere port city. The arrival of plague, cholera, or yellow fever could spell death but also global isolation and the total collapse of colonial economies. This threat produced increased controls over any travel and trade from non-European ports and overwhelming surveillance of colonial populations to prevent the spread of these diseases.

By the passage of the Venice International Sanitary Convention of 1897, which responded mostly to the spread of plague, it was accepted in the minds of the signatories that the reservoirs of both cholera and plague lay beyond the borders of Europe. Unlike cholera, when plague emerged in Hong Kong, germ labs around the world became focused on isolating the bacteria.[7] Unlike other global epidemic diseases like cholera, the emergence of plague was met by the relatively swift acceptance on the part of scientists around the world of its etiology and treatment strategies.[8] The knowledge that the plague bacterium could be isolated in the blood, spleen, liver, and lymph nodes was to become vital in accurately diagnosing outbreaks of plague as distinct from other diseases as it spread around the globe. Plague and cholera had their roots in the Himalayas and India while yellow fever was prevalent in Africa, and North and South America. The International Sanitary Conventions made possible, and thinkable, a global effort to prevent these diseases from ever appearing in Europe. Rather than maintaining the established practice prior to 1888 of quarantining local populations afflicted with illness to cordon sanitaires within national boundaries, the signatory parties, buoyed by the new scientific knowledge of plague and cholera spread, could maintain a system of medical monitoring and control before diseased bodies could reach their shores.[9]

The quarantining of vessels and goods traveling across borders presented a commercial threat to many imperial interests and drove demand for standardized practices across several empires, most notably within the British Empire. As the dominions of the British were the most affected by plague and cholera, the threat of these diseases to the empire was particularly significant. Though the conventions only presided over the signatory nations, the first notification of the regulation urged that all colonial dominions outside of Europe also accept its terms.[10] The responses to the Venice Convention of 1897, which expanded the earlier 1894 Paris Convention to control the spread of plague, was especially significant for the British Empire.

Racism(s) at the Core of Epidemic Orientalism

If the last chapter explored the ways in which infectious disease was capable of remapping relations in the modern world, constructing new visions of East and West while burnishing Western visions of modernity through the aegis of infectious disease control, this chapter considers the ways in which international regulations around infectious disease and the concern for these threats organize systems of political subject formation at the sites of epidemic. In many of the sites of epidemic spread in the late nineteenth and early twentieth centuries (as well as in the present), responses were articulated and organized along lines of existing racial orders. The examples in this chapter expose that, beyond racism solely being a force for organizing labor according to the political economic systems already in place, the racial policing of diseases and their spread in fact rationalized novel systems of human subjugation for their own ends in addition to serving wider local and global economic needs. We see this in the cases of race- and caste-based governance of epidemic threats in British India, American colonial Hawaii, and most specifically British-controlled Cape Town at the turn of the twentieth century. As Zygmunt Bauman writes, "Racism manifests the conviction that a certain category of human beings cannot be incorporated into the rational order, whatever the effort."[11] In the face of the teleological progressive narrative of controlling disease and sanitary improvement, disease—broadly across the world colonized by Europe, but especially epidemic diseases capable of threatening global trade and traffic—operated as a bright-line division between the civilized and the hopeless others. Racism isolates particular categories of people as the unreachable by modern progress.

While conversations at the International Sanitary Conferences may have highlighted the particular distinctions between East and West that played out through logics of disease control and economic and biological concerns, at the sites of epidemics, difference and disease were too often mapped along the internal fissures of race and caste already in operation. While linked to the wider imperial concerns for colonial economic exploitation, racialized and caste approaches to disease control also functioned through practices of sovereign rule imposed through colonial rule. The isolation, control, and separation of racialized populations blamed for spreading disease were carried out too often under systems of colonial regulations located in practices of settler and extractive colonialism rather than solely those methods laid out in the International Sanitary Conventions. While, on a global scale, the International Sanitary Conventions may have envisioned an epidemic Orientalist system of international political and economic relations, at colonial sites of epidemic spread beyond Europe, these visions were often articulated through racial regimes of difference, cutting up the world and its people along different lines. Racialized regimes of infectious disease control, beyond ultimately being seen by colonial actors as essential to the adherence to the International Sanitary Conventions, also supported the white supremacist aims of colonial settlement and remote sovereignty. In most cases, epidemic threat became an opportunity to consolidate sovereign power over life, death, and movement, and to impose that power, especially on those populations rendered as racialized others within colonial systems.

Racializing Geographies

In connection to the rising economic threat of the diseases notifiable under the International Sanitary Conventions, the threat of non-European persons in their dissemination came to quickly be associated with the demise of colonial holdings. This triggered a concern for the economic viability of colonial sites on top of the obvious biological threats to life. On May 24, 1897, the British government sent out a circular dispatch to the governing bodies of each of its self-governing colonies[12] detailing the proceedings of the Venice conference and requesting that they observe the convention.[13] Correspondence between Britain and its colonies regarding the Venice International Sanitary Convention of 1897 demonstrates the economic and political threat posed by the spread of plague. Plague within colonial zones represented not only a medical peril but also the threat of isolation from both Britain and the empire more broadly, and most colonies accepted the terms of the convention. Certain colonial states like Hong Kong and parts of Australia rejected the regulations based on their structural inabilities to maintain the necessary facilities for quarantine, while others refused them because they were too lax. Ceylon's colonial government saw the potential emergence of plague in their one port of Colombo and the economic consequences of having all of their exports delayed, quarantined, and possibly destroyed as catastrophic:

> If the plague broke out at Colombo, most vessels would doubtless cease to call there, and there would be no means, except at excessively high freight of

exporting tea and other produce. This would mean disaster if not ruin. . . .
Before the Venice Convention there was no general agreement even among
experts regarding the origin of the disease, the manner by which it could
be transmitted and the period of incubation. Each nation judged for itself
and as trade with Europe was far more important to this colony than trade
with Western India, it was decided to sacrifice the latter in order to ensure
the former.[14]

In later correspondence between Ceylon and Britain, the particular concern of colonized populations freely moving across territory drove the colonial administration to prophesize the downfall of the tea industry and by
extension, the colony itself:

> Regarding the proposed adherence of Ceylon to the Venice Sanitary Con-
> vention, and to state that the principal difficulty in adopting the convention
> arose out of the fact that the immigration of Coolies for Tea Estates, even if
> the Plague should break out in the Districts whence they came, could not be
> stopped without great injury, if not ruin to the Tea industry.
> I assumed that the Rules of the Convention of Venice would apply to these
> arrivals in which case there would have been great peril to the Colony for
> these Coolies being free immediately on landing to spread over the island
> would scatter the seeds of disease as they went.[15]

In order to maintain trade with Europe, the colonial government of Ceylon's restrictions on India prior to 1897 were more stringent than those outlined in the convention, largely due to a decision to isolate itself from India
rather than risk a local epidemic. As the correspondence between Ceylon's
government and Britain reflects, the economic penalties of such ostraciza-
tion were most severe. News of plague and cholera, spread via telegraph,
took a matter of days to reach all ports in Europe, and the long quarantine
or destruction of goods meant heavy losses to colonial corporations and
the colonies themselves. Infected port cities would often wait until the last
possible moment once all other causes had been exhausted to report the
outbreak.

The enforcement of quarantine practices and the other preventive measures of the Conventions outlined in Chapter 1 had to then be carried out immediately by the colonies accepting of it. Though quarantine was no longer a particularly desirable practice in Europe,[16] the acceptance of the International Sanitary Conventions within the colonies made such practices a necessity in the sites afflicted by plague and cholera in order to avoid economic repercussions. The pace of information spread by telegraph meant that once one of these diseases had infected a new site, it was highly unlikely that ships leaving colonial ports in the Southern Hemisphere could arrive at their European ports before restrictions were imposed. Clippings from public health reports show that within a single week of an outbreak being reported in a colonial site, other countries around the world established restrictions in keeping with the conventions.[17]

In the Western Hemisphere in Honolulu during an outbreak of plague in 1900, doctors, colonial administrators, and the general colonizing population lamented the emergence of the disease as they feared the city may become associated with the cities of Asia where plague was currently present rather than the urban centers of Northern Europe.[18] As plague spread in Honolulu and countries around the world closed their borders or quarantined any and all vessels arriving from its port, the city administrators embarked on a full quarantine of the city's Chinatown, allowing no one to leave. This quarantine placed significant hardships on those within, limiting employment options, movement, and access to supplies. The area of quarantine encompassed all Chinese and non-American properties immediately near the harbor but avoided white-owned buildings and businesses that were immediately connected to sites of quarantine.[19] Ultimately, the burning of contaminated buildings by the public health authorities spread beyond their control and consumed most of Chinatown in flames.

This system of control reflected an epidemic Orientalist vision of protecting Europe and America first and foremost from the trade and traffic of colonial sites. The requirements in the conventions were unidirectional, protecting the interests of Europe while leaving their dominions without a clear method of sanitary management for ships entering from Europe or the management of intercolonial trade. While the International Sanitary

FIGURE 1: Honolulu Chinatown Fire of 1900. Source: Brother Bertram. Wikimedia Commons.

Conventions were effective in standardizing trade to Europe, the old challenges of quarantine were left for colonial sites beyond Europe to negotiate themselves:

> A careful examination of the Convention discloses two very important lacunae:— the Chapter relating to countries outside Europe contains no rules as to arrivals and the chapter relating to countries in Europe contains no rules for departures from plague infected ports in Europe. . . . India intended no doubt all along to join the Convention and it might be said that rules for arrivals must surely have been provided for countries outside Europe. But during the meetings of the Conference, the question of the rules to be provided for arrivals in ports outside Europe was not discussed and I think that it was never present in any definite manner to the Delegates' minds. They were concerned with keeping the plague out of Europe

without interfering unduly with navigation and trade. . . . From the purely local point of view, I think that a vessel arriving at a port of a Signatory Power from a port outside Europe abiding by the rules for departures from plague-infected ports could claim Convention treatment, quite apart from the treatment accorded in that port outside Europe to arrivals. But if that port imposed on arrivals restrictions greater than those declared by the Convention to be sufficient for the protection of public health in Europe, I think that a Signatory Power would have very good grounds, from what may be called a political point of view, for refusing Convention treatment to ships coming from the port in question. There are no essential, but only accidental differences in sanitary matters between countries in Europe and out of Europe and it appears to me quite unreasonable, and indeed illogical, that, say, India or Ceylon because they are by accident outside of Europe, should expect to obtain, in European ports under the convention, a more favorable treatment than they themselves are prepared to give.[20]

The effects of this perspective, raised by the Secretary of State for India, Francis Hamilton, were often evident in North African port sanitation protocols. The International Quarantine Directory of 1934 highlights how the ports of Algeria and Tunisia served as sanitary buffer zones for transit to France. All native Algerians traveling to France were required to complete sanitary inspection prior to boarding for France.[21] A tiered pricing system for sanitation fees privileged ships arriving from European ports while charging higher fees for oceangoing or Eastern vessels.

"Note.– Contrary to the preceding provisions, and providing the fees are in no case more than those indicated in the three preceding paragraphs, ships calling in an Algerian port are subjected to a fixed fee of 75 fr. if they come from a European port, and of 150 fr. if they are engaged in ocean traffic up to the amount of 100 tons; above this figure the fees indicated in the preceding paragraphs are applicable. None but ships which only touch at a single Algerian port on their way to a foreign port can benefit from this special tariff. Steamers calling on the coasts of France to take in or land passengers: If they come from a European port :

Per passenger taken on board or landed. . . . . Fr. 1))

Per ton of goods landed up to 5 tons. . . . .)) 2))

If they come from an extra-European port :

Per passenger taken on board or landed.)) 2))

Per ton of merchandise landed up to 5 tons. . . . .)) 3))[22]

The pressures placed on colonial dominions to maintain trade while preventing the emergence or spread of disease provoked drastic measures of social control by governments already well versed in quelling any anticolonial dissent.

Plague in India

Much like in the case of cholera, during epidemics of bubonic plague in the late nineteenth century, India's epidemic control was a particular focus both of European attention as well as British imperial concern. The Indian colonial government faced two drastic problems from the International Sanitary Conventions during the plague outbreak: economic isolation and health emergency. While the conventions set the maximum standards for quarantine and prohibition of particular imports, European concerns over the spread of plague to Europe by Indian pilgrims en route to Mecca provoked a concern for both trade and traffic, which threatened to leave the colony isolated from its imperial lifelines.

In response to this outbreak and the overwhelming concussive effects that the colonial government feared it may have, the British government of India formulated the Epidemic Diseases Act to apply to all of British India in 1897.[23] These powers allowed the colonial authority to destroy any goods, homes, and property potentially carrying plague and to cancel any and all public gatherings.[24] Thousands of homes were destroyed, and these control efforts were often carried out by the Indian military. The plague regulations under the epidemic diseases act reflected a microcosm of the ideologies present within the International Sanitary Conventions broadly while also reflecting the ideologies inherent to British colonial rule. All activities of Indians thought to be responsible for spreading plague were controlled, and private property could be seized and destroyed. Anyone suspected of carrying the

plague or found in homes affected by plague could be quarantined.[25] Failing
to cooperate with medical officials was punishable by imprisonment of up
to six months in certain areas.[26]

There were also significant controls in domestic travel across India. Railways and water routes were heavily controlled, usually employing the Indian
caste system as a mode of dividing populations and assessing disease threat.
In Madras, medical inspectors at railway stations were empowered to detain
any person suspected of carrying the plague, and any person leaving from
a suspected plague area was required to hold a passport that the traveler
was expected to present daily to the sanitary authority of their destination
for ten days.[27] Local villages were also required to keep detailed ledgers of
every person arriving from an infected area. Among the data required in the
register was father's name and caste:

> The Headman of every village shall keep himself promptly informed of the
> arrival of every person from an infected area without a passport, and shall
> deal with him as in the preceding clauses of this regulation to which such
> person shall be bound to submit himself. (vii) A register shall be main-
> tained by each local authority in the following form:—
>
> (1)   Date and receipt of Intimation.
> (2)   Name of traveler.
> (3)   From what infected area arriving.
> (4)   Date of arrival of traveler.
> (5)   Number, date and place of issue of passport.
> (6)   How long kept under observation.
> (7)   State of health of the traveler and other persons living in the
>   house in which he is or has been residing.
> (8)   Date of departure to the local authority of the place of destination.
> (9)   Date of intimation of departure to the local authority of the place
>   of destination.
> (10) Date of dispatch of the passport to the Tahsildar [Inspector].
>
> (viii) In the case of persons passing through a Railway Frontier Inspection Sta-
> tion, the medical officer in charge shall arrange to record the following infor-
> mation in respect to every traveler from an infected area who is not detained

by him under the provisions of Regulation 14 and send it without delay—if possible by the railway guard of the same or next train—to the District Medical and Sanitary Officer of the district to which such traveler is proceeding:–

(1) Name and Date of arrival.
(2) Name of traveler.
(3) Father's name.
(4) Caste.
(5) Age.
(6) Whence Coming.[28]

It was also suggested that carriages holding lower-class travelers should be scrutinized more aggressively for plague.

Under the auspices of the plague regulations, the British colonial authorities deployed novel techniques of biometric surveillance and data collection. Prior to the first effective employment of fingerprint analysis in criminal cases,[29] fingerprinting to ascertain the validity of plague vaccination certificates was enforced in response to the outbreak. The first fingerprint bureau was established in Calcutta in 1897 and was put into service quickly to monitor any populations suspected of carrying disease.

Bubonic Plague and Smallpox in Cape Town

While British India imposed novel forms of population control that navigated and operated along caste lines, an epidemic of bubonic plague in Cape Town provoked the production of novel technologies of racial control that reflected both a colonial concern for trade isolation while also mapping onto long-existing anxieties around racial mixing and the free movement of non-white people in the city. The Cape Town bubonic plague epidemic of 1901 was a formative event in the history of racial subjugation in South Africa, and the period is seen as a major transition to state-organized, urban racial governance.[30] However, the divergent responses to epidemics of plague and smallpox at the same moment in 1901 Cape Town also reflect in stark terms the effects of global sanitary controls and the International Sanitary Conventions on racial forms of governance. On March 12, 1901, due to the fear of the spread of plague from within the city's poorer urban neighborhoods, the Cape government forcibly removed 6,000 Black Africans (likely Xhosa and Nguni speaking peoples) under armed guard and transferred them to Uitvlugt, a temporary quarantine site that was later made into a permanent township known as Ndabeni. This evacuation occurred without concern for actual infection or based on exposure to the disease. Removal was solely conditional on race and housing situation.

While plague was indeed a serious and major threat, Cape Town had been experiencing one of the city's largest smallpox epidemics in its history prior to the outbreak of plague. Though plague produced some of the most aggressive sanitary controls ever seen in the city, smallpox was left largely untreated beyond vaccination. The different responses to each of these out-breaks can be explained by the differing perceptions of their threat of spread to Europe and the threat posed by plague to the economic isolation of the British-controlled Cape Colony.

Where plague was a disease marked through the International Sanitary Conventions as threatening to its signatory powers, smallpox was seen as ubiquitous around the globe and less threatening to Europeans.[31] The case of plague in Cape Town shows how global networks of medical actors were mobilized to respond to threats to the international sanitary regime, prompt-ing much more aggressive and significant responses than to other seemingly destructive epidemics. These divergent responses to these twin epidemics also show how powerful epidemic Orientalism was for organizing perspec-tives on disease threat and structuring responses to diseases that served the interests of European powers.

In response to the arrival of plague in Cape Town, the colonial authorities imposed a novel urban model of colonial population control that would echo throughout history as one of the most totalizing and oppressive structures of the twentieth century: the township.[32] Though it was claimed that the segre-gated space of Uitvlugt was a temporary site, the Cape government deferred the decision to close the area until 1902, when the legislature established it as a permanent site. All movement in and out of Uitvlugt, later known as Ndabeni, was prohibited without a pass, echoing the practices of British India and a bitter precursor of what was to come in the form of the pass laws in Apartheid South Africa.[33]

The Cape Town plague epidemic marks a pivotal moment in which medical practices calibrated with imperial concerns over the maintenance of health in white European populations to produce novel forms of racial governance that would later be reproduced across South Africa. These actions transformed the urban space of the city and produced the blueprint for the first state-monitored and regulated, racially delineated, enclosed residential space in South Africa—the first township. The responses to the Cape Town plague epidemic of 1901 were facilitated in large part through the systems of disease control mandated by the Venice International Sanitary Convention of 1897.

Smallpox had been ravaging Cape Town since 1882, when it killed up to 4,000 people that year.[34] Between 1882 and 1902, the disease regularly infected several thousand annually. While smallpox was certainly a serious local threat to public health, the emergence of bubonic plague was a global phenomenon eliciting widespread concern from various European and Asian empires.[35] It was the global aspect of the disease that produced new forms of disease control and led to the aggressive racial quarantining and surveillance in Cape Town.

The global threat of plague to European economic interests and to the continued success of the British Cape Colony provided the justification to enact the local quarantining and permanent surveillance of Black African persons in Cape Town. These actions were seen by the medical actors in Cape Town as necessary for protecting imperial interests around the world. For these reasons the City of Cape Town marshaled vast resources toward fighting plague. Medical expertise, rooted in epidemic Orientalism from both within Cape Town as well as foreign authorities, and understandings of previous plague outbreaks in India and elsewhere viewed the arrival of plague in Cape Town as a consequence of racial mixing, which guided the local responses to the epidemic, ultimately producing the first urban township in the city. Where smallpox was a localized issue, the response to plague marshaled medical experts from around the world versed in the management of the disease, prompted global concerns for its spread, and cost the small colony a great deal financially. It also transformed the racial cartography of South Africa forever. International concerns for the spread of plague, which isolated the Cape Colony, melded with latent racial anxieties to provoke one of the most aggressive disease controls of its time.

Contrasting Responses to Plague and Smallpox

The first case of plague was discovered in Cape Town on February 2, 1901. By the February 4, Dr. John Gregory, the acting medical officer for the colony, had confirmed the diagnosis of plague pending a full bacterial analysis. In order to coordinate plague prevention activities, the Cape Sanitary Authority formed the Cape Plague Advisory Council and met regularly to provide guidance to the Cape government and report on health activities. This council was composed of the mayors of each municipality as well as Dr. Gregory and Dr. William Simpson, the chief advisor to the plague council. The council met twenty times until July 10, whereupon the members decided it was no longer necessary to convene as the plague threat had dissipated.[36] The City of Cape Town took on the full financial burden for the outbreak, which was at its conclusion to total over £300,000 or the equivalent of £30,000,000 today. What resulted was an almost total lockdown of the city.

From the first case of plague, Dr. Simpson and Dr. Gregory had a significant remit to quickly enact policy and operated largely unchecked by other authorities. Upon the announcement of the outbreak, Gregory began circulating pamphlets to the public on the prevention and recognition of plague. These pamphlets largely focused on personal hygiene within the home, cleanliness, and how to eradicate rats. These handbills were delivered by a newly enlisted force of sanitation personnel, largely made up of poor Black persons and the city's convicts, under the authority of a district medical officer. Very early in the outbreak, health responses galvanized around a racialized logic that placed heightened levels of disease surveillance among the city's poorest while reducing the monitoring of Europeans to a minimum. Among the sanitation team's responsibilities were the eradication of rats and the daily inspections "of all lower class houses, and a less frequent inspection of the houses of better class Europeans."[37] Once again, the laborers conducting these inspections were already, prior to the forced removals, racialized with prisoners and poorer Black laborers making up the vanguard of this dangerous and invasive work. Many of these homes were populated by recently migrated Black Africans from other regions of southern Africa, and inspections galvanized around the concerns of overcrowding within houses occupied by Black people.

The daily inspections of lower-class houses were often carried out in the middle of the night, the logic being that the occupants would have a more difficult time hiding the evidence of overcrowding.[38] Such inspections took place on a daily basis for several months after the initial case of plague. The process of isolating cases of the plague was equally as swift and forceful. All known or likely cases of plague were removed from their homes, along with all other contacts within the dwelling as well as from some adjoining houses. Initially they were moved to the newly equipped plague hospital. The houses of infected persons were disinfected and sanitized, a process often taking several days or weeks. All houses labeled unfit for human habitation were permanently shuttered. All infected articles of clothing or goods were either disinfected or destroyed at the will of the medical authorities. All Capetonians attempting to leave the city, either by rail or by ship, were stopped and their baggage and their persons searched.[39] Removals from infected homes were proving disastrous for the former inhabitants, as those either released from quarantine at the hospital or awaiting the disinfection of their homes were forced effectively into homelessness. The Plague Advisory Council saw this as a major threat of further disease spread.[40]

The health authorities ultimately decided that wholesale segregation of the Black urban population in Cape Town, regardless of health status or proximity to the infected, was a justifiable response to plague. On March 12 all Black Africans inhabiting the city's poorest urban areas were forcibly removed and transferred to the area immediately surrounding the Plague Hospital in a former sewage station known as Uitvlugt. By the end of May roughly 6,000 Black persons were removed to Uitvlugt.

The reaction to smallpox was very different, even though it too was deadly. The first major outbreak of smallpox swept through Cape Town in 1713. This outbreak wiped out a quarter of the European populace and roughly a third of the enslaved population, while also having utterly devastating effects on the KhoeKhoe and San peoples.[41] Later epidemics produced drastic and near-equally deadly consequences in 1735, 1755, and 1767. Epidemics were also common in the early nineteenth century occurring in 1807, 1812, 1840, and 1858.[42] In 1801 inoculation against smallpox became common practice in Cape Town. However, as the century progressed, the challenges in transporting effective smallpox cultures from British calf lymph nodes could mean that inoculation required a rather painful invasive medical process that proved unpopular: required tissue drawn from live patients and through arm-to-arm inoculation.[43] This process was quite painful for the donor,[44] and the practice of inoculation drew widespread ire.

An outbreak of smallpox in 1882 would prove to have the most significant consequences on the public health system of any disease prior to the plague outbreak of 1901. In 1882 the *Drummond Castle* landed in the Cape with a case of smallpox onboard, leading to one of the largest outbreaks in the history of the city and the most deadly since the first epidemics of the disease in the eighteenth century.[45] According to various estimates, this outbreak took between 1,000 and 4,000 lives, equating to a mortality rate within the population of Cape Town of between 2 and 5 percent.[46]

The Cape government attempted to implement a quarantine. However, disorganization and heavy storms slowed efforts to remove contacts to quarantine sites.[47] There were, prior to the outbreak, no quarantine centers in and around Cape Town and no legislation to coordinate such a large health crisis. The New Somerset Hospital, the main point of treatment, also had no facilities in which to isolate patients. Tent cities were established at Paarden Eisland, a cut-off area by the port, which became even further isolated due to poor weather making it almost impossible to access.[48] A farm was offered as a quarantine facility by a local landowner, but this area soon became too small to support the rising infection rate and had to increase the number of beds at the farm by almost one hundred. The city's sanitation authorities were overwhelmed. Within the quarantine facilities, patients were segregated according to race while smallpox lymphs used for inoculation were only taken from white children.[49]

Unlike in other outbreaks of smallpox discussed earlier, in Cape Town the disease reflected a rising concern for the disease's ability to travel from colonized to colonizer. It was during this outbreak that calls for segregation, primarily of the Malay population, reached fever pitch. Arguments for segregation focused on racial difference while hailing the incommensurability of modern settler populations to coexist with non-European peoples. Letters in both in the *Cape Times* and the *Lantern*, two prominent periodicals of the time, called for the residential segregation of the nonwhite population from Europeans. An anonymous letter published under the name "Friend of the Free State" in the *Cape Times* stated that "it is high time that the White people of the Metropolis built a town for themselves and left the present town for [a] location for the Malays, Mozambiques . . . et hoc genus omne [*and everyone else of this kind*] . . . to breed fever."[50]

Despite the end of the 1882 epidemic, the racial animus surrounding smallpox did not cease to exist. When sanitation authorities advocated closing the cemeteries within the boundaries of Cape Town in 1885 and 1886, the focus of blame for contagion shifted to the Muslim burial practices of the Malay[51] population. The primarily nonwhite-European but often racially mixed Malay population mobilized to protest the closing of the cemeteries and met with significant resistance from Cape police. Muslim burial ceremonies in Cape Town were large and were a central community practice.[52] The protests were cast in the public media as "Oriental fanaticism," equating Muslim practice with obstinacy in the face of health threats to the larger community and the Malay as insanitary as a result. While preventing burial ceremonies, the closures of the cemeteries also eliminated a major nonwhite display of political unity and communal practice.

Plague and Smallpox Responses Reconsidered

Explanations for the imposition of racial segregation as a response to the outbreak of plague in 1901 Cape Town have focused primarily on how epidemic emergency and the threat of massive urban contagion were employed to justify racial separation. Maynard Swanson's 1977 work *The Sanitation Syndrome* articulates clearly how the specter of epidemic outbreak became a powerful metaphor for rationalizing racially specific urban segregation policies in early twentieth-century Cape Town. Epidemic outbreaks provided an opportunity for segregationists to justify their positions by arguing that cohabitation of urban spaces by different races presented a public health concern to the European population of the city.[53] Scholarship on this moment of early urban racial separation has primarily explored the role of public health in promoting segregationist aims.[54]

While epidemic moments were indeed periods in which segregationists attempted to coopt health concerns with racial animus, not all outbreaks engendered the same response. Smallpox is a key example. Calls for segregation had been voiced as early as 1882, and despite racial animus in response to the threat of smallpox, segregation never materialized. Instead, as noted above, smallpox was treated with more traditional forms of quarantine.

Prior to the outbreak of smallpox in 1882, the Cape sanitary and health authorities had little power with which to disperse funds to support health responses or centralize activities, which explains why this particular outbreak did not result in segregation.[55] After the outbreak of 1882 slowed, the Cape government ratified the Public Health Act of 1883, which established a permanent position of sanitary health officer and required by law that all persons receive smallpox inoculations. The act was amended in 1897 to provide significantly more powers to colonial health authorities during epidemic events, guaranteeing essentially unlimited government funds to enact reforms and protect the city. The Public Health Act of 1897 No. 15 was ultimately enforced in 1901 to provide colonial medical officers the authority to enact a racial quarantine of Cape Town. However, after 1883, and most importantly in 1901, the legal conditions to enact segregation were the same for both plague and smallpox. During this time smallpox still remained a serious threat to the Cape population, yet it was not met with the responses mobilized against plague in 1901.

From 1897 to 1901, Cape Town reported up to 2,000 cases of smallpox per year. In 1900, there were 2,200 cases, alone almost equaling case totals from the 1882 outbreak. Most of Cape Town's public health legislation was formed to prevent the spread of smallpox, and the disease was, prior to 1901, associated with the city's non-European population. In spite of increasing infection rates, a legacy of racial stigma toward smallpox, and the state's capacity to enact sweeping reforms to combat the spread of the disease, racial quarantine measures were never pursued in the case of smallpox between 1897 and 1901.

Existing medical knowledge drawn from the time also fails to explain why plague would be met with these particular forms of racial governance

TABLE 2: Number of Cases from Smallpox and Plague in
Cape Town, 1896–1901.

Cases per year	Total cases
Smallpox 1896	3349
Smallpox 1897	545
Smallpox 1898	699
Smallpox 1899	799
Smallpox 1900	2211
Smallpox 1901	868
Plague 1901	766
Plague prior to removals	88

Note: Reproduced with the consent of *Social Science History.*
Sources: All smallpox data from Vivian Bickford-Smith, "South African
Urban History, Racial Segregation and the Unique Case of Cape Town?,"
Journal of Southern African Studies 21, no. 1 (1995): 63–78; Vivian Bickford-
Smith, Elizabeth van Heyningen, and Nigel Worden, *Cape Town in the
Twentieth Century: An Illustrated Social History* (Cape Town: David Philip,
1999); Elizabeth van Heyningen, "Public Health and Society in Cape Town
1880–1910" (Dissertation, University of Cape Town, 1989); Maynard W.
Swanson, "The Sanitation Syndrome: Bubonic Plague and Urban Native
Policy in the Cape Colony, 1900–1909," *Journal of African History* 18, no.
3 (1977): 387–410. All bubonic plague data from J. A Mitchell, "Small-Pox
and 'Amaas' in South Africa," *The Lancet* 200, no. 5172 (October 14, 1922):
808–12, https://doi.org/10.1016/S0140-6736(01)01096-0; van Heyningen,
"Public Health and Society in Cape Town."

as opposed to smallpox. Doctors of the period perceived smallpox to be
much more interpersonally contagious as opposed to bubonic plague, for
which rats were considered the primary vector.[56] A memorandum sent to
house owners at the outbreak of plague in Cape Town suggests that personal
interaction was less likely to spread plague than smallpox:

Plague is not a highly infectious disease in the sense that small-pox, scarlet
fever and spotted typhus are. There is no infection in the air of a clean and
well-lighted room in which a Plague patient is lying, nor is there the slight-
est danger to the persons who nurse or move the patient, as long as they are

careful to wash and disinfect their hands, and to disinfect the discharges of the patient and the cups and spoons and other utensils.[57]

This position is derived from a medical paper written a year prior to the outbreak by Dr. William Simpson, the man who would become the consulting medical officer to the Cape on plague.

> Plague is not a highly infectious disease in the sense that small-pox, scarlet fever and spotted typhus are and the measures which have proved effective against the latter have proved a signal failure in the case of Plague. Why? Because neither small-pox, scarlet fever, nor typhus are diseases of house vermin: Plague on the other hand is, and therefore unless we can eliminate this element in the sanitary problem, all other efforts are bound to be futile.[58]

These statements would suggest a stronger argument for the quarantining of smallpox patients rather than those infected with plague, as interpersonal contagion would generally mandate a greater need to isolate infected persons capable of spreading the disease through their own agency. The Plague Advisory Council was aware that the greater threat of plague stemmed from both surfaces and rodents, yet the focus of interventions came to center on the removal of Black Africans, the prevention of their unsurveilled movement around the city, and the concealment of cases.

The 1901 Plague Outbreak: The Arrival of a Global Threat

By the time plague arrived in Cape Town in 1901, it had already swept through Bombay and other parts of India as well as Hong Kong. This had crippling effects on the populations affected but also threatened to destabilize global maritime trade as the concern for the spread of plague from the Southern Hemisphere to Europe grew in the eyes of European nations. Prior to the emergence of bubonic plague, the Cape Colony was subject to the International Sanitary Conventions of 1897, which brought the added economic pressures to control the diseases that were discussed in Chapter 1.

The Venice Conference of 1897, prompted by the devastating effects of the plague outbreak in Bombay that accounted for roughly 15 percent of all

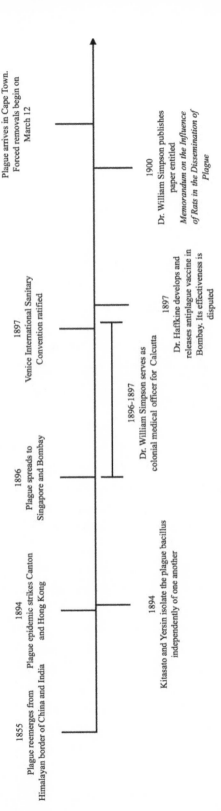

FIGURE 2: Timeline of the Third Bubonic Plague Pandemic Prior to Cape Town Epidemic. Made by author. Reproduced with the consent of *Social Science History*. From White, Alexandre I. R. (2018) "Global Risks, Divergent Pandemics: Contrasting Responses to Bubonic Plague and Smallpox in 1901 Cape Town." *Social Science History* 42(01):135–58.

Sources: Echenberg, Myron J. (2002) "Pestis redux: The initial years of the third bubonic plague pandemic, 1894–1901." *Journal of World History* 13 (2): 429–49.

Echenberg, Myron (2007) *Plague Ports: The Global Urban Impact of Bubonic Plague, 1894–1901*. New York: New York University Press.

Gregory, A. John, and William John Richie Simpson (1901) *Memoranda by the Acting Medical Officer of Health for Cape Colony and Professor W.J. Simpson. M.D., F.R.C.P. on the Outbreak of Plague in Cape Colony and the Precautions Taken in Connection Therewith*. Office of the Medical Officer of Health for the Colony, Cape Town. CO 897/67/2. London: National Archives at Kew.

Mayor, E., et al. (1897) International Sanitary Convention, Signed at Venice, March 18, 1897.

Simpson, William John Richie (1900) *Memorandum on the Influence of Rats in the Dissemination of Plague*. Cape Town: Richards.

of India's deaths that year[59] and the risk of plague spreading to Europe from India traveling through the Persian Gulf and Red Sea,[60] focused solely on plague. Prior to the Venice Conference there was no formal consensus on how plague was transmitted.[61]

A greater understanding of the pathology of bubonic plague shifted the focus in Europe from containment after infection to the prevention of transference of the disease to European locales. The convention sought to achieve this through rigorous medical inspections of persons and vessels incoming from plague ports and the isolation and quarantine of those infected if the disease was found to be present.[62] The presence of an epidemic of either plague or cholera meant isolation from necessary trade routes and the elimination of exporting power for the duration of the outbreak.

Disease, Epidemic Orientalism, and Colonial Dominance: Dr. William John Ritchie Simpson and the Cape Town Epidemic

The threat of plague to imperial interests forced the British Empire to carefully monitor plague outbreaks within their domains and mandated responses within colonies to be reported back to London.[63] The efficacy of responses was judged not only by the state of health within distant colonies but also by the methods employed to fight them by governmental leaders in Britain.[64]

In sites of plague outbreak within the British Empire, medical consultants with previous experience tackling the plague were often called upon to develop policies.[65] A letter from University College Liverpool to the secretary of state for the colonies dated February 12, 1901, ten days after plague was first diagnosed in the Cape, suggests the competitive nature of these positions and the desire on the part of research institutions to capitalize on these opportunities:

> Seeing there is a probability of Cape Town becoming infected by Plague I have the honour to inform you that we have here Dr. Balfour Stewart who, should you require an expert on Plague would be willing to proceed to Cape Town. Dr. Balfour Stewart was out in India in charge of Plague operations and was also for some time assistant to Professor Haffkine. Since returning home he has been attached to this Laboratory and also serves the Liverpool Corporation as Assistant Bacteriologist and in that capacity he has more

than anyone else contributed to preventing the entry of Plague into the port of Liverpool. . . . I need not allude to the importance of Bacteriological Diagnosis which in the case of plague is sometimes the only method of Diagnosis, and in any case is a final proof. I have, &c., (Sgd) Rubert Boyce, Dean of the Liverpool School of Tropical Medicine[66]

While Dr. Stewart ultimately did not receive the posting, his previous experience of treating plague internationally in India, his role as a bacteriologist capable of diagnosing plague, and his medical relationship to Dr. Haffkine, a noted plague doctor, provided the primary support for his candidacy for a medical position in Cape Town. Professor William Simpson, appointed by the colonial secretary as the leader of the plague response in Cape Town, was previously the colonial health officer in Calcutta as well as a lecturer at and cofounder of the London School of Tropical Medicine. In 1900 Dr. Simpson published a paper titled "Memorandum on the Influence of Rats in the Dissemination of Plague,"[67] which was the first to link rats to the spread of plague in scientific terms.

Simpson and Gregory operated freely to direct Cape funds to their policy directives as a result of the public health laws in place in the city.[68] The choice of Dr. Simpson as the primary medical consultant to the Cape government who was given overwhelming responsibility to enact disease controls[69] was central to the imposition of racial quarantine in Cape Town. Simpson's own experiences in other British dominions as well as his perspectives on the role of race in preventing disease spread tessellated with the racial anxieties of both the Plague Advisory Council and much of the European population of Cape Town. Dr. Simpson's role in the Cape Town epidemic and his future endeavors demonstrate the global circulation of the epidemic Orientalist discourse among medical experts and colonial spaces.

Simpson's approach at forced removals in Cape Town was not his first foray into large-scale evacuations, and the racist approach to public health and hygiene taken in the city was not to be his last. In almost every previous and future placement, regardless of the disease present at the time, Simpson advocated for the separation of the white European population from the local one whenever it could be practicably implemented as a strategy to prevent any disease spread affecting colonial interests. Simpson was an aggressive advocate for the segregation of tropical colonial cities, both in the interest of malaria prevention and due to the ever-present threat caused by what he saw as the insanitary habits and environments of the local people.

Prior to his posting in Cape Town, Simpson was the chief medical officer of Calcutta, where he unsuccessfully conducted an evacuation of a plague-afflicted area.[70] The size of Calcutta's population also rendered the wholesale removal of people from a certain area almost impossible. In Cape Town, however, the scale was far more manageable for such an undertaking.

After leaving the Cape, Simpson was stationed in Hong Kong to consult on the continued epidemic of plague in the city. Here he recommended the constant inspection of "emigrant homes" regardless of cases of illness and the construction of segregated hospitals to accommodate patients:

> Outside the Sanitary Department and in the domain of hospital which is ably and admirably controlled by the Principal Improvement Medical Officer of the Colony, is the Government Infectious Hospital, to which the plague patients are sent for treatment. This hospital was not originally built for the purpose for which it is now used and is consequently deficient, in many respects, in the accommodation necessary for such institutions, . . . It is necessary in a well-arranged infectious hospital that separate buildings be provided for each of these diseases, both for Europeans and Chinese.[71]

Soon after his appointment in Hong Kong, Simpson returned to Africa to consult in both West and Central Africa on health, sanitation, and urban planning in the tropics. It was at this time that he wrote several books on the topic of health in the region. Twice more he advocated strongly for the segregation of colonial urban spaces:

> There are certain important points in connection with dwelling houses in the tropics which should be borne in mind when either leasing or building a house. First, the houses should not be surrounded by nor close to native huts. Native children are seldom not infected with malaria, and hence living in a dwelling house in this position increases the risk of infection from that

disease. For this reason a dwelling house among native huts is an unhealthy house, apart from the fact that it will also always be in the midst of other insanitary conditions.[72]

Secondly, the segregation of the residential quarters of the Europeans away from the native town. The business quarters, if in the neighbourhood of the natives, should only be occupied during the day.[73]

In this same piece, Simpson calls for strict racial controls akin to the pass laws that were later implemented both in Cape Town and throughout South Africa and were previously extant during the Cape's period of enslavement:

For Europe and other countries advanced in sanitary organization, these regulations secure a very considerable degree of protection, but for tropical countries with their different conditions, and often with no proper sanitary organization, certain modifications are desirable in order to prevent the importation of plague by land or sea. These are, that native passengers from an infected point should at the time of embarkation and inspection by the medical officer of the port produce a certificate of having been inoculated at least a week previously; and that natives from an infected area should not be admitted into healthy areas without passports indicating that they have been inoculated.[74]

Simpson's justifications for segregation in response to disease stemmed from both an argument about cultural incommensurability and biological justifications for why European bodies were at heightened risk from local diseases:

It has to be recognized that the standards and mode of life of the Asiatic do not ordinarily consort with the European, whilst the customs of Europeans are at times not acceptable to the Asiatics, and that those of the African unfamiliar with and not adapted to the new conditions of town life will not blend with either. Also that the diseases to which these different races are respectively liable are readily transferable to the European and vice versa, a result especially liable to occur when their dwellings are near each other. In the interests of each community and of the healthiness of the locality and country, it is absolutely essential that in every town and trade centre the town planning should provide well defined and separate quarters or wards for Europeans, Asiatics and Africans, as well as those divisions which are necessary in a town of one nationality and race, and that there should be a neutral belt of open unoccupied country of at least 300 yards in width between the European residences and those of the Asiatic and African.[75]

Simpson's recommendations were ultimately accepted and enacted by the Cape colonial government.

Without the larger global focus on plague and the significant monitoring imposed by the British Empire after pressure imposed through the International Sanitary Conferences and Conventions to prevent its spread, William Simpson would not have been appointed as the senior advisor on plague to Cape Town. The circulation of experts to plague sites around the Southern Hemisphere was driven by the larger concerns of Europe to halt its spread, as evidenced in the perspectives and concerns that drove the Venice Convention of 1897.

Racial Mixing and the Threat of Plague in Cape Town

In Cape Town, the particular threat of plague-spread to all racial groups within the city reflected a threat to white colonial dominance that was echoed by the economic perils posed by the continued presence of epidemic. As already examined, the presence of plague in a port city mandated, under the Sanitary Conventions, an almost total embargo of all goods to and from the city and strict quarantines of any vessels arriving from that port. This would cause severe financial burden on the colonial city, in some cases tantamount to total colonial collapse.[76] This further stoked the long-held concerns of white Europeans over the racial integration of urban space. The melding of the imperial concerns about disease control and the role of racial segregation, perceived as a necessary technology for the management of colonial and colonized populations espoused by Dr. Simpson, aligned with the long-held white Capetonian concerns about how to manage and control an increasing Black population in the face of epidemic emergency, producing the first township in the city.

The concerns of plague as a threat to both health and colonial stability were evident in the statements made about the disease even prior to its arrival in Southern Africa. Nearly two years before the major outbreak of plague in Cape Town, calls for racial segregation and limitations to immigration in the hopes of preventing major outbreaks were levied both in government and by the general European public. Drawing on existing language from the Venice Convention, a council comprising representatives not only of the Cape Colony but from all of the territories of South Africa addressed the particular concern of Indian immigration as a potential cause of plague-spread at an interstate conference on the disease, held in Pretoria in 1899:

> This Conference recommends that steps be immediately taken by all South African Governments to provide for the prohibition or restriction of immigration into this country from countries in which Plague is prevalent; to place under proper, and sufficient restrictions the moving about of persons likely to contribute to the more rapid spread of the infection of Plague within their territories.[77]

This position, while not accepted by the Cape Colony delegation, demonstrates the concern for plague's arrival from other ports via the travel of persons rather than trade and goods. Though plague, as stated earlier, was less interpersonally contagious, the threat of immigration particularly of Indians and South and East Asian people was ultimately perceived as a colossal risk.[78]

The South African League, a British nationalist organization writing in the *Cape Times*, raised comparisons between the hygienic conditions in Bombay and Cape Town publicly as justification for outright segregation:

> In conclusion let me remind your readers that many of the unsanitary conditions of Bombay are in evidence in the crowded, dirty, and ill-ventilated dwellings of our poorer coloured folk, and that plague, once domiciled amongst us, would lead to an appalling mortality and to enormous expense, for no measure short of wholesale segregation, and demolition of many houses in toto, would even shorten the epidemic.[79]

Plague was simultaneously recognized as a threat that can and would spread from far away through ports and with people that could radically destabilize the Cape. In drawing comparisons between the sanitary conditions in Bombay as cause of the outbreak there and urban nonwhite poverty in the Cape, plague and both the medical and economic effects it would bring were recognized as the inevitable consequence of racial mixing in the city. This particular recognition of plague being a disease not only preventable through racial hygiene and separation but also recognized as a foreign threat to domestic economic interests reflects a global comprehension of disease unseen in the language and fears associated with other diseases. This particular fear of disease emerging out of the poorer, racially mixed or non-European centers of town was further stoked when the disease landed on South African shores.

The concern that racial mixing in residential areas might drive and perpetuate the spread of plague was reinforced by claims made by foreign plague experts central to the development of health responses in the city. Dr. William Simpson himself, prior to his appointment to the Cape as the primary advisor on the plague outbreak, stated from afar before the epidemic broke:

> Next to Bombay, Cape Town is one of the most suitable towns I know of for a plague epidemic. . . . Situated in one of nature's most beautiful spots in the world it has grown up uncared for and neglected so that for its size it has an extraordinary proportion of filthy slums, full of dirty and unsanitary houses. . . . (Occupied by) a heterogeneous population of natives, coloureds, Indians, Malays, and whites of almost every nationality.[80]

While conservative white-supremacist groups stoked racial animus within the white European population prior to the epidemic in Cape Town, the epidemiological threat of plague only added fuel to the fire. In contrast to smallpox, the racial heterogeneity of plague cases was significant.

As Table 3 shows, while smallpox produced a far greater number of cases, the outbreak was largely confined to non-European populations. However, plague cases were far less isolated. Plague was a disease of great

TABLE 3: Number of Cases from Smallpox and Plague in Cape Town-1896–1901 by Race.

Cases per year	European	Colored	African	Asiatic and Chinese	Total cases
Smallpox 1896	151	3198	N/A	N/A	3349
Smallpox 1897	32	513	N/A	N/A	545
Smallpox 1898	29	670	N/A	N/A	699
Smallpox 1899	12	787	N/A	N/A	799
Smallpox 1900	23	2188	N/A	N/A	2211
Smallpox 1901	30	838	N/A	N/A	868
Plague 1901	207	380	157	22	766
Plague prior to removals	30	18	40	N/A	88

Note: Reproduced with the consent of *Social Science History.*

Sources: All smallpox data from T. James, "The Year of the Plague in Cape Town," *South African Medical Journal = Suid-Afrikaanse Tydskrif Vir Geneeskunde* 44, no. 50 (1970): 1432. All bubonic plague data from J. A Mitchell, "Small-Pox and 'Amaas' in South Africa," *The Lancet* 200, no. 5172 (October 14, 1922): 808–12, https://doi.org/10.1016/S0140-6736(01)01096-0; Elizabeth van Heyningen, "Public Health and Society in Cape Town 1880–1910" (Dissertation, University of Cape Town, 1989).

medical concern to the European population, and the Black African populations were seen as responsible for its spread. Though smallpox at the time remained largely isolated to non-Europeans, plague reflected a disease capable of transcending the boundaries of race that smallpox did not. It was the threat from racial mixing of the disease and the financial perils borne out of the arrival of plague that marked it as separate and triggered concerns that had lingered since the emergence of the colony. Once plague arrived in Cape Town, responses focused very heavily on the threat of non-European populations, both to white Europeans and as vectors of disease spread.

The first case of plague was discovered in Cape Town on February 2, 1901, at roughly the same time that Dr. John Gregory, the acting medical officer for the Colony, was notified of a large incidence of rat mortality at the port.[81] Public health reports from that week show that by February 9, London, Berlin, and Washington, DC, were notified of the outbreak and would have at that time imposed restrictions in accordance with the Venice Convention.[82] From this point, the implementation of the Venice Convention as well as more recent methods to stamp out plague went into swift effect. On February 14 the Cape Peninsula Plague Advisory Council met for the first time.

The emergence of plague triggered preexisting fears of Black and Colored subterfuge and mendacity, which provided significant justification for the forced removals that were to take place. In the minutes of the Plague Advisory Council there were numerous references to the threat of free-moving Black Africans and non-Europeans:

> Dr. GREGORY informed the Board that the death at Sir Lowry's pass of a Kafir who recently reached there with a few others, had been reported: that the District Surgeon had held a post-mortem and diagnosed Plague as the cause of death; and as there were traces of coal dust on the corpse it was probable that the kafirs had escaped from the Docks, especially as they gave evasive answers as to where they had come from . . . and he (Dr. Gregory) remarked that these instances supported his view that the Kafirs were concealing cases, and emphasized the necessity for instituting a daily surprise visitation of all Kafir dwelling-places in each municipality. (Meeting Minutes of the Plague Advisory Council 20th February 1901)[83]

These statements by Dr. Gregory were made in the meeting prior to the ultimate decision to compel the Cape government to remove the Black population. The medical knowledge on rats became the justification for why existing smallpox regulations were unfit to prevent the further spread of plague. In the same meeting of February 20, Dr. Simpson remarked:

> Plague was primarily a rat disease, but rats could infect human beings, who could then in turn affect other persons and also rats. Thus the measures, which were sufficient for coping with a smallpox outbreak, were not comprehensive enough for an outbreak of Plague. . . . Rats were not

great travelers, but of course if infected animals were conveyed with goods by ship or train the disease might be spread far and wide through their agency.[84]

By the meeting of February 27, it was further agreed by the council that the slum areas populated primarily by the Black population were too infested with both rats and plague-infected homes and materials to remain, and they were to be razed.[85] The melding of the three concerns over rats, race, and plague's ability to travel found in the minutes of the Plague Advisory Council guided the actions of the Cape government. Ultimately, the logic surrounding the threat of rats was mirrored in the justifications for racial quarantine:

He (Dr. Gregory) was of the opinion however, that fresh cases were bound to occur, especially as in one house, with forty Kafir inmates, from which patients had been removed, most of the remaining residents had scattered before they could be collected and isolated. He also represented that a scare had arisen among the Kafirs in the town and that numbers wished to go back to their Districts, but that every effort was being made to dissuade them and to gain their confidence and that the Railway Authorities and Shipping Companies were cooperating by refusing conveyance. In conclusion, he reported that the Uitvlugt camp was well staffed and in good working order, and was capable of a substantial enlargement if required.[86]

Similar concerns about non-European populations as the agents of plague-spread were voiced, not only by members of the Advisory Council, but also by corporate interests in the further reaches of the Cape Colony such as the town of Paarl:

The CHAIRMAN [sic] read a letter from the General Manager of Railways, enclosing a proposal from the Traffic Manager, Paarl that aboriginal natives should not be allowed to travel by rail from the Cape Peninsula. (Meeting Minutes of the Plague Advisory Council 18[h] February 1901)[87]

In the period immediately prior to and during the forced removals, the concerns not only over racial mixing but also the unsurveilled travel of Black Africans became the primary concern of the Cape government and health actors alike. These concerns formed the focal point for the largest and most drastic disease response in the city's history. For plague, the Cape government imported outside medical support in the form of Dr. Simpson, who commanded much of the city's response and enacted a civic transformation that deprived many of the Cape's residents of rights and movements previously recognized and tolerated.

The continued presence of plague in Cape Town presented a clear and present threat to the greater Cape economy. So long as plague was present, all vessels and shipments leaving from Cape Town would continue to be subject to the scrutiny, quarantine, and controls laid down by the Venice Convention. This would have the effect of delaying shipments or losing them to sanitary destruction all together. As the Plague Advisory Council deliberated, it became very clear that to them, the unsurveilled travel of Black Africans was a foremost concern in shaping plague prevention policies. So significant was the concern for racial mixing that the desires for segregation in the aftermath of the epidemic reflected a regret that such separation was not enacted on ethnically separate European populations as well. Simpson, in justifying his perspective on the dangers of racial mixing. argues in his summary of the plague responses in the Cape after the epidemic:

> There can be little doubt that, if it had been possible for a similar measure on a more extensive scale to have been undertaken with regard to some of the most overcrowded, most insanitary and most infected quarters inhabited by Malays and the poorer class of Europeans and coloured people, the disease could have been as effectually stamped out among these as it has among the natives. These Europeans are seldom of British origin, but are foreigners from every part of the Continent, consisting largely of Portuguese, Italians, Levantine and Polish Jews. They are extremely dirty in their habits, live under the most insanitary conditions and herd together with the poorer coloured people, who are equally dirty and insanitary.[88]

Conclusion: Epidemic Orientalism
and Economic Concerns in Colonial Spaces

The cases of plague in Cape Town, Honolulu, and India reflect the micro-dynamics of epidemic Orientalism and colonial concerns for economic stability that structure epidemic responses. Prior to the outbreak of plague disease, Cape Town did not have state-mandated urban racial separation,[89] and though racial inequalities and de facto segregation did exist,[90] Cape Town was largely an outlier among other African colonial cities. The forced removals and establishment of Ndabeni were not the creation of a racially determinist order but rather the reinscription of it, linking latent racist motivations with medical authority. Prior to 1834, the Cape Colony had maintained a labor system organized significantly around enslaved labor.[91] The conditions of slavery established a racialized system of economic and social engagement. Slavery at the Cape was marked by a system of "constant surveillance"[92] as well as anxiety regarding the potential actions of unsupervised and unattended enslaved peoples. The Cape Slave Codes, first established in 1754, required all those enslaved to carry passes to enter town. Such acts are reminiscent of later regulations as well as some other more literal forms of discipline that provided a level of visibility to the enslaved. After dark, all enslaved persons were required to carry torches, to prevent them from having "conspiratorial conversations in darkened corners."[93]

When slavery was fully abolished in 1838, anxieties over the free movement of former enslaved persons grew within the landholding community. By the 1840s academic literature and local Cape newspapers like the *Zuid Afrikaan* began reporting on the threats of degeneration that could emerge from new European immigrants living in close proximity to nonwhite populations in Cape Town, who will "become mixed up with, and run the risk of their children imbibing the filthy, immoral, and degraded habits of the much to be pitied coloured population"[94]

Racial mixing and disease formed a powerful terrain upon which the risks of civilizational and racial degradation could be signified. Prior to the emergence of plague and spurred largely by the South African war raging in other parts of the country, large numbers of predominantly Xhosa and Nguni speaking Black refugees had entered Cape Town seeking employment and housing. According to reports of the time, 1,500 migrants were living in barracks along the docks and 8,000 lived in overcrowded and cramped conditions elsewhere.[95] This rise of Black migrants, seeking refuge from war and uncertainty elsewhere, was interpreted by colonial authorities as a vector of contagion and a threat to empire more broadly. Comments such as those made in the *Zuid Afrikaan* above mirrored those made both by members of the public local government and foreign medical elites such as Dr. Simpson over half a century later.

Cape Town's formation primarily as a port, relying from an early period on enslaved labor that prompted Europeans, Asians, and Africans to live in close proximity to one another, differed greatly from that of other contemporary African colonial cities. Many colonial cities in West Africa were initially designed to enforce segregation so as to prevent malarial spread, placing European settlements at higher altitudes than those of the local population.[96] The threat of plague to societal order and colonial stability, made present not solely through disease but also the global responses to it, made a reinscription of governmentally controlled and monitored racial order a justifiable solution on the part of the Cape Plague Advisory Council. This threat of residential racial mixing to both the public and economic health of Cape Town, as a result of the global scrutiny placed on infected sites, meant that plague was no longer solely a Capetonian problem but a British imperial one, which in the minds of the medical authorities mandated a racial solution in order to maintain white control of the colony. The Cape medical authorities were very conscious of how plague had damaged the global esteem of Bombay and hindered its economic output greatly. Cape Town could ill afford such restrictions.

What ultimately made plague so different from smallpox in Cape Town was that it was a disease capable of destabilizing the existing colonial order where smallpox could not. The focus on the disease through the International Sanitary Conventions encouraged an aggressive and rapid response to the outbreak. Through copious inoculation and because it was a disease already common in Europe, smallpox rarely produced high rates of mortality within the European population of Cape Town.[97] In effect it was a disease that maintained or failed to shake colonial power. Plague, however, in two strikingly divergent ways threatened the legitimacy of the colonial elites of the Cape, both in the high European mortality rates as well as through the threat of isolation from a global economy on which they relied. It also threatened to permeate the assumed boundary between colonized and colonizer. Plague was in effect understood through epidemic Orientalist discourse as an anticolonial disease that had the capacity to challenge existing economic, political, and social power relationships, where smallpox was not. The threat to the existing social relations of racial mixing was about more than racial anxieties: plague threatened the ability to control, monitor, and constrain nonwhite persons in the ways previously available during slavery. The township model provided both a way to limit the spread of disease that was acceptable to international medical regulations and the consulting medical officials and a way to reestablish a racialized system of labor control. The pass laws issued for those within Ndabeni that allowed for travel out of the zone for work, while restrictions were made for all other movements,[98] reflect a reemergence of the control and regulation over nonwhite Europeans that occurred under slavery.

The case of the responses to plague in Cape Town demonstrates the far-reaching affect that the International Sanitary Conventions and epidemic Orientalism had on disease responses at the points of outbreak. Aggressive reactions to plague generating racially motivated responses were also seen in Hawaii and San Francisco.[99] Outbreaks of the three diseases of concern in the conventions prompted swift and overwhelming responses to them in order to prevent an economic isolation that could threaten the viability of colonial sites as much as the physical threats of the disease itself. Plague in Cape Town mobilized not only racial anxieties that aligned with concerns over the economic and biological effects of disease but also a global network of scientists to advise on the response. Due to all of these factors, plague, once it arrived in Cape Town, was enveloped in a constellation of dense global networks of knowledge, trade, and travel, significantly altering the nature of the responses to it.

3 EPIDEMICS UNDER THE WHO

THE FIRST HALF OF THE TWENTIETH CENTURY was a fractured time for the international management of infectious diseases. If the first two chapters aimed to explain the emergence of a discourse of infectious disease control rooted in the relative threat of the world east of the Suez canal, then this chapter examines how, despite the multipodal pull of different interests relating to health in the early twentieth century and the development of new control practices, epidemic Orientalism persisted as a discursive frame as the World Health Organization (WHO) took over authority for the International Sanitary Conventions. Prior to the formulation of the WHO, the international health world was marked by four major forces: the International Office of Public Hygiene (Office International d'Hygiène Publique, OIHP), who presided over the International Sanitary Conventions; the International Sanitary Bureau, later the Pan American Sanitary Bureau and then Pan American Health Organization (PASB/PAHO); the Rockefeller Foundation; and the League of Nations Health Organization (LNHO). However, two world wars and numerous geopolitical catastrophes would affect the shape of international health prior to the emergence of the WHO. The intervening years between the beginning of the twentieth century and the emergence of the WHO produced a plethora of philosophical perspectives on infectious disease control. During this time, novel concepts of social medicine emerged as a potential way of managing endemic threats with epidemic potentialities. This chapter seeks to address why, despite the rise of significant concepts and ideas of infectious disease control and what would become global health emerging out of much of Africa, China, and Asia broadly, the International Sanitary Conventions retained their fundamental perspectives and structures as they transitioned into the International Sanitary Regulations, and later International Health Regulations under the emergent WHO.

US colonial and domestic endeavors into disease eradication led to the belief that all infectious disease could one day be eradicated. At the same time, the growing powers in the Americas recognized the limitations of the International Sanitary Conventions in responding to their concerns. At the Pan-American Sanitary Conferences, numerous ideas were discussed that would go on to shape the field of international health, from disease eradication to the management of endemic diseases, the development of resolutions regarding drinking water, and sanitary system design.[1] Meanwhile, the period between World War I and II has been described by several as a moment of greater regionalism in the domain of international health.[2]

World War I and the devastating 1918 influenza pandemic shook the international health community, and during World War II, while armies were still marching across Europe and the rest of the world, the specter of postwar epidemics would become central to the justification for a new globally consecrated health organization, which would ultimately become the WHO. A post–World War II world would yield a radical change in many approaches to international health. Out of prewar colonial experiments and military strategies for disease control, a new focus on disease eradication as a solution to health disparities around the world came to highlight the WHO's activities between the 1950s and 1980s.[3] These clashed with ideas of rural and social medicine that emerged especially out of West Africa and South and Southeast Asia.[4] In the late 1970s health equity and universal healthcare came to be benchmarks of global health movements around the world.[5] Historians such as Nancy Stepan, Iris Borowy, and Randall Packard have demonstrated that the origins of these late twentieth-century projects were rooted especially in early twentieth-century movements that emerged outside of the concerns of solely European and US interests. While the over-arching project of international health would shift greatly in the second half of the twentieth century from its prior orbit largely around sanitary controls, the International Sanitary Conventions were reinscribed in new form under the WHO. Yet despite all of these global transformations, a focus on postwar epidemics and the need for a return to global infectious disease control, the International Sanitary Regulations, and the later International Health Regulations of 1969 that replaced the International Sanitary Conventions under the authority of the WHO all would remain quite similar in the scope of diseases and perceptions of disease threat.

This chapter charts how the WHO, in assuming authority over and re-forming the International Sanitary Conventions, reproduced the Orientalist discourse that guided the earlier conventions while in the process incorpo-rated new forms of disease control into the operations of the regulations. Epidemic Orientalism, a discourse formerly primarily focused on distinctly European concerns and interests, came to expand to incorporate the Western Hemisphere and would then be inscribed in the practices of control written into the International Health Regulations.

Over the course of the early twentieth century and most acutely during World War II, the contours of a formal, consolidated, international organiza-tion devoted to the question of health was conceived and debated by senior actors within the LNHO, OIHP, and the earlier instantiations of PAHO. In addition to the philosophical perspectives on international health that emerged in the early twentieth century, by 1951 when the first International Sanitary Regulations were ratified under the authority of the WHO, the world witnessed a dramatic transformation in world powers. As European empires were declining in direct power, a variety of different priorities were emerg-ing. In no small part the interests of powerful nations in the Americas came to shape the vision of infectious disease control globally. The International Sanitary Regulations under the WHO would adopt many of the same prin-ciples of the earlier conventions as well as the same overarching Orientalism, now expanded from a purely Eurocentric to a Western Hemispheric project. Further, in spite of significant epidemiological developments and several opportunities for reform, the regulations under the WHO maintained the focus upon plague, cholera, and yellow fever as three of the primary diseases of international concern. As much of the international health community transitioned toward a health system development model for health engagement, prioritizing local general public health improvements and development strategies in the later twentieth century, the International Sanitary Regulations, later renamed the International Health Regulations, remained very similar in scope to the International Sanitary Conventions until the twenty-first century.

The early twentieth century would produce new International Sanitary Conventions as well as regional Pan-American Sanitary Conventions regarding US states and territories. While similar in form and in many cases adopting much of the International Conventions,[6] these Pan-American codes and conventions adhered more closely to the concerns of the western Atlantic. A central aim in the production and ratification of the International Sanitary Regulations under the WHO was the consolidation of all of these related though distinct conventions into a single, binding treaty for international epidemic disease management.[7]

In the transformation of the International Sanitary Conventions to the International Sanitary Regulations, the WHO asserted a global vision for the organization of the natural world to facilitate the sanitized transmission of goods and bodies across space. The additions to the International Sanitary Conventions in the updated regulations were novel. Rather than operating under multilateral agreements between nations and imperial actors as with the previous sanitary conventions, the member nations of the World Health Assembly formed a covenant between themselves and the WHO directly. Thus, the WHO became the authority over of the regulations and the disseminating agent of disease surveillance knowledge. This, as we will see in following chapters, had far-reaching effects for how diseases are managed and disease threats are prioritized. In the mid-twentieth century, the authorities governing the regulations within the WHO, facing challenges to the acceptance of the regulations themselves, retained the Orientalist vision of the world produced during the establishment of the first international sanitary conventions.

TABLE 4: Significant International Conventions Pertaining to Infectious Diseases 1892–1969.

1892	International Sanitary Convention signed at Venice
1893	International Sanitary Convention signed at Dresden
1894	International Sanitary Convention signed at Paris
1897	International Sanitary Convention signed at Venice
1903	International Sanitary Convention signed at Paris replacing the 1892, 1893, 1894, and 1897 International Sanitary Conventions
1905	Inter-American Sanitary Convention
1912	International Sanitary Convention replacing the 1903 Conventions
1924	Pan American Sanitary Code
1926	International Sanitary Convention, modifying the 1912 International Sanitary Convention
1927	Additional Protocol to the Pan American Sanitary Convention
1928	Pan American Sanitary Convention for Aerial Navigation
1933	International Sanitary Convention for Aerial Navigation
1934	International Convention for Mutual Protection against Dengue Fever
1938	International Sanitary Convention, amending the 1926 International Sanitary Convention
1944	International Sanitary Convention, modifying the 1926 International Sanitary Convention
1944	International Sanitary Convention for Aerial Navigation, modifying the 1933 International Sanitary Convention for Aerial navigation
1951	WHO International Sanitary Regulations
1969	WHO International Health Regulations

Source: All data reproduced from Norman Howard-Jones, *The Scientific Background of the International Sanitary Conferences, 1851–1938* (Geneva: World Health Organization, 1975), http://apps.who.int//iris/handle/10665/62873; David P. Fidler, "The Globalization of Public Health: The First 100 Years of International Health Diplomacy," *Bulletin of the World Health Organization* 79, no. 9 (2001): 845.

International Sanitary Authority under the WHO: Taming Space and Bodies

What marked the most significant difference between the International Sanitary Conventions and the International Sanitary Regulations under the authority of the WHO was their approach to the application of sanitary controls. While the International Sanitary Conventions, through the threat of strict quarantine controls and embargoes from fellow signatory empires and nations, motivated the imposition of at times brutal sanitary controls in colonized sites exhibiting outbreaks, the International Sanitary Regulations envisioned the same ends but through different means. The ability to impose the Orientalist vision laid out in the International Sanitary Conventions was made possible through colonial power relations that pushed quarantines formally located at European ports to colonial sites and mandated aggressive responses to plague, cholera, and yellow fever at sites of outbreak in order to avoid economic isolation. In what would ultimately become the absence of formal authority over colonial spaces under direct or indirect rule of imperial authorities, the responsibility for convincing nations to adhere to sanitary order transitioned to the WHO. This in turn shifted the nature of the application of power to a mode of rule devoted to maintaining the sanitary controls of the past through the cleansing of frontier spaces, ports, and the vessels leaving them and rendering the potentially infected traveler visible and subject to sanitary manipulation.

Under the conventions, empires imposed strict disease surveillance through swift telegraphic reporting of outbreaks around the world, aggressive local responses against colonized populations, and port sanitation. However, without the rule of empire and the particular remote governing imperial structures that they could allow, not all of these tactics were available. The International Sanitary Regulations of 1951 were also embedded within the logics of disease eradication of the time, recognizing that the regulations would be needed until the "true object of epidemic control," eradication, had been achieved.[8] At the same time, the WHO called for independent nations to control and eradicate endemic diseases within their own borders, leaving the regulations as an international vehicle to operate largely outside of domestic domains. The WHO, lacking the ability to impose direct controls upon entire nations, focused on the management and sanitation of areas and bodies at ports and national borders as well as the management of those bodies in transit through the interstitial spaces between nations. In turn the WHO shifted in its strategy, narrowing the sanitary gaze and concentrating racist and xenophobic anxieties, made material in the sanitary conventions, on these areas in the International Sanitary Regulations.

Theorist of science studies Sheilah Jasanoff suggests that boundary conflicts over the production of knowledge and impositions of standards never emerge out of a tabula rasa but rather at moments when competing epistemologies seek compromise.[9] Like the International Sanitary Conferences before them, the WHO revisions of the conventions were an exercise in world making, the establishment of a novel sanitary paradigm that dictated not only the diseases that were to be subject to regulations but also the practices of controls and the managements of persons required to maintain the sanitary boundaries envisioned by the regulations themselves. In order to standardize a new, universal set of sanitary regulations, the WHO member nations as well as actors within them had to achieve consensus on several issues necessary for the formulation of standards.

The member nations of the WHO had to agree to standard definitions not only of diseases, the scale of epidemics, and sanitary practices, but also for infected areas, infected persons, and categories of travelers who would be, as a result, subject to divergent levels of surveillance and controls under the conventions. Several member nations of the WHO actively disputed the stated aims and methods of the International Sanitary Regulations, prompting division. The International Sanitary Regulations, once passed, represented the melding of a variety of differing approaches to disease control that would ultimately synthesize into an overarching and globally accepted set of controls.

While the International Sanitary Conventions endured until their incorporation under the authority of the WHO in 1947, international health practices were being standardized around the world in addition to the formal mechanisms imposed by the conventions. As this chapter will expand upon, in addition to Pan-American Sanitary Conventions produced in the western Atlantic, two further visions for the global management of disease were being developed in the period between the turn of the century and World War II in parallel to the International Sanitary Conventions. One was the disease eradication model, used most notably by the United States in its overseas territories and at home by US-based international sanitary bodies.

This model prioritized the imposition of strict disease control and sanitation practices to eradicate the agents of particular diseases, notably malaria and yellow fever. These practices were often imposed by military authorities for the maintenance of colonial projects and protection of foreign authorities in sites where these diseases occurred.[10] The second vision focused on holistic development of public health systems. This model, known at the time as "social medicine,"[11] was articulated primarily by the LNHO, the International Plague Conference held at Mukden China in 1911, the Pan-African Health Conferences of 1932 and 1935, and the Bandoeng Health Conference of 1937. Each of these global health strategies needed to be considered and incorporated by the initial framers of the WHO International Sanitary Regulations in the midcentury as they posed a challenge to the model of the conventions.

Complementary Orientalism: US Responses to Infectious Disease Management

The role of sanitation in the Americas and within the US empire has received thorough and important treatment from many scholars including Marcus Cueto, Randall Packard, Warwick Anderson, John Lindsay-Poland, among others.[12] Rather than explore in as great a detail as these important scholars have previously, I will summarize the activities of US sanitation authorities and the PASB in order to demonstrate the relations of these actors to the International Sanitary Conventions.

From the end of the 1907 until the formulation of the WHO in 1947, the management of the International Sanitary Conventions fell under the authority of the OIHP, which was primarily responsible for maintaining, updating, and standardizing the conventions as well as disseminating disease surveillance information to the signatories of the convention. However, the particularly European focus of the International Sanitary Conventions meant that plague and cholera received far more attention at international sanitary conferences and in the conventions themselves than yellow fever, the major threat in the western Atlantic. This left the Americas and the International Sanitary Bureau based in Washington, DC (later to become the PASB and ultimately PAHO), whose primary concern was yellow fever, to organize the management of the disease priorities of the Americas themselves. Where the

International Sanitary Conventions advocated for the control of diseases crossing international borders through trade and travel, allowing for the imposition of aggressive sanitary regimes on colonial sites outside Europe, the International Sanitary Bureau in conjunction with the Rockefeller Foundation's International Health Board were moving steadily toward disease eradication policies and sanitary conventions in the Americas.

The success of US colonial actors in eradicating mosquito-borne diseases from Panama during the Panama Canal excavation as well as in US colonial sites such as Cuba and the Philippines[13] provided the justification for eradicationist approaches to disease. Employing primarily a military sanitation regime by which soldiers would drain standing water and distribute pesticides to eradicate the mosquito vectors of disease, US sanitary practices began to operate on the same or larger scale as European actions taken in Africa and Asia.[14] Architects of malaria and yellow fever eradication campaigns, such as the surgeon general of the US Army William Gorgas, became significant health actors in global conversations around disease control.

These strategies of disease control employed similar colonialist discourses that bound the actions under the International Sanitary Conventions. While the International Sanitary Conventions focused largely on international threats, the practices of disease eradication focused very significantly on the control and management of nonwhite and native populations and implicitly upon the understanding that indigenous actors in malarial or yellow fever zones were incapable of maintaining a sanitary order. This discourse motivated and was critical to the application of sanitary practices. Historian Randall Packard notes that these early disease eradication strategies imposed unilateral sanitation regimes that were aimed at protecting the health of colonial personnel while leaving broader public health concerns to missionaries and noncolonial actors.[15] These practices took on a larger racial dimension as the architects of disease eradication saw them as critical to establishing permanent white settlement in tropical areas. Gorgas, the architect of the Panama Canal sanitary responses, in his book *Sanitation in Panama* noted:

> The discovery of the Americas was a great epoch in the history of the white man, and threw large areas of fertile and healthy country open to his

settlement. The demonstration made at Panama that he can live a healthy life in the tropics will be an equally important milestone in the history of the race, and will throw just as large an area of the earth's surface open to man's settlement, and a very much more productive area.[16]

In US colonial incursions in the Philippines, it was also suggested that the survival of certain races was largely specific to the environment in which they originated. Thus tropical areas were seen as uninhabitable to white people for long durations so long as the afflictions of the tropics remained.[17] Similar to the motivations of the International Sanitary Conventions, which saw plague and cholera as capable of destabilizing the colonial project both economically and epidemiologically, US visions of disease eradication viewed malaria, yellow fever, and hookworm as critical to the success of the imperial project. It was medical officers such as Gorgas, vice-president of the Rockefeller Foundation Selskar Gunn, and others who developed their sanitary acumen through US governmental and Rockefeller Foundation projects that would go on to produce policies and strategies of PAHO and later still the WHO.

While Pan-American interests were not in any way exclusively led by the interests of the United States, as we will see in the next section, the United States in the late nineteenth and early twentieth centuries reflected a concerted Orientalist concern with regard to disease that operated through immigration law. Two notable legislative acts circumvented the need in the eyes of US leaders to manage diseases arriving across the Pacific through quarantines and sanitary controls: the Page Act of 1875 and the more commonly known Chinese Exclusion Act of 1882. Since the mid-nineteenth century, immigrants traveled from across Asia to the United States. They were primarily male laborers and faced not only interminable working conditions as they constructed the infrastructure and built up the wealth of the western United States but also significant racism and oppression. Chinese (as US racial ideology homogenized most Asian peoples into a single group) immigrants were blamed for the taking of jobs and the corruption of the moral fiber of white Americans, especially with regard to sexuality.[18] Chinese women under the racial politics of the late nineteenth century came to signify both sexual difference and disease threat. The presence of Asian sex workers in the 1870s in California represented a sexualized racial danger capable of ruining white domestic virtue and moral and racial pollution. Not only this, but there was also the belief that in particular, Chinese sex workers carried more virulent strains of venereal disease. In 1876 the American Medical Association declared that the strain of the sexually transmitted disease syphilis arriving from China was more dangerous than the disease already present in the United States, capable of "poisoning the Anglo-Saxon blood."[19] Historian Sucheta Mazumdar has argued that the racialized white US conception of the family and familial morality in the late nineteenth century emerged through the Orientalist positioning of Asian immigrants as corrupted, racialized others.

In 1875 the Page Act was passed that ostensibly banned the immigration of women from Asian nations to the United States. Concerns for disease, sexual habits, and cultural differences merged with race science of the time

FIGURE 3: Friedrich Graetz, 1840–1913, "The Kind of 'Assisted Emigrant' We Can Not Afford to Admit." Printed in 1883 in *Puck*. Wikimedia Commons.

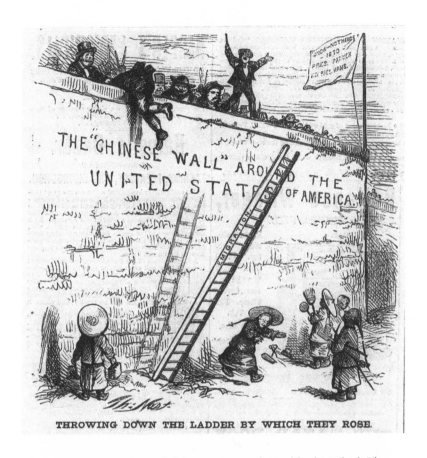

THROWING DOWN THE LADDER BY WHICH THEY ROSE.

FIGURE 4: Thomas Nast, "Throwing Down the Ladder by Which They Rose." 1870. Source: The Miriam and Ira D. Wallach Division of Art, Prints and Photographs: Picture Collection, New York Public Library. Public domain.

in the conceptions that Chinese immigrants were fundamentally racially inferior and, like the recently emancipated African Americans,[20] incapable of attaining the civilization of the Caucasian race.[21] The evocative combination of racist anxieties interwoven with disease and pathologized beliefs around sexual immorality were central to the passage of the Chinese Exclusion Act of 1882, which effectively banned immigration from China. This was the first racially specific immigration control enacted in the United States. These

A STATUE FOR *OUR* HARBOR.

FIGURE 5: Two coastal visions of epidemic Orientalism. In the first, the specter of cholera arrives on American shores of New York City as a Turkish immigrant, and in the second, a critique of American xenophobic immigration polices in the late nineteenth century as European immigrants throw down the ladder of emigration to block Chinese entry. In the third by Keller, a Chinese man is depicted atop the statue of liberty, this time located in San Francisco Harbor clutching an opium pipe and a torch that reads in the rays emanating from it from right to left: Filth, Immorality, Disease, Ruin to, White, and Labor. The evocative linkings of disease, race, immigration and labor located in American visions of nineteenth-century immigration. Source: George Frederick Keller, "A Statue for Our Harbor." 1881. Wikimedia Commons.

controls, while limiting immigration, also had the effect of maintaining the same epidemic Orientalist discourse at work through the International Sanitary Conventions that perceived the diseases emerging from the Middle East and Asia as representing the greatest threats to Western civilization.

Although the strategies of disease eradication and the International Sanitary Conventions differed in their responses to infectious diseases, much of their ideological underpinnings were very much the same. Both US sanitary campaigns and the International Sanitary Conventions had at their roots a vision of infectious disease control composed of targeted interventions against specific diseases seen to be dangerous to actors external to the environments from which they emerged. Located within this vision was the same Orientalist discourse and distinct racist approach that privileged interventions for the protection of white persons while imposing increased sanitary scrutiny upon nonwhite people for the purposes of disease control.

The International Sanitary Bureau and the Making of Western Hemisphere Sanitary Conventions

In the absence of commensurate attention paid to the Americas in the International Sanitary Conventions, the nations of the Americas beginning in 1902 convened the First International Sanitary Conventions of the American Republics. The US delegation to the Second International Conference of American States (held between October 1901 and January 1902) under the direction of US surgeon general Walter Wyman suggested that a conference be held to assemble a formal bureau of sanitation headquartered in the United States.[22] This project was enthusiastically supported by Eduardo Licéaga, the chair of the Superior Council of Health of Mexico. The first conference in 1902 led to the establishment of the PASB. Mexico's leadership and that of Licéaga in particular in conjunction with the United States was critical to the formulation of the bureau. This relationship between the US and Mexico and sanitary affairs extended to yellow fever eradication campaigns, which Wyman held up at the second sanitary conference in 1905 as a model of what should be done across the Americas.

At the same meeting, the first Pan-American Sanitary Conventions were produced, known as the Washington Sanitary Convention of 1905.

This convention drew heavily on the International Sanitary Conventions, adapting forty-six articles from the most recent 1903 Paris Convention while adding further sections on the management and control of yellow fever.[23] The later Pan American Sanitary Code of 1924 was developed from this initial convention. The convention itself was similar in scope to the International Sanitary Conventions, requiring notification of any event of plague, cholera, or yellow fever as well as measures for quarantine, monitoring, and disinfection. Operating somewhat in parallel to the International Sanitary Conferences of Europe, at the third International Conference of American States held in Rio De Janeiro in 1906, resolutions were adopted to obtain effective sanitation in cities and ports as well as the creation of national commissions of three health officers who, in conjunction with those of other states, would "constitute an international bureau of sanitary information."[24]

Rupert Blue became the second chairman (later known as director) of the International Sanitary Bureau in 1912. Blue was a veteran of several major US epidemics including a yellow fever outbreak in New Orleans and the more infamous epidemic of plague in San Francisco, which, much like in Honolulu, saw much of the city's Chinatown ravaged by racially specific quarantine and fire. Blue, however, arrived after these quarantines and unlike his predecessors advised sanitation and rat eradication campaigns over racially targeted controls.[25] In the first decade of the twentieth century, plague also visited the Americas several times, with epidemics occurring in Hawaii, Paraguay, New Orleans, San Francisco, Argentina, Brazil, Chile, Ecuador, Uruguay, and Peru. While these epidemics generally produced few deaths (with the exception of epidemics in Peru and Ecuador), Asia was recognized as a looming threat to the health of the Americas.[26]

In 1912 a major schism occurred between the United States and the OIHP over the International Sanitary Convention signed that year. At the root of the disagreement were what were perceived as "illogical" regulations pertaining to the definition of healthy, infected, and suspected vessels as well as the obvious Eurocentric nature of the trade interests protected under the convention.[27] The United States would ultimately refuse to be a signatory to the revised convention. In the intervening years between 1912 and 1945, the PASB and later PAHO would go on to produce parallel sanitary conventions pertaining more closely to what were seen as the concerns of the Americas. This, however, did not preclude American nations from signing the International Sanitary Conventions. Indeed the Pan American Sanitary Codes and Conventions were largely similar in spirit to the International Sanitary Conventions, though more focused on internal health affairs and the strengthening of hygienic systems than the International Sanitary Conventions under the OIHP.

In 1920 after World War I, US surgeon general Hugh S. Cumming was appointed director of the International Sanitary Bureau. The postwar United States found itself in a position of relatively greater power globally as well as within the bureau. As formerly powerful European nations and empires disappeared or lost strength after World War I, the primacy of the United States in international health matters was emerging. At the same time, the formerly major power within the bureau, Mexico, was in the midst of a revolution that led in part to the diminution of their role.[28] Under Cumming's stewardship and with the support of increasingly more delegates from Latin America, the International Sanitary Bureau would be renamed the PASB and pass a series of important regulations around infectious disease control in the Americas. The most significant was the Pan American Sanitary Code of 1924 and subsequent Pan American Sanitary Conventions on Aerial Navigation, which preceded those produced by the OIHP.

Social Medicine, Rural Hygiene, and the League of Nations Health Organization

As the PASB melded philosophically with the perspectives in the International Sanitary Conventions, a new strand of public health emerged outside of Western imperial nations that would ultimately come to be the antecedents of much modern global health practice.[29] While the OIHP was devoted to the management of quarantine and disease controls, and the International Sanitary Bureau imposed a particular vision of health that benefited foreign actors, the League of Nations began a movement toward social health between World War I and World War II.[30]

The LNHO was the first world health organization with a vision to address a vast array of health issues. While the LNHO suffered from less funding and lacked several prominent member nations including the United States,[31] it was at times able to present innovative practices for health around the world.[32] Social medicine, focusing on healthcare that targeted what we would now call the social determinants of ill health, became a major priority of the organization due to demographic transitions and from an emerging understanding of the health effects of poverty brought on by the Great Depression. Rather than focusing on the health factors and diseases critical to maintaining systems of empire and networks of trade, the LNHO put forward an agenda that sought to explore which social conditions would be needed in order for people to live healthy lives. This priority would not return to the world stage again until the formulation of the WHO and even then would not be formalized effectively until the 1978 conference in Alma-Ata.[33]

A notable focus of the LNHO's social medicine objectives was rural hygiene. During the 1930s the LNHO facilitated several major conferences on rural health and social medicine. Two of these conferences were pan-African in scale, held in Cape Town in 1932 and Johannesburg in 1935. The first of these conferences suggested an altogether different modus operandi for colonial health management that focused on preventative health measures and targeted diseases unlikely to spread outside of their areas of endemicity, such as sleeping sickness, tuberculosis, and malaria.[34] While the Cape Town Conference of 1932 stressed a focus on yellow fever spreading across Africa and ultimately the Indian Ocean as a result of increased air travel, these two conferences suggested economic uplift as a mode by which disease must be controlled:

> It must not be forgotten that, without raising the economic status of the vast bulk of the population of Africa as a whole, there can be no hope of applying successfully on a continental scale the results of research or of markedly improving the position of great populations with regard to malaria as a disease.[35]

The conferences also suggested the involvement of local populations in the management and treatment of health issues. The Johannesburg Conference of 1935 explored both yellow fever and plague while suggesting responses also inclusive of social uplift as a method of sanitary control and management. While still driven by the force of colonial authority, these conferences, by focusing upon diseases carried between animals and humans as well as typhus and malaria, prioritized diseases of importance to colonized subjects and not only the colonizers themselves. These conferences, while managed by the LNHO, were an opportunity for actors from the OIHP and other international health agencies as well as colonial medical officers to organize together and share health information.[36] Throughout the early twentieth century the central actors of the LNHO, OIHP, Rockefeller Foundation, and PASB often circulated between their respective organizations as well as their home ministries of health. At the Cape Town Conference, representatives from colonial governments, the Rockefeller Foundation, LNHO, and (despite internecine battles and disagreements between it and the director of the LNHO[37]) the OIHP were all represented. The OIHP in particular was responsible for considering the risks of the spread of yellow fever and maintained its outward-looking approach to international health.[38]

The collaboration of international health actors was most prevalent at the final LNHO health conference in 1937. The third major conference held in Bandoeng, Indonesia, in 1937 further stressed the importance of social issues to effective health policy. Prior to the conference a preparatory committee chaired by the secretary of the Federated Malay States, A. S. Haynes; former dean of the Faculty of Medicine of Batavia, Dr. C. D. De Langen; and Dr. E. J. Pampana of the League of Nations Health Secretariat set off on a five-month tour across East and Southeast Asia to explore the problem of rural medicine.[39] As a stark contrast to the African conferences, this conference almost solely focused on the issues of health as they related to internal populations of the territories in question. This report also recognized the manner in which health priorities, especially within colonial spaces in Asia, had prioritized the control of diseases capable of spreading overseas and interrupting trade. The management of epidemic diseases as they have been organized in the Asian region was a pressing concern, and the committee suggested that the mobilization of significant health forces to fight an epidemic were not also enlisted to conduct preventative work.[40] Disengaging from the concerns of the International Sanitary Conferences, the intergovernmental conference in Bandoeng lamented the way in which the epidemic concerns diverted attentions and funding for control over holistic healthcare provision:

> In India, for example, each district has a population of about one million, and contains so many villages that, even if every district had its own health officer, he would have to spend his whole time in touring the villages, in order to visit each of them were it but once a year. Under such conditions, the district health officer obviously cannot hope to get into touch with the people in his charge and can only concentrate his activities on areas in which epidemics threaten. In the vast majority of cases, he has only two types of assistant staff—sanitary inspectors and vaccinators. The sanitary inspector can help the health officer to discover and investigate infectious cases; he can assist him in the health supervision of the district; but he is not qualified, for example, to do any useful maternal and child welfare work. As for the vaccinator, he is almost wholly untrained, and can do even less.[41]

In addressing these concerns, the conference suggested the provision of free healthcare and critiqued the imposition solely of Western biomedicine onto Asian regions. The report of the conference argued that preventive medicine was a far more common and natural concept in what they defined as Asian medicine than in Western medicine, which would allow for more equitable social medicine:[42] "What is important is, not that social medicine should be taught as a separate subject in the curriculum but that it should permeate all clinical instruction."[43] Contrasting epidemic Orientalist approaches so evident at the International Sanitary Conferences, the report of the Bandoeng Conference made special mention of the raising of public health and sanitation standards across East Asia through non-European or Western means.[44] Perhaps most striking in the departure from most of the debates within the sanitary conferences was the attention to the importance of and argument for the interrelation between differing philosophies of medicine:

European medical science is everywhere invading Asia where it encounters what has remained the old medical lore of Hindu medicine, the Arabian school and the old Chinese institutions, all of them based upon traditional empiricism. The importance of all this should not be underestimated and official medical science, over-confident of its own infallibility and of the inferiority of this ancient popular medicine, has made a mistake of scorning it. Yet many an old precept can be found which accords with our own views, even though put in somewhat different form. Thus, frequently we strongly oppose the use of the medicinal herbs and other substances of popular Eastern medicine, forgetting that our own pharmaceutical industry has produced, in addition to sound and valuable medicines, much that it would have been better never to administer to any sufferer.[45]

Though still ascribing a particular vision of difference between Western and Asian medicine, rooted especially in a vision of non-Western medical traditions being old and premodern, the report of the preparatory committee for the Bandoeng Conference sought to speak to an equity of value of medical traditions beyond those produced in European and Western spaces.

At this conference, attended by over one hundred participants from the LNHO member nations as well as participating organizations, recommendations were made for the improvement of rural housing through education initiatives, cheap credit facilities for the support of farmers and sanitary reform, wholesale sanitary land reform akin to that used to drive out malaria in Italy, and the provision of large-scale health services across states.[46] These conferences discussed here, as well as the Mukden International Plague Conference of 1911,[47] not only addressed access to healthcare but also challenged the fundamental issues associated with ill health.[48] Such measures, while novel and distinct at the time, are certainly familiar to most familiar to global health today as these concepts form the bedrock of contemporary health and development initiatives. The long-term effects of these conferences to direct health policy prior to World War II were scuttled due to turbulent relationships with the PASB, resulting in a significant defunding of the LNHO, which limited any significant transformation of health practices.[49]

The Final Prewar International Sanitary Conventions

The final International Sanitary Convention was drafted in 1926 and ratified by over fifty countries in 1944. This sanitary convention shifted approaches to infectious disease control more formally away from quarantines toward disease surveillance as the mode of control, with regional offices around the world organizing disease surveillance information. They also were the first conventions to more formally connect the three major powers in international health—the LNHO, OIHP, and PAHO—in agreement with one another.[50] The conventions continued to require the automatic reporting of any cases of plague, cholera, and yellow fever found to be present within a nation and compelled both the PASB and the LNHO to comply with any and all disease surveillance demands. For the first time epidemics of typhus and smallpox also required reporting to health authorities and the parties to the convention. These diseases were included after significant epidemics of each occurred in the aftermath of World War I. The member nations of the PASB were particularly central to the shift toward information sharing and disease surveillance and away from quarantine as the dominant mode of control. At the conference proceedings, Dr. Carlos Chagas—famed parasitologist and discoverer of Chagas disease, director general at the time of the National Department of Public Health of Brazil, and a Brazilian representative at the conference—argued for the shifting away from quarantine and disinfection toward observation and disease surveillance. Rejecting the need for costly quarantines and particular forms of sanitary control at borders, Chagas argued:

> At present, nothing can justify the confidence hitherto given to terminal disinfections, recognized as being the most powerful weapon against communicable diseases. Some countries are already beginning to recognize the anachronism of such a measure and follow, in their sanitary regime, the indications of the new doctrines; but this is not the case for all nations, and several public health administrations still keep the old practice of fumigations and broad disinfections with antiseptic solutions. From the point of view of doctrine, this constitutes an error; from a practical point of view,

it is absurd that a large part of the state's resources should be unnecessarily spent on prophylactic measures, the results of which are more than doubtful.[51]

The development of new and more effective scientific knowledge around disease transmission as well as effective treatment for diseases rendered traditional quarantine measures somewhat unfashionable. Ultimately the push by the American nations would reduce the focus on quarantine in the 1926 Convention. Most references to quarantine in the convention would be replaced with observation:[52] "the keeping and isolation of a person either on board or in a sanitary station before they are given free pratique [passage]."[53]

The one glaring exception to this were the sections in Title II of the convention referring to the Hajj and travel through the Suez Canal and Red Sea.[54] In these we see the maintenance of the Orientalist impulse to keep Easterners static in place or under significant surveillance. The maintenance of these controls received little pushback from the Americas, with US Surgeon General for Public Health Cumming noting in a report on the convention published in the *American Journal of Public Health* that the rise of Islam in tropical regions where epidemics occur posed a particular threat to Europe:

> The fact that the Mohammedan Religion spread through the Far and Near East, particularly those tropical portions of Asia which were endemic centers of such pestilential diseases as plague and cholera, and along the littoral both of the Mediterranean and Black Seas, influenced not only the political but the epidemiological history of Europe. Pilgrims coming to the holy places of Arabia from such endemic centers as the valley of the Ganges and the Dutch East Indies were crowded upon vessels or traveled in Caravans with no provision for sanitation or ordinary hospital care. At the holy places pilgrims from Southern Russia, Turkey, the Balkans and elsewhere were thrown into immediate contact with these infections under the terrible conditions, existing around the holy places, and they returned to their native countries carrying with them plague and cholera infections which were spread along the caravan, river and sea routes to western Europe.[55]

Cumming, while not quite as explicitly associating pilgrims from India and the Middle East with unsanitary and uncivilized habits, still signifies them as agents of disease spread, carrying illness by their action and religious fervor to unsuspecting, naïve, and unspoiled populations from southern Russia, Turkey, and the Balkans only for them to carry disease westward to the gates of Europe.

In these sections the role of quarantine in the Mediterranean, Suez Canal zone, and Red Sea remained in force, requiring uninfected vessels travelling from plague- or cholera-afflicted ports to submit to quarantine procedures. However, these controls were not equal depending on the direction of travel. At the center of the distinctions were the definitions of uninfected ships, uninfected ships coming from infected ports, uninfected ships coming from uninfected ports as well as distinctions made between vessels for trade, shipping, and the movement of troops (ordinary vessels) and pilgrim vessels. Depending on the designation given to a ship and port, a variety of travel controls could occur.

Uninfected ships travelling from Europe or the Mediterranean basin from a plague- or cholera-afflicted port would be required to submit to quarantine, but suspected or infected ships would be subject to the determinations of the Sanitary, Maritime and Quarantine Board of Egypt.[56] While these requirements were more strict though similar for "ordinary" ships travelling through the Suez Canal from the Red Sea, for vessels carrying pilgrims, the controls were different. In Title III of the Convention, the maximum sanitary controls on pilgrims remained strict. Ships carrying nonpilgrim passengers or upper-class pilgrims were designated as ordinary vessels and subjected to similar controls as that of other vessels. However, vessels that did not meet these criteria were required to process through quarantine, medical examination, and, if required, cholera vaccination. On uninfected but suspicious pilgrim vessels travelling from the south toward Mecca, stops were required at the sanitary station of Camaran off the coast of Yemen, where all persons would be required to bathe and have soiled clothing and baggage disinfected.[57] These measures were, however, unnecessary if all persons on board were vaccinated against plague and smallpox. For infected ships upon which people were afflicted with plague or cholera within the last five or six days, the controls were more significant. All persons were to disembark at Camaran, where the ill would be separated from the seemingly uninfected. Those not exhibiting symptoms would further be isolated into "groups comprising as few persons as possible" and remain in quarantine for five days from the last case of cholera or six days for plague.[58]

Ships travelling southbound carrying pilgrims from Europe would face no quarantine if uninfected and be immediately granted passage through to their destination. In the event that plague or cholera was suspected, they would stop at the sanitary station at El Tor on the southeastern Egyptian coast of the Red Sea. For the return journey northward for pilgrims on Hajj, the controls were more stringent than those departing to Mecca. If no plague or cholera epidemics had occurred either in Hedjaz (the region in which Mecca is located) or at the port of departure, they would be subjected to disembarkation at El Tor, disinfection, and observation not exceeding seventy-two hours.[59] If plague or cholera was found at the port of departure or in Hedjaz, then all pilgrims would be subjected to six full days of observation, isolation into groups, and disinfection. This quarantine could repeat in the event that a new case was discovered during observation, resetting the six-day clock.

The International Sanitary Conventions' power had waned as they proscribed at the time no controls for the burgeoning domain of air travel. The PASB sanitary codes found widespread support as their air regulations, passed in 1933, were ratified by all the nations involved in their drafting and provided clear systems for the control of plague, cholera, yellow fever, smallpox, and typhus.[60] The applications of the Pan American Sanitary Codes were complicated by the air travel regulations in the 1944 revised International Sanitary Conventions. By the establishment of the WHO in the late 1940s, there were thirteen conventions relating to management of disease spread.[61] Much like in the time prior to the first International Sanitary Conventions, sanitary regulations were fracturing and disjointed. In addition to the philosophical differences evident in the divergent strategies of the globe's three major health regulatory authorities, the International Office for Public Hygiene, the PASB, and the LNHO, the WHO upon its instantiation also faced the task of bringing the divergent sanitary codes under one set of regulations.

Reconceiving the International Health Terrain during World War II

World War II would ostensibly halt most of the international health efforts occurring across the major health organizations. While the LNHO would come to focus on the refugee programs from its location in neutral Switzerland, the OIHP was overrun and rendered ostensibly defunct during and after the Nazi occupation of Paris. However, even the LNHO, left largely without funding, was forced to operate with a skeleton crew of clerical workers and two men, Raymond Gautier and Yves Biraud. Gautier joined the LNHO in 1924 and served as the director of the Eastern Office in Singapore from 1926 to 1930, where he established the radio service of epidemiological information.[62] He would go on to be the assistant director-general of the WHO from 1948 until 1950. Biraud was a French epidemiological expert and would eventually go on to serve as the director of Epidemiological Services at the WHO. From 1941 until the end of the war, Biraud and Gautier would exchange a series of correspondences devoted to imagining a postwar international health organization. Joined in this correspondence were a host of other actors including senior Rockefeller Foundation health official Selskar Gunn; Dr. R. H. Hazeman, who would go on to senior positions at the WHO; and Hugh S. Cumming. Cumming served as the US surgeon general for public health from 1920 until 1936, as a member of the permanent committee of the OIHP in the 1930s, and as director of the PASB before his death in 1947. He also served internationally as an immigration health official. He also most dubiously served on the advisory board of the US Eugenics Committee, and as surgeon general was responsible for implementing the Tuskegee Study of Untreated Syphilis in the Negro Male. Cumming was also a staunch critic of global health cooperation, the LNHO, and the formation of the WHO in particular. These men among others would go on in large part to envision the structure of the WHO. Biraud and Gautier in collaboration and consultation with one another produced a proposal that would become the basis of the constitution of the WHO. Through lobbying at international conferences for postwar organizing such as Dumbarton Oaks (which provided the mandate for the founding of the United Nations) and support from a variety of nations, most notably Brazil and China, the WHO received its mandate for existence within the UN Charter.

Central to the focus of a future health organization was the reestablishment of epidemiological surveillance and the International Sanitary Conventions, motivated in no small part because of the epidemics that occurred after World War I and the anticipated mass migrations to occur at the close of the World War II. In October 1943, Dr. Oscar Forel, a noted psychotherapist and member of the French Resistance, sent a proposal for a postwar World Health Center. In his preamble to the proposal, he highlights that famine and epidemics in the years following the armistice of World War I killed more people than the war itself.[63] At the center of his concerns for the postwar health future was the possibility for the rapid spread of disease as a result of large-scale resettlement of refugees and soldiers returning home:

> From the armistice we will witness powerful migrations, the return of millions of deported human beings, voluntary exiles and evacuees. To this will be added the exodus of prison camps, the number of which already exceeds 5 million, and the liberation of concentration camps, internment and work camps. It is therefore necessary to foresee a movement of populations such as the history of humanity has never known. To this will be added enormous difficulties of transport, so that repatriates organized under conditions of proper hygiene can not be staggered for long months after the armistice. . . . It is likely to lead to a catastrophe if these millions spread in their way the contagious germs they carry, not to mention the risk of avoiding much more than the disorderly return of millions of men who, in 1919, relapsed pell-mell by any means, this poor motley crew, covered with vermin, carriers of contagious germs, contributed powerfully to the dissemination of post-1914–1918 epidemics, a cruel and costly experience, but minimal in comparison with what is developing in the shadow of this "total war."[64]

In a memorandum originally drafted in 1942 but rewritten in 1944, Biraud lays out his arguments for the amalgamation of the major international health organizations (the LNHO and OIHP) into one. He justifies the amalgamation in no small part due to "the tremendous task arising out of the sanitary situation in Eastern and Central Europe" that "could only be carried out by an international health institution with a broad statute and strong political and financial support fitting it for action."[65] The pressing concern for postwar reconstruction that both motivated the creation of the United Nations Relief and Rehabilitation Administration and undergirded much of the justification for the formulation of the United Nations also motivated actors beyond the orbit of the LNHO's offices in Geneva in addition to a cadre of senior health figures at the international organizations. Though forced out as head of the LNHO and largely excluded from the planning of the WHO, physician, humanitarian, and evangelist of social medicine Ludwick Rajchman called for a United Nations Health Service in an article printed in the *Free World*, in which he advocated for a World Health Service to attend to the challenges of postwar Europe but also connected these issues to those of postwar trade and traffic:

> It is obvious that in the coming years, air and sea traffic, particularly intercontinental transit, must be under the strictest surveillance if disease and disease carriers prevalent in one area are not to be spread all over the world. Who could perform this service as effectively as the organization suggested? Both colonial and traffic services might need their own regional research laboratories and training schools. . . . The total staff might well be several thousand strong, since the colonial and epidemiological branches would need to be numerous.[66]

Rajchman locates the role of disease control as closely tied to a world dominated largely by colonial systems of health control and management, anticipating a future in which these structures would continue to guide the mechanisms of international health. However, at the level of state policy deliberations, in the United States the role of disease in a postwar world as well as its effects on the possibilities for US hegemonic economic power presented powerful justifications for joining in any proposed world health organization. Trade and access to new markets for economic expansion proved an important motivator for the emergent superpower in the postwar climate. Citing relief as "an essential part of the plan to cushion the shock of postwar economic adjustments,"[67] president of the American Public Health Association and future consultant to the WHO Charles-Edward Winslow suggested that an international health organization was critical to heading off a disaster akin to the Black Death in Europe.

By December 1945 the US House of Representatives and Senate passed a joint resolution unanimously calling for the organization of a conference to create a world health organization due to the lessons learned from epidemic disease after the armistice of 1918 and the influenza pandemic of 1918 among other outbreaks as well as the risks and challenges posed by epidemics to global trade:

> Disease does not respect national boundaries. Particularly in our shrinking world, the spread of disease via airplane or other swift transport across national boundaries gives rise to ever present danger. Thus to protect ourselves that we must help wipe out disease everywhere. . . . The records of our export trade show that countries with relatively high living standards buy most of our goods. If the rest of the world continues in ill-health and abject poverty our own economy will suffer.[68]

With the support of significant postwar nations such as Brazil, China, the United States, Britain, and forty other countries, the WHO was formed out of the ashes of World War II but remained very much wedded to the same attitudes and disease priorities shaped by nineteenth-century imperialism. The same authorities that put forward the blueprints for a world health organization during the war years from the LNHO, OIHP, and PASB would go on to senior positions there. Biraud, Gautier, and even later Rajchman would take central positions within the WHO. The structures of the old international health orders would endure in no small part as a result.

From Conventions to Regulations

Of all the major battles faced in the early drafting of the International Sanitary Regulations, the debate over whether the regulations should facilitate disease eradication within nations or solely sanitary controls at borders was the most significant. It is in this moment in the drafting of the International Sanitary Regulations that a major component of the practices rationalized by epidemic Orientalist discourse become formalized into standard global regulations. In Chapter 2 I showed that the nature of the conventions shifted the management of sanitary controls from European ports of entry to the colonial points of departure, in effect imposing significant economic restrictions on colonial sites. These in turn led to overwhelming and punitive controls on colonial subjects in those areas in order to protect colonial interests. In the battles over how the International Sanitary Regulations were to approach disease control, the transfer of the responsibility of disease measures shifts formally to the dichotomous relationship established by earlier colonial relations. Where previously imperial metropoles compelled their territories to adopt and manage their colonized populations with a focus on limiting the presence of disease and thereby economic effects of outbreak, the International Sanitary Regulations as an agreement between the WHO and its member states reproduced this system of relations by imposing similar controls on countries exhibiting outbreak, albeit through different methods and practice.

In reproducing this set of relations, the drafting members of the International Sanitary Regulations established new definitions for the purpose of standardized controls for the management of infectious disease, thereby introducing a vision for a sanitized international sphere.

The Second Interim Committee of the WHO ultimately provided the authority for the WHO to reform the International Sanitary Conventions in 1946. The organization of the revision was conducted under the authority of the Expert Committee on International Epidemic Control and Quarantine.[69] Reporting to this committee were a set of separate committees devoted to exploring the ways in which the epidemiological state of the world had changed since the last full drafting of the conventions in 1926. The first meeting of this committee was attended by members of the major international health agencies, the International Office of Public Hygiene, PASB, and International Civil Aviation Organization (ICAO); Brock Chisholm, the first director of the WHO; as well as representatives from Norway, France, the United Kingdom, Brazil, India, and Egypt.[70] The committee was tasked with revising the regulations and updating them to the latest epidemiological knowledge and sanitary controls while also consolidating existing regulations under a single, uniform code. For these reasons the PASB was represented as well as the ICAO, reflecting the importance placed on effective air-travel controls to the new regulations. It was at this first meeting that the mandate of the International Sanitary Regulations, to ensure the maximum security against international transmission of infectious diseases with the minimum interference to trade and traffic, was reinvoked from the sanitary conventions to form the basis of the revised regulations. In these early expert committee meetings, the members started to situate themselves and their regulations among the constellation of other activities taking place at the WHO. Namely, the expert committee saw itself in coordination with disease eradication strategies taking place within the other areas of the WHO. In a draft forwarded to the International Sanitary Regulations written by the Secretariat of the WHO in 1949, they remark:

> The final aim of the International campaign against epidemics is the eradication of pestilential diseases. It is only by maintaining an offensive against the permanent seat of these diseases that this result will be obtained. Prolonged efforts will be required and until success has been achieved, it will be necessary to maintain a sanitary organization similar to that which has so far rendered it possible to limit the extension of the major epidemic diseases throughout the world. Nevertheless, this sanitary organization should be progressively adapted to take account of all substantial progress in the field of health.[71]

While this framing of the regulations situates it within a larger trajectory of disease-free health for all, the vision implied by the secretariat pertained solely to the eradication of the diseases representing a threat to international concerns by their particular valences to trade and traffic. These continued to be the three central diseases—plague, cholera, and yellow fever—as well as the twentieth-century additions of smallpox, typhus, and relapsing fever. While the development of internal controls was seen as critical to this long-term project, it was very clear that the maintenance of effective sanitary controls at the borders of nations was the primary concern of the regulations. This placed the expert committee at odds with several of its member nations, who saw a possibility for the International Sanitary Conventions to move beyond reproducing the Orientalist gaze of the past and shift from their focus on surveillance and travel controls to more health development services. Directly referencing this aspect of the preamble, representatives of Venezuela, criticizing the historical agenda of the International Sanitary Conventions to establish defensive borders against the spread of disease, sought to eradicate diseases at their source, thereby rendering costly quarantine practices unnecessary:

> The notion of attack against communicable diseases should replace the conception of defensive barriers against them. WHO should be entrusted with the task of delineating the endemic areas and with that of attempting, at the same time, in collaboration with the countries concerned, to eliminate foci of infection—a less costly method than maintaining quarantine barriers.[72]

Once the major drafting committees were convened, this vision of disease eradication was suggested as representative of the most modern epidemiological knowledge. Certain members of the committee, suggesting that diseases like cholera, plague, and yellow fever had all been rendered curable or preventable through vaccine, argued that the practice of quarantine was no longer a desirable response in light of effective public health measures. At the second meeting of the drafting committee in 1951, Dr. Gear, a representative of the South African delegation, suggested that raising the standard of health in all nations would render quarantine unnecessary, especially given the relative unimportance of the major diseases covered under the existing conventions. The delegation of Egypt, however, suggested this vision was utopian in scope and could not be achieved under the organizational constraints of the regulations:

> Dr. El-Halawani (Egypt) said that the Utopia referred to by Dr. Gear of raising the standard of health in all countries, while desirable, could not be achieved so rapidly as was hoped and, therefore, international sanitary

regulations could not be dispensed with. It should be remembered that the diseases covered by the draft Regulations caused a high mortality and disorganized trade and traffic in countries in which they broke out, as had been demonstrated by the cholera epidemic in Egypt in 1947. In his opinion, countries should be protected against epidemic diseases by tightening up certain articles in the present draft.[73]

Little would come from these protestations to change the overall approach in the regulations. Though the issue of the effectiveness of quarantine had been consistently raised in opposition to the International Sanitary Conventions in the nineteenth and twentieth centuries, and often by American nations, halting the travel of disease at borders and ports rather than local health system development would remain the central aim. The International Sanitary Regulations of 1951 make no dispensation for the institution of long-term effective healthcare systems but rather established the requirements for effective and constant disease reporting from areas where outbreaks of the quarantinable diseases occur or are endemic. Endemic control of disease would be left to eradication strategies external to the regulations. In the same discussion over the principle interventions to be taken over disease control, the US delegation suggested the method for imposing global disease surveillance over all sites affected by six quarantinable diseases:

Mr. Stowman introduced a proposed amendment to Article 3. The United States Government considered that complete epidemiological information was essential for preventing the spread of diseases with the minimum of restriction on traffic. The United States proposals were therefore intended, first, to extend to the whole world a reporting system for international port and airport cities similar to that of the Singapore Epidemiological Intelligence Station, which had proved invaluable for twenty-five years; secondly, to give smallpox, which at present was more widespread than the other diseases mentioned, an equal rating and, thirdly, to omit relapsing fever. The third point might be discussed in connexion [sic] with Articles 87 and 88. It was proposed that Article 3 read as follows:

Article 3 1. Each health administration shall notify to the Organization by
telegram:

(a) the first case of plague, cholera, yellow fever, or smallpox recognized in
its territory, designating the location of the case;

(b) the occurrence of a foyer of typhus designating the area, or areas,
affected;

(c) the first discovery of rodent plague in an area which has been free from
this infection during the previous six months.

2. Any such notification shall be made by the health administration as
soon as it is informed of the occurrence and at the latest within twenty-
four hours of the receipt of such information. Each first case notified
shall be confirmed by laboratory methods as far as resources permit.

3. In addition to the notifications required under paragraphs 1 and 2
of this Article, each health administration shall report to the Organization by telegraph the number of cases of epidemic diseases and
deaths therefrom which are known to have occurred during the previous week in each of its seaport or airport cities open to inter-national
traffic. The absence of such cases shall be reported, and such negative
reports may be sent by airmail.[74]

This draft article would form the basis for establishing the embargos
necessary to impose sanitary restrictions. It required the establishment of
definitions for what would be considered an infected area, an infected person, and the threshold of disease burden necessary to impose restrictions
upon sites of outbreak. This practice delineated the world into areas afflicted
by any of these diseases and those regions unaffected. Any outbreak of these
diseases was required to be reported to the WHO, and in so doing any nation
suffering an epidemic subjected itself to sanitary controls deemed necessary to protect the rest of the world from the outbreak. In order to facilitate
the effective implementation of the regulations, the persons within these
affected areas were defined in relation to their disease status or potential
for infection. This method of determination imposed a subject position
that rendered persons in areas of outbreak visible to control on the basis of

potential disease threat. These practices also provided the modes through which ports were rendered sanitized and therefore open to trade and traffic.[75] In the definitions section of the International Sanitary Regulations, the WHO redefines disease episodes of global significance only in terms of the epidemic diseases covered in the regulations and its victims solely in relation to these regulations:

> "foyer" means the occurrence of two cases of a quarantinable disease derived from an imported case, or one case derived from a non-imported case; the first case of human yellow fever transmitted by Aëdes aegypti or any other domiciliary vector of yellow fever shall be considered as a foyer;
>
> "health administration" means the governmental authority responsible over the whole of a territory to which these Regulations apply for the implementation of the sanitary measures provided herein;
>
> "health authority" means the authority immediately responsible for the application in a local area of the appropriate sanitary measures permitted or prescribed by these Regulations;
>
> "imported case" means a case introduced into a territory;
>
> "infected local area" means (a) a local area where there is a foyer of plague, cholera, yellow fever, or smallpox; or (b) a local area where there is an epidemic of typhus or relapsing fever; or (c) a local area where plague infection among rodents exists on land or on craft which are part of the equipment of a port; or (d) a local area or a group of local areas where the existing conditions are those of a yellow-fever endemic zone;
>
> "infected person" means a person who is suffering from a quarantinable disease, or who is believed to be infected with such a disease[76]

(Re-)Orientalizing the Pilgrim

Where these particular definitions and the associated articles that dictated the sanitary responses required to prevent the spread of disease were significant, nowhere were they more totalizing in their sanitary control than in the management of pilgrims during Hajj. As happened previously under the International Sanitary Conventions, the discourse surrounding disease control interpolated the Muslim pilgrim as the greatest threat to Western sanitary order. Prior to the drafting of the final International Health Regulations, the major Arab nations represented especially by Egypt voiced objections about the Orientalist gaze of the International Sanitary Conventions and the provisions pertaining solely to the Hajj. In the official suggested revisions, Egypt argued that the new International Sanitary Regulations should

> Incorporate all provisions concerning the Mecca pilgrimage in the new Sanitary Regulations without grouping them under a special chapter, in order to do away with a discriminatory procedure which the Moslem people find unacceptable.[77]

While this reservation was recognized in the drafting process, nevertheless a separate section of the International Sanitary Regulations was devoted to the Mecca pilgrimage in isolation, and an expert subcommittee devoted to the Hajj was established to draft their regulations. In doing so the WHO inserted itself significantly into all aspects of the pilgrimage itself, reproducing the Muslim pilgrim as the always-already disease vector threatening the globe. Where the International Sanitary Conventions primarily covered the transit of pilgrims on Hajj traveling through the Suez Canal and the Red Sea, the International Sanitary Regulations expanded their dictates to require increased sanitary surveillance of all Muslims participating in the Hajj from anywhere in the world. These particular regulations existed in addition to those in the general sanitary regulations. The failure to submit to regular sanitary checks of all vaccination certificates or the provision of any and all required stool or fluid samples could result in quarantine for the duration of the pilgrimage at any of the required sanitary outposts between Egypt and Mecca. All pilgrims were required to be immunized at ports before departure or would be unable to take part in the pilgrimage. Where in other cases only persons traveling from or to sites where one of the six diseases was in epidemic form were required to be vaccinated and require such sanitation measures, the pilgrimage regulations required it of all participants. In order to regulate the pilgrimage to Mecca, the routes, means of transportation, and definition of the pilgrimage and pilgrims themselves had to be redefined through the lens of epidemic Orientalism:

> "pilgrim" means a person making the Pilgrimage, and, in the case of passengers on board a pilgrim ship, includes every person accompanying or traveling with persons making the Pilgrimage;
>
> "pilgrim ship" means a ship which (a) voyages to or from the Hedjaz during the season of the Pilgrimage; and (b) carries pilgrims in a proportion of not less than one pilgrim per 100 tons gross;
>
> "Pilgrimage" means the pilgrimage to the Holy Places in the Hedjaz.[78]

These definitions, as stated earlier, affected whether an individual could actually fulfill the pilgrimage itself. If traveling by ship, all pilgrims were required to stop at Port Said on the northern end of the Suez Canal for inspection or at a relevant inspection port south of the Suez Canal.[79] If a single case of one of the quarantinable diseases were found on board, the ship would be forced to stop at an intermediate port for further inspection en route to Hedjaz, the final port before Mecca. Any persons found to be without the vaccination certificates against yellow fever and the other diseases required for transit to Mecca would be vaccinated and detained until the vaccine was deemed to be effective. These measures applied to any intermediate port or Hedjaz itself. All pilgrims en route to Mecca underwent several sanitary screenings during their passage to and from Mecca. These modes that controlled the movement of persons also applied to their vessels, which had to maintain strict sanitary codes in order to pass through ports to and from Mecca. While many of these regulations were reproduced from earlier sanitary conventions, the strict passage and control of pilgrims, to the point of redefining the pilgrimage through sanitary eyes, was a product of these new International Sanitary Regulations. While the definition of "pilgrim" in the regulations was meant as a form of bureaucratic shorthand, it produced very real effects. Refusal of any of the regulations set out for the Hajj would likely result in detention. A pilgrim thus became one who consented to the power of the regulations and thereby, through fulfilling their obligations, could participate in the Hajj. It would not be until the passage of the International Health Regulations of 1969 that the explicit and separate controls for the Hajj were dropped from the regulations.

After Ratification: The Effects of
the International Sanitary Regulations

The International Sanitary Regulations were ratified unanimously by the sixty-four governments of the World Health Assembly in 1951, thereby establishing a unified set of sanitary regulations for the control of epidemic diseases across borders.[80] These regulations reproduced the epidemic Orientalism of earlier periods of global disease control, imposed the systems of relations that informally existed under the International Sanitary Conventions, and globalized their scope. The passage of the regulations also set up long-standing divisions between the International Sanitary Regulations and the broader operations of the WHO. In the years after the passage of the International Sanitary Regulations, this approach was embraced by the members of the committees active in the management of the regulations. The salience of maintaining the system of colonial relations extant in the International Sanitary Conventions and replicated by the International Sanitary Regulations under the authority of the WHO became even more desirable by members of the quarantine committees. As formerly colonized nations shook free from their colonial rulers, the committees recognized a sudden vulnerability of developed nations in relation to their newly independent counterparts. The removal of colonial authority, especially in tropical areas where the quarantinable diseases were active, posed a threat to the existing modes through which the WHO and imperial powers had previously imposed their will. Decolonization quickly became justification to suggest further scrutiny upon formerly colonized subjects. In a review of the International Sanitary Regulations in 1967, the Expert Advisory Panel on International Quarantine highlighted the threat to sanitary controls posed from decolonization:

> The continued existence in the developing countries of the communicable diseases in general and the quarantinable diseases in particular, still present a threat to all countries because of high speed traveling of aeroplanes with

more passenger load and capacity. . . . The following Suggestions are made for improving the operation of the International Sanitary Regulations:

(1) There is a need to stir up interest in national quarantine services. This can help to eliminate the excessive measures which some states feel bound to take.

(2) The responsibility of Governments to ensure the hygiene and sanitation of ports and frontier stations open to international traffic needs stressing to ensure the more effective institution of control measures within the over-all context of community health care.

(3) Improvements in the collection, analysis and dissemination of epidemiological information to and from Governments in respect of the quarantinable diseases especially smallpox, cholera and yellow fever.[81]

This became justification for the maintenance of the standardized epidemic surveillance system. This was especially critical to countries concerned with the importation of yellow fever. The definition of what constitutes an infected area had been of great concern to the members and their representative nations in the drafting of the International Sanitary Regulations.[82] These concerns were especially acute for South Asian nations, whose region was home to the mosquitos capable of carrying the disease but had never had a significant outbreak. Many nations lobbied to consider an entire nation an infected area so as to provide for the maximum sanitary scrutiny, quarantines, and controls to be placed upon all goods and peoples traveling from a region where the disease was endemic. So significant was this concern that British-controlled Ceylon, in voicing its reservations much like it had over fifty years earlier,[83] suggested the threat of a single unsurveilled traveler represented an economic and epidemiological disaster:

Therefore when the Additional regulations come into force, it is possible that the countries or areas which fall into the yellow-fever endemic zone may not be declared as infected local areas, or may subsequently be declared as free from infection after a period of three months has elapsed. . . . The periods now prescribed for determining freedom from yellow-fever infection are too short. . . . The information provided in this publication indicates that, year after year, yellow fever is a constant and continuous problem in various parts of Latin America. Secondly the possibility of a person getting out of a jungle area, leaving by plane and arriving at an airport in a receptive area within the incubation period, has always to be borne in mind.[84]

These particular concerns, voiced not only by Ceylon but also South Africa and Australia, provided justification for increased controls on all persons leaving tropical areas for yellow-fever-receptive zones.

However, the Orientalist vision for global health control established by the International Sanitary Regulations dictated an ordering of the world largely incongruous with other disease management strategies that fell beyond the scope of the regulations. This set up a series of palace wars in the period after ratification between various members of the communicable disease community within the WHO. By targeting solely six diseases, the regulations legitimated these pathogens as worthy of international cooperation to prevent their spread. The International Sanitary Regulations compelled nations to act aggressively to prevent the spread of infectious disease or face international consequences. Though without the ability to sanction, the regulations aimed to dictate very specific and, in some cases, totalizing responses to diseases considered to be a global threat. In maintaining the diseases previously associated with the International Sanitary Conventions as the primary diseases slated for control, these regulations reflected almost exclusively a level of economic and sanitary protectionism that benefited solely nations not exhibiting outbreak while prioritizing the management of these diseases in the nations suffering an outbreak.

In the intervening years between the passage of the International Sanitary Regulations of 1951 and the International Health Regulations of 1969, the next major reform of the regulations, this concern was often raised. In prioritizing the control of the six diseases in the regulations (bubonic and pneumonic plague, cholera, yellow fever, typhus, relapsing fever, smallpox), the nations exhibiting outbreaks ignored the management of other public health crises for the explicit control of the regulated diseases. However, the epidemiological importance of these six diseases continued to wane in the first two decades of the International Sanitary Regulations.

The lessening epidemiological severity of the six diseases prompted the WHO Division of Malaria Eradication and the Communicable Diseases Division more broadly to call for the reform of the regulations. The Malaria Eradication Division lobbied aggressively in the 1960s for malaria's inclusion in the International Sanitary Regulations as a notifiable disease, suggesting that the particular imperial perspective inherited from the sanitary conventions limited the efficacy of the regulations:

> The International Sanitary Regulations, as they stand at present are still tinged with the out-dated motives and health policies which produced the original International Sanitary Conventions and similar arrangements. By outdated health policies we mean the defensive aspect which appears in the Regulations against the introduction of disease into clean and usually developed areas from other areas notoriously infected and under-developed. The current trend in health policy is not defensive. The positive approach to health clearly defined in the Constitution of the WHO indicates that an attack on the diseases where they exist and the strengthening of the general health services is the greatest safeguard against the spread of disease. By out-dated motives we mean the unjustified priority that still continues to be given to the six quarantinable diseases which now constitute only a minor threat to the lives of people and against which efficient prophylactic measures at present exist. Moreover, for four of them effective curative measures are now available.[85]

While the Malaria Eradication Division leveled this critique as justification for malaria being incorporated as one of the notifiable diseases under the regulations, other bodies saw the particular defensive orientation of the regulations as justifications for full-scale reform. Citing the rapid increase in populations and the increased pace of trade and traffic, others suggested that the International Sanitary Regulations allow the WHO and its member nations to take a more active role in managing international outbreaks of any important epidemic threat, not limited to the six quarantinable diseases.[86] Largely ignored at the time, this approach would ultimately form the later basis of the International Health Regulations of 2005.

Envisioning Total Surveillance

At the height of imperial power in the late nineteenth and early twentieth centuries and even into the mid-twentieth century, totalizing controls akin to the India plague regulations and the Cape Town forced removals could be readily applied by authoritarian colonial regimes. However, World War I and II left much of Europe increasingly less critical to infectious disease control. As decolonization swept the world in the mid-twentieth century, the dilemma of how to effectively police the masses seen as agents of global disease spread without imperial authority became one of the central concerns of those responsible for drafting the regulations. In the deliberations over the International Sanitary Regulations and later instantiations as the International Health Regulations, disease surveillance for this reason became a central concern of the members of the divisions of communicable diseases at the WHO responsible for the management of the International Sanitary Regulations. Practices for sanitation and hygiene, developed in sites such as India, the Red Sea, and South Africa, returned and were incorporated by WHO actors into the International Sanitary Regulations. K. Raška, director of the Division of Communicable Diseases, encapsulates this Orientalism in a document charting the future disease threats for the globe:

> The tremendous development of science and technology has provided means for the efficient control and prevention of most of the communicable diseases of the world. In practice, however, recent developments in the control and prevention of communicable diseases had materialized to a varying degree depending on different socio-economic and cultural situations in different parts of the world, and discrepancies between the developed and developing countries in the health field are steadily increasing. The problems of communicable diseases are also continually changing. In several well-developed countries some diseases are approaching the stage of disappearance but in the developing countries the same diseases flourish, without systematic application of known control measures (vaccination against diphtheria, whooping cough, poliomyelitis, etc.). The public health

services in most developing countries have still not sufficient trained staff and material resources. In some of the countries all existing communicable diseases are not yet recognized and it is not known what is the relative importance of each diseases in the given country per se in relation to possible control and prevention measures.[87]

The effective adherence to the International Sanitary Regulations demanded the taming of space and bodies deemed by their proximity to outbreaks of the six diseases to be unsanitary. Shifting from the controls of all territory, incumbent upon colonial sites under the International Sanitary Conventions if they were to maintain trade abroad, the International Sanitary Regulations moved their focus to the sanitation and cleansing of areas around frontier ports for trade and travel. This practice of making land safe for international enterprise has its roots in colonial medicine but more recently explicitly in the disease eradication practices of the Panama Canal and the US empire, which focused on making tropical geographies safe for colonial enterprise through the application of colonial power.[88] This was in keeping with the major developments that had occurred since the drafting of the first regulations.

The sanitation of ports and frontier spaces through both effective disease surveillance of all vessels and persons leaving or entering ports and surveillance of any areas in which an outbreak is occurring preserved these spaces as open for global trade and travel. While the policies for the sanitary control of ships and persons entering foreign ports untouched by the six diseases may have appeared to shift the responsibility for controls from colonial or formerly colonial sites back to Europe and American metropoles, the International Sanitary Regulations maintained the focus of scrutiny on these sites through a more significant development of disease surveillance.

What the new International Sanitary Regulations of the WHO would produce was a universally accepted and rationalized vision for the management of disease in the international arena. Where the International Sanitary Conventions dictated a particular vision for the management of disease and populations across the globe, the revisions of the International Sanitary Conventions into the International Sanitary Regulations of the WHO reconsidered the existing codes of sanitation and a desire to impose a new system of standards and practices to routinize all of the existing regulations under one global set of regulations. While seventeen of the most economically powerful nations were signatories to the most recent 1944 Sanitary Convention, the other regulations extant across the globe failed to consolidate any standard agenda for disease control, especially across the Atlantic. In order to facilitate global consensus under the aegis of the WHO, a new model had to be devised. This model ultimately reified the epidemic Orientalism first emergent in the eighteenth and nineteenth centuries and imposed by the International Sanitary Conventions, while drastically increasing the scope and application of the regulations by insuring total universal acceptance across the member states of the World Health Assembly. However, as we will see in the next chapter, the limitation of the power of sanitary controls and a focus only on a small number of infectious agents would ultimately challenge the WHO's authority as the dominant actor in the field of international disease management.

4 THE BATTLE TO POLICE DISEASE

SO FAR IN THIS BOOK WE HAVE seen how infectious disease regulation emerged out of particular regional European concerns over the threat of infectious disease, not only to life but also to imperial and global systems of trade and traffic. The development of the first International Sanitary Conventions, arising both out of Eurocentric concerns for the diseases most devastating for their interests and the practices of control made possible by colonial systems of disease management, made international disease control a realizable political project. The discourse that mobilized this project I have termed *epidemic Orientalism*. In the last chapter we traced the development of the International Sanitary Conventions to their incorporation into the wider architecture of the World Health Organization (WHO). In that chapter we saw how, through the development of other international and regional health bodies in the early twentieth century, a more global conception of disease control developed and was consolidated in the first International Sanitary Regulations under the WHO. The passage of these regulations saw the globalization in no small part of the Orientalist logics first emergent in Europe but also in the Americas and then inscribed in the practices set out in treaty form under the International Sanitary Regulations. Between the passage of the first International Sanitary Regulations in 1951 and the early 1990s, the International Health

Regulations (IHR) remained largely unchanged, save for two periods of reform in 1969 that removed relapsing fever and typhus from the list of quarantinable diseases and later in 1983 that removed smallpox. The reform in 1969 also changed the name of the International Sanitary Regulations to the present-day IHR. When the IHR 1969 were revised in 1983, the three original diseases (plague, cholera, and yellow fever) of the International Sanitary Conventions returned to primacy as the only diseases covered. In 1995 the WHO passed resolution WHA 48.7, calling for a revision of the IHR, and ushered in a ten-year reform period that drastically changed the nature of international disease control and management. In 2005, those new regulations, the ones currently in operation (as of publication) were passed: the IHR (2005).[1]

This chapter will attempt to put the revision of the latest IHR 2005 in the context of the wider histories and developments discussed in this book so far. The IHR (2005) introduced a completely new practice for infectious disease threat assessment. Instead of prioritizing three main diseases for control, the WHO developed an algorithm in the IHR to determine which threats constitute a Public Health Emergency of International Concern (PHEIC, pronounced *P-HEIC*). While dispensing with the now far less globally threatening plague, cholera, and yellow fever, the diseases of imperial anxieties of the past, these current regulations can define any biowarfare or epidemic threat as a potential public health emergency requiring international coordination to control. In this chapter we will examine the development of this device, its effects, and how and why the current IHR takes the shape that it does. I argue that even in moving away from the practices and priorities of earlier conventions, reforming considerably from the old regulations, the IHR (2005) still perpetuates the old epidemic Orientalism of the past. While the next chapter will show how epidemic Orientalism as a discourse continues to operate in relation to the declaration of a PHEIC, this chapter will show how the new regulations and the practices enshrined within the treaty developed out of the political and organizational priorities of the WHO at a time when its power was diminishing as an international body. Since 2005 the WHO has been the only organization capable of deliberating over and declaring which major epidemics of infectious disease require large-scale international efforts to defeat. Yet the WHO operates on a budget of less than most major American hospital systems.[2] How can an international organization with so few fiscal resources maintain such a central role as a global authority on infectious disease threat?

Without the totalizing systems of colonial rule and governing control of extraterritorial dominions, the WHO did not have the ability to police populations directly through a small group of imperial powers, and therefore it focused its jurisdiction on port and border spaces. In this chapter we explore how the WHO retained its primacy as the authority on international infectious disease control, increasing its role in disease surveillance.

Where previously only three diseases fell under the purview of the IHR and warranted compulsory reporting on their outbreaks to be delivered to the WHO, both the early drafts as well as the final IHR (2005) require the reporting to the WHO of all unusual or potentially epidemic disease outbreaks that could spread internationally. Further, the WHO in the IHR (2005) placed itself at the center of both disease surveillance and response by establishing a decision matrix by which reported outbreaks would be assessed for overall global threat and subsequently categorized by the WHO. If an epidemic appears to be spreading beyond the initial controls emplaced, the director-general of the WHO can determine the threat to be a PHEIC. The designation of this term under the IHR (2005) allows the director-general to issue nonbinding recommendations and call aggressively for international interventions and aid into areas of outbreak, as has been done in the cases of Zika virus in 2016 in Latin America and the West African Ebola virus disease outbreak from 2014 to 2016, among others.[3]

In reforming the IHR, the framers of the new regulations greatly expanded their mandate and scope, giving the WHO power to classify and assess international epidemic risk while also attempting to assert itself as the clearing house for all disease surveillance information from around the world. This was a major transformation from the previous tradition of prioritizing the control and management of a few individual diseases seen to be a threat. The IHR (2005) expanded the scope of the regulations to consider any potential international threat, thus leaving the WHO with the definitional power to assess outbreaks.

Dominant arguments for why the WHO chose to begin transforming the IHR at this time suggest that the continuing HIV/AIDS pandemic and emerging diseases such as Ebola virus disease were provoking concern from member states, showing the weakness of the organization to respond to emergent threats and new infectious disease outbreaks. The increased pace of trade and traffic around the world due to globalization is also a cited factor in the decision to reform.[4]

Under the Orientalist discourse that pervades international disease controls, the international health regulations were no longer effectively maintaining the sanitary borders that separated the diseases of the tropics from the Northern Hemisphere. The three original diseases under the purview of the regulations, plague, cholera, and yellow fever, were no longer as great a threat to the globe, while emergent infectious diseases such as Ebola and HIV/AIDS tested the capacity and utility of the existing regulations. The emergence of these epidemics and the IHR's limitations in disease surveillance allowed for new actors to enter the space of international disease control, challenging the WHO for its authority in this realm on the basis of the WHO's inability to contain the threats of the Global South. In addition, the mishandling of an epidemic of plague in Surat, India, and challenges to the implementation of airborne pesticide requirements laid out in the regulations weakened the authority of the WHO as the arbiter of disease controls. These attacks upon the WHO's dominance produced a new field of global infectious disease control in which member nations of the World Health Assembly as well as other international organizations sought to claim the dominant role.

In reforming the IHR, the WHO sought to take advantage of the mechanisms for collecting infectious disease surveillance data and the authority to arbitrate levels of epidemic threat, regarding not only the three diseases previously in focus but all potential epidemics. This knowledge made the WHO indispensable in its central role as the global authority on infectious disease response. The ultimate reform of the IHR into the IHR (2005) made the WHO the center of the knowledge apparatus that collects information on infectious disease and organizes responses to threats, claiming expert knowledge that only it is capable of assessing.

As early as the first informal meetings in which reform was discussed, the future trajectories and departures from the old IHR model became evident. The IHR would no longer be a set of regulations for limiting isolated diseases but would become a formal apparatus for locating, surveilling, and responding to any potential international threat as defined by the WHO. The decision to revise the IHR in 1995 and the ensuing transformation of the regulations signaled a radical shift in international disease response. These changes were a vehicle by which the WHO could cement authority and maintain power over the field of infectious disease control, no longer solely through the management of control measures at ports and borders but through disease surveillance and the strategic employment of expert knowledge. The WHO, through its expertise over surveillance knowledge, assumed the authority to define and classify infectious disease risk on a global scale. This power to define is central to the maintenance of the WHO's authority in the field of infectious disease control and conceals a system of power relations that exists between international organizations, relevant international actors, and their member states.

The IHR within the WHO

While the WHO went through a variety of philosophical and political shifts in the twentieth century, the IHR remained oddly static. Most historians and theorists of the WHO and global health recognize the organization to be a relatively amorphous and at time a very weak entity. It is an organization often seen as weakly governed and overly regionalized with little centralized power.[5] The funding structure of the WHO is rarely secure and requires in most cases a complex set of political and strategic approaches to manage the continued or increased flow of funding to its programs. Unlike other international entities like the International Monetary Fund or World Bank, it lacks sanctioning power over any member nations or bodies.

However, as Gostin, Sridhar, and Hougendobler have written, its largely unparalleled expertise in the field of health and broad mandate gives it significant normative and discursive power to shape priorities around health and health policy.[6] These very often result in soft, nonbinding norms being incorporated into domestic policy. Few historians of the WHO have invested significant research into the IHR and their development. While impressive histories of the organization have been written, upon which a great deal of this work is scaffolded,[7] few have examined the reform of the IHR in the late twentieth century. Indeed, the IHR seem to be an outlier among the mechanisms at work within the WHO. While most of the authority of the WHO comes from its soft capacity to affect norm building, the IHR, since their instantiation in the WHO in 1951 (as the International Sanitary Regulations), have been one of the three examples of hard treaties requiring affirmative obligations from sovereign nations.[8] Though this chapter will examine the broad threats to the authority of the IHR, their role is remarkably clear and provides the organization with significant power relative to its other practices. Under Article 21 of the WHO constitution, the WHO is empowered to adopt regulations on sanitation, quarantine, and other interventions to prevent the international spread of disease. More significantly, under Article 22 of the constitution, all regulations enter into force for all members of the World Health Assembly after a certain period unless individual nation reservations are delivered to the director-general of the WHO within a given time. In other words nations, should they wish to reject the regulations, must "proactively opt-out or they are automatically bound" to the law.[9] Gostin, Sridhar, and Hougendobler note that this might be the only instance in international law that permits the imposition of a binding treaty obligation on a nation without their express assent.[10] Nevertheless, the IHR have always lacked any express sanctioning or further coercive power, making their legitimacy in no small part a function of the normative authority that the WHO holds over the member nations of the World Health Assembly to affect assent. As this chapter will demonstrate, and is even clearer in the next, the maintenance of this authority held by an increasingly fragile institution requires a host of political calculations that ultimately affect the shape of the regulations themselves.

Global Politics, the WHO, and the International Health Regulations

Between the formulation of the WHO and the 1990s when the revisions to the IHR first began, a number of critical geopolitical shifts occurred, and within them the WHO saw itself move from an almost unchallenged entity in world health to an actor among many. The development of disease eradication strategies, made possible through both early twentieth-century public works interventions but more acutely insecticide and chemical-based approaches, led to disease eradication being one of the fundamental tenets of the WHO's operations in its first few decades.[11] Smallpox, polio, yellow fever, yaws, Guinea worm, and malaria were all slated for a much-vaunted and ambitious campaign of disease eradication.[12] While the eradication of smallpox may have been the most impressive feat organized by the WHO to date, the relatively prolonged disappointments of the other eradication campaigns reflect the limitation of such endeavors.

While the last chapter largely left us chronologically at the end of the 1960s, as Nitsan Chorev has written, the 1970s reflected a major shift in the political winds in global health with massive effects upon the WHO. The rise of new, independent nations and the fall of direct colonial rule across much of the world increased the voice of these new nations within the governing body of the WHO, the World Health Assembly. The 1970s saw the increased power of newly decolonized, independent nations in the production of global policy and the shifting responsibility of industrialized nations to foster economic development globally.[13] In terms of policy, leadership within the World Health Assembly was dominated by the objectives and goals of the these newly independent nations.

With respect to the WHO, this meant that the WHO under Director-General Halfdan Mahler proceeded with an ambitious plan of living up to the objective laid down for the organization in its constitution: the attainment of all peoples of the highest possible level of health.[14] This was most ambitiously realized at the Twenty-Ninth World Health Assembly in 1976 where Mahler put forward his vision of Health for All by the year 2000, which was later adopted as a World Health Assembly resolution that all nations and the WHO should work toward a level of health that would allow for "a socially and economically productive life."[15] This proposal led to the WHO adopting universal primary healthcare as one of its major health goals to aid in its broader objective of health for all by 2000. The Declaration of the Alma-Ata Conference on Primary Health Care of 1978 attempted to attend to the crippling inequalities across nations by returning to a similar philosophy as envisioned earlier by the adherents of social medicine under the LNHO. While the Alma-Ata Declaration called attention to the gross inequalities in the health status of peoples between developed and developing nations, it was very much reliant upon those nations developing their own plans of action toward greater health equity.[16] Embracing community-led health practices. it also simultaneously advocated for maximum self-reliance in these initiatives, requesting that all governments "should formulate national policies, strategies and plans of action to launch and sustain primary health care as part of a comprehensive national health system and in coordination with other sectors."[17] This would require the mobilization of political will and government support within countries to achieve these efforts.

While policies and philosophies shifted from costly and relatively ineffectual eradication campaigns toward a social health agenda between the 1950s and the 1970s, the WHO since the 1960s has faced limitations due to its diminished funding from the member nations of the World Health Assembly. During the late 1960s and more decisively in the following decades, the policy leadership of the so-called developing world met resistance from the industrialized world that had more authority over the purse strings of international development. This is in no small part due to the neoliberal turn in the late 1970s and 1980s, which saw a global shift away from government-funded programs as a strategy for development and toward free market approaches complemented by the reduction in domestic expenditure to public programs. While newly independent nations had called for the development of the public sector as well as for developed nations to play a role in the economic development of the nations from which they had extracted massive wealth under colonialism, many industrialized nations in the West, especially the United States and United Kingdom, rejected this approach, deeming it socialist in nature.[18] US operatives under the Reagan administration dubbed the United Nations as "being dominated by a coalition of Third-World developing countries and Soviet bloc nations."[19] The invocation of public expenditure, international organizations for development, and the support of socialism at a peak moment of the Cold War allowed conservative American and British politicians to call for the reduction of mandatory funding for UN organizations and international organizations more broadly while at times also calling for withdrawal from the WHO. From 1970 through the 1980s the US government, at the time one of the largest funders of the United Nations, reduced its support so dramatically as to imperil the whole organization. During this period, support for the expansion of the WHO budget waned and the organization, with its lofty goals of health equity and health for all, operated as a largely a normative force and unfunded mandate.[20] Unpaid contributions in the 1980s by the United States, Soviet Union, and others further contributed to challenges.[21] In the 1990s the WHO under Gro Harlem Brundtland would adapt to this neoliberal environment broadly by shifting from a social approach to health toward an overarching organizational logic that viewed health in economic terms, seeking both cost-effective solutions as well as ways to justify health interventions in terms that saw health only as a social merit if it increased economic productivity.

The Return of Pandemics: HIV/AIDS

After the successful eradication of smallpox in 1980, there was great optimism that the era of infectious disease may well and truly be ending for the human race.[22] While deaths from reemerging or newly discovered infectious diseases were on the decline globally in the 1970s, since the late 1980s new infectious diseases have been discovered at the rate of roughly one per year.[23] The emergence of HIV/AIDS and the ensuing devastation brought on from its ongoing pandemic, as well as the rise of other diseases such as hemorrhagic fevers like Ebola causing outbreaks in the 1970s, 1980s, and 1990s, dampened expectations for the demise of infectious diseases. Reflecting on the lack of understanding of the cause of AIDS, Dr. Anthony Fauci, one of the central HIV/AIDS researchers responsible for the discovery of the virus and its treatment, suggested in 1982 that examining illnesses for familiar syndromes (clusters of symptoms) may be an effective response to combating new and reemergent diseases for which a cause is unknown: "Because we do not know the cause of this syndrome, any assumption that the syndrome will remain restricted to a particular segment of our society is truly an assumption without scientific basis"[24]

The emergence of HIV/AIDS and Ebola provided a clear signal that the era of infectious diseases was far from over and that the constant, looming threat of disease emerging from formerly colonial sites remained. Further, these diseases, entirely separate and heretofore unmonitored by the WHO, existed well beyond the purview and reporting network of the IHR. Once again, the threat of new diseases transmitted from people traveling from far-flung tropical lands arose, like it had in the 1960s and the nineteenth century before that, and spurred concern among Western nations over the efficacy of the present disease controls maintained through the IHR.

An emergent group of global health experts began developing the case for global disease surveillance. Dr. Joshua Lederberg, the Nobel-laureate microbiologist, was one of the first to call for a shift away from the ways in which the international community had responded to infectious diseases. While Lederberg suggested a policy shift and a novel approach to the practice of disease control, the justifications for these changes were not particularly new. Rather, they reflected a reproduction of the Orientalism of the earlier International Sanitary Conventions and IHR and the methods that ensured their success: the constant monitoring and policing of nonwhite peoples within spaces of former European colonial domination. Re-presenting the same Orientalist gaze and noting the increased spread of humans into previously untouched areas and the increased rate of travel and trade, Lederberg stated in 1988:

> Opening of wild lands to human occupation has exposed people unaccustomed to viruses. . . . Such research should be done on a broad international scale to both share the progress made in advanced countries and amplify the opportunities for fieldwork at the earliest appearance of outbreaks in the most afflicted areas. No matter how selfish our motives, we can no longer be indifferent to the suffering of others. The microbe that felled one child in a distant continent yesterday can reach yours today and seed a global pandemic tomorrow. "Never send to know for whom the bell tolls; it tolls for thee."[25]

The quickly shifting terrain of international health risks away from the three reportable diseases under the IHR and the realization that the potential global risks from infectious disease not only threatened the planet but also challenged the capacity of the IHR to respond to threats. This by extension questioned the authority of the WHO as the arbiter of infectious disease response between nations. As mentioned earlier, this period represents one of the first and most significant times that actors outside of the WHO had actively contested the authority and role of the IHR. At this moment the WHO found itself within a contested space, battling for its central role as the global health authority of first and last resort.

While the structural inability of the IHR to respond to HIV/AIDS presented a foundational problem for the regulations, the WHO as a whole faced a larger problem regarding its broad HIV/AIDS response. The WHO was slow to recognize the pandemic potential of HIV/AIDS, especially in Africa.[26] The WHO would only become actively involved in any form of HIV/AIDS response in 1985, two years after the causal virus of AIDS was discovered[27] and long after the threat of an immune deficiency syndrome had been recognized. In 1987 the UN General Assembly designated the WHO as the lead organ for fighting the disease. The WHO Global Program on AIDS (GPA) focused on education and prevention, and between 1987 and 1990 became the largest operation within the WHO; it was seen by others within the organization as crowding out much of the other campaigns for funding and resources.[28] As the GPA was ultimately corralled through the ousting of its leader, the limited financial power of the WHO to directly engage in local, targeted anti-HIV activities and a broader push from global donors interested in supporting a worldwide organization for HIV/AIDS response crowded the WHO out of the field.[29] The ultimate establishment of a separate entity for coordinating the global AIDS response, UNAIDS, threatened the authority of the WHO in the domain of the most pressing infectious disease threat of the late twentieth and early twenty-first centuries, rendering the WHO marginal to the global HIV/AIDS response relative to other international organs.

National Interests

In the eyes of the WHO's member nations, it could no longer be relied upon to provide effective and practical outbreak information or establish effective sanitary protocols to prevent the spread of threatening diseases. The rise of new forms of national disease surveillance systems challenged the WHO's ability to maintain the Orientalist perspective that the greatest threats to global disease spread emerge from the unsurveilled masses in the now formerly colonized world and that surveillance was the most effective response to these threats. While the threats were still being perceived as arriving from distant and exotic lands beyond the West, the diseases of concern had shifted.

The late 1980s produced several critical conferences organized outside the purview of the WHO that reassessed the medical and international communities' role in the prevention of epidemic spread. In May 1989 the Rockefeller Foundation and US National Institutes of Health hosted a conference on *Emerging Viruses: The Evolution of Viruses and Viral Diseases*, which aimed to "consider the mechanisms of viral emergence and possible strategies for anticipating, detecting, and preventing the emergence of new viral diseases in the future."[30] The conference concluded that rapid, constant surveillance to identify and categorize threats worldwide through a network of integrated research and health centers was of vital importance.[31]

The results of this conference were distilled and published in a book entitled *Emerging Infections: Microbial Threats to Health in the United States*, which laid out both a plan for disease surveillance and recontextualized the threat of infectious disease in new terms:

> There is nowhere in the world from which we are remote and no one from whom we are disconnected. Consequently some infectious diseases that now affect people in other parts of the world represent potential threats to the United States because of global interdependence, modern transportation, trade and changing social and cultural patterns. . . . Rather than organize the report around specific diseases the committee decided to focus on factors that are implicated in the emergence of infectious diseases in the US.[32]

At the same time, Canada and other nations around the world were also questioning the IHR's focus on only three diseases and also set about developing a method for disease surveillance.[33] In 1987 the Canadian Advisory Committee on Epidemiology established a subcommittee to review which communicable diseases should be surveilled by their medical authorities.[34] Suggesting that the existing IHR reporting criteria focusing solely on cholera, plague, and yellow fever were inadequate, Canada developed a points scoring system by which threats would be assessed.

The presence of disease surveillance systems that not only expanded upon but also increased the surveillance character of the IHR posed a serious challenge to the efficacy and scope of the regulations. For the first time in nearly a half century, the WHO found its role as the central figure in international disease management challenged by its member states. Major member nations such as the United States and Canada were actively attempting to protect their borders and contain diseases beyond the scope of the existing regulations, compromising the usefulness of the WHO in matters of infectious disease control.

Direct Challenges to the WHO and IHR Adherence

While the emergence of new and very grave infectious disease threats with pandemic potential such as HIV/AIDS and Ebola forced nations to consider whether the existing IHR went far enough to actually live up to their mandate of ensuring "the maximum security against the international spread of diseases with a minimum interference with world traffic,"[35] divergent interpretations of the regulations themselves were producing disputes between nations. While Canada and the United States' proposals to expand their disease surveillance criteria looked beyond the IHR for disease controls, they did not directly challenge the existing components of the regulations themselves. One of the primary mechanisms of disease control was the management and control of diseases at ports and airports. In the early 1990s the means by which vector borne-insect diseases were managed at airports became a controversial element of the IHR. The countervailing factors of the ineffectiveness of the surveillance scope of the IHR and the dispute over the sanitary policing of disease at air and seaports challenged the WHO on two fronts. The WHO found itself in competition over its disease management authority as nations, international airline associations, and corporations began to resist adherence to the IHR.

In 1992 a number of cases came to light of civilian airline passengers becoming ill from airborne pesticide spraying in planes shortly before flights to control for disease-carrying insects. This practice, known as "blocks away" disinsection, whereby pesticide is sprayed in passenger cabins directly before take off, was the recommended practice of the IHR.[36] Under Articles 25 and 67 of the IHR 1969, any port in a nation in which the mosquito capable of carrying yellow fever is found must actively disinsect any craft leaving for foreign ports:

> 2. Every aircraft leaving an airport situated in an infected area shall be disinsected in accordance with Article 25, using methods recommended by the Organization, and details of the disinsecting shall be included in the Health Part of the Aircraft General Declaration, unless this part of the Aircraft General Declaration is waived by the health authority of the airport of arrival. States concerned shall accept disinsecting of aircraft by the approved vapor disinsecting system carried out in flight.
>
> 3. Every ship leaving a port in an area where *Aedes aegypti* still exists and bound for an area where *Aedes aegypti* has been eradicated shall be kept free of *Aedes aegypti* in its immature and adult stages.[37]

While this practice explicitly aims to control yellow fever spread, disinsection also guards against any mosquito-borne disease carried by the mosquito *Aedes aegyptii* including dengue fever, chikungunya, and Zika virus. As the regional overlap of yellow fever and malaria is quite significant, this method also aims to protect against cases of malaria either spreading or disseminating within and beyond ports of entry.[38]

In 1994 US newspapers reported on several cases of chemical sensitivity and illness in passengers visiting countries practicing blocks away disinsection.[39] Citing breathing difficulties and in some cases neurological disorders that lasted for years, US passengers such as Julia Kendal complained that while the practices of disinsecting airplanes once fully boarded was eliminated as a method in the United States, US and foreign airlines as well as travel agents did not notify passengers ahead of time that they would be sprayed with pesticide on board when departing from countries that actively spray on planes. British passengers also complained of similar effects and even deaths associated with the spraying of pesticides during travels to and from Australia.[40]

The concern by passengers over the potential health hazards of blocks away disinsection produced a number of medical and regulatory dilemmas for WHO member nations, and airlines and their organizing body and signatory to the IHR, the International Civil Aviation Organization (ICAO), over how to administer and interpret the IHR. In the case of the United States and its airlines, contradicting the IHR's demands for disinsection put them in a difficult position. While no American passengers were being sprayed on US soil, the US government, Environmental Protection Agency, and Centers for Disease Control (CDC) could not challenge the authority of sovereign nations to spray within aircrafts at foreign ports, thus putting US passengers at risk. The only way to protect US passengers from these pesticides on US carriers would be to eliminate all routes to such destinations, ostensibly eliminating all travel to much of the Caribbean, South America, Southern and Southeast Asia, Australia and New Zealand, and much of sub-Saharan Africa. The economic implications for airlines would be disastrous.[41] This became a contested issue among the World Health Assembly. Countries with especially fragile or yellow-fever-susceptible environments such as India, Pakistan, China, New Zealand, and Australia actively endorsed the practice of blocks away disinsection to protect their populations from the spread of disease.[42]

In May 1994 this issue came to a head in the United States when the US Congress passed a concurrent resolution urging that ICAO end all in-flight spraying:

> The overwhelming support, both in Congress and the administration, for ending this unnecessary chemical exposure should be a clear signal to the international community that American travelers will not travel to countries that welcome them with an insecticidal spray.[43]

On May 18, 1994, Representative Peter DeFazio and Senator Patrick Leahy drafted a letter to President Clinton on behalf of Congress requesting the president suggest reforms to the IHR and directly confront the WHO on this matter:

> We respectfully request that you take the most expeditious steps possible, to change the World Health Organization (WHO) regulations which endorse the spraying of insecticides on international commercial flights. . . . This policy is based on WHO regulations which endorse the spraying of insecticides on boarded aircraft for pest and disease control. We believe the WHO policy regarding in-flight spraying of insecticides is ineffective as a means of pest control and potentially harmful to human health. . . . Countries across the world look to WHO for guidance when establishing public health protection policies. The labels on airline disinsectants themselves use WHO's regulations in describing the proper use of those products. It is imperative that those regulations provide public health protection.[44]

While the scope of the IHR was being tested by individual nation-states, this particular challenge by the United States to disinsection and the general confusion caused by the international nature of this problem directly questioned the IHR's legitimacy in the eyes of its member states. The ambiguity as to how and when to apply blocks away disinsection as well as what sort of information to provide to passengers prior to spraying showed the regulations to be ineffective in the modern environment.[45] The increased pace of travel and the sheer volume of commercial flights meant that the rare neurological effects of disinsection could not be ignored in the face of a rapidly growing jet-set population and massive airline and tourism industry. The regulations that had existed for so long in a framework developed in the 1960s were no longer workable.

A Weakness in Confronting Outbreaks

By the time the decision to ultimately reform the IHR was made in May 1995 at the World Health Assembly, the WHO's foremost international infectious disease regulations had come under major international strain and delegitimized the WHO as a regulatory body. Outbreaks of plague in India had proven the existing regulations weak at managing the spread of the diseases established within its protocols, while threatening and high-profile outbreaks of Ebola in Zaire evaded the scope of the regulations altogether.[46] These outbreaks were being reported on by news agencies, often faster than by the WHO, which also increased the perception of the weakness of the WHO to respond to crises. Reporting from new disease surveillance entities such as the global surveillance network Program for Monitoring Emerging Diseases (ProMED)[47] also highlighted the limitations of the WHO's surveillance capacities in cases of outbreaks. The outbreak of Ebola in Kikwit, Zaire, was in large part the final nail in the coffin of the previous regime of the IHR. A key drafter of the IHR (2005) and one of the authors of the resolution that called for the reform of the IHR, in speaking on the Kikwit outbreak, said in an interview with me:

And the stimulus for this [Resolution WHA 48.7] was the 1993 Kikwit outbreak of Ebola and I think folks at WHO—I was at WHO then, I was seconded there from CDC. And my job was to help internationalize the response to, the strategy for responding to, infectious diseases. And this all goes back to the 1992 Institute of Medicine or National Academy of Sciences report on emerging infectious diseases. So CDC had taken up this cause and very quickly realized they needed an international component to it, so I was seconded there to help set that up, and over the course of the four years (I was there from 1992 to 1996), there was a number of internationally important outbreaks of emerging diseases that really drew international attention and set the stage for a receptive audience to realize that the existing IHR were too limited in their scope and pretty inflexible as far as what could be done to coordinate an international response. So I think all of this then led to the passage in 1995 of the resolution, then for literally the next decade the negotiations over what the new IHR should be and what the context should be. But at the end of the day that allowed the WHO greater flexibility both in terms of identifying what was appropriate to respond to and actually initiating response, even in spite of governments' perhaps reluctance to share key information. And then, you know, I guess another element just in setting the stage—this was about the time that ProMED was coming online, and information was becoming available much more

rapidly and without the bureaucratic hurdles that had hampered official reporting previously. And it was also the change in technology. You might recall that during the 1993 Kikwit outbreak there were real news reports from
the front lines, so what had previously been an unknown, exotic disease
became common knowledge because it was being reported in real time in
the news. . . . Certainly the Kikwit outbreak was certainly the highest profile
incident, but you'll recall that was about the same time that plague occurred
in India that caused a tremendous amount of economic impact. That was
the discovery of the Hendra virus and nipah. So there was a lot of diseases
that appeared that had not only public health implications but significant
economic drawbacks as well. So all of these things got peoples' attention
even beyond the health sector.

These emergent outbreaks without an effective entity to coordinate international responses left a power vacuum that was being filled in limited
capacities by the CDC among others as the WHO appeared ineffective. Em-
barrassed by the rise of novel disease surveillance groups like ProMED and
the ability of twenty-four-hour news teams to arrive on the scene of outbreaks
prior to the WHO, the organization, through reform of the IHR, needed to
find a way to reestablish itself as a key agent over these disparate actors and
knowledge sources.

WHO Reform Strategies

In reforming the IHR beginning in 1995 and ultimately ending in 2005, the
WHO undertook a radical transformation of a set of regulations that had
largely gone unchallenged for over one hundred years. The WHO developed a plan to confront the challenges to the IHR head on but also in so
doing to return the WHO to a central authority on disease control across
borders. Ultimately what emerged was a much larger mandate for the
WHO and a redefinition of the environment of international disease control and management. The WHO expanded its mandate by consolidating
the authority to assess disease risk that emerges from disease surveillance
systems.[48] In the new IHR and through the reform process the WHO developed a novel disease risk criterion that would be managed by the WHO

secretariat and mandated that all disease threats meeting its criteria be submitted to the WHO for review.

The limitations of the IHR explained earlier presented several obstacles to the reform of the document. The scope of the IHR being limited to only three diseases was inadequate to the variety of infectious threats around the globe, but the WHO also suffered from poor reporting on infectious disease outbreaks. Surveillance over outbreaks would have to be greatly strengthened if the WHO were to expand its mandate. Further, the role of the IHR as a toolkit for sanitation authorities at ports and border crossings had become both contested and obsolete as evidenced by both the increased pace of travel and the battles over blocks away disinsection. Dr. Brian Gushulak, a consultant at work on an early draft of the IHR revisions, reflected:

> The 1969 IHR amended in 1973 and 1981 had become an ineffective tool for its purpose, for instance by limiting immediate reporting to three specified diseases. It is now clear that international infectious disease control is more effectively undertaken by surveillance and intervention strategies taking advantage of the considerable evolution in communications technology, laboratory science, and in diagnosis, treatment and control of infections, rather than by the application of quarantine practices or other inappropriate measures at sites distant from the source of infection.[49]

The IHR had been found wanting on an ever-changing disease frontier.[50] In shifting from a mandate to monitor three diseases to monitoring all potential threats, the WHO was preparing to take on a much larger role in disease control. Further, by aiming to make control and surveillance the top priority of the IHR rather than sanitary measures, the power of the IHR aimed to shift from a control of practice to a control of knowledge: the management and consolidation of surveillance data.

During an informal consultation to review the application of the IHR held on December 14, 1995, the members of the informal working group remarked, in light of calls for the abolition of the IHR, that without such a regulatory structure there would be no guiding authority by which countries would manage outbreaks and that member states would "feel themselves permitted to take absolutely any ad hoc measures without even having to account for them and no one would know what to expect on going to a country."[51] The WHO sought to claim that authority in order to maintain a standardized frame by which disease threat would be confronted and managed globally. This authority was all the more important in the cases of the most serious global epidemic threats.

The mode and means by which the WHO would now assess disease threat in this new deductive context became a challenge for the members of the revision committee to define in the early stages of reform. While the criticisms of the IHR reflected the same concerns over the unsurveilled movements of people in the Southern Hemisphere, the ability of the WHO to police these threats was actively being questioned. However, the movement away from existing practices left the WHO in the position of having to assess which diseases would trigger significant responses and why. The revisions of the IHR were moving the WHO into a position of being able to define and effectively triage global disease threats, not according to a rigid list of three or six diseases but through some other form of knowledge control derived through rigorous disease surveillance conducted by member states and consolidated by the WHO.

In seeking advice on these matters, the WHO reached out to their member state actors for comment. In a letter to the director-general of the WHO Dr. Hiroshi Nakajima, the minister of health for Mongolia Dr. D. P. Nymadawa suggested that the list of diseases be directly revised to include a broader range of diseases such as hemorrhagic fevers and expand the surveillance criteria to any illnesses causing high fatalities, atypical microbial isolates, and unusual clinical presentations.[52] This was found too limiting in the scope of the responses. Ultimately the WHO reformers chose to adopt the philosophical perspectives on the utility of global disease surveillance more similar to those put forward by Lederberg, the Canadians, and US surveillance advocates.

The debates over one of the more respected early models for the IHR relied on a method of disease surveillance and reporting known as *syndromic surveillance*, a method by which, in lieu of accurate diagnostic information, the WHO could assess the relative threat of outbreaks by the syndromes presented by the disease prior to full lab analysis. This would allow the WHO to triage risk of global spread prior to the diagnosis of disease and thereby act quickly. Such a method relies on timely reporting to the WHO of all outbreaks by member states. While not what was ultimately accepted as the strategy for assessing risk to the WHO, syndromic surveillance provided an early model for the diagnostic criteria that the WHO would ultimately adopt in the 2005 IHR revision. In the draft of the initial strategy for syndromic reporting, Dr. Gushulak, representing the Canadian Quarantine Health Services, suggested that the threat of disease spread and the disease itself be assessed and prioritized based not only on medical and etiological criteria but also on the sociopolitical and economic climate of the site of outbreak, the possible threats the disease may pose to trade and traffic, technological capacities to treat the outbreak, and the risks associated with each given a potential global epidemic.[53]

By providing expert consensus opinion and analysis, the IHR can become an internationally accepted standardized framework that guides national health providers in the management of epidemic outbreaks. Diversity in control activities, which may occur as different national health authorities attempt to deal with the same situation, can adversely affect multinational efforts to deliver a balanced and scientifically appropriate response to an acutely developing situation. Due to the fact that many of these episodes will involve emerging or re-emerging infectious disease illnesses where knowledge and clinical experience may be limited, guidelines and collectively approved recommendations can be a useful tool. They prevent or moderate the introduction of unnecessary or inappropriate measures that can interfere with international commerce. They can also provide global standards for disease control that can be used as national models. The availability of internationally consistent disease control measures will assist national authorities in the maintenance of public confidence in time of international emergency. Additionally they will greatly facilitate the decision-making process faced by national health authorities by providing a widely accepted framework of response measures. In this manner, they will support the efficient and effective allocation of resources directed at international control efforts in areas where action is required. At the same time they can clearly delineate the lack of necessity for inappropriate or unnecessary control measures.[54]

This model transformed the disease threat, previously represented as the mere presence of the disease for which there would be clear responses, into a dynamic heuristic whereby the WHO would directly assess the risk of spread and develop practical responses based upon that risk. The creation of this classificatory schema relied significantly on meeting the challenges that all organizations traditionally have to face. The concerns of the members of the Informal Working Group over the rapid reporting of outbreaks reflected the particular anxieties of the WHO at the time. The rapid dissemination of information about outbreaks leading to a secondary epidemic of panic spread by the emergent twenty-four-hour media was a pressing concern. The recent 1994 outbreak of pneumonic plague in India produced a great deal of media speculation without a cohesive assessment from WHO experts. This weakened the WHO's capacity to control the modes of information dissemination on the outbreak. The urgent issue of media optics melded with the concerns over the overall mission of the IHR to limit the threat of disease to trade and traffic. As such, both the early and final versions of the IHR considered media coverage in its risk assessment of outbreaks.

Media role in Syndromic reporting:

Public concern:

F) Is there grave concern about the syndrome among the public or the media leading to discriminatory actions in business or social transactions?

G) Is there international media coverage and concern

H) Is international aid being sought?

When at least one criteria in any two groups are satisfied a health problem would be reportable. . . .

What is the justification of these criteria?

Concern leading to discriminatory actions: Rumors and misunderstandings leading to inappropriate actions at home and at frontiers/ports would require classification and monitoring and WHO should be able to give the true story to other countries who are instituting or contemplating such inappropriate measures.[55]

While this particular formulation of syndromic surveillance would prove to be unpopular, the model itself, of retaining control over the risk assessment of different diseases, would come to be the accepted form of disease control within the 2005 IHR. Ultimately syndromic reporting was scrapped due to the infeasibility of implementing such a rapid reporting system under the present institutional constraints of the WHO.

> Syndromic reporting will likely result in more reports of disease outbreaks. Management of political and economic concerns and reassurance of worried citizens will be critical. . . . WHO and member nations will almost certainly receive more requests for assistance. This will impact on already limited resources.[56]

A pilot study in twenty-two countries in all WHO regions (completed in 1999) field tested syndromic surveillance. As the result of an interim review, it was concluded that syndromic reporting, although valuable within a national system, was not appropriate for use in the context of a regulatory framework, mainly because of difficulties in reporting syndromes in the field test, and because syndromes could not be linked to preset rules for control of spread. The political and economic risks of declaring a multiplicity of threats was considered too significant an undertaking on the part of the WHO and could present a major challenge to their credibility if too many emergencies were triggered. In addition, the WHO concluded that an excess of emergencies could trigger collateral effects to trade and traffic.

Ultimately the reformers of the IHR settled upon a very specific and topdown mode of disease control and management. The clear issues associated with earlier drafts of the IHR reflected the need to be able to assess and declare threat according to a particular criterion. The IHR needed to embrace epidemiological concerns as well as the social, political, and economic factors associated with epidemic risk, including the costs that the WHO would have to bear. Early drafts for disease management and threat assessment that included syndromic reporting recognized the need for the WHO to claim its role as the authority over the control of international disease spread; however, how that authority would be exercised proved to be a central challenge.

The WHO decided to assess the threat of outbreaks based on a reproducible algorithm to determine the level of global risk. In place of the previous model in the IHR by which any outbreaks of plague, cholera, or yellow fever would receive the highest levels of control and scrutiny, the WHO settled on the designation of PHEIC in the sole control and authority of the director-general of the WHO.

In addition to this classificatory structure for assessing disease threat, the WHO further consolidated its command over surveillance knowledge through the formulation of the Global Outbreak Alert and Response Network to act as a clearing house for all incoming disease and surveillance information. A novel component of the notification system that emerged in the 2005 IHR is the ability of the WHO to accept surveillance data from nonstate actors. This significantly increased the capacity of the WHO to assess threat but also challenged the authority of their member states to hide, conceal, or control surveillance data from the WHO. Thus, reporters, health actors, or NGOs can send reports and information to the WHO without notifying or confirming with the national government in question. Such a model of reporting had never been in place previously and further solidified the WHO's control over the employment and management of surveillance knowledge in the absence of other forms of sanction or direct power.

In addition the IHR 2005 also created a structure between the WHO and each of the 196 national signatories to the regulations for constant epidemiological surveillance known as National IHR Focal Points, which allow for a single source and chain of reporting from a national agent directly to the WHO.[57] This streamlines the system of communication between national actors and the WHO and consolidates surveillance data at single points to be directed to the WHO.

Surveillance Authority

The fundamental discourse that oriented the International Sanitary Conventions was the inherent and constant threat posed by infectious diseases emanating from the heart of European-controlled colonies, interrupting patterns of trade and ultimately reaching European shores. Thus far we have seen how this same Orientalism, reproduced by actors like the CDC, the Canadian Advisory Committee on Epidemiology, as well as the emergent disease surveillance community and global news agencies, reflects this dominant belief that the major disease threats to the West require the aggressive policing of those threats that emanate from beyond their territories. Like the Orientalist frame that separated colony from metropole and colonizer from colonized in order to protect Europe from disease, the same epidemic Orientalism reifies similar boundaries in a world where they are less visible in the absence of explicit empire. These logics maintain themselves as the underlying ideology of the domain of international infectious disease control.

The International Sanitary Regulations and first IHR (1969) under the WHO condensed the force of these earlier controls to border spaces and restricted the sanitary gaze almost exclusively to those traversing national borders. The concern for the emergence of diseases such as Ebola, HIV/ AIDS, and Nipah virus, among others, emanating from postcolonial tropical areas once again triggered anxieties over the unobserved movement of nonwhite peoples around the world. The same epidemic Orientalism that emboldened segregation efforts in Cape Town in 1901 and the aggressive sanitary policing of Muslims on Hajj remains in the twenty-first century. As the field of infectious disease management emerged, the WHO was challenged for its inability to effectively surveil the masses that would bring disease to the rest of the world and establish regulations accordingly while also (as in the case of disinsection) imposing undue harm to Western bodies. This prompted the reformers of the IHR to attempt, through the reconstitution of the regulations, to reclaim their authority through a number of revisions and through dominance over the means of disease surveillance. This empowered the WHO, through the IHR, to define and classify disease threat through the same epidemic Orientalist realm as previously, rendering a constellation of economic, political, and epidemiological considerations as *common-sense*.

As the reform of the International Sanitary Conventions under the authority of the WHO had reproduced the Orientalizing gaze of previous sanitary eras, the lingering concerns over the unsurveilled movement of people beyond these zones in the absence of colonial rule remained. The solution to this power vacuum was the establishment through the IHR of the WHO as the collector and sole arbiter of disease threats around the world, responsible for maintaining the Orientalist discourse enabled through the International Sanitary Conventions. While the practices and approaches to disease regulation altered drastically, the particular focus and scrutiny on formerly colonized sites as the spaces from which threats will emerge remained. Rather than acquiesce to the demands of their member states and detractors, the reformers of the IHR attempted to entirely reshape the domain of infectious disease control by placing it at the center of how infectious outbreaks are assessed for risk, classified, and ultimately managed. Recognizing the WHO's capacity to appraise global threat and thus its authority, the reformers of the IHR returned the WHO from a tenuous position to a central body to arbitrate over the use and power of that surveillance data for disease control. The recognition of the WHO and its experts of its role in a growing, contested battle over the authority to police disease in competition with nongovernmental and state actors produced these particular reforms. The relative difficulty and power of the director-general to assign PHEICs (based on the recommendations of the Emergency Committees) also demonstrate the symbolic power and latitude that the WHO maintains in deciding which outbreaks become a threat requiring international cooperation to stop. The enhanced requirements to mandate reporting on any suspicious outbreaks by their member states permanently place the WHO at the center of international disease control, where the previous instantiation of the IHR risked placing it very much at the periphery.

The IHR (2005), like its predecessors, represent the only binding international agreement on public health.[58] Several scholars have pointed to the inherent disjointedness and weakness of the WHO as an organization in recent times.[59] Critics have concluded that its lack of sanctioning power, small budget,[60] and decentralized operating structure, with regional blocs operating semiautonomously from the central headquarters. limits its role as a central actor in global health.[61] However, the recent responses to epidemic outbreaks have challenged this understanding that the WHO and the IHR are marginal in the space of global health. The WHO retains a powerful role in proliferating health norms and practices throughout the globe.[62] This is especially the case in establishing best practice procedures for the treatment and surveillance of diseases by making direct recommendations to member states.

The authority of the WHO is even more explicit in the domain of the IHR. This examination into the power of the IHR demonstrates that while the WHO may not wield sanctioning power over its member states, it retained prior to the COVID-19 pandemic significant might as a normative regulatory actor in the larger field of global health. The IHR remain at the present, in spite of the embattled position of the WHO, "the only legally binding instrument to prevent the trans-boundary spread of infectious diseases."[63]

5 EPIDEMICS, POWER, AND THE GLOBAL MANAGEMENT OF DISEASE RISK

THE PRECEDING CHAPTERS HAVE EXPLAINED which forces govern the practices and responses to particular epidemic threats. Epidemic Orientalism, which structures the responses to diseases and organizes the perception of disease threat, has for most of this book been the dominant discourse through which infectious threats were seen. In the current era, where disease threats are assessed based on the threat designation Public Health Emergency of International Concern (PHEIC), what sort of epidemics compel the international community to act? And further, is this designation powerful enough to compel action? How do these priorities affect which outbreaks become a focus for actors like the World Health Organization (WHO) and which outbreaks receive comparatively less global attention? Who becomes the focus of the power of the International Health Regulations (IHR)? While epidemic Orientalism, the guiding discourse of the International Sanitary Conventions, and the WHO's IHR have thus far explained why certain disease threats are prioritized over others, this theory alone cannot explain why certain diseases interpolated as international concerns garner more attention than others. To answer these questions, this chapter examines the deliberation process behind the highest infectious disease threat designation, the PHEIC, as the management of symbolic power by the WHO. The previous chapter explored how the WHO managed to retain, through the reform of the IHR, its dominance over the field of infectious disease control in no small part through the revisions to the IHR in 2005. Through the revisions of the IHR in the 1990s and 2000s, the WHO was able to recapture a level of global disease surveillance that had been missing since the first International Sanitary Conventions. At the same time, the WHO was a weakened and complementary actor within the field of international health rather than the sole actor that it had been in this space in the mid- and late twentieth century.

Since 2007[1] the WHO has employed the PHEIC to classify the highest level of public health emergencies. The designation of this term under the IHR (2005) mandates that the WHO and in some instances its member nations to commit to extraordinary measures to combat the health threat. The WHO upon this declaration is empowered to coordinate the disease response, offer regular guidance and technical support to the affected regions, suggest or challenge the emplacement of travel and trade barriers, and facilitate the gathering of resources from its member nations to combat the threat. While this designation technically covers all manner of health threats including biohazard and biological warfare, it has only been declared in response to moments of epidemic outbreak.

Since the passage of the IHR (2005), seven epidemics have received the designation PHEIC: the 2009 outbreak of H1N1 Influenza, the resurgence of wildtype polio in 2014, the West African Ebola virus disease outbreak of 2014–2016, the Zika microcephaly epidemic of 2016, the Ebola virus disease epidemic currently under way in the Democratic Republic of Congo, and the pandemic of SARS-CoV 2 (COVID-19) that is also ongoing (as of May 2022) and the recently declared epidemic of Monkeypox. Each of these diseases was determined to be a PHEIC by the director-general of the WHO after deliberation with an emergency committee of experts. However, two diseases have come before the director-general and emergency committee that did not receive the designation PHEIC: yellow fever in 2016 and the sporadic epidemics of MERS coronavirus (MERS-CoV) of the 2010s.

All of these diseases would seem to fit the criteria of a global disease threat through the lens of epidemic Orientalism, as all derive from former colonial areas and reflect a threat from those spaces that can travel to the "developed" world. This is not to say that epidemic Orientalism is not still at work in the practice of disease control. Quite the opposite, in fact. Each PHEIC has been determined and responses have been structured under the understanding that the countries affected can no longer help themselves or require international responses. As neither yellow fever nor MERS-CoV triggered a PHEIC designation, another causal mechanism must be at work.

In deciding to recommend a PHEIC, members of the emergency committees must contend with and manage the perception of the designation and the effects that it may have on the outbreak response as well as subsequently the patterning of epidemic spread itself. The effects of employing the designation produces repercussions that not only challenge the future legitimacy of the WHO but also affect the efficacy of anti-outbreak responses. By considering the power of the PHEIC designation that produces consequences that must be attended to and are difficult to anticipate, the PHEIC itself, amid a constellation of human, state, and organizational actors, produces an understanding of the epidemic and alters epidemic response. By considering or even declaring a PHEIC, the perception of threat and the epidemic itself is altered even if epidemiologically there is no change. Within these calculations, the relative power of the WHO and its ability to effectively coerce responses commensurate with the PHEIC designation by the nation-states of the world becomes critical.

Explaining why epidemics triggered alerts but may or may not have received the designation of PHEIC is critical to the understanding of how disease risk is assessed on a global scale and to demonstrate how the normative power of the WHO is employed. The PHEIC designation is more than solely a signal that compels the international community to act in response to an epidemic crisis. It is also a mechanism for maintaining or curbing challenges to world trade and travel as well as organizing the activities of the WHO. Similar to the original International Sanitary Conventions that aimed to halt the production of uncoordinated quarantine practices in Europe, the PHEIC is often employed, or not, to limit the actions of member states that are incongruous with the desired aims of the WHO. The International Sanitary Conventions compelled aggressive disease control measures from colonies exhibiting outbreaks of particular diseases; so too does the PHEIC designation decide not only which diseases warrant concern from the international community but also which epidemics demand an aggressive response.

TABLE 5: Outbreaks Prompting Emergency Committee Meetings and Their Outcomes.

Disease	Date of first meeting	Number of emergency committee meetings	No. of members	Countries affected	Decision
H1N1	April 25, 2009	9	15; 1 advisor	Pandemic-global	Declared a PHEIC upon first meeting
Poliomyelitis	May 5, 2014	13; ongoing	15; 5 advisors	Pakistan; Afghanistan; Nigeria/Lake Chad Region	Declared a PHEIC upon first meeting
MERS-CoV	July 9, 2013	10	17; 7 advisors	Algeria; Iran; Jordan; Netherlands; Saudi Arabia; UAE; USA; Qatar; South Korea	No PHEIC declared
Ebola virus disease	August 8, 2014	9	13; 9 advisors	Guinea; Liberia; Sierra Leone; Mali; Senegal; Italy; Spain; UK; USA; Nigeria	Declared a PHEIC upon first meeting
Zika micro-cephaly	February 1, 2016	5	13; 10 advisors	Most of North and South America; East Africa; parts of Asia	Declared a PHEIC upon first meeting
Yellow fever	May 16, 2016	2	8; 3 advisors	Angola; Democratic Republic of Congo; China	No PHEIC declared
Ebola virus disease	May 18, 2018	4	12; 5 advisors	Democratic Republic of Congo	PHEIC Declared after 3rd meeting

TABLE 5: (*continued*)

Disease	Date of first meeting	Number of emergency committee meetings	No. of members	Countries affected	Decision
Outbreak of novel coronavirus (n-CoV 2019)	January 23, 2020	2	15; 7 advisors	Global	PHEIC declared after 2nd meeting

Source: World Health Organization, "List of Members of, and Advisor to, the International Health Regulations (2005) Emergency Committee Concerning Influenza Pandemic (H1N1) 2009," 2009, 1, https://cdn.who.int/media/docs/default-source/documents/ihr/ihr-committee-members-h1n1-orginal-list.pdf; World Health Organization, "MERS-CoV IHR Emergency Committee," 2013, https://www.who.int/groups/mers-cov-ihr-emergency-committee; World Health Organization, "Members of, and Advisers to, the International Health Regulations (2005) Emergency Committee on Yellow Fever," 2016, https://www.who.int/docs/default-source/documents/ihr/ihr-committee-members-yellow-fever.pdf; World Health Organization, "Statement on the 1st Meeting of the IHR Emergency Committee on the 2014 Ebola Outbreak in West Africa," 2014, https://www.who.int/news/item/08-08-2014-statement-on-the-1st-meeting-of-the-ihr-emergency-committee-on-the-2014-ebola-outbreak-in-west-africa; World Health Organization, "Statement on the October 2018 Meeting of the IHR Emergency Committee on the Ebola Virus Disease Outbreak in the Democratic Republic of the Congo," https://www.who.int/news-room/detail/17-10-2018-statement-on-the-meeting-of-the-ihr-emergency-committee-on-the-ebola-outbreak-in-drc; World Health Organization, "Statement on the 9th IHR Emergency Committee Meeting Regarding the International Spread of Poliovirus," 2016, https://www.who.int/news/item/20-05-2016-statement-on-the-9th-ihr-emergency-committee-meeting-regarding-the-international-spread-of-poliovirus; "COVID-19 IHR Emergency Committee," https://www.who.int/groups/covid-19-ihr-emergency-committee.

It was the objective of the WHO, in the production of the PHEIC and the decision-making algorithm of the instrument, to create a reproducible method by which to assess the risk of international spread of infectious disease. The PHEIC designation process brings together key experts in the fields of medicine and epidemiology to respond to the data produced from disease surveillance sources around the world in order to determine at that time if an outbreak constitutes an international public health emergency. As noted in Table 5, the sizes of these emergency committees are small and the discussions quite intimate. The application of a standardized classificatory system to routinize the designation of disease risk is the objective of the PHEIC designation process.

Key to the WHO's legitimacy on the world stage is its power to leverage its normative authority. As the most significant international agency devoted to health and commissioned by the United Nations, the WHO has the power to establish global standards, provide technical guidance and expert knowledge, negotiate treaties, define and classify health situations and diagnostic criteria, and coordinate responses to health emergencies.[2] Over the last six years in particular, the WHO has come under significant scrutiny over its management of epidemic emergencies like the West African Ebola virus disease outbreak of 2013–2016 and the more recent Zika and yellow fever outbreaks of the last several years.[3] Perceptions of poor management resulted in significant calls for reform and weakening the organization's position as the normative authority over infectious disease response, namely, the utility and effectiveness of the classificatory system it uses in declaring health emergencies. The condemnation received by the WHO over its management of the West African Ebola virus disease epidemic led to organization-wide reform and the establishment of several independent advisory committees on world health emergencies.[4] No epidemic event has more significantly challenged the WHO in recent times, or threatened the overall stability of the organization, than the current pandemic of COVID-19. At the center of this struggle for authority and legitimacy is the careful management of the PHEIC declaration in order to productively manipulate nations of the world into complying with WHO recommendations. This requires both the careful recognition of the strategies and priorities of member nations while also explicitly recognizing the dynamics of epidemic Orientalism that guide certain member nation responses. It is these factors that the members of the WHO emergency committees must navigate.

By conducting interviews with senior members of the WHO emergency committees that deliberate over the threat of international disease spread, I examine the factors that determine how epidemic risk is assessed, finding that the symbolic, classificatory power of the PHEIC designation is an important force to be mediated by emergency committee members in order to derive sound health responses. Members of the WHO emergency committees engage in a complex negotiation that incorporates concerns for the potential effects of the designation itself on the outbreak and the responses to it from nations.

Significance of a PHEIC

The declaration of a PHEIC can drastically alter the conditions of outbreak response. Under the designation, the WHO takes responsibility for coordinating the international response to the outbreak. The effect of this was particularly evident in the Ebola response in West Africa. While the WHO was slow to respond to the outbreak, the designation of the PHEIC galvanized international support and coordinated a range of national and nongovernmental actors under a single authority, which streamlined communication and activities. The other major function of the PHEIC designation is to manage the economic fallout of outbreaks. This requires the management of responses of trade partners and other nations to an epidemic. As this book has shown, the risk of epidemic to trade concerns has been catastrophic, especially for colonial sites and nations in the developing world seeking trade with the West. An outbreak of pneumonic plague in Surat, India, in 1994, though small and relatively isolated, resulted in $2 billion of economic losses to India over the course of the outbreak, including trade embargoes and tourism losses to the region.[5] Fears of plague in India, though it was a very small epidemic, mobilized old epidemic Orientalist fears of disease spread from the Indian subcontinent and halted shipping of Indian goods through the Persian Gulf and Suez Canal for a period. The SARS epidemic of 2003 resulted in losses of up to 1 percent of gross domestic product in Singapore, Hong Kong, China, and Taiwan. The scope and scale of outbreak responses managed on an international level is modulated by the PHEIC designation, and effective responses can hinge on the guidance of actors within the WHO.

The Formal Criteria of a PHEIC Declaration

In a document titled "WHO Event Management for International Public Health Security Operational Procedures," the WHO lays out a "reproducible

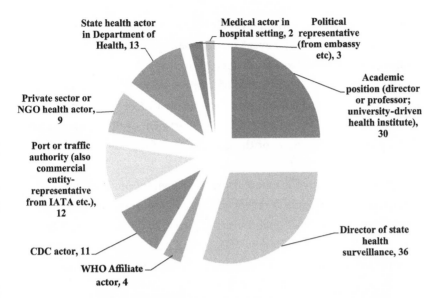

FIGURE 6: Professional Affiliation of Emergency Committee Membership.

Source: Margaret Chan, "WHO Director-General Summarizes the Outcome of the Emergency Committee Regarding Clusters of Microcephaly and Guillain-Barré Syndrome," February 1, 2016, http://www.who.int/mediacentre/news/statements/2016/emergency-committee-zika-micro cephaly/en/; World Health Organization, "Statement on the 1st Meeting of the IHR Emergency Committee on the 2014 Ebola Outbreak in West Africa"; World Health Organization, "List of Members of, and Advisers to, the International Health Regulations (2005) Emergency Committee Concerning Middle East Respiratory Syndrome Coronavirus (MERS-CoV)"; World Health Organization, "List of Members of, and Advisor to, the International Health Regulations (2005) Emergency Committee Concerning Influenza Pandemic (H1N1) 2009"; World Health Organization, "Members of, and Advisers to, the International Health Regulations (2005) Emergency Committee on Yellow Fever"; World Health Organization, "List of Proposed Members and Advisers to International Health Regulations (IHR) Emergency Committee for Pneumonia Due to the Novel Coronavirus 2019-NCoV."

process for managing acute public health events" that may affect the international community.[6] The document provides a framework for how events should be monitored and how the WHO should assess risk regarding international epidemic events. In efforts to be reproducible and transparent, the document lays out standardized questions and actions by which threats are assessed for potential risk. Events are managed by a diverse group of actors coordinated around the world through WHO headquarters. Threats are assessed and managed by an event management group, an ad-hoc network composed of experts in outbreak control from the WHO country office of the affected member state, regional offices, and ultimately WHO headquarters.[7] The event management group is coordinated by an event manager designated by the director-general, the Department of Epidemic and Pandemic Alert and Response, or the coordinator of the Alert and Response network.

Upon verification of an outbreak event through specific protocols further established by the WHO,[8] the event is assessed for its potential risk. The risk of an outbreak of international concern is primarily evaluated under the rubric laid out under Annex 2 of the IHR (2005). According to this algorithm, potential PHEICs are to be judged based on four major conditions:

1. Is the public health impact of the event serious?
2. Is the event unusual or unexpected?
3. Is there a significant risk of international spread?
4. Is there a significant risk of international restriction(s) to travel and trade?[9]

While these questions make up the focus of the algorithm and are predicated on a further list of subquestions, there are a set of additional considerations necessitated in the risk assessment that consider not only the medical risks associated with the outbreak but also the geopolitical situation in the country(s) of outbreak as well as the public perception of risk and the potential risks associated with the WHO not taking action. At the outcome of the risk assessment, having considered the alert delivered by the member nation struck by outbreak or by a confirmed source, the WHO event management group may choose one of six responses:

1. Discard the event if there is no risk of international spread
2. Continue to monitor the event
3. Assist by providing technical assistance

4. Disseminate information to the international community to prevent similar events

5. Escalate the level of intervention

6. Advise the WHO senior management to initiate a PHEIC determination procedure[10]

If a PHEIC determination procedure is requested, then an emergency committee will be formed, the director-general will appoint a chair under the conditions of Article 48 of the IHR (2005), and the director-general will decide whether the event constitutes a PHEIC by considering the following:

1. Information provided by the member state(s)

2. The IHR (2005) Annex 2 rubric

3. The advice of the emergency committee

4. Scientific principles, available scientific evidence, and other relevant information

5. An assessment of the risk to human health, international spread of disease, and interference with international traffic[11]

If the event is determined to be PHEIC after this protocol is enacted, then international cooperation will likely be required and requested by the WHO to take a response decided to be appropriate for the outbreak.

The first significant appraisal of the validity of the PHEIC designation system was carried out in 2012.[12] The analysis compiled 175 unique infectious disease events and provided details of these events to three key experts in the field of infectious disease management. Based on the decision-making instrument in Annex 2 of the IHR, they were asked to provide yes or no answers to questions on whether these outbreaks constituted a PHEIC. In addition to providing affirmative or negative answers to these questions the experts were required to state their confidence in their assertion based on a five-point Likert scale (1 = strongly disagree to 5 = strongly agree).[13] While the experts were unaware of the outcomes and effects of the hypothetical emergency scenarios, such scenarios were ultimately based on real-world situations. The result was that of the 46 unique disease events determined to be of international concern by the experts involved, 44 of them would have been reported using Annex 2 of the IHR (2005). This is a 95.6 percent sensitivity under the conditions put forward by the test.[14]

While this research tested the reproducibility of the diagnostic criteria of Annex 2 of the IHR, it did not establish the validity of the underlying assumptions over what makes an international health event, namely, the four conditions central to the algorithm. This study did not challenge the underlying ideological or discursive positions that determined the four conditions for a PHEIC declaration. Several doctors and medical experts have challenged the way in which the PHEIC designation and the strategic employment of emergency committees operate as powerful consensus-building engines as well as a vehicle to shed light on outbreaks and draw attention to their importance.[15] PHEIC designations carry with them a powerful geopolitical weight that in and of itself structures how the international community may respond to threat, affecting the epidemiological course of outbreak.

The Interviews

To understand the complexities of the deliberation process over the PHEIC designation, interviews were requested from members of the emergency committees of each outbreak that provoked a meeting, including those that did not produce PHEIC declarations. The members of each emergency committee are listed on the WHO website along with their biographies. Contact was attempted with every member of each committee for whom contact information was available,[16] via email and in more formal settings at scientific conferences. Interviews with those who responded to the request were carried out between January and August 2017. Particular priority was assigned to those members who have served on multiple committees, as their experience with emergency committees spans several health emergencies. Through this period roughly 10 percent of all active committee members were interviewed. While this percentage may seem low, the focus of this research was not to survey the whole population on certain matters but rather to understand the process of designation and the considerations brought to bear on each issue.[17]

Disease Threat, Epidemic Orientalism, and the Power of the PHEIC

While each outbreak of a major epidemic or biothreat could potentially trigger a PHEIC, every case is different, producing very different contexts from which to deliberate the scope of the threat. The IHR and Annex 2 of the regulations were designed to address this. In addition to the designation, the emergency committee members have to acknowledge a variety of exogenous factors that produce secondary effects to the designation itself and end up modulating the decision making of the committee. Central among these is the complex negotiation of the potential effects of the catalyzing power of the PHEIC designation itself, which, as interview subjects will demonstrate, can have either beneficial or highly negative effects on the ability to coordinate outbreak responses. Though the epidemiological, economic, and political threats posed by an outbreak may represent their own health emergency in and of themselves, the application of the PHEIC designation produces second-order externalities that transform the nature of the outbreak itself. Very often the members of the emergency committee are forced to manage the perspectives that world nations may take toward epidemics. In recognizing this, emergency committee members absorb these considerations and modulate their responses. The three key areas in which emergency committee members must anticipate these concerns are in relation to managing the potential responses of the global community to the threat of a potentially global outbreak, managing the economic fallout from the designation of a PHEIC, and managing media and information dissemination during times of outbreak. These are the modes through which emergency committee members manage and manipulate the effects of the PHEIC in order to effect different outcomes from actors at the sites of epidemic as well as their broader community of member states. The nature and dynamics of these wider concerns reflect the enduring force of epidemic Orientalism as well as the ways in which the practices of international infectious disease response still operate through this discursive frame.

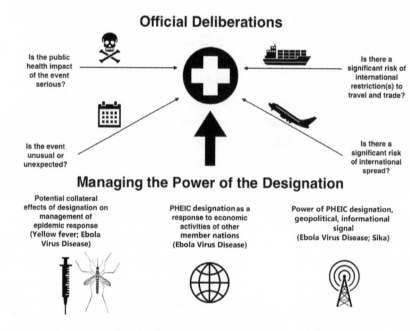

FIGURE 7: Formal and Informal Considerations Involved in Declaring PHEIC.

Source: World Health Organization, "WHO Guidance for the Use of Annex 2 of the International Health Regulations (2005)," WHO, 2010, http://www.who.int/ihr/publications/annex_2 _guidance/en/.

Managing the Responses of the Global Community

While the mandate of the IHR is to control the spread of disease and minimize the effects on trade and travel, the WHO and emergency committee members must not only respond to the potential economic impact of an outbreak, which may or may not increase the likelihood of a PHEIC designation, but also recognize that the designation alters the global perspective on the outbreak. This may in some cases positively increase the levels of international response and cooperation or in some cases may exacerbate the already devastating epidemiological effects of outbreak. These concerns were central to the deliberations concerning the yellow fever outbreak concentrated in Angola and the Democratic Republic of Congo and the Ebola virus disease outbreak in West Africa.

A member of the Yellow Fever Emergency Committee suggested that the effect of a PHEIC designation in response to the yellow fever outbreak would have limited the response capacity of the WHO to the outbreak. Though yellow fever is a preventable disease with a very effective vaccine, the scale of this urban outbreak, the largest of its kind in several decades, posed very serious concerns for the global vaccine supply. While mass vaccination was possible, it required supplies of stockpiled vaccines to be shifted to the site of outbreak in order to prevent high death rates as well as the possibility of further spread to yellow-fever-susceptible areas such as China, North America, South Asia, and Europe. In the committee deliberations, the possibility of a PHEIC designation negatively affecting the ability to mobilize the vaccine supplies needed to carry out an effective response was a focus of discussion:

> Therefore if we introduce those things [mass vaccination campaigns] as West Africa did in those parts of Africa then we can actually reduce to a large extent the possibility of the spread of yellow fever. And if we know that anybody who has come into the endemic area gets themselves vaccinated before coming, then the chances are somewhat more reduced. The alternative would have been to have declared a PHEIC and said "Yes, it is a public health emergency." What would have happened would have been a cascade of activities in which many countries would now be asking for vaccines. Supposedly countries that don't really need it would now be asking for vaccines, and we are now in a state of vaccine shortage that would have compounded the issue. We would have not had enough vaccines to take care of DR Congo, Angola, and those other places, and that would have left opportunities for the disease to spread. And those are the things that we looked at. In taking a position on that. Yes, it is an emergency, but it is not a PHEIC, and if we do what is right we can actually nip that in the bud. (Yellow Fever Member 1)

This decision not to upgrade the yellow fever threat to a PHEIC in order to maximize access to the much-needed vaccines to combat the outbreak in the affected nations displays the power of the PHEIC designation to mobilize the international community into action. It also demonstrates the lingering power of the threat of Orientalist perspectives around disease threats and the careful line WHO officials must tread to appease the epidemic Orientalist anxieties of the nations of the world. Members of the emergency committees must actively grapple with the epidemic Orientalism of nation-states in appraising what will be the most effective route to disease control. In this case, concerns around elevating the concern for yellow fever reflected the possibility of prompting vaccine nationalism and other counterproductive measures. While that is exactly what it is actually designed for, the response of national actors to the invocation of a PHEIC can produce negative externalities that may harm efforts to control outbreaks due to the ongoing discursive effects of epidemic Orientalism. Instead, the WHO coordinated what amounted to one of the largest vaccination campaigns in modern history prior to COVID-19.[18]

Conversely, the power of the PHEIC partially justified the maintenance of the designation in the context of the West African Ebola outbreak. Some have argued that the PHEIC designation in that case heightened the economic penalties incurred on the main three countries affected, due to border closures.[19] However, the maintenance of the designation was also used as a signal to maintain vigilance in the waning months of the outbreak:

Particularly at the end [of the epidemic]. Should we lift the PHEIC? At what stage should we lift the PHEIC? Particularly to reopen the doors for travel and trade. . . . But with respect to travel and trade it's always a big decision to declare a PHEIC. And in our case and you may recall we had a meeting just before the holidays, just before Christmas/New Year, and the epidemiological situation was pretty well improved then. And if we would have had to declare a new PHEIC at that stage, we probably would have decided no, that's not a PHEIC. But if you already have a PHEIC, it's a question of if you terminate a PHEIC, would then the people feel suddenly feel "OK then, it's no longer an important health problem"? No longer a public health concern of any value? And particularly with respect to the holidays, we decided just to keep it on because we had some concerns that otherwise many people in the three countries affected and elsewhere as well possibly would just go on a vacation and say, "OK now it's over, we don't need to deal with it." And so

if you may recall we continued with the PHEIC until early March. (Ebola
Committee Member 1)

In the case of the diminution of the Ebola threat, the risk of complacency
brought on in part from seasonal holidays prompted a longer PHEIC period than was necessarily medically required. While the medical threat
had diminished, it was the power of the designation itself that prolonged
a heightened state of vigilance toward the outbreak. Here we see the WHO
managing the anticipated behavioral and social responses to the diminution of threat, attempting to regulate action. It is at moments like this that
the domain of epidemiological knowledge of threat cannot be separated
from the social context for understanding that threat.

PHEIC and Its Economic Effects

A particularly challenging role for the emergency committee to navigate is
that of managing the economic effects of outbreak. Once again these economic effects are read through the extant discourses of epidemic Orientalism. A central consideration of a PHEIC designation is the potential risk
to trade and traffic of a particular threat. This can in and of itself produce
the designation. Historically, international epidemics have been economically disastrous for the nations affected, as other countries embargo products and institute travel bans prohibiting the movement of people.[20] These
effects compound the human devastation wrought by such events. While
the PHEIC provides a powerful signal to the global community to divert
resources to the outbreak, often this designation may also elicit trade and
border responses on the part of the WHO member nations. One of the
actions that the WHO may take upon designating a PHEIC is to instruct
nations to open or close borders. However, with no enforcement or sanctioning power, the WHO must leverage the power of the PHEIC effectively
so as to produce the most effective responses from their member nations.
This places the emergency committee members in a difficult position of
having to manage the concerns for the nations affected and the wider economic community while also anticipating the actions of other nations that
may act to secure their borders:

Yeah well you see, different countries react differently to PHEIC. I think . . . let me tell you where I am coming from. . . . I look at it as each country has a right to protect its own people if there is an epidemic going on somewhere else. And there is an initial reaction that I don't want to bring people in from somewhere else because that could become a problem in my country. . . . The country that cares about its people will want to do whatever it needs to do to ensure that nothing comes into the country. While the signs of it may not be right, the first reaction is exception: what is the easiest way of not getting diseases in my country? It's not to go where the disease is. So don't bring in people from there. And they have the facilities to quarantine or do whatever, but suppose those people escape my quarantine? So we must give in to the countries themselves. They have a right to first of all consider their people. That was the point I had to tell my colleagues there, that if we fail to do what is right and countries decide to do what they think is right for themselves, you can't blame them. If we discover we are not able to curb our epidemics and become international, then we must pay for whatever decision. This is a personal opinion. I know what the international organization [WHO] says, but at the same time I think we need to balance that. Countries have a right to protect themselves by whatever means they can. There are many international regulations that have been broken today. What is anybody doing about it? When you look at international regulations, there are also national concerns, and that's why I feel very strongly that before an issue becomes an international concern, countries themselves must look at it as if it is a national concern and do something about that. (MERS-CoV Member 1)

This particular issue, in attempting to anticipate the responses of nations to PHEICs, is made more complex by the lack of enforcement mechanisms in the IHR. Unlike the World Trade Organization and World Organization for Animal Health, which have significant sanction and enforcement mechanisms, the WHO relies on international pressure from its member nations and good faith to assert its recommendations. For this reason, the practice of navigating the effect of a PHEIC designation requires a complex calculus that mediates whether to declare a PHEIC:

Well, they [WHO] say the rules are that determines . . . for example, they talk about that if a foreign epidemic is going on in place, you should not ban travel, you should not ban commerce and industry. But then you remember, with animal diseases for example, if my country has the foot and mouth disease, and I'm exporting meat to your country, the rule also says I cannot, because you want to protect your own animal population. Therefore, that's why I think the OIE [World Organization for Animal Health] is a little more aggressive, more realistic than what the human side is talking about. If you have foot and mouth disease, you have rinderpest, you're automatically banned from exporting disease to another country. It's there in their regulations. Although you can't compare animals to humans, we are talking about similar economic things and things of that nature. And your cost by not doing your duty is exposing me to danger, and it's also an economic issue. (MERS-CoV Member 1)

This matter became central to the justifications to declare a PHEIC in response to Ebola in West Africa. However, the capacity of the WHO and the emergency committee to put pressure on nations implementing travel bans was limited:

And we have seen that particularly in the United States and also in Caribbean countries (and also some others by the way) where there was an overreaction, which had a negative impact on travel and trade. . . . That was certainly not helpful. Neither to the global community, nor to the persons involved, and particularly not to the three countries involved. As until now they do have some handicaps and they got stigmatized. . . . We had actually before and after the meeting [1st Ebola Emergency Committee Meeting] a prolonged discussion on how we should try to convince those nations to abandon the unnecessary and illogical measures. The problem was that very often these for instance small Caribbean nations would not even reply to requests of the WHO. And when the WHO sent more and more urging notes that they should immediately reply and they should immediately act—well, there was just no action. And that was truly frustrating. So some of us tried through personal connections to contact people in these nations to try and convince them, but very often we found out that there was just a basic fundamental nonscientific fear that Ebola could be introduced. (Ebola Committee Member 1).

This challenge of limiting the economic effects of epidemic is particularly acute for the WHO, an organization without the level of direct enforcement power of other global entities. Where the PHEIC designation for Ebola emerged in part to reduce the scale of the economic effects to the three affected West African nations, the outbreak continued to provoke trade and travel controls at ports of entry around the world.[21] The economic responses to the West African Ebola epidemic were also, as pointed out in the excerpt above, mobilized by a variety of Orientalist suppositions about the specter of an African Ebola epidemic reaching American shores. In this moment the PHEIC was also an instrument to counteract the epidemic Orientalism of the wider global community.

PHEIC as Global Signal

A final critical mode through which the power of a PHEIC operates, in addition to driving international resources, providing technical support and coordination, and issuing trade and travel advisories, is in the more ersatz realm as information disseminator and signaling. A PHEIC represents a marker to the global community that a major outbreak is occurring and that the world should take notice.[22] In many cases the convening of an emergency committee in and of itself attracts greater global interest to the outbreak and thereby conveys the seriousness of a threat. The importance of knowledge dissemination and the ability of the WHO to craft the narrative around the disease are critical to the future success and implementation of an effective response to a PHEIC. Both the declaration of a PHEIC and the convening of emergency committee meetings are critical tools that the WHO uses strategically to elicit support and coordinate responses to these outbreaks. Emergency committee members are acutely aware of the historical role that media and information plays in these outbreak scenarios:

Well, I think any time you can one of these events and make it known to the general public, then they feel interested. And I think that then facilitates, or makes it easier for governments to contribute funds and resources. Not just money but technical support as well. Now, that said, that was already in place before the press really got involved, but I think as it became more and more apparent that these were global issues of international importance and they were being talked about in the national press literally around the world, I think political leaders saw this. And I think part of this is why the Europeans actually got that much more involved, because they saw that they had resources they'd invested in their own scientific, technical capabilities. They wanted to be sure that they were participating in these outbreaks as well. And there is a long history of some scientific and medical centers collaborating on the research. The original discovery of Ebola, for example, was an international partnership as well. As these became more common knowledge to the general public and the politicians, it was easier for governments to play a larger role in supporting their institutions. (Ebola Committee Member 2)

In the case of the Zika microcephaly outbreak concentrated in South America, a disease for which there was at the time of the PHEIC designation very little knowledge, the effective dissemination of information by highlighting the threat proved a critical component of the response itself:

The WHO took immediate action compared to other epidemics we have had before. And I mean one thing is very little was known about Zika before, and the other thing is at least with the public, with those kinds of meetings we are creating public awareness, and that, I hope, helped a lot to keep the world alert of an impending epidemic, or rather pandemic. (Zika Microcephaly Committee Member 1)

In the deliberations over Ebola in West Africa, the role of the PHEIC in effectively driving awareness of the disease was both critical and unique to the disease itself. As it was both deadly and incurable at the time, a wide, accurate public understanding of how the virus spreads was central to effective health responses:

> Imagine if Ebola had spread into Nigeria. It would have been more disastrous. And I think the situation in Nigeria—let's look at it. While Nigeria did what was right, there was also the element of luck. The guy who brought Ebola into Nigeria actually fell sick at the airport: he collapsed at the airport and therefore was seen almost immediately on arrival. At that time when he came the hospitals were closed because they were on strike. And so he didn't go into a public hospital; he went to a private hospital. But when you look at what happened in the private hospital, we still had a risk of the hospital staff getting infected. When they saw that he was coming from an Ebola country, that proper steps be taken, not waiting three or four days before we began to suspect it was Ebola. So it is through that fear which we learned that a lot of African diseases follow the same pattern [as Ebola]. The first thing you think of is malaria fever and other diseases. So given that maybe the awareness or quick response to certain exotic or dangerous diseases have not been brought online, it was necessary to have a Public Health Emergency of International Concern so people's awareness would have gone up. And remember for Ebola we didn't have the vaccine, we didn't have a drug, so it would have been more difficult. If you're going to have epidemic spread, I suppose it's possible around the world. So I feel the emergency was justified. (Ebola Committee Member 3)

The power of the PHEIC as a signal to the global community to take notice, which focuses attention on the actions and expertise of the WHO, is a critical component of disease responses. The employment of the rhetorical power of both the PHEIC and emergency committee meetings ideally allows the WHO to construct and control the narrative and technical information about an outbreak, dismissing rumors or conjecture in exchange for a clarified message. As a result, the PHEIC designation and the process that forms it itself drastically affects the nature of the outbreak going forward.

The PHEIC designation is a classification of the highest international disease threat. Declared by the director-general of the WHO under the advisement of emergency committees established on a case-by-case basis, the PHEIC designation grants the WHO authority to manage and centrally coordinate outbreak responses between the nations affected, international organizations, and their member nations. It also provides greater authority for the WHO to make temporary recommendations on travel guidance and trade restrictions. These formal aspects of the PHEIC fit broadly within the mandate of the IHR to maximize the prevention of infectious disease across borders while minimizing the risks to trade and traffic.

However, beyond the explicit parameters of the PHEIC classification structure lies a far more complex matrix of decision making and concerns that operate in conjunction with any epidemiological knowledge of an outbreak. These structure the deliberations of WHO emergency committees and affect how PHEICs are themselves designated. The designation of a PHEIC, while acting as a powerful signal to the global community to respond to a universal risk, also has the power to limit and weaken responses, thereby affecting the epidemiological course of outbreak. In the case of the yellow fever outbreak located primarily in Angola and the Democratic Republic of Congo, the potential fallout of vaccine stockpiling driven by the increased threat level of a PHEIC would have made it more difficult to carry out effective health campaigns. Alternately, the de-escalation of the Ebola PHEIC designation provoked concern that a too-rapid decline in epidemiological vigilance could provoke a secondary outbreak. The economic effects of outbreaks may also be compounded or alleviated by the PHEIC designation. As the WHO has no major enforcement authority with respect to the IHR or the implementation of PHEIC recommendations, the manner which the emergency committee and director-general respond to the PHEIC designation produces significant effects on this aspect of epidemic control. Finally, the PHEIC can also be wielded deftly as a powerful signaling tool to the larger world, allowing for ease of resource acquisition to fight outbreaks while also coordinating the global message and technological knowledge about a disease. The PHEIC designation, given the authority it conveys to the WHO and the weight it holds on the global stage, often makes the negotiation of its effects on outbreak response unwieldy.

This constellation of secondary considerations surrounding the WHO's highest international threat designation shows the ways in which the spheres of the social, economic, and medical world are less distinct but rather co-constitutive of one another. The PHEIC designation is the most powerful tool in the WHO's arsenal for compelling the nations of the world to act in a manner it most desires. These modulate the classification of what is on its surface seen as an epidemiological decision presided over by public health experts. The fusing of health concerns with diplomatic and economic concerns is not novel in the history of infectious disease responses.[23] However, understanding the contours by which a disease meets the conditions of a PHEIC demonstrates the lingering interconnections that these factors play in the production of scientific consensus around outbreaks and how they govern global health action against potentially devastating epidemics.

Epilogue: COVID-19

This chapter has considered how and what forces affect the declaration of a PHEIC designation. PHEIC designations in their triggering, the timing of the declaration, as well as the nondesignation can have significant effects on epidemic responses as well as on the overall authority of the IHR and the WHO. In the response to the global COVID-19 pandemic, the WHO has faced its toughest epidemic challenge to date, which has threatened the organization and its activities in the space of epidemic infectious disease control to its core. At the center of the crisis emerging from the WHO has been a political feud between one of the WHO's largest funders, the United States, and one of its most emergent funders, China.

On December 30, 2019, several hospitals in Wuhan, China, held an emergency meeting regarding the treatment of patients exhibiting pneumonia with an unknown cause. A novel emergent coronavirus was suspected. While SARS, the epidemic disease first emerging in 2003, was feared to be the initial cause of the disease, by January 3, cases were increasing in China beyond Wuhan and travel screenings involving temperature checks were being employed in neighboring countries in the region.[24] By January 8 as 59 cases in Wuhan were being treated in hospital, 7 in critical condition, the virus we have come to know as SARS-CoV-2 (the causative agent of the illness

COVID-19) was isolated. While this was an extremely fast result, as little was known of the virus still in terms of severity or the process of transmission.

The WHO convened the first emergency committee meeting on what was then still called 2019-nCoV or novel coronavirus 2019. The first meeting, convened on January 23, did not yield a PHEIC declaration as the emergency committee diverged in their opinions on the matter. At the meeting the emergency committee received updates from the Ministry of Health of the People's Republic of China, Japan, Thailand, and the Republic of Korea.[25] At that point in time the Ministry of Health for China reported 557 confirmed cases with a fatality rate of 4 percent. At this meeting the WHO reported that the extent of human-to-human transmission remained unclear. The committee cautiously decided that it was too early to declare a PHEIC, though it provided a series of recommendations.

In the report on the meeting, the committee urged the support of ongoing investigations into the animal source of the disease as well as extended surveillance and screening efforts. In the statement from the emergency committee, concern was also expressed for the PHEIC designation system itself, suggesting an overall frustration with the strictures of the IHR (2005) deliberation system. In the statement from the meeting, a call was made for a more nuanced system of assessing threat. The binary nature of the PHEIC designation was at the root of this concern:

> In the face of an evolving epidemiological situation and the restrictive binary nature of declaring a PHEIC or not, WHO should consider a more nuanced system, which would allow an intermediate level of alert. Such a system would better reflect the severity of an outbreak, its impact, and the required measures, and would facilitate improved international coordination, including research efforts for developing medical counter measures.[26]

The statement makes clear a significant challenge to the PHEIC designation system itself, which is the problem of conveying significant authority over suggestions and responses beyond sounding the loudest alarm at the WHO's disposal. The need for an intermediate level of alert would in theory cohere the global community around a threat without necessarily having to declare it the greatest of threats. Without this option, the WHO was left providing recommendations but without a full PHEIC declaration after this first meeting.

The WHO recommended that the People's Republic of China actively collaborate on all levels with the WHO in the sharing of data on cases, genome sequences, and disease surveillance, and investigate the evolution of the outbreak. The WHO advised other countries to prepare for containment, active surveillance, and early detection systems to prevent the global spread of the disease.[27] The committee stopped short of advocating for travel restrictions to or from certain countries. The meeting, though closing without a PHEIC declaration, continued into a second day of discussions when the committee reached the same result.[28]

While the first meeting ended with a plan to reconvene in approximately ten days, the next emergency committee meeting was held on January 30, exactly a week after the first meeting. In the statement of the second meeting, the emergency committee noted the quick, strong, effective measures that China had taken to identify and control the virus that were "good for the country and good for the rest of the world" and "that the declaration of the PHEIC should be seen in the spirit of support and appreciation for China, its people, and the actions China has taken on the front lines of this outbreak, with transparency, and, it is to be hoped, with success."[29] As part of the recommendations under the PHEIC, which included the increase of scientific research collaboration and enhanced screening, contact tracing, and surveillance, the WHO again did not recommend any travel or trade restrictions.

At this point, as we arrive at the discussion of COVID-19, we can consider the ways in which these statements must be read in the context of the discourse of epidemic Orientalism, which, while long existent as the dominant discursive frame in infectious disease control, has been made much more visible during this ongoing pandemic. Within the recommendations under the PHEIC, the WHO cautioned explicitly against state actions that would promote stigma or discrimination. On January 30, the same day as the PHEIC declaration, the Danish newspaper *Jyllands-Posten*, noted for publishing controversial cartoon images of the prophet Mohammed, published an image of the Chinese flag with viruses in place of the yellow stars on the official state flag. Across the United States, United Kingdom, and Europe, anti-Asian violence and racist attacks had increased significantly since the beginning of the outbreak. By March, a Kansas county commissioner suggested that pandemic restrictions could be lessened because, unlike in what was at the time the epicenter of the pandemic, Italy, there were not a lot of Chinese people living in central Kansas, so there was less risk of disease spread.[30] While the WHO's statements of support and solidarity with China were aimed in no small part at heading off such racist and xenophobic sentiment, it was also an attempt to appease a growing contributor to the organization.

As we have seen in the last chapter, the battle over the authority and priorities of the WHO has been fought in no small part by the United States leveraging its weight as the largest national donor to the WHO. However, under the Trump administration and more broadly since the Reagan administration, US support for international organizations in terms of funding has decreased.[31] While China has not been one of the top donors to the WHO, its donations to the organization have been increasing, rising by 52 percent since 2014 to $86 million in 2019.[32] Conversely the US contributions were roughly $531 million in 2019.

More specifically, rising tensions between the United States and China provided President Trump with a convenient scapegoat to heap blame on as the world watched COVID-19 overwhelm the health system of the United States, becoming the epicenter of the pandemic. Since early in the epidemic, it was suggested widely by both the media and health experts alike that Chinese wet markets were to blame for the spread of the virus as the first case was said to be linked to that source. In addition the associations between mask wearing and homogenized *Asian* culture became a central element for online harassment and mocking, and may have had an effect on resistance to masking overall in the United States. In March 2020, on Twitter and in his daily press briefings on the pandemic, President Trump began referring to COVID-19 as the "Chinese virus." President Trump first tweeted the stigmatizing term on March 16, 2020. Recent research of the effects of the president's tweets describing the disease in these terms have demonstrated that Trump's actions led to a robust increase in anti-Asian Twitter hashtag use.[33]

While the previous president and his administration's use of derogatory language and resistance to practices like social distancing, school and business closures, and masking had a devastating effect on the COVID-19 response in the United States, the president leveraged the WHO's support of China's response to call for the halt of support and ultimate withdrawal of the United States from the WHO altogether. On May 29, 2020, while the COVID-19 epidemic in the United States continued to rise with record daily infections and deaths, the president announced that the United States would leave the WHO and "redirect funds to US global health priorities."[34] This was a move that would isolate the country from global vaccine distributions as well as disease surveillance information. Much like the challenges raised by the United States to the WHO in the twentieth century, the president's justification for this decision was that the WHO failed to make the reforms recommended and required, while accusing the WHO of being too wedded to the goals and objectives of China. At the center of the president's justification was the slow action of the WHO to contain the pandemic, including what was perceived as a hesitance to declare a PHEIC.[35]

While the threat by the United States to leave the WHO was perhaps the most devastating outcome of IHR deliberation and action with regard to pandemic response, the securing of relations between the United States and WHO would ultimately be a significant policy platform in the 2020 presidential election and a campaign rallying cry of then candidate Joe Biden.[36] Almost exactly a year to the day of the first SARS CoV-2 Emergency Committee meeting, President Biden rededicated the United States to the WHO.

Like the response to Ebola virus disease in West Africa, the COVID-19 response by the WHO and the subsequent contestations regarding the WHO's actions have led to a review of their emergency response by the Independent Oversight and Advisory Committee for the WHO Health Emergencies Programme (IOAC). While clearly the coordinated response by the WHO lacked the resources and political support to contain and control COVID-19, the failure of the IHR in particular has led to the formal call for its revision. In the IOAC statement to the World Health Assembly in May 2021, the committee called attention to the primary role of member states in "preparing for, and responding to, outbreaks and emergencies."[37] While the report applauded the WHO's increase in emergency operations and the joint coordination of global vaccination delivery through COVAX,[38] the statement also reflected on the critical issue that the WHO lacks the funding to adequately respond to all of the tasks required of it in emergency response.

A large component of the committee's statement was reserved for the reform of the IHR and in particular the reform of the PHEIC designation structure. A year earlier, the 73rd World Health Assembly called for a comprehensive review and revision of the IHR in light of the COVID-19 pandemic.[39] The reservation of the SARS CoV-2 Emergency Committee that reflected the unwieldy nature of a binary PHEIC designation remain a critical point of concern. The IOAC reflected that, as a mechanism, it provides little operable indication for action on the part of member states while also being vague in terms of scale of an emergency. The broad design of the PHEIC designation presents unique challenges, as it must cover anything from regional epidemics such as Ebola virus disease in West Africa to a pandemic on the scale of COVID-19.[40] A May 2021 report from an IHR review committee, presented to the 75th World Health Assembly, calls for a full review of the PHEIC designation structure while calling for an intermediate tier of alert that would raise awareness and proportional assessment of risk.[41] The report, however, hastens to add that this secondary alert structure might provoke further confusion.

At the core of the current issues raised by the ongoing revisions of the IHR in light of COVID-19 are many of the same more intangible concerns that have been persistent themes across their history: the need to coerce and compel member nations to act, the surveillance of populations at the sites of outbreak, and the navigation of national sovereignty. The overall responsibility for implementing the IHR remains with state actors, and very few nations have complied with the IHR mandate to increase national preparedness since 2005. The sovereignty over disease surveillance information as well as the application of remote sanitary controls on foreign spaces has been a consistent challenge for the WHO since its instantiation. Under the global world system of empire, as shown in Chapter 2, the response to epidemics capable of threatening global trade and traffic were managed within colonial sites in often violent and aggressive ways, limiting their spread to Europe. The IHR retain in so many ways this implicit assumption that responses can be remotely dictated. In the absence of this colonial power, however, this lacuna in the management of infectious disease remains a point of contention between the WHO and the member nations of the World Health Assembly. The IHR is currently being comprehensively reviewed. As seen throughout this book, these revisions can take many years, if not decades. An effective future IHR must attempt to both confront and rid itself of the shackles of its imperial mindset and its epidemic Orientalism.

6 PRICING PANDEMICS

IN THIS CHAPTER WE DEPART FROM the World Health Organization and the International Health Regulations (IHR) altogether to explore how logics of epidemic Orientalism operate or change in other contexts. This chapter explores how rationalities of the world of finance and insurance modulate the perceptions of risk in international infectious disease control. This chapter encounters a linked but also different discourse of infectious disease control, located both in histories of epidemic response but also in legacies of slavery and the appraisal of financial value in human form. I call this particular discursive formation *necrofinance*: the recognition and appraisal of disease risk in terms of quantifiable human value in death and life. If epidemic Orientalism is marked by notions of Western difference, non-Western threat, modernist conceptions of progress, and racialized forms of control, then necrofinance reflects a particular mode through which we can see these aspects link epidemics, economic risk, and complex financial risk mitigation products. These are not exclusively the same projects, though it should become clear how epidemic Orientalism and necrofinance engage from similar discursive positions. While the IHR exist to manage threat and control spread, as we consider the domain of infectious disease control after COVID-19 and its economic upheaval, market-based approaches to disease control may continue to develop.

In the Pandemic Emergency Financing Facility (PEF), a program at least temporarily consigned to the dustbin of global health interventions, we find an attempt by the juggernaut of international development, the World Bank, to enter the space of pandemic response. Seeing the weakness of the IHR to sufficiently finance epidemic responses, the World Bank attempted to implement a financial instrument that would pay out a certain amount of aid support to nations afflicted by certain epidemics once certain markers of epidemic spread were met—primarily the numbers of cases and deaths. This financing facility sought to create a market for pandemic risk speculation by issuing bonds to sophisticated private investors, which, if certain criteria were met, would be paid out to nations afflicted by epidemic. In the event that they did not, they would provide returns for investors.

An Ebola Epidemic in the Shadow of Another

The global response to the West African Ebola epidemic of 2014–2016 was roundly criticized by global health actors and the media alike.[1] Much of the blame was levied on the World Health Organization for their hesitation to declare a Public Health Emergency of International Concern (PHEIC) and their incapacity to respond to the epidemic with fully funded responses. However, this funding shortfall could not be blamed on the WHO's agencies or secretariat. In April 2014, a month after the epidemic was first reported, the WHO requested $4.8 million from international governments and aid agencies. By November that call would rise to $1.5 billion and $4 billion by January 2015.[2] However, the Report of the Ebola Interim Assessment Panel drafted by a group of independent experts determined that the WHO was financially hobbled from the outset and continues to lack the capacity to effectively respond to health emergencies.[3] While the passing of the IHR (2005) was meant to equip the WHO with the financial authority necessary to respond to epidemic events as well as voluntarily strengthen health system capacity around the world, the organization was falling short, and not always as a result of its own weaknesses. The interim panel found that less than 25 percent of WHO's budget derives from required, assessed contributions from member states of the World Health Assembly and that the rest had to be made up from voluntary donations,[4] making it a weak entity to functionally respond to an epidemic emergency. The organization's funding dilemma was reflected in massive shortfalls of funding for the WHO to disburse to health agencies and governmental bodies in Liberia, Guinea, and Sierra Leone. Between April 2014 and January 2015, only 40 percent of the pledged $2.9 billion had been disbursed to West Africa.[5] By October 31, 2015, of the $8.9 billion pledged to the WHO for Ebola response, only $5.9 billion had been delivered, reflecting a total disbursement of 66 percent of total pledged funds.[6] While the WHO had acted too slowly to declare a PHEIC, it was also structurally ill equipped to manage the response. Though the interim panel would ultimately call for the strengthening of the WHO's epidemic response capacity after the outbreak had largely subsided,[7] a new actor who had previously provided health support in the form of lending and had donated $200 million to the Ebola response in Liberia as of December 2014 was already mobilizing to become a central force in defining epidemic emergency and determining response: the World Bank.

On October 10, 2014, the World Bank Group president put out a press release calling for a new PEF:

The world has an IMF to coordinate and work with central banks and ministries to respond to financial crises. . . . When it comes to health emergencies, however, our institutional toolbox is empty: There's no such center of knowledge and skill for response and coordination. . . . Also, until very recently, the plans to fight them [epidemics] were either non-existent or inadequate. And, inaction is literally killing people—one because of the rapid spread of a deadly virus, the other from the poisoning of the atmosphere and the oceans. And finally, perhaps most critically from our point of view, resolving these problems is essential to development, whether from the perspective of human suffering, economic growth, or public health. . . . We must maintain this commitment because increasing global fragility and volatility will challenge us more and more every day. In our march to end extreme poverty—conflict, typhoons, floods, droughts, financial shocks and epidemics may, at times, slow us. But they will not stop us. The Bank will be aggressive and creative and apply large-scale solutions to help states manage, prepare for, recover from and conquer these risks, so they can grow and flourish.[8]

While the Ebola Interim Assessment Panel called for greater funding for the WHO to tackle epidemic emergencies and for the organization to have greater authority in this regard overall, the support for a formal epidemic response system headed by the World Bank was gaining support within the international community. At the 2015 G7 annual meeting at Schloss Elmau in Germany, the ongoing Ebola epidemic in West Africa was a key topic, and the members roundly endorsed the development of a PEF to be organized by the World Bank.[9]

On May 21, 2016, the World Bank announced the development of the first-ever PEF to prevent the worst humanitarian and economic effects of epidemic emergencies.[10] The PEF is a twofold structure: a cash window that can pay out up to $50 million to support early response to escalating epidemic crises, and a much larger insurance window that provides up to $425 million to afflicted countries,[11] aid agencies, and nongovernmental organizations (NGOs) to facilitate support. This novel funding strategy was designed to limit the deadly delays and false promises of country pledges to support epidemic response and provide swift funding within a matter of days. The head of derivatives and structured finance for the World Bank's Capital Markets Department, Michael Bennett, stated that "if the pandemic emergency financing facility (PEF) had existed in 2014, some $100 million could have been mobilized as early as July."[12] However, when faced with the 2018–2019 Ebola epidemic in the Democratic Republic of Congo, the largest set of funds, the potential $425 million contributed nothing to the effort to control the spread of the disease. Though the WHO declared a PHEIC in July 2019, as of September, the World Bank had contributed $50 million from the PEF cash window and an additional $100 million from the World Bank's International Development Association.[13] It has only been during the recent pandemic of COVID-19 that the bulk of the PEF's funds have been disbursed, contributing $195.84 million to COVID-19 interventions in April 2020, three months after the start of the global pandemic. How does the largest funded epidemic response facility in the world, designed in the shadow of an Ebola epidemic, fail to pay out for another while operating too slowly for meaningful change during the largest pandemic of the twenty-first century?

The Roots of Pandemic Speculation: Catastrophe Bonds

When the World Bank launched their PEF, they ushered in a new modality for apprehending disease risk. For the first time the risk of disease spread could be appraised in explicitly financial terms. The World Bank created a market for speculating on the probability of pandemic events. As such the speculation on epidemic risk has now been infused and incorporated into all corners of the global economy.

The Pandemic Emergency Financing Facility Insurance Window operates through a mechanism that the World Bank has colloquially named a "pandemic bond." A pandemic bond is a mutation of a catastrophe bond, which is a financial instrument to protect insurance companies and reinsurers from the risk of default in the event of an acute major catastrophe. Historically, when insurance companies that insure property have purchased insurance for the insurance company itself, they do so to offset the risk of default or insolvency from the possibility of having such a high number of costly claims at once that they cannot afford to pay out with their existing funds. While traditionally insurance companies derive the funds to cover insurance claims from the collection of premiums from clients and disburse them accordingly, it is possible that a claim or multiple claims are too large to be covered by the accrued collected premiums. For this reason an insurance company will purchase insurance to offset this risk and provide additional funds to cover their losses and keep the company solvent.

However, what happens in the event of a loss being so great that even the reinsurance agent cannot cover the losses? This question was answered in the first early hints of the devastating effects of cataclysmic events linked to climate change: Hurricane Andrew. The category 5 storm would produce insurance claims payouts totaling $15.5 billion in 1992 prices, but models had suggested the insured losses would only total $4–5 billion at most.[14] This event led to numerous insurer and reinsurer insolvencies.[15] In the aftermath of the climate and humanitarian catastrophe that precipitated a corporate one, the catastrophe bond was born.

A catastrophe bond operates in effect as a hedge against loss, an insurance for reinsurers against high payouts from catastrophic claims. It is an insurance swap. A bond fundamentally is an instrument by which a company (or nation) can sell debt in exchange for immediate funds. The issuer of the bond essentially is a borrower who owes the holder of the bond (the creditor) the price of the bond (the principal) plus interest in the form of a regularly paid coupon until the maturity date (typically three years) when the bond is paid off. A special purpose entity, a subsidiary, is created by the sponsor of the bond (either an insurance or more commonly a reinsurance company) to pool (securitize) debt separately from the parent company so investors can be assured of repayment without the risk of those funds being used for the daily activities of the company. When a sponsor wishes to sell its insurance risk, the special purpose vehicle issues a catastrophe bond, which is purchased by an investor at the face value price of the bond (the principal). The proceeds from this sale are held in the collateral account of the special purpose vehicle. The coupons (interest payments) on the bond are paid by the sponsor into the special purpose entity's account, where it is then disbursed to the investor at regular intervals. To cover the effects of inflation over time to the maturity of the bond, the funds in the collateral account are usually invested in some sort of low-risk Treasury money market fund.[16] In the event of a catastrophe predefined prior to the issuance of bonds between the sponsor and investor, the bond is triggered, a portion or all (depending on the severity of the catastrophe) is liquidated and delivered to the sponsor to cover their losses. If the bond reaches maturity without it being triggered, the funds held in the collateral account return to the investor.

What a catastrophe bond achieves, which was not possible prior to their development, is the transference of insurance risk out of the hands and accounts of a reinsurance company to capital markets. The argument for their existence is that acute natural disasters and catastrophes represent the possibility for losses far greater than the financial capacity of the greater insurance market, but that those are relatively small compared to the financing available from the wider global financial markets.[17] In exchange, investors normally receive higher than usual interest rate payments on the bond, as the risk of

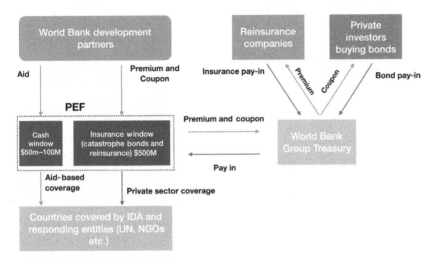

FIGURE 8: The Pandemic Emergency Financing Facility.

Source: Felix Stein and Devi Sridhar, "Health as a 'Global Public Good': Creating a Market for Pandemic Risk," BMJ 358 (August 31, 2017): j3397, https://doi.org/10.1136/bmj.j3397.

losing the principal is greater than most bonds. Most bonds or long-term debt-based instruments usually pay out according to capital market indices or national interest rates, which rise and fall according to market growth or decline. However, as natural disasters are wholly uncorrelated with movements in the market, these bonds represent a way to diversify risk within larger portfolios with assets invested across global capital markets. As such, catastrophe bonds have been very popular with mutual and pension funds as a risk abatement measure. The outstanding market for catastrophe bonds sat at $39.3 billion as of the end of the second quarter of 2019.[18]

The high demand for these bonds, from both the desire for a risk abatement strategy for insurance and reinsurance companies and the potentially high returns to be gained from this risky investment, has produced a secondary market for catastrophe risk modeling data and information in order to effectively price the bonds and determine interest rates, as well as predict potential environmental disasters.[19] This has generated a boutique industry for catastrophe modeling companies who attempt to predict the potential financial exposure to these sorts of risks.

In addition to providing risk abatement opportunities for corporate enti-ties like reinsurance companies, novel catastrophe instruments have been developed to protect sovereign risk for countries seeking to rebuild in the aftermath of disaster and gain access to insurance through capital markets in cases of emergency where their national coffers may not be able to cover the costs. Operating as the special purpose entity and intermediary between the International Bank for Reconstruction and Development's[20] (IBRD) mem-ber nations and investors, the largest issuer for sovereign catastrophe bonds (as they are known) is the World Bank. As of 2019 the bank has facilitated roughly $4 billion of catastrophe bond risk transactions.

Catastrophe bonds and sovereign catastrophe bonds have been very suc-cessful in distributing the risk of environmental disaster from the insurance company or nation to the much larger world of capital markets. Catastrophe bonds and to a lesser extent insurance more broadly allows for environmental disaster to be seen and subsequently appraised in financial terms. The dev-astation of a hurricane can be realized through the risk exposure a nation or insurer understands through property loss in monetary terms. Devastation can be financially quantified and subsequently indemnified against that loss. Likewise a nation can be indemnified against not only property loss but also the lost productivity of the economy and slowing of economic growth as a result of an environmental disaster. The World Bank can provide support to get factories, markets, and commerce back online. However, in the case of epidemics, how is loss quantified, what is the risk, and what constitutes an epidemic worthy of triggering the bond have all been reimagined.

The Pandemic Emergency Financing Facility

As figure 8 demonstrates, the structure of the PEF is similar to standard catastrophe bonds. However, they differ in some important ways. The PEF is more complex than the standard model of catastrophe bond. As shown in figure 8, the PEF is made up of a cash window and an insurance window. The cash window is supported by aid donations from World Bank Group development partners, namely, the governments of Japan and Germany. The cash window provides supplemental financing and can be distributed in advance of the activation criteria being met.[21]

TABLE 6: Pandemic Emergency Financing Facility Operations Manual

Coronavirus maximum coverage: $195.83m	Pay-in based on: Aggregate number of confirmed deaths within IBRD/IDA countries		
	At 250	At 750	At 2,500
Regional (outbreaks affecting 2 to 7 countries)	29% (US$56.25m)	57% (US$112.5m)	100% (US$195.83m)
Global (outbreaks affecting 8 or more countries)	34% (US$65.63m)	67% (US$131.25m)	100% (US$195.83m)
Filoviridae maximum coverage: US $150m	Pay-in based on: Aggregate number of confirmed deaths within IBRD/IDA countries		
	At 250	At 750	At 2,500
Regional (outbreaks affecting 2 to 7 countries)	30% (US$45m)	60% (US$90m)	100% (US$150m)
Global (outbreaks affecting 8 or more countries)	35% (US$52.5m)	70% (US$105m)	100% (US$150m)
Other diseases (Rift Valley, Lassa fever, Crimean Congo) Maximum coverage: $75m	Pay-in based on: Aggregate number of confirmed deaths within IBRD/IDA countries		
	At 250	At 750	At 2,500
Regional (outbreaks affecting 2 to 7 countries)	30% (US$22.5m)	60% (US$45m)	100% (US$75m)
Global (outbreaks affecting 8 or more countries)	35% (US$26.25m)	70% (US$52.5m)	100% (US$75m)

Source: Pandemic Emergency Financing Facility Steering Body, "Pandemic Emergency Financing Facility Operations Manual."

The insurance window represents the more traditional aspect of a catastrophe bond. It provides coverage to nations suffering from an epidemic and support for NGOs operating in response to the outbreak up to $500 million through two primary methods, bond and swap issuances of a period of three years (2017–2020 for the initial issuance).[22] The insurance window is funded through two mechanisms, reinsurance entities who collateralize the risk of these bonds through reinsurance and a pandemic bond issued by the World Bank Treasury.

Where standard catastrophe bonds and the PEF differ are in the nature of the criteria used to activate the swaps and payouts on the bond. While traditional catastrophe bonds shift the risk of massive insurance payouts due to cataclysmic property damage to capital markets, the PEF seeks to shift the risk of mass death, the macroeconomic costs of epidemic disaster, and the costs of disease response from foreign aid and country pledges to capital markets. As such, rather than property damage, the "activation" criteria for the PEF is measured in cases and deaths over a certain period and geographies.

The Calculus of Pandemic Risk

When the World Bank set out to develop the PEF, they worked with parties that were well versed in how to bring this form of risk to market. Swiss Re and Munich Re, two of the largest reinsurance firms in the world, underwrote the bonds for the PEF and served as the book runner, coordinating the issuance of the bonds. Swiss Re has developed mortality catastrophe bonds in the past,[23] which, similarly to the PEF, are designed to offset the risk of massive loss of life, in this case to collateralize life insurance risk. Swiss Re had previously developed two similar bond products to hedge against the risk of mass death for life insurance companies. These bonds were triggered based on a certain aberration in mortality rates within an age- and gender-weighted population, which breaks the bounds of the expected parameters for the life insurance policies within the portfolio.[24]

However, for the PEF, the World Bank needed to develop a new set of parameters to assess the scale of an epidemic and the conditions under which a pandemic catastrophe bond might trigger. For this they turned to AIR Worldwide, a catastrophic risk modeling firm that provides consultation services on the financial and economic risks associated with cataclysm. Central to their operations has been the quantification of pandemic risk based on a variety of deterministic and stochastic models.[25] AIR Worldwide was brought in to model outbreaks and establish parameters for the triggering of the PEF bond.

What AIR Worldwide produced was a probabilistic simulation model known as the AIR Pandemic Model, which "generates potential infectious disease outbreak events in accordance with their estimated relative probability of occurrence."[26] For the PEF, AIR Worldwide captured the potential loss of life and financial risks associated with major global outbreaks of influenza, coronaviruses such as severe acute respiratory syndrome (SARS) and Middle East respiratory syndrome (MERS), filoviruses (Ebola virus disease, Marburg virus), cholera, Rift Valley fever, Crimean Congo hemorrhagic fever, bubonic plague, Lassa fever, and meningitis.[27] The AIR Worldwide model is complex, drawing on numerous sources both historical and contemporary as well as passenger travel data, migratory bird data, and land use data to simulate 500,000 years and over 1 million pandemic events. From this catalog of simulated pandemics, Swiss Re and Munich Re's experience with underwriting catastrophe-linked bonds, and the World Bank's role as a market maker, the four institutions in conjunction with the WHO created the PEF and produced two novel bond offerings.

The Class A Floating Rate Catastrophe-Linked Capital at Risk Notes (Class A Notes) is the first and largest pandemic bond available. It has an aggregate nominal amount of $225 million and was issued in minimum denominations of $250,000. These Class A Notes cover risks associated with epidemics of influenza exclusively. A second smaller bond, the Class B Floating Rate Catastrophe-Linked Capital at Risk Notes (Class B Notes), has an aggregate nominal amount of $95 million and can likewise be purchased in minimum denominations of $250,000. The Class B Notes cover the risks associated with coronaviruses, filoviruses, Lassa fever, Rift Valley fever, and Crimean Congo hemorrhagic fever. These bonds were issued in 2017 and matured in 2020.

The triggering mechanism for these bonds is complex, and the bonds are separated out into two classes as they reflect two different categories of risk (See Table 6). A number of events must occur in order to trigger the bond. First, an event would have to be designated by the WHO, which acts as the reporting source. An event is any case of the covered diseases as reported by the WHO. When an eligible event occurs, the IBRD provides a written notice to AIR Worldwide, the event calculation agent, which assesses whether the event has exceeded the parameters necessary to trigger the bond. For the Class A Notes for Flu, to trigger the bond-swap the following Activation Criteria must be met:

(a) There must be at least 5,000 confirmed cases (counted from all countries worldwide) within a rolling 42-day period. For these cases, the virus needs to satisfy the following conditions:

   i. WHO Report states that such Virus is an influenza A virus (either through a statement or by denoting such influenza Virus with an "A" prior to its genetic subtype);

   ii. Such WHO Report states either:

- influenza A virus is a new or novel influenza A virus with a new or novel genetic subtype, and no Case of or Death relating to such influenza A virus has been reported in any WHO Report published prior to July 2017; or

- that such influenza A virus is an influenza A virus whose hemagglutinin gene is antigenically distinct, due to an antigenic shift, from those in seasonal influenza viruses circulating in the 35 years prior to July 2017; and

   iii. Such WHO Report states that the influenza A virus is experiencing sustained or effective human-to-human transmission.

(b) The Growth Rate needs to be greater than zero after the first 42 days and the Growth Rate Mean needs to be greater than or equal to 0.265, for any day after the first 42 days.[28]

Once these criteria are met and confirmed by the external reporting agent (WHO) and the event calculation agent (AIR Worldwide), 100 percent of the total $275 million, which includes the full $225 million of Class A Notes plus an additional $50 million in reinsurance swaps, will be released for delivery to the nations affected and collaborating NGOs. These funds, and those of the Class B Notes, are available to any of the International Development Association (IDA) borrowing countries.

However, for the Class B Notes, the criteria for releasing the funds are somewhat different. While the process of event reporting is ultimately the same, the funds are paid out in tranches reflecting different activation criteria for each covered disease. The total funds disbursed, including pandemic bond and insurance payouts, are differentiated by disease. Filovirus epidemics can receive $150 million, coronaviruses receive $195.83 million, and all other diseases are capped at $75 million.[29] For non-flu-related events, twelve weeks must transpire from the date of the event to the date of fund release. Further, the outbreak has to be in more than one country, with each nation having greater than or equal to twenty confirmed deaths. In addition:

(f) The Growth Rate needs to be greater than zero to ensure that the outbreak is growing at a specific statistical confidence level

(g) The Total Confirmed Death Amount needs to be greater than or equal to 250

(h) The Rolling Total Case Amount needs to be greater than or equal to 250

(i) The Rolling Confirmed Case Amount needs to comprise a minimum percentage of the Rolling Total Case Amount[30]

Further dispensations are made to specify the relative severity and concomitantly differentiate the pay-out amount between "regional" and "global" events. Regional outbreaks affecting two to seven nations activate payout amounts in three tranches, but global outbreaks that affect more than eight countries provide higher funding levels at the earlier two triggers.[31]

When these notes were listed and then purchased via the Luxembourg Stock Exchange, they created the first market for epidemic risk, potentially diffusing some or all of the financial costs for epidemic response and economic losses to capital markets. And capital markets were overwhelmingly receptive. In order to reflect the risk of holding one of these bonds, and for bond holders to receive the maximum returns on the risk of holding these bonds, the coupons provide an annual return of 6.5 percent over the six-month US LIBOR[32] for the pandemic influenza Class A Notes and 11.1 percent over US LIBOR for the Class B Notes.[33] These returns are on average much higher than most traditional bonds and many catastrophe bonds. As a result the appetite for these bonds on the market was significant, and the bond issue was oversubscribed by 200 percent, meaning that twice the number of bonds were requested as were available.[34] The market for these bonds lay largely with dedicated bond investors for the Class A Notes, while a plurality of the Class B Notes were purchased by pension funds. This signals that these products have been widely diffused across and into the global financial

TABLE 7: IBRD Pandemic Bonds Distribution by Investor Type and Location

Distribution by investor type	Class A	Class B
Dedicated catastrophe bond investor	61.70%	35.30%
Endowment	3.30%	6.30%
Asset manager	20.60%	16.30%
Pension fund	14.40%	42.10%
Distribution by investor location	Class A	Class B
US	27.90%	15.00%
Europe	71.80%	82.90%
Bermuda	0.10%	2.10%
Japan	0.20%	0.00%

Source: World Bank, "World Bank Launches First-Ever Pandemic Bonds to Support $500 Million Pandemic Emergency Financing Facility," June 28, 2017, http://www.worldbank.org/en/news/ press-release/2017/06/28/world-bank-launches-first-ever-pandemic-bonds-to-support-500 -million-pandemic-emergency-financing-facility

network and are intertwined in the lives of everyday people from around the world within pension and retirement portfolios. Overwhelmingly the bulk of these notes have been purchased by investors in the United States and Europe. The bonds did not pay out to the Democratic Republic of Congo, which was suffering the second largest Ebola virus epidemic in history. This epidemic, though it existed within a country the size of Western Europe, has not crossed a national border and as such has not triggered an activation event. It was only after the mandated twelve weeks had passed from the start of the COVID-19 epidemic that the PEF finally paid out $195.84 million from its Class B Notes. By this point this fund was far smaller than the disbursements that had already been released around the world in response to the COVID-19 pandemic.

Future Possibilities for the PEF

The PEF has been roundly criticized for the criteria established for activation.[35] The primary critiques of the PEF lie in the opaque and stringent activation criteria that are too constricted to provide funds when needed[36] and that the facility has effectively found an avenue to pay private investors with public funds, primarily coming from Germany, Japan, and the World Bank.[37] To attend to this, any future bonds, while not anticipated, will require looser activation criteria and perhaps remove the multicountry requirement for the Class B Notes. This would, however, almost certainly increase the riskiness of these bonds, which would invariably increase the coupon rate and annual returns for investors to accommodate for an increased risk tolerance. The former concern thus compounds the latter issue of support for private investor speculation with public funds. By supporting the PEF with funds from the World Bank and notably Germany and Japan, the facility diverts funds that could otherwise be directly contributed to aid agencies or health sector strengthening in "lower-income countries" toward speculation on mortality derived from a small group of infectious diseases. A report produced by Swiss Re prior to the formal release of the PEF suggests that in the next bond offerings, the overall scope of the PEF could be increased to accommodate more diseases and open the fund to more countries beyond the initial IDA borrower nations:

In its first three-year phase (Figure 3), G7 donor countries will provide premium support to the World Bank, allowing the PEF to purchase insurance coverage on behalf of the developing countries (defined as the 77 countries currently eligible for World Bank International Development Assistance) to cover the costs of containing disease outbreaks. This phase will cover four main disease classifications: Filovirus, coronavirus (including SARS/MERS), ADOM, and pandemic influenza (i.e. severe multi-country outbreaks of non-seasonal flu). Subsequent phases will attempt to expand the facility to cover more countries (with middle-income countries paying at least a portion of their own premiums) and additional disease classifications as modeling capabilities improve. In order to maximize the effectiveness of the PEF and ensure that it most effectively provides the basis for the development of a mature pandemic insurance market, it is necessary to examine the evolving landscape of pandemic risk.[38]

As disease surveillance and modeling improves over time, it will enable the insurance market to expand to cover a wider spread of disease outbreak risks. Currently, the PEF will cover most of the diseases that the WHO identified as in need of "urgent action" in December 2015. In the future, the PEF could expand to cover Nipah virus (NiV), which is a member of the family Paramyxoviridae, genus *Henipavirus*, which is also on the list of diseases needing urgent attention. It could also expand to cover chikungunya, severe fever with thrombocytopenia syndrome and Zika, which were listed as serious diseases "necessitating further action" as well. Once the dynamics of how these diseases spread and how much cash would be needed to address them are understood, reinsurance companies like Swiss Re will be able to include them in their coverage.[39]

If a mature market for pandemic were to develop the market for pandemic risk, public funds devoted to the provision of investor returns would increase and likely reshape a large swath of health financing.

A Transformation in Logics of Response

In the PEF we see a transformation in how epidemic threat is quantified, how those suffering are constituted and realized in the responses to epidemic. Prior to the PEF and explicitly under the logics of the IHR (which are still in operation), the designation of a PHEIC was a gesture of symbolic power that an event will require the global community to act—in the aid world, the equivalent of a call to arms. However, the glaring weaknesses in the West African Ebola virus disease response exposed the limits of the PHEIC and the reliance on global charity. Rather than devoting significant funds to health system development or holistic strategies of epidemic prevention, the World Bank sought to find a solution in the domain of finance and capital market speculation. In doing so, it produced a novel form of global finance, one for which the lives of populations can be abstracted to financial value and risk.

Necrofinance

Achille Mbembe first articulated the concept of *necropolitics* to define how the departure of contemporary forms of subjugation differ from those demonstrated by the Foucauldian notion of biopolitics.[40] Mbembe deploys necropolitics and necropower to account for the various ways in which, in our contemporary world, weapons are deployed in the interest of maximum destruction of persons and the creation of death-worlds, new and unique forms of social existence in which vast populations are subjected to conditions of life conferring upon them the status of living dead.[41]

Reengaging the concepts of biopower through a consideration of colonial violences and the plantation, Mbembe produced one of the most profound treatises of political theory of the twenty-first century. Mbembe challenges and rearticulates the role of sovereignty in biopolitical action as the capacity to define who matters and who does not, and thereby who is "disposable" and who is not.[42] This turn in the definition of sovereignty posits important questions of the concept of biopolitics. If the sovereign in Foucault's articulation is those who have the authority to kill or let live, Mbembe's concept broadens to engage sovereignty formally as the ability to impose death as a limit to freedom and subject formation (as opposed to liberal notions of citizenship, rights etc.)—in effect the sovereign production of the *living dead* whose conditions of life are predicated on their "subjugation of life to the power of death."[43]

While I do not want to suggest that the dynamics of the PEF function as a necropolitical order, necropolitics as a concept is critical for theorizing the affective worldview manifested by the PEF. The similarities between what I term *necrofinance* and Mbembe's *necropolitics* lie most substantively in how the PEF reconstitutes the nature of subjects living under an epidemic through particular logics of financial speculation as well as how this has shifted the constitution of epidemic response through discourses of financial analysis. I thus lean heavily on the definitions of necropolitics to derive my own definition for necrofinance.

In the formulation of the PEF, we have an expression of financial power: necrofinance, the capacity to speculate on the lives and deaths of others in order to dictate who may live and who may die. Necrofinance is the speculative logic through which economic value is conferred in life and loss in death, abstracted from the lived experience of those who perish. Central to necrofinancial systems is the reconstitution of human life into quantifiable metrics for the purposes of speculation. Where necropolitics examines the production of the necropolitical order of things through the question of sovereignty, I expand on the concept of commodity fetishism to explore how the PEF produces novel subjects for financial speculation.

An undertheorized aspect of scholarship on political economy is the role of financial instruments to constitute subjects.[44] Baudrillard identified the concept of commodity fetishism in Marx's *Capital* as the lived ideology of capitalist society: the moment when "the capitalist system denies, abstracts and 'alienates.'"[45]

> Thus the fetishization of the commodity is the fetishization of a product emptied of its concrete substance of labor and subjected to another type of labor, a labor of signification, that is, of coded abstraction (the production of differences and sign-values). It is an active collective process of production and reproduction of a code, a system, invested with all the diverted, unbound desire separated out from the process of real labor and transferred onto precisely that which denies the process of real labor. Thus fetishism is actually attached to the sign object, the object eviscerated of its substance and history, and reduced to the state of marking a difference, epitomizing a whole system of differences.[46]

In Baudrillard's semiotic conception of commodity fetishism, the commodity is emptied of its material relationship to the labor of its production and subjected to signification in which commodity becomes invested in the meanings and concepts brought on by their *exchange-value* or price, their value at market, and divested of any meaning that would have previously existed that constituted its "substance and history." Matory critiques Marx for alienating enslaved Black people almost entirely from their labor and role in the making of modern Europe by elevating the European factory worker as the agent of economic history par-excellence. In doing so we lose the ways in which financial speculation and the pricing of humans has been a formative part of the making of markets. Crucially we also ignore the vital ways in which the quantification of lives and deaths of people have been processed through economic lenses. Scholars of economic history and of slavery have demonstrated that indemnification against the financial risk of lives lost during the Middle Passage of the transatlantic slave trade and the development of insurance pricing methods were critical to the expansion of the transatlantic slave trade in the eighteenth century.[47] Sowande' Mustakeem and Stephanie Smallwood have explored how the painful journey through the slave trade, from capture and imprisonment in Western Africa to transport aboard ships to point of sale, were all part of a process of dehumanization for the enslaved and simultaneously a process of turning human into commodity.[48] Smallwood demonstrates that the practice of the commodification of human life, rather than abstract, is a physically violent process that enslaved people resisted at every step along the path. The history of the explicit commodification of human bodies, lives, and their labor that runs through histories of slavery and colonialism.

As economic sociologist and historian Viviana Zelizer notes "life insurance became the first large-scale enterprise to base its entire organization on the accurate estimate of the price of death."[49] It was the first to transform human life into a quantifiable object for financial gain and ultimately for speculation. However, while life insurance policies attempt to place a financial value on human life, they do so for the benefit of those loved ones who may lose their own to an untimely demise—the monetary compensation offsetting lost wages or future earnings, quantified through the complexity of actuarial tables. While insurance companies are able to speculate ultimately on the nature of one's demise and reap premiums from a long life lived, the benefits are largely returned to those closest to the policy holder. It was not truly until viaticals were made legal in the early twentieth century that third parties could gain from the speculation on the value of human life.[50] Viatical settlements allow for investors to speculate on the lifespan of individuals by allowing for the right to purchase insurance policies of others in exchange for paying the premium and some lump sum to the originator of the policy, the viator. This speculation became profitable during the height of the HIV/AIDS epidemic in the United States when young people with significant life insurance policies began to die at very young ages. This had the effect of paying out large amounts while also reducing the amount investors had to pay in premiums due to the swift death that the disease caused. Profits decline the longer the viator lives. While viaticals can and have been packaged and purchased for purposes of creating markets and speculating on life for large-scale financial gain, this is largely the end result. However, in the case of viatical settlements, the valuing of the lives covered by insurance is not the underlying asset that is being speculated on—the insurance contract is. Though the insurance policy is based on a large and lengthy actuarial analysis of the likelihood of death and speculation on healthy lifestyles, the asset that derives value is not the life or death of a person but rather the contract. Even in the case of mortality bonds, the market for these products exists as a hedge against losses incurred from insurance payouts, not loss of life. The life and death of the policy holder is only valuated in the production of the insurance contract, but the value lies not explicitly in the life of the policy holder but the contract that guarantees funds in the event of that policy holder's death.

In the case of the PEF, the calculus is different. As a solution to the slow or incomplete fulfillment of aid burdens needed for epidemic response and recovery, the World Bank has funneled what could be aid funding toward a way of spreading the risk of epidemic to broader capital markets. However, the primary unit upon which these bonds are activated and which ultimately affects whether investors continue to receive payments or lose their invested principal to aid responses is the mortality and rates of deaths of others. This prompts a vastly different structural logic of epidemic response. Discourses of epidemic Orientalism or the conceptions of difference rooted in tropical medical treatises examined the threat of others in terms of a potential possible vector of disease or a risk to European commercial interests. With PEF the specter of the diseased other from beyond Europe is transmogrified once more not as a direct corporeal threat but abstracted as a bare life subject, whose relative value to the wider political economic system is measured either in their prolonged existence, (thus conferring wealth to investors in these notes) or as a risk and functionally economic loss (whose value is then as a representation of a threat requiring aid support).

Thus the victim of disease is fetishized through the mechanisms of finance, constituted as an abstracted object of and for speculation. As commodity fetishism divorces the commodity from the forces of labor that produced it,[51] so too is the person at the site of epidemic: those who make up the number constituting the statistics in an event report are emptied of all form and content and replaced by a binary, alive or dead, with relevance to the PEF. The victim of disease becomes a fetish object of financial speculation within a necrofinancial schema that only derives financial value from the bare-life abstraction of the epidemic subject, conferring loss in death but financial returns in survival. Those aspects that make the epidemic subject human beyond their own mortality by disease are made irrelevant to the calculus of aid delivery through the PEF.

Moreover, in the fetishization of the speculative epidemic subject, a double necrofinancial move is executed. The funds reserved for a response are only released once a certain number of deaths occur and in multiple sites (especially in the case of Class B Notes). Thus in the absence of further aid support, the speculative epidemic subject becomes a prospect for salvation in death and representative of a parochial threat in life. Further, we see a differential valuation of life and death. As we have seen in the case of the 2018/19 Ebola epidemic in the eastern Democratic Republic of Congo, though over two thousand deaths were reported since the beginning of the epidemic, the lack of twenty confirmed deaths in another country withheld the support from the World Bank and increased earnings of PEF investors. In the case of its ultimate deployment during the COVID-19 pandemic, we see this intervention providing far too little and at far too late a time. In this we find a particular exertion of some form of biopolitical order within the PEF: the bloodless accounting structure of the PEF relies on disease surveillance information to bear witness to epidemic disaster but only intervenes through its insurance window after a sufficient number of deaths occur over a border.

The fetishization of epidemic subjects is not uniform in its gaze. Only two European countries were represented as IDA borrower nations at the time of the PEF's operation: Kosovo and Moldova.[52] The overwhelming majority lie in Africa, East Asia, and the Caribbean. The fetishization of non-European bodies carries with it the broader legacies of the histories of epidemic Orientalism. The fetishization of non-European life and more explicitly death by epidemic disease reflects back on the producers and investors in the PEF a variety of anxieties that should now be familiar to us. Valuing the deaths of those across borders as integral to their activation criteria is once again an anxiety about the threat of global spread as critical to any meaningful engagement by the global community, or more specifically capital market actors. In addition, the constitution of life in these bare terms, separated from any humanitarian objectives, reflects a history rooted in the imperial pasts of international disease control that saw colonial subjects only as agents of contagion spread or worthy of medical aid relative to their economic value.

Necrofinance and Epidemic Orientalism

Necrofinance marks the rationalization of financial logics into discourses of pandemic risk. However, it is not a complete departure from the discursive framings we have become familiar with. The PEF was designed only to trigger and support nations primarily in the Global South and outside of Europe, providing funds for epidemics in the developing world. At the same time, the absence of epidemics in these sites would provide the opportunity for wealthy private actors to make financial gains from publicly provided funds that could otherwise have been delivered in the form of aid or myriad other vehicles to address urgent issues. In this necrofinancial schema, like under epidemic Orientalism, the risks of threat still are envisioned as arising from beyond the shores of Europe and North America.

While the PEF does not reflect a need to control bodies in the manner consistent with the International Sanitary Conventions, it does allow for speculation on the likelihood of death of persons living in areas of outbreak, providing value in life and much-needed aid should deaths occur. While epidemic Orientalism facilitates the constitution of subjects for the purpose of surveillance and sovereign control, necrofinance organizes the making of novel subject positions for the purposes of financial speculation. As such the incentives and processes are different under these schemas. However, these two framings of disease threat still articulate a similar vision of division with regard to global relations. The world beyond the Western and Northern Hemispheres requires careful management and control due to the epidemic threats it poses. Both framings still retain a colonialist mindset that differentially values human life based on these geographic distinctions, clearly reflected in the assumptions and practices built into the PEF.

CONCLUSION

I WISH TO REFLECT ON WHAT has been covered in this book as well as to provide some thoughts on the nature of international infectious disease control after COVID-19. Indeed, perhaps the pandemic of COVID-19, more than any book ever could, exposes the terrifying nearness of the nineteenth century, its violences, pandemics, and loss of life. The past worlds described in this book perhaps bear less of a chronological relation to our current times than a palimpsestic one: modified or written over to make way for the new, while showing the obvious traces of what was there before. In this we find the endurance of epidemic Orientalism, that discursive framework that like a shadow is cast upon global responses to disease threats.

I have argued that the management of infectious disease is not solely the manifestation of economic and trade concerns intersecting with disease threat but also a space of international affairs through which the West could project its own visions of its superiority to the rest of the world and thereby reflect a mythology of its own supremacy over disease back to itself. COVID-19 has done more than merely expose the underlying xenophobia and racisms evident in the history of international infectious disease control: the discourse of epidemic Orientalism has quite literally boomeranged to imperil those living in the West. While much of Europe and North America has engaged in an epidemic Orientalist framing of China, South Africa, and other nations as marked by plagues, unsanitary behaviors, and as a threat to the rest of the world, the pandemic of COVID-19 found its epicenter in the United States, killing over one million people as of August 2022. This devastation has not been felt equally, with minoritized populations in the United States and in much of the West suffering far higher rates of severe illness and death. However, the myths of Western superiority in the face of plagues made possible by the 175-year-old discourse of epidemic Orientalism reproduced a lie that has left the West complacent *and* decimated.

The framing of China as a land of wet markets, its people as carriers of disease, and its politics rooted in ideologies foreign to a unified and ossified West does not expose a novel moment of xenophobic and racist fervor brought on by a more populist world. Rather, the pandemic has exposed the depth and centrality of these beliefs to our discursive understanding of disease control. To confront the pandemics of the future effectively, it is not satisfactory to merely apply novel forms of practice, develop and expand international health authority, or increase technological expertise. The fundamental perspectives and objectives of international infectious disease control need to be reconsidered. We have to challenge the discursive formation of epidemic Orientalism that stubbornly guides disease response at a global level.

This should raise further questions of the ways in which we casually periodize eras in international health. As this book demonstrates, the end of formal systems of colonialism and remote sovereignty retained many of the same anxieties, desires for sovereign power, and ideologies that were at work previously. The transference of the International Sanitary Conventions into the International Sanitary Regulations under the WHO in some ways ensured this transition of perspectives. While this book is not a history of the present, in attempting to understand where we sit at this particular pandemic moment relative to the past, we see the ways that those elements which we have consigned to history remain in operation or continue to structure relations. The stickiness of these histories should be recognized and considered as we resist the desire for progressive narratives or easy periodizing. We may not have moved as far past the past as we would wish to believe. Rather, this work seeks to understand long-term continuity through change to uncover the politics of international infectious disease control at both the foundational and surface levels.

Throughout this book we have seen the ways that international infectious disease control as understood through attempts to regulate disease spread has intersected with concerns for trade and travel, capitalist expansion, and colonial systems of relation, organized around a perspective that the lives that are most needing of saving are those in the wealthy Western world. However, I do not doubt we see epidemic Orientalism at work in the deeply flawed belief that lifesaving vaccinations, that marker of scientific modernity, if given to the Western world without delivery to all peoples everywhere will successfully protect the world, let alone those in the West. The practice of delineating populations, delineating risk groups, and valuing some above others yields only the reinforcement of the myth that the West is capable of protecting itself through the exiling and isolation of others. We can recall in our moment the protest made by Salih Effendi at the 1866 International Sanitary Conference when responding to the motion to isolate Muslims on Hajj from sea-borne transportation, leaving them stranded in the Arabian desert in the event of a cholera outbreak, that "towns of living sentient beings would be soon transformed into necropoli."[1] Beyond this self-proclaiming vision that Western triumph over disease is only rooted in its technological superiority to disease and its need to preserve its own interests, both in its economic concerns and white ethnocentrist responses, we see how this toxic relationship ultimately harms in crippling ways any effective pandemic response. While this book hopefully provides some useful approaches for theorizing our present moment—certainly it provides a framing to understand the vaccine nationalism and intellectual property protectionism that we are seeing—I hasten to add that other works have explored these phenomena in far greater detail.[2]

At the same time, this book solely considers one aspect of the space of global health. It does not consider whether epidemic Orientalism operates in other arenas. If it does, I leave it to other thinkers to explore, should they so choose. Though I draw broadly across time, this book remains focused upon the making of the International Sanitary Conventions, International Health Regulations, and Pandemic Emergency Financing Facility. While organizations like UNAIDS, the Global Fund, the Bill and Melinda Gates Foundation, and Médecins Sans Frontières are mentioned, my focus on the regulatory aspects of infectious diseases rather than a single entity devoted to managing other health threats (or even other infectious health threats) marks this intervention as both different from others and stressing sites where further inquiry is needed. Further research could and should be done in the spaces that were not taken up in this work. Despite this book's length, all books fall short of providing a complete story. I hope you see this less as a failing than a space for more research. I did not address in great detail the practice of colonial medical knowledge production and its relation to the International Sanitary Conventions. Nor does this book focus as much as others might on Asian continental framings of disease threat that may counter or have countered the epidemic Orientalism of Western powers. While some moments are referenced, more work can be devoted to this endeavor.

As a final consideration, I hope this book presents a rebuke of forms of thought and modes of operating that rely on a vision of division in order to develop practice. Such discursive formations lead to violence, harm, and the valuing of certain lives above others. There is a way of seeing infectious disease control through the lens of those concerns most pressing to the West, and this way of seeing has organized so much knowledge creation around infectious disease to support this perspective. Challenging this hegemonic vision will be as critical to any future pandemic control as any form of preparedness or regulatory framework, lest our actions and our epidemic Orientalism continue to transform worlds into necropoli.

NOTES

Preface

1. Mark Harrison, *Disease and the Modern World: 1500 to the Present Day* (Cambridge, MA: Polity, 2004); Sheldon Watts, *Epidemics and History: Disease, Power and Imperialism* (New Haven, CT: Yale University Press, 1999).

2. It deserves more than a footnote and deserves serious mention that many people living with HIV and the activists and citizen-scientists who spoke out at the silences of the political and medical community to HIV/AIDS in the 1980s and 1990s in the United States have spoken out and recognized the violence behind this myth that major epidemics cannot occur in the West. Katharine Swindells, "We Hope Covid-19 Will Lead to a Better World. But Those Who Remember the Aids Crisis Are Less Sure," *Prospect*, May 21, 2020, https://www.prospectmagazine.co.uk/politics/covid-19-aids-crisis-epidemic-pandemic-2020; Gregg Gonsalves, "Beating Covid-19 Will Take Coordination, Experimentation, and Leadership," *The Nation*, April 23, 2020, https://www.thenation.com/article/society/coronavirus-hydroxychloroquine-treatment-hiv/.

3. Sylvia Wynter, "Unsettling the Coloniality of Being/Power/Truth/Freedom: Towards the Human, After Man, Its Overrepresentation—An Argument," *CR: The New Centennial Review* 3, no. 3 (2003): 260, https://doi.org/10.1353/ncr.2004.0015.

4. Colin Freeman, "'I Would Sit next to Ebola Sufferer on Tube', Says Scientist Who Discovered Deadly Virus," *The Telegraph*, July 31, 2014, https://www.telegraph.co.uk/news/worldnews/ebola/11002041/I-would-sit-next-to-Ebola-sufferer-on-Tube-says-scientist-who-discovered-deadly-virus.html.

5. Médecins Sans Frontières International, "Ebola: Pushed to the Limit and Beyond," March 23, 2015, http://www.msf.org/en/article/ebola-pushed-limit-and-beyond.

6. World Health Organization, "Health Security and Health Systems Strengthening—an Integrated Approach," https://www.who.int/csr/disease/ebola/health-systems-recovery/health-security-infographic.pdf.

7. Paul Richards, *Ebola: How a People's Science Helped End an Epidemic* (London: Zed Books, 2016).

8. Mark Doyle, "Ebola Outbreak: How Liberia Lost Its Handshake," *BBC News*, September 21, 2014, http://www.bbc.com/news/world-africa-29260185.

9. Claire Laurier Decoteau, *Ancestors and Antiretrovirals: The Biopolitics of HIV/AIDS in Post-Apartheid South Africa* (Chicago; University of Chicago Press, 2013).

10. "SA's Zuma 'Showered to Avoid HIV,'" *BBC*, April 5, 2006, http://news.bbc.co
.uk/2/hi/africa/4879822.stm.

11. Phillip Rucker, "Trump Beats a Retreat on Opening Country as Coronavirus
Data, Images Show Dark Reality," *Washington Post*, March 29, 2020, https://www.wash
ingtonpost.com/politics/trump-coronavirus-guidelines-easter-elmhurst/2020/03/29/
c15c21f2-7215-11ea-87da-77a8136c1a6d_story.html.

12. Madeline Holcombe, Jen Christensen and Joe Sutton, "CDC Removes Guidance
on Drugs Touted by Trump to Treat Coronavirus," *CNN*, April 8, 2020, https://www
.cnn.com/2020/04/08/health/cdc-coronavirus-hydroxychloroquine/index.html.

13. William J. Broad and Dan Levin, "Trump Muses About Light as Remedy, but
Also Disinfectant, Which Is Dangerous," *New York Times*, April 24, 2020, https://www
.nytimes.com/2020/04/24/health/sunlight-coronavirus-trump.html.

Introduction

1. Mary Wollstonecraft Shelley, *The Last Man*, vol. 2 (London: Henry Colburn,
1826), 211, http://tinyurl.galegroup.com/tinyurl/BN4XH4.

2. Alan Bewell, *Romanticism and Colonial Disease* (Baltimore, MD: Johns Hopkins
University Press, 1999), 296.

3. Bewell, *Romanticism*, 298.

4. I employ the term *epidemic* rather than *pandemic*, as the concept of a pandemic
is both a relatively recent phenomenon and one that does not maintain the same regulatory force as an epidemic. While the declaration of COVID-19 as a global pandemic
has led to the much wider use of the term, the WHO's declaration of a pandemic does
not produce direct policy outcomes or shifts in approaches (except in the case of the
management of pandemic influenza under the International Health Regulations of
2005). However, terms like *Public Health Emergency of International Concern* invoke
and mandate certain responses. In addition, while a pandemic implies a continental
or global scope, much of this work is devoted to understanding why certain epidemics
or moments of disease emergence produce international or global responses. An epidemic needn't be pandemic in its scale to provoke global concern, and for these reasons
I primarily employ the term *epidemic*. In employing my concept of *epidemic orientalism*, which I developed from my dissertation in 2018, I am aware of one earlier independent academic employment of the term in Varlick Nükhet's 2017 piece "'Oriental
Plague' or Epidemiological Orientalism? Revisiting the Plague Episteme of the Early
Modern Mediterranean," in which the author argues that plague in the 19th century
was a marker for distinguishing the civilized West from a diseased Orient in the historical and literary framing of "Oriental Plague." This concept put forward in this book of
Epidemic Orientalism, while engaging in depth with Ottoman and Western European
relations at the International Sanitary Conferences, draws in a wider history connecting geographies beyond the Ottoman empire and also the framings of other diseases
beyond plague in relation to epidemic orientalism. While Nükhet and I both draw on
Edward Said's critiques of Orientalism to examine 19th century disease imaginaries, this

book also looks at the persistence of epidemic orientalism from the early 19th century to the present and the framing of infectious disease threats through the lens of the eyes of a constructed "west." Nükhet's chapter is a deeply informative and exacting look at literary imaginings of epidemic frontiers in both medical treatises and travel writings, the primary focus upon the Ottoman empire as opposed to Asia more broadly as well as parts of Africa and the Pacific highlight the divergent geographical framings of our two concepts. Though the terms "epidemiological orientalism" and "epidemic orientalism" explore similar periods and literatures, they should be read as separate. The terms *Epidemic Orientalism or Epidemiological Orientalism* has also been discussed in Germany in November of 2020 by Maximilian Mayer, Marina Rudyak, and Marius Meinhof as Epidemische Orientalismus in *Cicero, The Magazine for Political Culture.*

5. Isaac Reed, *Interpretation and Social Knowledge: On the Use of Theory in the Human Sciences* (Chicago: University of Chicago Press, 2011).

6. Vanessa Ogle, *The Global Transformation of Time: 1870–1950* (Cambridge, MA: Harvard University Press, 2015).

7. Norman Howard-Jones, *The Scientific Background of the International Sanitary Conferences, 1851–1938* (Geneva: World Health Organization, 1975), http://apps.who.int//iris/handle/10665/62873.

8. Socrates Litsios, "Malaria Control, the Cold War, and the Postwar Reorganization of International Assistance," *Medical Anthropology* 17, no. 3 (May 1, 1997): 255–78, https://doi.org/10.1080/01459740.1997.9966140; Randall M. Packard, *A History of Global Health: Interventions into the Lives of Other Peoples* (Baltimore, MD: Johns Hopkins University Press, 2016); Javed Siddiqi, *World Health and World Politics: The World Health Organization and the UN System* (Columbus: University of South Carolina Press, 1995).

9. David P. Fidler and Lawrence O. Gostin, "The New International Health Regulations: An Historic Development for International Law and Public Health," *Journal of Law, Medicine & Ethics* 34, no. 1 (March 1, 2006): 85–94, https://doi.org/10.1111/j.1748-720X.2006.00011.x; Special Committee established by the third World Health Assembly to consider the Draft International Sanitary Regulations, "Draft International Sanitary Regulations: Proposal for the Machinery to Review the Functioning of the International Sanitary Regulations and the Settlement of Disputes Arising Therefrom Presented by Dr Raja, Delegate for India," 1951, https://apps.who.int/iris/handle/10665/100844.

10. Fidler and Gostin, "The New International Health Regulations"; World Health Organization, *International Health Regulations*, https://www.who.int/health-topics/international-health-regulations#tab=tab_1.

11. World Health Organization Department of Epidemic and Pandemic Alert and Response and United States Agency for International Development, *Communicable Disease Surveillance and Response Systems: Guide to Monitoring and Evaluating* (Geneva: World Health Organization, 2006), 10, https://apps.who.int/iris/handle/10665/69331.

12. David P. Fidler, "From International Sanitary Conventions to Global Health Security: The New International Health Regulations," *Chinese Journal of International Law* 4, no. 2 (January 1, 2005): 325–92, https://doi.org/10.1093/chinesejil/jmi029.

13. L. O. Gostin, D. Lucey, and A. Phelan, "The Ebola Epidemic: A Global Health Emergency," *JAMA* 312, no. 11 (September 17, 2014): 1095–96, https://doi .org/10.1001/jama.2014.11176; D. Lucey and L. O. Gostin, "A Yellow Fever Epidemic: A New Global Health Emergency?," *JAMA* 315, no. 24 (June 28, 2016): 2661–62, https:// doi.org/10.1001/jama.2016.6606; Médecins Sans Frontières International, "Ebola: Pushed to the Limit and Beyond," March 23, 2015, http://www.msf.org/en/article/ ebola-pushed-limit-and-beyond.

14. S. J. Hoffman, "The Evolution, Etiology and Eventualities of the Global Health Security Regime," *Health Policy and Planning* 25, no. 6 (November 1, 2010): 514, https:// doi.org/10.1093/heapol/czq037.

15. At the time of the influenza pandemic, the virus responsible for the pandemic had not been isolated, and much work was conducted at the time to ascertain the mechanisms by which it spread.

16. For an important exception, as well as further analysis of why pandemics rarely produce sociological inquiry, see Robert Dingwall, Lily M. Hoffman, and Karen Staniland, "Introduction: Why a Sociology of Pandemics?," in *Pandemics and Emerging Infectious Diseases*, ed. Robert Dingwall, Lily M. Hoffman, and Karen Staniland (Malden, MA: John Wiley & Sons, 2013), 1–7, http://onlinelibrary.wiley.com/ doi/10.1002/9781118553923.ch1/summary.

17. Paula A. Treichler, *How to Have Theory in an Epidemic: Cultural Chronicles of AIDS* (Durham, NC: Duke University Press, 1999); Claire Laurier Decoteau, *Ancestors and Antiretrovirals: The Biopolitics of HIV/AIDS in Post-Apartheid South Africa* (Chicago: University of Chicago Press, 2013); Susan Sontag, *AIDS and Its Metaphors* (New York: Farrar, Straus and Giroux, 1989); Deborah Gould, "When AIDS Began: San Francisco and the Making of an Epidemic," *American Journal of Sociology* 111, no. 6 (May 2006): 1973–76, https://doi.org/10.1086/506218; Vinh-Kim Nguyen, *The Republic of Therapy: Triage and Sovereignty in West Africa's Time of AIDS* (Durham, NC: Duke University Press Books, 2010).

18. Nitsan Chorev, *The World Health Organization between North and South* (Ithaca, NY: Cornell University Press, 2012).

19. Stuart Hall, "The West and the Rest: Discourse and Power [1992]," in *Essential Essays, Volume 2*, ed. David Morley (Durham, NC: Duke University Press, 2018), 141–84, https://doi.org/10.1215/9781478002710-009. By describing this binary as such, I in no way mean to denigrate the world outside of the Northern and Western Hemispheres. Rather I employ the bifurcation as Hall does, as a way of reflecting the epistemic and political power imbalances often at work on our planet.

20. Nancy Leys Stepan, *Eradication: Ridding the World of Diseases Forever?* (Ithaca, NY: Cornell University Press, 2015); Iris Borowy, "International Social Medicine between the Wars: Positioning a Volatile Concept," *Hygiea Internationalis: An Interdisciplinary Journal for the History of Public Health* 6, no. 2 (December 1, 2007): 13–35.

21. The role of colonial sites as centers of knowledge production, extraction, and experimentation has a rich and important history that I do not detail closely in this

work. For important references that discuss some of these aspects in greater detail, see Helen Tilley, *Africa as a Living Laboratory: Empire, Development, and the Problem of Scientific Knowledge, 1870–1950* (Chicago: University of Chicago Press, 2011); Deirdre Cooper Owens, *Medical Bondage: Race, Gender, and the Origins of American Gynecology* (Athens: University of Georgia Press, 2018); Londa Schiebinger, *Secret Cures of Slaves: People, Plants, and Medicine in the Eighteenth-Century Atlantic World* (Stanford, CA: Stanford University Press, 2017); Pablo F. Gómez, *The Experiential Caribbean: Creating Knowledge and Healing in the Early Modern Atlantic* (Chapel Hill: University of North Carolina Press, 2017); Philip D. Curtin, "Medical Knowledge and Urban Planning in Tropical Africa," *American Historical Review* 90, no. 3 (June 1, 1985): 594–613, https://doi.org/10.2307/1860958; Philip D. Curtin, *Disease and Empire: The Health of European Troops in the Conquest of Africa* (Cambridge: Cambridge University Press, 1998); Douglas Melvin Haynes, *Imperial Medicine: Patrick Manson and the Conquest of Tropical Disease* (Philadelphia: University of Pennsylvania Press, 2001), http://site.ebrary.com/id/10748515; Packard, *A History of Global Health*.

22. Stepan, *Eradication*; Borowy, "International Social Medicine between the Wars"; J. Jenson, "Getting to Sewers and Sanitation: Doing Public Health within Nineteenth-Century Britain's Citizenship Regimes," *Politics & Society* 36, no. 4 (December 1, 2008): 532–56, https://doi.org/10.1177/0032329208324712.

23. Packard, *A History of Global Health*. Packard provides an important and sustained critique of this phenomenon in the first chapter of this work.

24. Warwick Anderson, *Colonial Pathologies: American Tropical Medicine, Race, and Hygiene in the Philippines* (Durham, NC: Duke University Press, 2006); Tilley, *Africa as a Living Laboratory*.

25. Ruth Rogaski, *Hygienic Modernity: Meanings of Health and Disease in Treaty-Port China* (Berkeley: University of California Press, 2014); Nükhet Varlik, "'Oriental Plague' or Epidemiological Orientalism? Revisiting the Plague Episteme of the Early Modern Mediterranean," in *Plague and Contagion in the Islamic Mediterranean*, ed. Nükhet Varlik (Arc Humanities Press, 2017).

26. Rana A. Hogarth, *Medicalizing Blackness: Making Racial Difference in the Atlantic World, 1780–1840* (Chapel Hill: University of North Carolina Press, 2017); Megan Vaughan, *Curing Their Ills: Colonial Power and African Illness* (Stanford, CA: Stanford University Press, 1991); Curtin, "Medical Knowledge and Urban Planning in Tropical Africa"; Suman Seth, *Difference and Disease: Medicine, Race and the Eighteenth-Century British Empire* (Cambridge: Cambridge University Press, 2018).

27. Alexandre I. R. White, "Global Risks, Divergent Pandemics: Contrasting Responses to Bubonic Plague and Smallpox in 1901 Cape Town," *Social Science History* 42, no. 1 (2018): 135–58, https://doi.org/10.1017/ssh.2017.41; Maynard W. Swanson, "The Sanitation Syndrome: Bubonic Plague and Urban Native Policy in the Cape Colony, 1900–1909," *Journal of African History* 18, no. 3 (1977): 387–410; James C. Mohr, *Plague and Fire: Battling Black Death and the 1900 Burning of Honolulu's Chinatown* (New York: Oxford University Press, 2006); Guenter B. Risse, *Plague, Fear, and Politics in San*

Francisco's Chinatown (Baltimore, MD: Johns Hopkins University Press, 2012); Alison Bashford, *Imperial Hygiene: A Critical History of Colonialism, Nationalism and Public Health* (Houndsmills, UK: Palgrave Macmillan, 2004); Valeska Huber, "The Unification of the Globe by Disease? The International Sanitary Conferences on Cholera, 1851–1894," *Historical Journal* 49, no. 2 (2006): 453–76.

28. Packard, *A History of Global Health*; Andrew Lakoff, *Unprepared: Global Health in a Time of Emergency* (Oakland: University of California Press, 2017); Huber, Valeska. "The Unification of the Globe by Disease? The International Sanitary Conferences on Cholera, 1851-1894." *The Historical Journal* 49, no. 2 (June 1, 2006): 453–76, Varlik, Nükhet. "'Oriental Plague' or Epidemiological Orientalism? Revisiting the Plague Episteme of the Early Modern Mediterranean." In *Plague and Contagion in the Islamic Mediterranean*, edited by Nükhet Varlik. Arc Humanities Press, 2017.

29. Chorev, *The World Health Organization between North and South*; Siddiqi, *World Health and World Politics*; Marcos Cueto, Theodore M Brown, and Elizabeth Fee, *The World Health Organization: A History* (Cambridge: Cambridge University Press, 2019).

30. Marcos Cueto, *The Value of Health: A History of the Pan American Health Organization* (Rochester, NY: University of Rochester Press, 2007).

31. Randall M. Packard, *The Making of a Tropical Disease: A Short History of Malaria* (Baltimore, MD: Johns Hopkins University Press, 2011); Stepan, *Eradication*; Paul Greenough, "Intimidation, Coercion and Resistance in the Final Stages of the South Asian Smallpox Eradication Campaign, 1973–1975," *Social Science & Medicine* 41, no. 5 (September 1995): 633–45, https://doi.org/10.1016/0277-9536(95)00035-6.

32. Neel Ahuja, *Bioinsecurities: Disease Interventions, Empire, and the Government of Species* (Durham, NC: Duke University Press, 2016); Packard, *A History of Global Health*.

33. Iris Borowy, *Coming to Terms with World Health: The League of Nations Health Organisation 1921–1946* (Frankfurt am Main: Peter Lang, 2009).

34. Nick Bingham and Stephen Hinchliffe, "Mapping the Multiplicities of Biosecurity," in *Biosecurity Interventions: Global Health and Security in Question*, ed. Andrew Lakoff and Stephen J. Collier (New York: Columbia University Press, 2008), 173–93, http://cup.columbia.edu/book/978-0-231-14606-7/biosecurity-interventions; Lakoff, *Unprepared*; Stephen J. Collier, Andrew Lakoff, and Paul Rabinow, "Biosecurity: Towards an Anthropology of the Contemporary," *Anthropology Today* 20, no. 5 (October 1, 2004): 3–7, https://doi.org/10.1111/j.0268-540X.2004.00292.x.

35. Ulrich Beck, *World at Risk* (Cambridge: Polity, 2009).

36. Andrew Lakoff and Stephen J. Collier, eds., *Biosecurity Interventions: Global Health and Security in Question* (New York: Columbia University Press, 2008), 21.

37. Ahuja, *Bioinsecurities*.

38. Chorev, *The World Health Organization between North and South*, 2012; Emma Whyte Laurie, "Who Lives, Who Dies, Who Cares? Valuing Life through the

Disability-Adjusted Life Year Measurement," *Transactions of the Institute of British Geographers* 40, no. 1 (January 1, 2015): 75–87, https://doi.org/10.1111/tran.12055.

39. Keith Breckenridge, *Biometric State: The Global Politics of Identification and Surveillance in South Africa, 1850 to the Present* (New York: Cambridge University Press, 2014); David Arnold, *Colonizing the Body: State Medicine and Epidemic Disease in Nineteenth-Century India* (Berkeley: University of California Press, 1993).

40. As of the time of publication.

41. Ann Laura Stoler, *Duress: Imperial Durabilities in Our Times* (Durham, NC: Duke University Press, 2016); Ann Laura Stoler, ed., *Imperial Debris: On Ruins and Ruination* (Durham, NC: Duke University Press, 2013); Ato Quayson, "The Sighs of History: Postcolonial Debris and the Question of (Literary) History," *New Literary History* 43, no. 2 (August 13, 2012): 359–70, https://doi.org/10.1353/nlh.2012.0021.

42. Walter D. Mignolo, "Delinking: The Rhetoric of Modernity, the Logic of Coloniality and the Grammar of De-coloniality," *Cultural Studies* 21, no. 2–3 (March 2007): 449–514, https://doi.org/10.1080/09502380601162647.

43. Aimé Césaire Mignolo, *Discourse on Colonialism* (New York: Monthly Review Press, 2000); Frantz Fanon, *The Wretched of the Earth*, trans. Richard Philcox (New York: Grove, 2004).

44. Edward W. Said, *Orientalism* (New York: Vintage Books, 1979), 3.

45. Said, *Orientalism*, 7.

46. Stuart Hall, ed., *Representation: Cultural Representations and Signifying Practices* (Thousand Oaks, CA: Sage, 1997), 44.

47. Hall, "The West and the Rest."

48. W. Montague Cobb, *The Laboratory of Anatomy and Physical Anthropology of Howard University* (Washington, DC: Howard University, 1936).

49. Mark Harrison, "Quarantine, Pilgrimage, and Colonial Trade: India 1866–1900," *Indian Economic & Social History Review* 29, no. 2 (June 1992): 117–44, https://doi.org/10.1177/001946469202900201; Adam Kamradt-Scott, "The Politics of Medicine and the Global Governance of Pandemic Influenza," *International Journal of Health Services: Planning, Administration, Evaluation* 43, no. 1 (2013): 105–21; White, "Global Risks, Divergent Pandemics"; L. O. Gostin, D. Sridhar, and D. Hougendobler, "The Normative Authority of the World Health Organization," *Public Health* 129, no. 7 (July 2015): 854–63, https://doi.org/10.1016/j.puhe.2015.05.002; Fidler and Gostin, "The New International Health Regulations."

50. Chinua Achebe, "An Image of Africa: Racism in Conrad's *Heart of Darkness*," *Massachusetts Review* 57, no. 1 (March 26, 2016): 14–27, https://doi.org/10.1353/mar.2016.0003; Neil Brenner, "Beyond State-Centrism? Space, Territoriality, and Geographical Scale in Globalization Studies," *Theory and Society* 28, no. 1 (1999): 39–78; Julian Go, "Global Fields and Imperial Forms: Field Theory and the British and American Empires," *Sociological Theory* 26, no. 3 (September 1, 2008): 201–29, https://doi.org/10.1111/j.1467-9558.2008.00326.x; Julian Go, *Postcolonial Thought and Social Theory*

(New York: Oxford University Press, 2016); Stuart Hall, "Race, Articulation, and Societies Structured in Dominance," *Sociology of Race and Ethnicity* 13 (2000): 40.

51. Said, *Orientalism*, 5.

52. Said, *Orientalism*, 3.

53. I am most grateful to Meghan Tinsley and Ricarda Hammer for the in-depth conversations we have had on this topic, without which I would have been unable to frame this analysis.

54. Henry Louis Gates, "Critical Fanonism," *Critical Inquiry* 17, no. 3 (1991): 457–70; Homi K. Bhabha, *The Location of Culture* (London: Routledge, 2004).

55. Bhabha, *The Location of Culture*.

56. Abdul R. JanMohamed, "The Economy of Manichean Allegory: The Function of Racial Difference in Colonialist Literature," *Critical Inquiry* 12, no. 1 (1985): 59–87; Benita Parry, "Problems in Current Theories of Colonial Discourse," *Oxford Literary Review* 9, no. 1/2 (1987): 27–58.

57. JanMohamed, "The Economy of Manichean Allegory," 68.

58. Frantz Fanon, *Black Skin, White Masks* (London: Pluto, 1952); Sut Jhally and Stuart Hall, *Race: The Floating Signifier* (Northampton, MA: Media Education Foundation, 1997).

59. Eli Park Sorensen, "Novelistic Interpretation: The Traveling Theory of Lukács's *Theory of the Novel*," *Journal of Narrative Theory* 39, no. 1 (2009): 57–85, https://doi.org/10.1353/jnt.0.0024; Edward W. Said, *The World, the Text, and the Critic* (Cambridge, MA: Harvard University Press, 1983).

60. Huber, "The Unification of the Globe by Disease?" I am indebted to the work of Huber and others for their critically important readings of the International Sanitary Conferences. Varlik, Nükhet. "'Oriental Plague' or Epidemiological Orientalism? Revisiting the Plague Episteme of the Early Modern Mediterranean." In *Plague and Contagion in the Islamic Mediterranean*, edited by Nükhet Varlik. Arc Humanities Press, 2017.

61. Vaughan, *Curing Their Ills*, 8.

62. Ann Laura Stoler, *Race and the Education of Desire: Foucault's History of Sexuality and the Colonial Order of Things* (Durham, NC: Duke University Press, 1995).

63. J.-A. Mbembe, "Necropolitics," trans. Libby Meintjes, *Public Culture* 15, no. 1 (2003): 11–40; Fanon, *Black Skin, White Masks*; V. Y. Mudimbe, *The Invention of Africa: Gnosis, Philosophy, and the Order of Knowledge* (Bloomington: Indiana University Press, 1988).

64. Mbembe, "Necropolitics," 2003; Achille Mbembe, *Necropolitics*, trans. Steve Corcoran (Durham, NC: Duke University Press, 2019).

65. Stoler, *Race and the Education of Desire*.

66. Mbembe, "Necropolitics," 23.

67. Mbembe, "Necropolitics," 24.

68. Michel Foucault, *The Birth of Biopolitics: Lectures at the Collège de France, 1978–1979* (New York: Picador, 2010).

69. Chorev, *The World Health Organization between North and South*; "Declaration of Alma-Ata International Conference on Primary Health Care, Alma-Ata, USSR, 6–12 September 1978," *Development* 47, no. 2 (June 1, 2004): 159–61, https://doi.org/10.1057/palgrave.development.1100047.

70. Adrien Proust, *La Défense de l'Europe Contre Le Choléra* (Paris, 1892), http://hdl.handle.net/2027/mdp.39015060800177.

71. Committee on International Quarantine, "Reservations to the Additional Regulations, 1955, Amending the International Sanitary Regulations, 1951," March 20, 1956, 2, WHO/IQ/33, World Health Organization.

72. J. Lederberg, "Medical Science, Infectious Disease, and the Unity of Humankind," *JAMA* 260, no. 5 (August 5, 1988): 685. Each of these quotations and their attendant effects will be discussed in greater detail in future chapters.

73. Hall, *Representation*; Jhally and Hall, *Race: The Floating Signifier*; Ferdinand de Saussure, *Course in General Linguistics*, ed. Roy Harris (LaSalle, IL: Open Court, 1998).

74. I. A. Reed, *Power in Modernity: Agency Relations and the Creative Destruction of the King's Two Bodies* (Chicago: University of Chicago Press, 2020), 237, https://books.google.com/books?id=3AbQDwAAQBAJ.

75. For notable exceptions see the work of historian Mark Harrison, *Contagion: How Commerce Has Spread Disease* (New Haven, CT: Yale University Press, 2013); Nicholas B. King, "Security, Disease, Commerce Ideologies of Postcolonial Global Health," *Social Studies of Science* 32, no. 5–6 (December 1, 2002): 763–89, https://doi.org/10.1177/030631270203200507.

76. Chorev, *The World Health Organization between North and South*; Bingham and Hinchliffe, "Mapping the Multiplicities of Biosecurity"; Lakoff and Collier, *Biosecurity Interventions*; Collier, Lakoff, and Rabinow, "Biosecurity." For exceptions see Packard, *A History of Global Health*; Siddiqi, *World Health and World Politics*; Borowy, *Coming to Terms with World Health*.

77. Paul Farmer, Jim Yong Kim, Arthur Kleinman, and Matthew Basilico, eds., *Reimagining Global Health: An Introduction* (Berkeley: University of California Press, 2013).

78. Paul Gilroy, *The Black Atlantic: Modernity and Double-Consciousness* (Cambridge, MA: Harvard University Press, 1995), 42.

79. Mary Louise Pratt, *Imperial Eyes: Travel Writing and Transculturation*. London: Routledge, 2007.

80. Nancy Stepan, *Picturing Tropical Nature*. London: Reaktion, 2001.

81. Rana A. Hogarth, *Medicalizing Blackness: Making Racial Difference in the Atlantic World, 1780–1840*. Chapel Hill: University of North Carolina Press, 2017; Mark Harrison, "'The Tender Frame of Man': Disease, Climate, and Racial Difference in India and the West Indies, 1760–1860." *Bulletin of the History of Medicine* 70, no. 1 (1996): 68–93.

82. Suman Seth, *Difference and Disease: Medicine, Race and the Eighteenth-Century British Empire*. Cambridge: Cambridge University Press, 2018.

83. Fanon, *The Wretched of the Earth*.

84. Sylvia Wynter, "Unsettling the Coloniality of Being/Power/Truth/Freedom: To-wards the Human, After Man, Its Overrepresentation—An Argument," *CR: The New Centennial Review* 3, no. 3 (2003): 268, https://doi.org/10.1353/ncr.2004.0015.

85. Wynter, "Unsettling the Coloniality of Being/Power/Truth/Freedom," 260.

86. Partha Chatterjee, *The Nation and Its Fragments: Colonial and Postcolonial Histories* (Princeton, NJ: Princeton University Press, 1993); Gilroy, *The Black Atlantic*, 3. Gilroy demonstrates most clearly how thinkers from W. E. B. Du Bois, Frederick Douglass, and many others apprehended and recognized the Enlightenment philosophies of modernity to make arguments for more radical and revolutionary forms of freedoms than the authors of the concepts of modernity could conceive. Similarly much scholarship on the Haitian Revolution and slave revolts in general have demonstrated how radical freedom was being conceptualized in more liberating and dynamic forms outside of the revolutions in Europe and in the spaces of ultimate bondage. Devastating critiques have also been leveled against the claims of modernity's progressive movement toward universal freedom. Sociologist Zygmunt Bauman, in his work *Modernity and the Holocaust*, demonstrates how the Holocaust presents a problem for scholars wedded to a progressive vision of history because the techniques, rationalities, and ideologies of modern society "was not the Holocaust's *sufficient* condition; it was however, most certainly its *necessary* condition." Zygmunt Bauman, *Modernity and the Holocaust* (Ithaca, NY: Cornell University Press, 2001), 19.

87. Partha Chatterjee, *Our Modernity*, SEPHIS-CODESRIA Lecture; No. 1 (Rotterdam, the Netherlands: SEPHIS; Dakar, Senegal: CODESRIA, 1997).

88. Decoteau, *Ancestors and Antiretrovirals*.

89. Paul Gilroy, *The Black Atlantic: Modernity and Double Consciousness*. London: Verso, 2002.

90. Gurminder K. Bhambra, "Historical Sociology, Modernity, and Postcolonial Critique," *American Historical Review* 116, no. 3 (June 1, 2011): 653–62, https://doi.org/10.1086/ahr.116.3.653; G. Bhambra, *Rethinking Modernity: Postcolonialism and the Sociological Imagination* (Basingstoke, UK: Palgrave Macmillan, 2007).

91. Walter Rodney, *How Europe Underdeveloped Africa* (London: Verso, 2018); Paul Gilroy, *The Black Atlantic: Modernity and Double Consciousness* (London: Verso, 2002); Cedric J. Robinson, *Black Marxism: The Making of the Black Radical Tradition* (Chapel Hill: University of North Carolina Press, 2000).

92. Henry A. Kissinger, "The Coronavirus Pandemic Will Forever Alter the World Order," *Wall Street Journal*, April 3, 2020, https://www.wsj.com/articles/the-coronavirus-pandemic-will-forever-alter-the-world-order-11585953005.

93. Mudimbe, *The Invention of Africa*.

94. Bruno Latour and other social theorists of science have examined the particular roles that scientific knowledge plays in the making of modernity. Science is critical to the modern project as it paves the way for rationalized ways of knowing the world outside of the confines of religious teachings. Scientific knowledge lights the way for the disenchantment with the sacred toward an understanding of a more ordered world.

Bruno Latour's analysis of the role of science in creating modernity persists largely as a critique of the ways in which modern science allows for the bifurcation between the human, social world and the natural one, creating analytic bifurcations of the two as separate entities without hybrid forms. This understanding to Latour allows for humans to imagine ourselves outside of the natural world, often with devastating and ignorant consequences constituting humans as agentic subjects in contrast to a natural world of objects. While scientific knowledge can certainly be mobilized for such purposes, we find through the history of infectious disease control that these knowledges are also mobilized to produce different human subjectivities for the purposes of disease management and control.

95. Wynter, "Unsettling the Coloniality of Being/Power/Truth/Freedom," 260.

96. Huber, "The Unification of the Globe by Disease?"; William F. Bynum, "Policing Hearts of Darkness: Aspects of the International Sanitary Conferences," *History and Philosophy of the Life Sciences* 15, no. 3 (1993): 421–34; Harrison, "Quarantine, Pilgrimage, and Colonial Trade."

97. Robert J. C. Young, *Postcolonialism: An Historical Introduction* (Oxford: Blackwell, 2001), 2.

98. While I draw primarily on the anticolonial and postcolonial scholarship of the latter twentieth century, I do not wish to exclude the work of prominent anticolonial writers such as Edward Blyden, numerous Haitian revolutionaries, as well as prominent African writers of the eighteenth and nineteenth centuries whose thought can be found in these works among many others: Edward Wilmot Blyden, *Hope for Africa. A Discourse, Etc. (From the Colonization Journal.).*, 1861; Edward Wilmot Blyden, *A Voice from Bleeding Africa on Behalf of Her Exiled Children* (G. Killian, 1856); Laurent Dubois, *Avengers of the New World: The Story of the Haitian Revolution* (Cambridge, MA: Belknap, 2004); Haiti 1805 Constitution, http://faculty.webster.edu/corbetre/haiti/history/earlyhaiti/1805-const.htm; W. E. B. DuBois, *The Suppression of the African Slave Trade to the United States of America 1638–1870* (New York: Cosimo Classics, 2007); Xolela Mangcu, *Biko: A Life* (London: I. B. Tauris, 2013).

99. Warwick Anderson, "The Possession of Kuru: Medical Science and Biocolonial Exchange," *Comparative Studies in Society and History* 42, no. 4 (October 2000): 713–44, https://doi.org/10.1017/S0010417500003297; Warwick Anderson, *Colonial Pathologies*; Warwick Anderson, "Making Global Health History: The Postcolonial Worldliness of Biomedicine," *Social History of Medicine* 27, no. 2 (May 1, 2014): 372–84, https://doi.org/10.1093/shm/hkt126.

100. Philomena Essed and David Theo Goldberg, *Race Critical Theories: Text and Context* (Malden, MA: Wiley-Blackwell, 2001); Gilroy, *The Black Atlantic*; Hall, "Race, Articulation, and Societies Structured in Dominance."

101. Ricarda Hammer, "Decolonizing the Civil Sphere: The Politics of Difference, Imperial Erasures, and Theorizing from History," *Sociological Theory* 38, no. 2 (2020): 101–21, https://doi.org/10.1177/0735275120921215.

102. Mbembe, *Necropolitics*, 2019.

103. Philip D. Curtin, *The Atlantic Slave Trade: A Census* (Madison: University of Wisconsin Press, 1969); Rodney, *How Europe Underdeveloped Africa*; Louis Sala-Molins, *Dark Side of the Light: Slavery and the French Enlightenment* (Minneapolis: University of Minnesota Press, 2006).

104. Saidiya V. Hartman, *Scenes of Subjection: Terror, Slavery, and Self-Making in Nineteenth-Century America* (New York: Oxford University Press, 1997); Young, *Postcolonialism*; Rodney, *How Europe Underdeveloped Africa*. In the words of philosopher Robert J. C. Young, this consisted of "the appropriation of territories and of land, of the institutionalization of racism, of the destruction of cultures and the superimposition of other cultures." The power of the colonial state and its sovereignty over occupied space derive from a power-knowledge relationship that produces knowledge for the purpose of colonial rule. Colonial sovereignty derives its legitimacy from its authority to both impose its own vision of its history and identity as well as enforce relations of subjection on colonial populations for the purpose of labor and economic exploitation. This links the modernist project with the colonial project even further. This practice is enforced through violence and the capacity to inflict it. Thinkers such as Edward Said and Frantz Fanon have shown that in order to make colonization an effective mode of domination, a variety of knowledge projects also had to occur to allow for the extraterritorial sovereignty necessary for imperialism to work. Walter Rodney's deeply complex and radical work *How Europe Underdeveloped Africa* links the exploitation(s) of slavery and colonialism in Africa not only to the enrichment of Europe but also foremost to the creation of Europe as an ontologically stable entity, capable only of being understood as a totality through its dialectic relationship to Africa. Thus while Europe underdeveloped Africa and made itself from an economic standpoint, it also was able to conceive of itself as Europe: the economic exploitation was also a phenomenological exercise in knowledge production. These knowledge projects were total ones, including the natural sciences, medicine, history, archaeology, and the social sciences to place the rest of the world as the object of study with a predominantly European (and at times Persian and Ottoman) viewpoint as the referent against which all others would be judged. Colonialism as a political economic and military practice also established the syntax, the rules of language through which colonial semiotics of relation could be thought. As I will show, it was through the International Sanitary Conferences that a particular transimperial vision of disease control emerged that was deeply rooted in the concerns and projects of European imperialism.

105. Hartman, *Scenes of Subjection*, 3; Young, *Postcolonialism*; Rodney, *How Europe Underdeveloped Africa*.

106. Jean Amery, *At the Mind's Limits: Contemplations by a Survivor on Auschwitz and Its Realities* (Bloomington: Indiana University Press, 1980).

Chapter 1

1. "Postcards: Ten Poems by Henry J.-M. Levet, Translated by Kirby Olson," *Jacket* 18 (August 2002), http://jacket1.writing.upenn.edu/18/levet.html.

2. Saurabh Mishra, *Pilgrimage, Politics, and Pestilence: The Haj from the Indian Subcontinent, 1860–1920* (New Delhi: Oxford University Press, 2011), 91.

3. Mishra, *Pilgrimage, Politics, and Pestilence.*

4. The particular relationships between imperial centers and colonial peripheries and sovereignty will be addressed most specifically in the next chapter.

5. Vanessa Ogle, *The Global Transformation of Time: 1870–1950* (Cambridge, MA: Harvard University Press, 2015).

6. Andre Gunder Frank, "A Theoretical Introduction to 5,000 Years of World System History," *Review (Fernand Braudel Center)* 13, no. 2 (1990): 155–248; Immanuel Wallerstein, *The Modern World-System I: Capitalist Agriculture and the Origins of the European World-Economy in the Sixteenth Century* (Berkeley: University of California Press, 2011).

7. Sheldon Watts, *Epidemics and History: Disease, Power and Imperialism* (New Haven, CT: Yale University Press, 1999); Dauril Alden and Joseph C. Miller, "Out of Africa: The Slave Trade and the Transmission of Smallpox to Brazil, 1560–1831," *Journal of Interdisciplinary History* 18, no. 2 (1987): 195–224, https://doi.org/10.2307/204281; Philip D. Curtin, *Disease and Empire: The Health of European Troops in the Conquest of Africa* (Cambridge: Cambridge University Press, 1998); Philip D. Curtin, "Medical Knowledge and Urban Planning in Tropical Africa," *American Historical Review* 90, no. 3 (June 1, 1985): 594–613, https://doi.org/10.2307/1860958; Mark Harrison, *Contagion: How Commerce Has Spread Disease* (New Haven, CT: Yale University Press, 2013); Mark Harrison, *Medicine in an Age of Commerce and Empire: Britain and Its Tropical Colonies, 1660–1830* (Oxford: Oxford University Press, 2010).

8. While I concur with Mark Harrison's analysis that the International Sanitary Conventions ushered in a new vision of Europeanness, my argument adds a racial and postcolonial dimension to his arguments in "Disease, Diplomacy and International Commerce: The Origins of International Sanitary Regulation in the Nineteenth Century," *Journal of Global History* 1, no. 2 (July 2006): 197, https://doi.org/10.1017/S1740022806000131.

9. Peter Baldwin, *Contagion and the State in Europe, 1830–1930* (Cambridge: Cambridge University Press, 2005).

10. Edward W. Said, *Orientalism* (New York: Vintage Books, 1979), 79.

11. Said, *Orientalism,* 91–92.

12. Said, *Orientalism,* 51–53.

13. Achille Mbembe, *Critique of Black Reason,* trans. Laurent Dubois (Durham, NC: Duke University Press, 2017), 28.

14. Rudyard Kipling, *Rudyard Kipling's Verse: Definitive Edition* (London: Hodder and Stoughton, 1940), https://books.google.com/books?id=vKqnxwEACAAJ.

15. Frantz Fanon, *The Wretched of the Earth,* trans. Richard Philcox (New York: Grove, 2004).

16. Said, *Orientalism,* 2.

17. Said, *Orientalism,* 2; Julian Go, *Postcolonial Thought and Social Theory* (New York: Oxford University Press, 2016).

18. Sut Jhally and Stuart Hall, *Race: The Floating Signifier* (Northampton, MA: Media Education Foundation, 1997).

19. Mary Louise Pratt, *Imperial Eyes: Travel Writing and Transculturation* (London: Routledge, 2007), 70.

20. Chapter 3 will more explicitly engage the dynamics of international disease control in the early twentieth century with respect to the Americas.

21. Alexandre I. R. White, "Global Risks, Divergent Pandemics: Contrasting Responses to Bubonic Plague and Smallpox in 1901 Cape Town," *Social Science History* 42, no 1 (November 2017): 1–24, https://doi.org/10.1017/ssh.2017.41.

22. Harrison, *Contagion*, 8. The Ordinances of Pistoia prohibited the trade of cloth and textiles from areas suspected of a plague outbreak.

23. Harrison, *Contagion*, 8.

24. Guy de Chauliac, *La Grande Chirurgie de M. Gui de Chauliac, . . . / Restituée Nouvellement à Sa Dignité Par M. Laurens Joubert . . .* , 1579, http://gallica.bnf.fr/ark:/12148/bpt6k79189f; Mary Douglas, "Witchcraft and Leprosy: Two Strategies of Exclusion," *Man* 26, no. 4 (1991): 723–36, https://doi.org/10.2307/2803778; Harrison, *Contagion*; Watts, *Epidemics and History*.

25. Scholars of the transatlantic slave trade have demonstrated how an understanding of the management of disease was critical to the growth of slavery in the seventeenth and eighteenth centuries, as the ability to avoid illness onboard slaving ships among crew and kidnapped people alike was a valued skill for ship captains. Managing disease on plantations as well as the adequate inspection of kidnapped Africans for disease formed a critical element of the system of commodifying people for sale. Sowande' Mustakeem, "'I Never Have Such a Sickly Ship Before': Diet, Disease, and Mortality in 18th-Century Atlantic Slaving Voyages," *Journal of African American History* 93, no. 4 (October 2008): 474–96, https://doi.org/10.1086/JAAHv93n4p474; Stephanie E. Smallwood, *Saltwater Slavery: A Middle Passage from Africa to American Diaspora* (Cambridge, MA: Harvard University Press, 2008); Daina Ramey Berry, *The Price for Their Pound of Flesh: The Value of the Enslaved from Womb to Grave in the Building of a Nation* (Boston: Beacon, 2017).

26. Charles de Secondat Montesquieu et al., *The Spirit of the Laws* (Cambridge: Cambridge University Press, 1989), 240–41.

27. Alden and Miller, "Out of Africa."

28. Mark Harrison, *Disease and the Modern World: 1500 to the Present Day* (Cambridge: Polity, 2004); Harrison, *Contagion*.

29. Sowande' M. Mustakeem, *Slavery at Sea: Terror, Sex, and Sickness in the Middle Passage* (Urbana: University of Illinois Press, 2016). Perceived resistance of enslaved people and most specifically certain Africans to disease also became an important justification for the expansion of the transatlantic slave trade as well as perceptions of racial difference between white colonizers and the enslaved in the sixteenth through the nineteenth centuries. For further reference see Suman Seth, *Difference and Disease: Medicine, Race and the Eighteenth-Century British Empire* (Cambridge: Cambridge University

Press, 2018); Rana A. Hogarth, *Medicalizing Blackness: Making Racial Difference in the Atlantic World, 1780–1840* (Chapel Hill: University of North Carolina Press, 2017); Patrick Tailfer et al., *A True and Historical Narrative of the Colony of Georgia, in America, from the First Settlement Thereof until This Present Period: Containing the Most Authentick Facts, Matters, and Transactions Therein: Together with His Majesty's Charter, Representations of the People, Letters, &c. and a Dedication to His Excellency General Oglethorpe* (Washington: P. Force, 1835), http://archive.org/details/truehistoricalnaootailf.

30. One major and glaring exception to this was the devastating effect of smallpox on kidnapped and enslaved peoples aboard ships. Disease on slaving ships and especially smallpox and yellow fever killed many kidnapped peoples of Africa throughout the duration of the transatlantic slave trade. Mustakeem, *Slavery at Sea*; Mustakeem, "'I Never Have Such a Sickly Ship Before'"; Marcus Rediker, *The Slave Ship: A Human History* (New York: Penguin Books, 2008).

31. Harrison, *Disease and the Modern World*; Harrison, *Contagion*.

32. Harrison, *Contagion*, 20.

33. Harrison, *Contagion*, 20.

34. Harrison, *Contagion*, 33.

35. Harrison, *Contagion*, 37. The thinly veiled jingoism that quarantine allowed for also poured forth renewed feelings of civic responsibility for the management of disease that delineated the role of foreign and citizen which would greatly affect the future production of disease responses. Dr. Damillo Samoïlowitz, a noted doctor and surgeon general of Moscow, in writing to Catherine the Great of Russia on the recent plague outbreaks, noted:

"As soon as the plague begins to reign in a city, would it not be unjust to refuse to all those who have no duty to fulfill in the civil state, or who are not obliged to reside there, some particular necessity, the freedom of exit? This liberty thus procures a considerable diminution over the totality of the Citizens, the Plague can no longer sacrifice so many victims. Those who are obliged by their duty or by their state to remain within their walls, have less to fear, in relation to the Provisions necessary for their subsistence; moreover, the police have less details, and it is easier to obviate the confusion and disorders which inevitably entail these times of fear and mortality. It is not the same with those which their state calls for the public good. If they were granted the freedom to leave their Places, who would now perform their duties with intelligence and foresight? who would order the necessary assistance to the poor peoples? who would ensure the maintenance of order, more than ever necessary in these times of crisis? who would oppose to the wicked the barriers which they would follow? Soon abuses would multiply on every side, and would concur with the plague, to the total ruin of a city so ill-policed, for in that time the police did not make use of all its authority; large disorders therefore, having dismissed from the commencement of the invasion of the plague the unnecessary part of the citizens, to refuse permission to go out to those who watch over the preservation of the Order and the happiness of the States. It is necessary to inflame the zeal of the People of Art, who devote themselves daily to the good of humanity;

we must encourage the efforts of all the true Patriots, in order to procure for their fellow-citizens all the reliefs, of which they may have need, we must above all, animate and warm feelings by example." Danilo Samoïlowitz, *Mémoire sur la peste, qui, en 1771, ravagea l'empire de Russie, sur-tout Moscou, la capitale, & où sont indiqués les remedes pour la guérir, & les moyens de s'en préserver* (Paris: Chez Leclerc; St. Petersburg: Chez M. Wilkowsky; Moscow: Chez M. Borissiakow, 1783), 204–6, http://archive.org/details/mmoiresurlapesoosamo.

While conceding the importance of state powers in managing disease threats, Samoïlowitz suggests that this disease was spread significantly by Turkish merchants.

36. Baldwin, *Contagion and the State in Europe*, 124–26.

37. Great Britain Poor Law Commissioners and E. Chadwick, *Report on the Sanitary Condition of the Labouring Population of Great Britain: A Supplementary Report on the Results of a Spiecal [Sic] Inquiry Into the Practice of Interment in Towns* (Clowes, 1843), https://books.google.com/books?id=2IYIAAAAQAAJ.

38. Baldwin, *Contagion and the State in Europe*.

39. Baldwin, Harrison, and others have expanded on the nature of the debates around sanitation and infectious disease control within European states. This chapter eschews a sustained inquiry into these debates, instead focusing on how the East came to be seen as the site from which disease threat emerges. Harrison, *Contagion*; Baldwin, *Contagion and the State in Europe*.

40. Gavin Milroy, *Quarantine and the Plague. Being a Summary of the Report on These Subjects Recently Addresed to the Royal Academy of Medicine in France; with Introductory Observations, Extracts from Parliamentary Correspondence, and Notes* (London: Samuel Highley, 1846), http://archive.org/details/b21365672.

41. David Arnold, *Colonizing the Body: State Medicine and Epidemic Disease in Nineteenth-Century India* (Berkeley: University of California Press, 1993), 162.

42. Arnold, *Colonizing the Body*, 162.

43. Watts, *Epidemics and History*, 67.

44. Harrison, *Disease and the Modern World*, 99.

45. Parliament of Great Britain, House of Commons. *Correspondence Relative to the Contagion of Plague, and the Quarantine Regulations of Foreign Countries. 1836–1843*. London: H.M. Stationery Office, 1843. https://books.google.co.uk/books?id=y1oSAAAAYAAJ.

46. Norman Howard-Jones, *The Scientific Background of the International Sanitary Conferences, 1851–1938* (Geneva: World Health Organization, 1975), http://apps.who.int//iris/handle/10665/62873; João Rangel De Almeida, "Epidemic Opportunities: Panic, Quarantines, and the 1851 International Sanitary Conference," in *Empires of Panic: Epidemics and Colonial Anxieties*, ed. Robert Peckham (Hong Kong: Hong Kong University Press, 2015), https://muse.jhu.edu/book/39842.

47. Baldwin, *Contagion and the State in Europe*.

48. Howard-Jones, "The Scientific Background of the International Sanitary Conferences"; Rangel De Almeida, "Epidemic Opportunities"; Nermin Ersoy, Yuksel

Gungor, and Aslihan Akpinar, "International Sanitary Conferences from the Ottoman Perspective (1851–1938)," *Hygiea Internationalis* 10, no. 1 (2011): 53–79.

49. Baldwin, *Contagion and the State in Europe.*

50. Ersoy, Gungor, and Akpinar, "International Sanitary Conferences from the Ottoman Perspective."

51. Ersoy, Gungor, and Akpinar, "International Sanitary Conferences from the Ottoman Perspective," 54.

52. Ersoy, Gungor, and Akpinar, "International Sanitary Conferences from the Ottoman Perspective," 54.

53. The Papal States, Sardinia, Tuscany, the two Sicilies, Austria, Great Britain, Greece, Portugal, Russia, Spain, Turkey, and France.

54. Howard-Jones, "The Scientific Background of the International Sanitary Conferences," 12.

55. It is important to note that many members of the national delegations retained their positions for multiple conferences, developing an institutional history and culture within the conferences themselves. Certain members became perennially associated with particular ideological and political positions. This was especially the case during the conventions toward the end of the nineteenth century and those conferences undertaken later by the Office International D'Hygiène Publique.

56. Ogle, *The Global Transformation of Time*; Rangel De Almeida, "Epidemic Opportunities."

57. Rangel De Almeida, "Epidemic Opportunities," 82–83.

58. Howard-Jones, "The Scientific Background of the International Sanitary Conferences."

59. Mark Harrison, "Quarantine, Pilgrimage, and Colonial Trade: India 1866–1900," *Indian Economic & Social History Review* 29, no. 2 (June 1992): 117–44, https://doi.org/1 0.1177/001946469202900201.

60. This perspective of British trade concerns in relation to sanitary controls is also reflected in Baldwin, *Contagion and the State in Europe.*

61. Howard-Jones, "The Scientific Background of the International Sanitary Conferences," 20.

62. Ersoy, Gungor, and Akpinar, "International Sanitary Conferences from the Ottoman Perspective."

63. Ersoy, Gungor, and Akpinar, "International Sanitary Conferences from the Ottoman Perspective"; Howard-Jones, "The Scientific Background of the International Sanitary Conferences."

64. Valeska Huber, "The Unification of the Globe by Disease? The International Sanitary Conferences on Cholera, 1851–1894," *Historical Journal* 49, no. 2 (2006): 462.

65. Baldwin, *Contagion and the State in Europe*, 230.

66. *Proceedings of the International Sanitary Conference Opened at Constantinople on the 13th February 1866* (Calcutta: Office of Superintendent of Government Printing, 1868), 63, http://hdl.handle.net/10973/23485.

67. Baldwin, *Contagion and the State in Europe.*

68. Ersoy, Gungor, and Akpinar, "International Sanitary Conferences from the Ottoman Perspective"; Howard-Jones, "The Scientific Background of the International Sanitary Conferences."

69. *Proceedings of the International Sanitary Conference Opened at Constantinople on the 13th February 1866*, 140.

70. "Annexure to the Minutes of the 29th Meeting: Report on the Measures to Be Adopted in the East in Order to Prevent a Renewed Invasion of Europe by Cholera: Drawn up by a Committee Consisting of Count De Lallemand, President; M. Kalegri, Secretary; M.M. De Krause and Vernoni, Diplomatists; and Drs. Bosi, Bykow, Fauvel, Polak, Salem, Sotto and Van- Geuns, Physicians," in *Proceedings of the International Sanitary Conference Opened at Constantinople on the 13th February 1866*, 402.

71. Italy, Greece, Austria, Prussia, France, the Netherlands, Russia, Egypt.

72. "Annexure to the Minutes of the 29th Meeting," 405.

73. "Annexure to the Minutes of the 29th Meeting," 406.

74. "Annexure to the Minutes of the 29th Meeting," 410.

75. "Annexure to the Minutes of the 29th Meeting," 410.

76. "Annexure to the Minutes of the 29th Meeting," 428.

77. "Annexure to the Minutes of the 29th Meeting," 451.

78. "Annexure to the Minutes of the 29th Meeting," 457.

79. "Annexure to the Minutes of the 29th Meetings," 455.

80. *Proceedings of the International Sanitary Conference Opened at Constantinople on the 13th February 1866*, 155.

81. *Proceedings of the International Sanitary Conference Opened at Constantinople on the 13th February 1866*, 466.

82. Harrison, "Quarantine, Pilgrimage, and Colonial Trade," 120.

83. Harrison, "Quarantine, Pilgrimage, and Colonial Trade."

84. Harrison, "Quarantine, Pilgrimage, and Colonial Trade," 123.

85. Harrison, "Quarantine, Pilgrimage, and Colonial Trade."

86. Adrien Proust was also the father of noted novelist and essayist Marcel Proust, himself a noted hypochondriac.

87. Adrien Proust, *La Défense de l'Europe Contre Le Choléra* (Paris, 1892), http://hdl .handle.net/2027/mdp.39015060800177.

88. International Sanitary Conference (7th: 1892: Venice, Italy), *Protocoles et procès-verbaux de la Conférence sanitaire internationale de Venise, inaugurée le 5 janvier 1892* (Rome: Impr. nationale de J. Bertero, 1892), 119, https://id.lib.harvard.edu/curiosity/ contagion/36-990113677780203941. I am grateful to Luis Aue of the WZB Berlin Social Science Center, who drew my attention to this particular quote.

89. S. Smith, "International Sanitary Conference," *Journal of Social Science; New York* 32 (November 1, 1894): 94.

90. Smith, "International Sanitary Conference," 97.

91. Huber, "The Unification of the Globe by Disease?"

92. Smith, "International Sanitary Conference," 98.

93. "Procès verbaux. International Sanitary Conference. 9th, Paris, 1894. Conférence sanitaire internationale de Paris, 7 février–3 avril 1894," 1894, 96–100, SPA.AD.O 25323 c.1; 64519 c.2, World Health Organization Archive.

94. Smith, "International Sanitary Conference," 98.

95. "Procès verbaux. International Sanitary Conference. 9th, Paris, 1894," 104.

Chapter 2

1. Philip D. Curtin, *Disease and Empire: The Health of European Troops in the Conquest of Africa* (Cambridge: Cambridge University Press, 1998); Philip D. Curtin, "Medical Knowledge and Urban Planning in Tropical Africa," *American Historical Review* 90, no. 3 (June 1, 1985): 594–613, https://doi.org/10.2307/1860958; Randall M. Packard, *White Plague, Black Labor: Tuberculosis and the Political Economy of Health and Disease in South Africa* (Berkeley: University of California Press, 1989); Jean Comaroff and John L. Comaroff, *Of Revelation and Revolution, Volume 2:The Dialectics of Modernity on a South African Frontier* (Chicago: University of Chicago Press, 1997); Jean Comaroff and John L. Comaroff, *Of Revelation and Revolution, Volume 1: Christianity, Colonialism, and Consciousness in South Africa* (Chicago: University of Chicago Press, 1991); Megan Vaughan, *Curing Their Ills: Colonial Power and African Illness* (Stanford, CA: Stanford University Press, 1991).

2. S. Smith, "International Sanitary Conference," *Journal of Social Science* 32 (November 1, 1894): 92–111.

3. Mayor et al., International Sanitary Convention, Signed at Venice, March 18, 1897.

4. Mayor et al., International Sanitary Convention, 9, 38.

5. Mayor et al., International Sanitary Convention, 38–44.

6. Mayor et al., International Sanitary Convention.

7. Myron J. Echenberg, "Pestis Redux: The Initial Years of the Third Bubonic Plague Pandemic, 1894–1901," *Journal of World History* 13, no. 2 (2002): 437.

8. Norman Howard-Jones, *The Scientific Background of the International Sanitary Conferences, 1851–1938* (Geneva: World Health Organization, 1975), http://apps.who.int//iris/handle/10665/62873; Valeska Huber, "The Unification of the Globe by Disease? The International Sanitary Conferences on Cholera, 1851–1894," *Historical Journal* 49, no. 2 (June 1, 2006): 453–76; Max von Pettenkofer, *Cholera: How to Prevent and Resist It* (London: Ballière, Tindall, & Cox, 1875).

9. Huber, "The Unification of the Globe by Disease?"

10. Mayor et al., International Sanitary Convention, 9.

11. Zygmunt Bauman, *Modernity and the Holocaust* (Ithaca, NY: Cornell University Press, 2001), 65.

12. Self-governing colonies had the power to elect executive officials and make most domestic decisions without the oversight of Britain. Foreign affairs and defense were still controlled by Britain.

13. Joseph West Ridgeway, "Letter to the Secretary of State for the Colonies, The Right Honorable Joseph Chamberlain M. P. from Ceylon Governor Joseph West Ridgeway Concerning Despatch No. 257," August 30, 1897.

14. Joseph West Ridgeway, "Letter to the Secretary of State for the Colonies, The Right Honorable Joseph Chamberlain M. P. from Ceylon Governor Joseph West Ridgeway," August 13, 1897, 2, 3, British National Archives at Kew, London.

15. Joseph West Ridgeway, "Letter to the Secretary of State for the Colonies, The Right Honorable Joseph Chamberlain M. P. from Ceylon Governor Joseph West Ridgeway," December 7, 1898, 65, FO 83/1691, British National Archives at Kew, London.

16. Huber, "The Unification of the Globe by Disease?"

17. *Public Health Reports: Volume 15, Issues 1–26* (U.S. Marine Hospital Service, 1901).

18. James C Mohr, *Plague and Fire: Battling Black Death and the 1900 Burning of Honolulu's Chinatown* (New York: Oxford University Press, 2006), 56.

19. Mohr, *Plague and Fire*, 67.

20. Francis Hamilton, "Francis Hamilton, Secretary of State for India to Under Secretary of State, Foreign Office 1898," February 26, 1898, 97–1318, British National Archives at Kew, London.

21. *International Quarantine Directory* (Office International d'Hygiene Publique, 1934), 3.

22. *International Quarantine Directory*, 5.

23. David Arnold, "Disease, Rumor and Panic in India's Plague and Influenza Epidemics, 1896–1919," in *Empires of Panic: Epidemics and Colonial Anxieties*, ed. Robert Peckham (Hong Kong: Hong Kong University Press, 2015), 113, https://muse.jhu.edu/book/39842; Elgin et al., "Government of India Home Department to the Right Honourable Lord George Francis Hamilton," December 23, 1897. It is interesting and important to note that this same act was reinvoked in response to the ongoing pandemic of COVID-19. Rakesh PS, "Implementing the Epidemic Diseases Act to Combat Covid-19 in India: An Ethical Analysis," *Indian Journal of Medical Ethics* 6, no. 1 (February 16, 2021): 13–17, https://doi.org/10.20529/IJME.2020.129.

24. Arnold, "Disease, Rumor and Panic in India's Plague and Influenza Epidemics," 113.

25. Government of India Home Department, "A Compilation of Regulations Issued by the Government of India and Local Governments in Connection with Plague," 1898, IOR/V/27/856/6A, British Library.

26. Government of India Home Department, "A Compilation of Regulations," 23.

27. Government of India Home Department, "A Compilation of Regulations."

28. Government of India Home Department, "A Compilation of Regulations," 25–26.

29. Simon A. Cole, "Witnessing Identification: Latent Fingerprinting Evidence and Expert Knowledge," *Social Studies of Science* 28, no. 5/6 (1998): 687–712.

30. Vivian Bickford-Smith, "South African Urban History, Racial Segregation and the Unique Case of Cape Town?," *Journal of Southern African Studies* 21, no. 1 (1995): 63–78; Sipokazi Sambumbu, "Reading Visual Representations of 'Ndabeni' in the Public Realms," *Kronos* 36 (2010): 184–206; Maynard W. Swanson, "The Sanitation Syndrome: Bubonic Plague and Urban Native Policy in the Cape Colony, 1900–1909," *Journal of African History* 18, no. 3 (1977): 387–410; Elizabeth van Heyningen, "Public Health and Society in Cape Town 1880–1910" (Dissertation, University of Cape Town, 1989); Elizabeth van Heyningen, "Agents of Empire: The Medical Profession in the Cape Colony, 1880–1910," *Medical History* 33, no. 04 (October 1989): 450–71, https://doi.org/10.1017/S0025727300049930.

31. Cole, "Witnessing Identification."

32. While racial segregation had been employed against workers in the gold- and diamond-mining camps of the Rand and Kimberley by corporate interests, this was the first time that urban racial segregation had been practiced against the general public by the colonial government of the Cape.

33. Geoffrey Bindman, *South Africa: Human Rights and the Rule of Law* (London: Pinter, 1988).

34. Swanson, "The Sanitation Syndrome."

35. Echenberg, "Pestis Redux"; Myron J Echenberg, *Plague Ports: The Global Urban Impact of Bubonic Plague,1894–1901* (New York: New York University Press, 2007); Mark Harrison, *Contagion: How Commerce Has Spread Disease* (New Haven, CT: Yale University Press, 2013).

36. Cape Peninsula Advisory Board, *Report and Proceedings, with Annexures, of the Cape Penninsula Plague Advisory Board Appointed to Advise the Government on Matters Connected with the Supression of Bubonic Plague, 1901* (Cape Town: W.A. Richards, 1901).

37. Cape Peninsula Advisory Board, *Report and Proceedings.*

38. A. John Gregory and William John Richie Simpson, "Memoranda by the Acting Medical Officer of Health for Cape Colony and Professor W. J. Simpson. M.D., F.R.C.P. on the Outbreak of Plague in Cape Colony and the Precautions Taken in Connection Therewith" (Office of the Medical Officer of Health for the Colony, Cape Town, May 22, 1901), 4. CO 897/67/2. British National Archives at Kew, London.

39. Cape Peninsula Advisory Board, *Report and Proceedings*, 138.

40. Gregory and Simpson, "Memoranda by the Acting Medical Officer of Health."

41. Cape Peninsula Advisory Board, *Report and Proceedings.*

42. Van Heyningen, "Public Health and Society in Cape Town"; R. J. Ross, "Smallpox at the Cape of Good Hope in the Eighteenth Century," Article / Letter to editor, *African Historical Demography* (1977): 416–28, https://openaccess.leidenuniv.nl/handle/1887/4200.

43. Van Heyningen, "Public Health and Society in Cape Town," 123.

44. Van Heyningen, "Public Health and Society in Cape Town," 127.

45. Van Heyningen, "Public Health and Society in Cape Town," 127.

46. Estimates as to the total number of deaths vary significantly between scholars on this matter. While Vivian Bickford Smith in *Ethnic Pride and Racial Prejudice in Victorian Cape Town* (Cambridge: Cambridge University Press, 2003) suggests that the total mortality was around 400 during the outbreak, van Heyningen argues based on reporting from the hospitals and news outlets of the time that mortality was likely closer to 1,400 (van Heyningen, "Public Health and Society in Cape Town"). Howard Phillips in *Epidemics: The Story of South Africa's Five Most Lethal Human Diseases* (Athens: Ohio University Press, 2012) argues for the highest estimate of roughly 4,000 dead due to this smallpox epidemic. While these estimates vary drastically, the small population of Cape Town at the time of around 45,000 reflects that even if the outbreak caused as few as 400 deaths, it would have reflected a drop of roughly 1 percent of the total population. Van Heyningen, "Public Health and Society in Cape Town," 132.

47. Bickford-Smith, *Ethnic Pride and Racial Prejudice in Victorian Cape Town*, 102; van Heyningen, "Public Health and Society in Cape Town," 135; Phillips, *Epidemics*, 157.

48. Van Heyningen, "Public Health and Society in Cape Town."

49. Bickford-Smith, *Ethnic Pride and Racial Prejudice in Victorian Cape Town*, 105.

50. *Cape Times*, August 31, 1882, quoted in Bickford-Smith, *Ethnic Pride and Racial Prejudice in Victorian Cape Town*, 75.

51. Within the colonial imaginary, the Malay, a term used to describe practicing Muslims, were seen as a model for the law-abiding nonwhite citizenry: law fearing and industrious, and much in contrast to the image of the "native" or Black African. Gabeba Baderoon, "The Underside of the Picturesque Landscape: Meanings of Muslim Burial in Cape Town, South Africa," *Arab World Geographer* 7, no. 4 (December 1, 2004): 262–63.

52. Bickford-Smith, *Ethnic Pride and Racial Prejudice in Victorian Cape Town*, 75.

53. Baderoon, "The Underside of the Picturesque Landscape," 266.

54. Swanson, "The Sanitation Syndrome," 387.

55. The cost of forcibly removing and separating the racial populations of the city became a pressing reason not to employ such action as it was unclear whether the government or other entity would pay for the removals. Segregation would also raise a constitutional issue around forcibly removing an enfranchised population Vivian Bickford-Smith, Elizabeth van Heyningen, and Nigel Worden, *Cape Town in the Twentieth Century: An Illustrated Social History* (Cape Town: David Philip, 1999), 229. Cape law at the time guaranteed franchise largely universally. Commercial interests raised further concerns that having their labor so far from their places of work would unduly encumber production. This may explain why the epidemic of 1882 did not result in segregation.

56. Cape Peninsula Advisory Board, *Report and Proceedings*.

57. Cape Peninsula Advisory Board, *Report and Proceedings*.

58. Cape Peninsula Advisory Board, *Report and Proceedings*, 15.

59. Echenberg, *Plague Ports*, 50.

60. Echenberg, *Plague Ports*, 79.

61. Joseph West Ridgeway, "Letter to the Secretary of State for the Colonies, the Right Honorable Joseph Chamberlain M.P. from Ceylon Governor Joseph West Ridgeway Concerning Despatch no. 257," August 30, 1897. FO 83/1641. British National Archives at Kew, London.

62. Ridgeway, "Letter to the Secretary of State for the Colonies."

63. Mayor et al., *International Sanitary Convention, Signed at Venice, March 18, 1897*; Echenberg, "Pestis Redux"; Nermin Ersoy, Yuksel Gungor, and Aslihan Akpinar, "International Sanitary Conferences from the Ottoman Perspective (1851–1938)," *Hygiea Internationalis* 10, no. 1 (2011): 53–79; Howard-Jones, "The Scientific Background of the International Sanitary Conferences, 1851–1938."

64. Parliament of Great Britain, House of Commons, *Parliamentary Papers: 1850–1908* (H. M. Stationery Office, 1902); Gregory and Simpson, "Memoranda by the Acting Medical Officer of Health"; R. Nathan, *The Plague in India, 1896, 1897 Volume III* (Simla: Government of India, Home Department, 1898); W. J Simpson, *Report on the Causes and Continuance of Plague in Hongkong and Suggestions as to Remedial Measures* (London: Waterlow, 1903), http://books.google.com/books?id=_j44AQAAMAAJ.

65. Great Britain Parliament House of Commons, *Parliamentary Papers*; Nathan, *The Plague In India, 1896, 1897 Volume III.*

66. Rubert Boyce, "Letter from Rubert Boyce to the RH. Joseph Chamberlain, Secretary of State for the Colonies," 02 1901, 1/469, Cape Town Archives Repository, National Archives of South Africa, Cape Town.

67. William John Richie Simpson, *Memorandum on the Influence of Rats in the Dissemination of Plague.* Cape Town: Richards, 1900.

68. Simpson, *Memorandum on the Influence of Rats in the Dissemination of Plague.*

69. A. John Gregory and William John Richie Simpson, "Memoranda by the Acting Medical Officer of Health for Cape Colony and Professor W. J. Simpson. M.D., F.R.C.P. on the Outbreak of Plague in Cape Colony and the Precautions Taken in Connection Therewith. Office of the Medical Officer of Health for the Colony, Cape Town." CO 897/67/2. British National Archives at Kew, London.

70. Van Heyningen, "Public Health and Society in Cape Town"; Swanson, "The Sanitation Syndrome."

71. Simpson, *Report on the Causes and Continuance of Plague in Hongkong and Suggestions as to Remedial Measures*, 113.

72. Sir William John Simpson, *The Maintenance of Health in the Tropics* (Wood, 1905), 32.

73. Simpson, *The Maintenance of Health in the Tropics*, 32.

74. William John Ritchie Simpson, *The Principles of Hygiene as Applied to Tropical and Sub-Tropical Climates and the Principles of Personal Hygiene in Them as Applied to Europeans* (London: J. Bales, Sons, & Danielsson, 1908), 371.

75. Simpson, *The Principles of Hygiene*, 359.

76. Curtin, "Medical Knowledge and Urban Planning in Tropical Africa," 611.

77. Ridgeway, "Letter to the Secretary of State for the Colonies, the Right Honorable Joseph Chamberlain M.P. from Ceylon Governor Joseph West Ridgeway Concerning Despatch No. 257," August 30, 1897. FO 83/1641, British National Archives at Kew, London; Ridgeway, "Letter to the Secretary of State for the Colonies, The Right Honorable Joseph Chamberlain M.P. from Ceylon Governor Joseph West Ridgeway," December 7, 1898. FO 83/1691, British National Archives at Kew, London.

78. Van Heyningen, "Public Health and Society in Cape Town," 297.

79. Quoted in van Heyningen, "Public Health and Society in Cape Town," 297.

80. Simpson quoted in T. James, "The Year of the Plague in Cape Town," *South African Medical Journal = Suid-Afrikaanse Tydskrif Vir Geneeskunde* 44, no. 50 (1970): 1432.

81. Gregory and Simpson, "Memoranda by the Acting Medical Officer of Health," (Gregory and Simpson 1901.)

82. *Public Health Reports: Volume 15, Issues 1–26.* In keeping with the convention, the Cape government was notified from the British Foreign Office that Italy and Belgium had applied restrictions on their vessels as per the Venice Convention on March 9, 1901 (Telegram of the Foreign Office 1901).

83. Gregory and Simpson, "Memoranda by the Acting Medical Officer of Health."

84. Cape Peninsula Advisory Board, *Report and Proceedings*, 22.

85. Cape Peninsula Advisory Board, *Report and Proceedings*, 23.

86. Cape Peninsula Advisory Board, *Report and Proceedings*, 29.

87. Cape Peninsula Advisory Board, *Report and Proceedings*, 22.

88. Cape Peninsula Advisory Board, *Report and Proceedings*, 22.

89. Gregory and Simpson, "Memoranda by the Acting Medical Officer of Health."

90. Swanson, "The Sanitation Syndrome"; Stanley Trapido, "The Origins of the Cape Franchise Qualifications of 1853," *Journal of African History* 5, no. 1 (1964): 37–54.

91. Bickford-Smith, "South African Urban History, Racial Segregation and the Unique Case of Cape Town?"; Harriet Deacon, "Racial Segregation and Medical Discourse in Nineteenth-Century Cape Town," *Journal of Southern African Studies – J S AFR STUD* 22, no. 2 (1996): 287–308, https://doi.org/10.1080/03057079608708492.

92. Baderoon, "The Underside of the Picturesque Landscape"; R. L. Watson, *Slave Emancipation and Racial Attitudes in Nineteenth-Century South Africa* (Cambridge: Cambridge University Press, 2012); Nigel Worden, *Slavery in Dutch South Africa* (Cambridge: Cambridge University Press, 1985).

93. Gabeba Baderoon, *Regarding Muslims: From Slavery to Postapartheid* (Johannesburg: Wits University Press, 2014), 11; John Edwin Mason, *Social Death and Resurrection: Slavery and Emancipation in South Africa* (Charlottesville: University of Virginia Press, 2003), 110.

94. *Zuid Afrikaan* March 27, 1840, in Baderoon, *Regarding Muslims*, 10–12.

95. Watson, *Slave Emancipation and Racial Attitudes in Nineteenth-Century South Africa*, 246.

96. Bickford-Smith, van Heyningen, and Worden, *Cape Town in the Twentieth Century*, 19.

97. Curtin, "Medical Knowledge and Urban Planning in Tropical Africa."

98. Cape Peninsula Advisory Board, *Report and Proceedings*, 57.

99. Cape Peninsula Advisory Board, *Report and Proceedings*, 57.

Chapter 3

1. Marcos Cueto, *The Value of Health: A History of the Pan American Health Organization* (Rochester, NY: University of Rochester Press, 2007), 40.

2. Anne Sealey, "Globalizing the 1926 International Sanitary Convention," *Journal of Global History* 6, no. 3 (November 2011): 431–55, https://doi.org/10.1017/S1740022811000404; A. Bashford, "Global Biopolitics and the History of World Health," *History of the Human Sciences* 19, no. 1 (February 1, 2006): 67–88, https://doi-.org/10.1177/0952695106062148.

3. These aspects will be discussed in greater detail in the next chapter. Nancy Leys Stepan, *Eradication: Ridding the World of Diseases Forever?* (Ithaca, NY: Cornell University Press, 2015); Randall M. Packard, *The Making of a Tropical Disease: A Short History of Malaria* (Baltimore, MD: Johns Hopkins University Press, 2011); Socrates Litsios, "Malaria Control, the Cold War, and the Postwar Reorganization of International Assistance," *Medical Anthropology* 17, no. 3 (May 1, 1997): 255–78, https://doi.org/10.1080/0 1459740.1997.9966140.

4. Arthur Stanley, George Ford Petrie, and Richard P. Strong, *Report of the International Plague Conference Held at Mukden, April, 1911* (Manila: Bureau of Printing, 1912), xiii, https://catalog.hathitrust.org/Record/001579593; Iris Borowy, "International Social Medicine between the Wars: Positioning a Volatile Concept," *Hygiea Internationalis: An Interdisciplinary Journal for the History of Public Health* 6, no. 2 (December 1, 2007): 13–35; Iris Borowy, *Coming to Terms with World Health: The League of Nations Health Organisation 1921–1946* (Frankfurt am Main: Peter Lang, 2009); Stepan, *Eradication*; William C. Summers, *The Great Manchurian Plague of 1910–1911: The Geopolitics of an Epidemic Disease* (New Haven, CT: Yale University Press, 2012); Packard, *The Making of a Tropical Disease.*

5. Randall M. Packard, *A History of Global Health: Interventions into the Lives of Other Peoples* (Baltimore, MD: Johns Hopkins University Press, 2016); Nitsan Chorev, *The World Health Organization between North and South* (Ithaca, NY: Cornell University Press, 2012).

6. Cueto, *The Value of Health.*

7. "Expert Committee on International Epidemic Control—Report on Its First Session" (Geneva, April 12, 1948), WHO.IC/Epid./8/Rev.1, World Health Organization Archive.

8. Interim Commission, "Draft Report of the Expert Committee on International Epidemic Control," April 16, 1948, WHO.IC/Epid./8, World Health Organization.

9. Sheila Jasanoff, *States of Knowledge: The Co-Production of Science and the Social Order* (London: Routledge, 2004), 19.

10. David P. Fidler, "From International Sanitary Conventions to Global Health Security: The New International Health Regulations," *Chinese Journal of International*

Law 4, no. 2 (January 1, 2005): 325–92, https://doi.org/10.1093/chinesejil/jmi029; Javed Siddiqi, *World Health and World Politics: The World Health Organization and the UN System* (Columbus: University of South Carolina Press, 1995).

11. Borowy, "International Social Medicine between the Wars."

12. Cueto, *The Value of Health*; Packard, *The Making of a Tropical Disease*; Packard, *A History of Global Health*; Anderson, "Excremental Colonialism: Public Health and the Poetics of Pollution," *Critical Inquiry* 21, no. 3 (Spring 1995): 640–69; Anderson, "The Possession of Kuru: Medical Science and Biocolonial Exchange," *Comparative Studies in Society and History* 42, no. 4 (October 2000): 713–44, https://doi.org/10.1017/S0010417500003297; Anderson, *Colonial Pathologies: American Tropical Medicine, Race, and Hygiene in the Philippines* (Durham, NC: Duke University Press, 2006); Lindsay-Poland, *Emperors in the Jungle: The Hidden History of the U.S. in Panama* (Durham, NC: Duke University Press, 2003); Malcolm Gladwell, "Fred Soper and the Global Malaria Eradication Programme," *Journal of Public Health Policy* 23, no. 4 (2002): 479, https://doi.org/10.2307/3343244; Litsios, "Malaria Control"; Steven Palmer, "Toward Responsibility in International Health: Death Following Treatment in Rockefeller Hookworm Campaigns, 1914–1934," *Medical History* 54, no. 2 (April 2010): 149–70; Siddiqi, *World Health and World Politics*.

13. Norman Howard-Jones, *The Scientific Background of the International Sanitary Conferences, 1851–1938* (Geneva: World Health Organization, 1975), http://apps.who.int//iris/handle/10665/62873; Packard, *A History of Global Health*.

14. Anderson, *Colonial Pathologies*; Gladwell, "Fred Soper and the Global Malaria Eradication Programme"; Packard, *The Making of a Tropical Disease*; Packard, *A History of Global Health*.

15. Packard, *A History of Global Health*, 22.

16. William Crawford Gorgas, *Sanitation in Panama* (New York; Appleton, 1918), 292.

17. Anderson, *Colonial Pathologies*; Lindsay-Poland, *Emperors in the Jungle*; Packard, *The Making of a Tropical Disease*.

18. Erika Lee, *At America's Gates: Chinese Immigration during the Exclusion Era, 1882–1943* (Chapel Hill: University of North Carolina Press, 2003), 26.

19. Sucheta Mazumdar, "Through Western Eyes: Discovering Chinese Women in America," in *A New Significance: Re-Envisioning the History of the American West*, ed. Clyde A. Milner and Allan G. Bogue (New York: Oxford University Press, 1996), 161.

20. F. L. Hoffman, *Race Traits and Tendencies of the American Negro*, Publications of the American Economic Association v. 11, nos. 1–4 (American Economic Association, 1896), https://books.google.com/books?id=N7MyAQAAMAAJ.

21. Lee, *At America's Gates*, 27.

22. Cueto, *The Value of Health*, 32.

23. Cueto, *The Value of Health*, 35.

24. "Third International Sanitary Convention," *Public Health Reports (1896–1970)* 22, no. 30 (1907): 1021–24.

25. Myron J. Echenberg, *Plague Ports: The Global Urban Impact of Bubonic Plague,1894–1901* (New York: New York University Press, 2007), 236.

26. Cueto, *The Value of Health*.

27. Hugh S. Cumming, "The International Sanitary Conference," *American Journal of Public Health* 16, no. 10 (1926): 976.

28. Cueto, *The Value of Health*.

29. "Declaration of Alma-Ata International Conference on Primary Health Care, Alma-Ata, USSR, 6–12 September 1978," *Development* 47, no. 2 (June 1, 2004): 159–61, https://doi.org/10.1057/palgrave.development.1100047; Summers, *The Great Manchurian Plague of 1910–1911*; Packard, *A History of Global Health*; Iris Borowy, "Shifting between Biomedical and Social Medicine: International Health Organizations in the 20th Century: International Health Organizations," *History Compass* 12, no. 6 (June 2014): 517–30, https://doi.org/10.1111/hic3.12162.

30. Borowy, "International Social Medicine between the Wars."

31. Borowy, "International Social Medicine between the Wars."

32. Historian Iris Borowy has written the comprehensive history of the organization, while other scholars such as Socrates Litsios also reflect that little has been written about the role of social medicine in the early twentieth century.

33. Socrates Litsios, "Revisiting Bandoeng," *Social Medicine* 8, no. 3 (2014).

34. Borowy, "International Social Medicine between the Wars"; Packard, *The Making of a Tropical Disease*.

35. Report of the Pan-African Health Conference, in Packard, *A History of Global Health*, 47.

36. Packard, *A History of Global Health*, 47, 55.

37. Borowy, *Coming to Terms with World Health*, 231.

38. George Buchanan, "Proposed International Conference of Medical Representatives of the Health Service of Certain African Territories at Cape Town on November 19th," October 11, 1932, R5920/8A/23475/23393, League of Nations Archive; "Meeting of Medical Officers of African Powers. Cape Town November 1932," November 1932, R5920/8A/40074/23393, League of Nations Archive.

39. Preparatory Committee, *Intergovernmental Conference of Far-Eastern Countries on Rural Hygiene. Report By Preparatory Committee* (Geneva: League of Nations, 1937).

40. Preparatory Committee, *Intergovernmental Conference*, 11.

41. Preparatory Committee, *Intergovernmental Conference*, 9.

42. Preparatory Committee, *Intergovernmental Conference*, 20.

43. Preparatory Committee, *Intergovernmental Conference*, 21.

44. Preparatory Committee, *Intergovernmental Conference*, 12.

45. Preparatory Committee, *Intergovernmental Conference*, 21.

46. Pan-African Health Conference, "Pan-African Health Conference," *British Medical Journal* 1, no. 3915 (January 18, 1936): 122–23.

47. The Mukden International Plague Conference of 1911 was a critical moment in health policy making in the early twentieth century, as it was the first international health conference held in China at a moment when Manchuria itself was being vied over for control by the Russian and Japanese Empires while also facing incursions from

the United States and European powers. Nevertheless the conference led by Dr. Wu-Lien Teh brought in health experts from around the world to facilitate critical developments in plague response and health infrastructure. The Mukden Conference was a critical site for the sharing of research on plague and led to the formulation of the North Manchurian Plague Prevention Service. The conference was also notable for seeking to bring the region in line with International Sanitary Convention procedures. Stanley, Petrie, and Strong, *Report of the International Plague Conference Held at Mukden, April, 1911.*; Summers, *The Great Manchurian Plague of 1910–1911.*

48. Theodore M. Brown and Elizabeth Fee, "The Bandoeng Conference of 1937: A Milestone in Health and Development," *American Journal of Public Health* 98, no. 1 (January 2008): 42–43, https://doi.org/10.2105/AJPH.2007.119222; Litsios, "Revisiting Bandoeng."

49. Brown and Fee, "The Bandoeng Conference of 1937."

50. Sealey, "Globalizing the 1926 International Sanitary Convention."

51. L'Office International D'Hygiène Publique, "Session Extraordinaire De Mai-Juin 1926 Du Comité Permanent De L'Office International D'Hygiène Publique: Procès Verbaux Des Séances" (World Health Organization Library, 1926), 14.

52. Sealey, "Globalizing the 1926 International Sanitary Convention."

53. "The International Sanitary Convention of 1926 with Annexes: Signed at Paris-June 21, 1926," 1926, 553, Library of Congress, https://www.loc.gov/law/help/us-treaties/bevans/m-ust000002-0545.pdf.

54. Sealey, "Globalizing the 1926 International Sanitary Convention," 445.

55. Cumming, "The International Sanitary Conference," 975.

56. "The International Sanitary Convention of 1926," 574–75.

57. "The International Sanitary Convention of 1926," 588.

58. "The International Sanitary Convention of 1926," 589.

59. "The International Sanitary Convention of 1926," 592.

60. Litsios, "Revisiting Bandoeng"; Packard, *A History of Global Health.*

61. Knud Stowman, "International Sanitary Regulations," *Public Health Reports* 67, no. 10 (October 1952): 972–76.

62. "Obituary: Raymond Gautier, M.D," *British Medical Journal* 1, no. 5027 (May 11, 1957): 1127.

63. Oscar Forel, "Proposal by Dr. O. Forel for a World Sanitary Centre to Yves Biraud and Raymond Gautier," October 8, 1943, R5920/8A/42128/41755, League of Nations Archive.

64. Forel, "Proposal by Dr. O. Forel. "

65. Yves Biraud, "Suggestions for the Post-War Amalgamation of International Health Institutions," October 27, 1944, R6150/8A/42169/41755, League of Nations Archive.

66. Ludwik Rajchman, "Why Not?: A United Nations Health Service," September 1943, R6150/8A/42169/41755, League of Nations Archive.

67. C.-E. A. Winslow, "International Organization for Health," January 23, 1945, R6150/8A/42169/41755, League of Nations Archive.

68. "Formation of an International Health Organization: Report to Accompany S. J. Resolution 89" (United States Senate, December 20, 1945), 2, R6150/8A/42169/41755, League of Nations Archive.

69. World Health Assembly, *International Sanitary Regulations: Proceedings of the Special Committee and of the Fourth World Health Assembly on WHO Regulations No. 2* (Geneva: World Health Organization, 1952), http://www.apps.who.int/iris/handle/10665/85636.

70. World Health Assembly, *International Sanitary Regulations*.

71. Interim Commission, "Draft Report of the Expert Committee on International Epidemic Control."

72. WHO Secretariat, "Draft of Forward to the International Sanitary Regulations," October 1, 1949, WHO/Epid/20, World Health Organization Archive.

73. Expert Committee on International Epidemiology and Quarantine, "Draft International Sanitary Regulations: Comments and Suggestions Regarding the Revision of the Conventions," November 28, 1949, 3, WHO/Epid./26, World Health Organization Archive.

74. World Health Assembly, *International Sanitary Regulations*, 39.

75. "*Article 20*
Every port situated in a yellow-fever endemic zone or a yellow-fever receptive area, and the area within the perimeter of every airport so situated, shall be kept free from Aëdes aegypti in their larval and adult stages.

2. Any building within a direct transit area provided at any airport situated in a yellow-fever endemic zone or in a yellow-fever receptive area shall be mosquito-proof.

3. Every sanitary airport situated in a yellow-fever endemic zone-

(a) shall be provided with mosquito-proof dwellings and have at its disposal mosquito-proof sick quarters for passengers, crews, and airport personnel;

(b) shall be freed from mosquitos by systematically destroying them in their larval and adult stages within the perimeter of the airport, and within a protective area extending for a distance of four hundred metres around that perimeter.

4. For the purposes of this Article, the perimeter of an airport means a line enclosing the area containing the airport buildings and any land or water used or intended to be used for the parking of aircraft." World Health Assembly, *International Sanitary Regulations*, 339.

76. World Health Assembly, *International Sanitary Regulations*, 42.

77. World Health Assembly, *International Sanitary Regulations*, 336.

78. Expert Committee on International Epidemiology and Quarantine, "Draft International Sanitary Regulations."

79. World Health Assembly, *International Sanitary Regulations*, 336.

80. World Health Assembly, *International Sanitary Regulations*, 360.

81. World Health Assembly, *International Sanitary Regulations*.

82. Expert Advisory Panel on International Quarantine, "Review of the International Sanitary Regulations: Comments from Members of the Expert Advisory Panel on International Quarantine," 1967, 4, IQ/WP/67.12, World Health Organization.

83. See pages 35–36.

84. Expert Committee on International Epidemiology and Quarantine, "Draft International Sanitary Regulations"; World Health Assembly, *International Sanitary Regulations*.

85. Committee on International Quarantine, "Reservations to the Additional Regulations, 1955, Amending the International Sanitary Regulations, 1951," March 20, 1956, 2, WHO/IQ/33, World Health Organization. WHO/IQ/33, World Health Organization Archive.

86. Division of Malaria Eradication, "Malaria and the International Sanitary Regulations" (Geneva: World Health Organization, 1967), 1, IQ/WP/67.9, World Health Organization Archive.

87. K Raška, "Considerations of the Future Trends in the International Spread of Communicable Diseases and Their Control" (Geneva: World Health Organization, 1967), IQ/WP/67.3, World Health Organization Archive.

88. Raška, "Considerations of the Future Trends in the International Spread of Communicable Diseases and Their Control," 2.

Chapter 4

1. While the International Health Regulations remain in effect as a global treaty, in September 2020 the World Health Assembly passed Resolution WHA73.1 calling for a comprehensive review of the COVID-19 response under the existing IHR (2005). It is anticipated that reforms to the IHR will follow the "Report of the Review Committee on the Functioning of the International Health Regulations (2005) during the COVID-19 Response," https://www.who.int/publications/m/item/a74-9-who-s-work-in-health-emergencies.

2. The WHO's total global operating budget for 2018–2019 was $4.422 billion, less than the budget of many of the hospital systems of single cities in the United States. In comparison the Gates Foundation distributed $5 billion in grants alone in 2018. WHO, "Budget and Finance," https://www.who.int/publications/i/item/programme-budget-2018-2019; Bill & Melinda Gates Foundation, "Foundation Fact Sheet," https://www.gatesfoundation.org/who-we-are/general-information/foundation-factsheet.

3. A deeper investigation of the PHEIC designation and the rationale for declaring a PHEIC will be investigated in detail in Chapter 5.

4. A. Bashford, "Global Biopolitics and the History of World Health," *History of the Human Sciences* 19, no. 1 (February 1, 2006): 67–88, https://doi.org/10.1177/0952695106062148; David P. Fidler and Lawrence O. Gostin, "The New International Health Regulations: An Historic Development for International Law and Public Health," *Journal of Law, Medicine & Ethics* 34, no. 1 (March 1, 2006): 85–94, https://doi.org/10.1111/j.1748-720X.2006.00011.x.

5. L. O. Gostin, D. Sridhar, and D. Hougendobler, "The Normative Authority of the World Health Organization," *Public Health* 129, no. 7 (July 2015): 854–63, https://doi.org/10.1016/j.puhe.2015.05.002; Javed Siddiqi, *World Health and World Politics: The World Health Organization and the UN System* (Columbus: University of South Carolina Press, 1995).

6. Gostin, Sridhar, and Hougendobler, "The Normative Authority of the World Health Organization."

7. Siddiqi, *World Health and World Politics*; Nitsan Chorev, *The World Health Organization between North and South* (Ithaca, NY: Cornell University Press, 2012); Marcos Cueto, Theodore M. Brown, and Elizabeth Fee, *The World Health Organization: A History* (Cambridge: Cambridge University Press, 2019). For exceptions see Andrew Lakoff, *Unprepared: Global Health in a Time of Emergency* (Oakland: University of California Press, 2017); Fidler and Gostin, "The New International Health Regulations."

8. Gostin, Sridhar, and Hougendobler, "The Normative Authority of the World Health Organization."

9. Gostin, Sridhar, and Hougendobler, "The Normative Authority of the World Health Organization," 855.

10. Gostin, Sridhar, and Hougendobler, "The Normative Authority of the World Health Organization," 855.

11. Socrates Litsios, "Malaria Control, the Cold War, and the Postwar Reorganization of International Assistance," *Medical Anthropology* 17, no. 3 (May 1, 1997): 255–78, https://doi.org/10.1080/01459740.1997.9966140.

12. Nancy Leys Stepan, *Eradication: Ridding the World of Diseases Forever?* (Ithaca, NY: Cornell University Press, 2015).

13. Chorev, *The World Health Organization between North and South*, 50.

14. Chorev, *The World Health Organization between North and South*, 58.

15. Chorev, *The World Health Organization between North and South*, 60.

16. "Declaration of Alma-Ata International Conference on Primary Health Care, Alma-Ata, USSR, 6–12 September 1978," *Development* 47, no. 2 (June 1, 2004): 159–61, https://doi.org/10.1057/palgrave.development.1100047.

17. "Declaration of Alma-Ata International Conference on Primary Health Care," 3.

18. Chorev, *The World Health Organization between North and South*, 126.

19. Chorev, *The World Health Organization between North and South*, 126.

20. Gostin, Sridhar, and Hougendobler, "The Normative Authority of the World Health Organization."

21. Chorev, *The World Health Organization between North and South*, 144.

22. Stephen S. Morse and Ann Schluederberg, "Emerging Viruses: The Evolution of Viruses and Viral Diseases," *Journal of Infectious Diseases* 162, no. 1 (1990): 1–7; Committee on Emerging Microbial Threats to Health and Institute of Medicine, *Emerging Infections: Microbial Threats to Health in the United States* (Washington, DC: National Academies Press, 1992).

23. Sara E. Davies, "Securitizing Infectious Disease," *International Affairs* 84, no. 2 (March 1, 2008): 298, https://doi.org/10.1111/j.1468-2346.2008.00704.x.

24. Anthony S. Fauci, "The Syndrome of Kaposi's Sarcoma and Opportunistic Infections: An Epidemiologically Restricted Disorder of Immunoregulation," *Annals of Internal Medicine* 96, no. 6_part_1 (June 1, 1982): 777–79, https://doi.org/10.7326/0003-4819-96-6-777.

25. J. Lederberg, "Medical Science, Infectious Disease, and the Unity of Humankind," *JAMA* 260, no. 5 (August 5, 1988): 685.

26. Chorev, *The World Health Organization between North and South*.

27. F Barre-Sinoussi et al., "Isolation of a T-Lymphotropic Retrovirus from a Patient at Risk for Acquired Immune Deficiency Syndrome (AIDS)," *Science* 220, no. 4599 (May 20, 1983): 868–71, https://doi.org/10.1126/science.6189183.

28. Chorev, *The World Health Organization between North and South*.

29. Chorev, *The World Health Organization between North and South*, 154.

30. Morse and Schluederberg, "Emerging Viruses," 1.

31. Morse and Schluederberg, "Emerging Viruses," 4, 5.

32. Committee on Emerging Microbial Threats to Health and Institute of Medicine, *Emerging Infections*, v.

33. Anne Carter, "Establishing Goals, Techniques and Priorities for National Communicable Disease Surveillance," *Canadian Journal of Infectious Diseases* 2, no. 1 (1991): 37–40.

34. Carter, "Establishing Goals, Techniques and Priorities for National Communicable Disease Surveillance."

35. World Health Organization, *International Health Regulations (1969)* (Geneva: World Health Organization, 1969), 5.

36. Norman G. Gratz, Robert Steffen, and William Cocksedge, "Why Aircraft Disinsection?," *Bulletin of the World Health Organization* 78, no. 8 (August 2000): 995–1004, https://doi.org/10.1590/S0042-96862000000800009; World Health Organization, *International Health Regulations (1969)*.

37. World Health Organization, *International Health Regulations (1969)*, 32.

38. Gratz, Steffen, and Cocksedge, "Why Aircraft Disinsection?"

39. Linda Bonvie and Bill Bonvie, "Aircraft Spraying," *Chicago Tribune*, June 4, 1994, https://www.chicagotribune.com/news/ct-xpm-1994-06-05-9406040300-story.html; Linda Bonvie and Bill Bonvie, "Count Disinsection among Risks of Travel," Baltimore Sun, March 5, 1994, https://www.baltimoresun.com/news/bs-xpm-1994-03-06-1994065234-story.html; Melissa Healy, "Insecticide Spraying of Passengers on Airliners Coming Under Scrutiny: Chemicals: Many Countries Require 'Disinsection' of Travelers. Political and Diplomatic Issues Face U.S. Officials Seeking Changes," *Los Angeles Times*, June 25, 1994, http://articles.latimes.com/1994-06-25/news/mn-8204_1_diplomatic-issue.

40. Bonvie and Bonvie, "Aircraft Spraying."

41. Bonvie and Bonvie, "Aircraft Spraying."

42. Maurice Williamson, "Opening Address to the New Zealand Air Facilitation Committee 50th National Conference," The Beehive, July 2, 1999, http://www.beehive .govt.nz/speech/opening-address-new-zealand-air-facilitation-committee-50th-national-conference.

43. Association of Flight Attendants AFL-CIO, "Re. Aircraft Disinsection," November 2, 2001, 8, http://ashsd.afacwa.org/docs/United.Pest.Nov01.pdf.

44. United States Congress, House Committee on Public Works and Transportation; Subcommittee on Aviation and Boston Public Library, "Airliner Cabin Air Quality: Hearing before the Subcommittee on Aviation of the Committee on Public Works and Transportation, House of Representatives, One Hundred Third Congress, Second Session, May 18, 1994," 10–11, http://archive.org/details/airlinercabinair00unit.

45. Robert Steffen, "IHR Meeting December 1995," November 21, 1995, E14/87/3, World Health Organization Archive.

46. Steffen, "IHR Meeting December 1995."

47. "ProMED—the Program for Monitoring Emerging Diseases—is an Internet-based reporting system dedicated to rapid global dissemination of information on outbreaks of infectious diseases and acute exposures to toxins that affect human health, including those in animals and in plants grown for food or animal feed. Electronic communications enable ProMED to provide up-to-date and reliable news about threats to human, animal, and food plant health around the world, seven days a week." Committee on Emerging Microbial Threats to Health and Institute of Medicine, *Emerging Infections*, v.

48. World Health Organization, "WHO Event Management for International Public Health Security Operational Procedures," 2008, web.archive.org/web/20220119091107/ http://www.who.int/csr/resources/publications/WHO_HSE_EPR_ARO_2008_1/en/.

49. Brian Gushulak, "Working Draft of IHR Revisions," October 17, 1996, 1, E14/439/4, World Health Organization Archive.

50. Fidler and Gostin, "The New International Health Regulations."

51. WHO Meeting to Review Epidemic Preparedness et al., "Report of a WHO Meeting to Review Epidemic Preparedness, Epidemic Control and Research in Outbreak Situations, Geneva, Switzerland, 25–17 September 1995," http://apps.www.who.int/ iris/handle/10665/65518.

52. D. P. Nymadawa, "Some Thoughts on Revision of the International Health Regulations (IHR)," Letter, August 15, 1995, E14/439/1, World Health Organization.

53. Brian Gushulak, "An Approach to International Disease Reporting by Syndrome," March 12, 1996, E14/439/4, World Health Organization.

54. Gushulak, "Working Draft of IHR Revisions."

55. Daniel Bleed, "Defining the 'Syndromic Approach' to Disease Reporting for the International Health Regulations (IHR)," June 30, 1996, 2. E14/439/4. World Health Organization Archive.

56. "Letter From Margaret Tipple to J. C. Alary," May 21, 1996, E14/439/4, World Health Organization Archive.

57. World Health Organization, "WHO Guidance for the Use of Annex 2 of the International Health Regulations (2005)," 2010, https://www.who.int/publications/m/item/who-guidance-for-the-use-of-annex-2-of-the-international-health-regulations-(2005).

58. Lawrence O. Gostin and Rebecca Katz, "The International Health Regulations: The Governing Framework for Global Health Security," in *Global Management of Infectious Disease after Ebola*, edited by Sam F. Halabi, Lawrence O. Gostin, and Jeffrey S. Crowley (Oxford: Oxford University Press, 2017).

59. Sam F. Halabi, Lawrence O. Gostin, and Jeffrey S. Crowley, *Global Management of Infectious Disease After Ebola* (Oxford: Oxford University Press, 2016).

60. Gostin, Sridhar, and Hougendobler, "The Normative Authority of the World Health Organization."

61. Ilona Kickbusch, "World Health Organisation: Change and Progress," *BMJ* 310, no. 6993 (June 10, 1995): 1518–20, https://doi.org/10.1136/bmj.310.6993.1518.

62. Gostin, Sridhar, and Hougendobler, "The Normative Authority of the World Health Organization."

63. Regional Office for South-East Asia World Health Organization, "Inaugural Address by Dr Samlee Plianbangchang, Regional Director, WHO South-East Asia, 29th Session of the WHO South-East Asia Advisory Committee on Health Research, Yangon, Myanmar, 14–16 June 2004," June 16, 2004, http://apps.www.who.int/iris/handle/10665/127138.

Chapter 5

1. This was the year the IHR (2005) went into effect.

2. L. O. Gostin, D. Sridhar, and D. Hougendobler, "The Normative Authority of the World Health Organization," *Public Health* 129, no. 7 (July 2015): 854–63, https://doi.org/10.1016/j.puhe.2015.05.002; Lawrence O. Gostin, "The World Health Organization's Historic Moment of Peril and Promise: Reimagining a Global Health Agency Fit for Purpose in the 21st Century," in "Reform of the World Health Organization," special issue, *Journal of Global Health Governance* 11, no. 1 (2017).

3. Daniel Chardell, "From Ebola to Zika: Why the World Needs WHO Reform," *Council on Foreign Relations – The Internationalist* (blog), February 17, 2016, https://www.cfr.org/blog/ebola-zika-why-world-needs-who-reform; Michelle Roberts, "WHO 'Unfit for Health Emergencies,'" *BBC News*, July 5, 2015, 20, http://www.bbc.com/news/health-33422635; World Health Organization, "Report of the Ebola Interim Assessment Panel—May 2015," May 2015, http://www.who.int/csr/resources/publications/ebola/ebola-interim-assessment/en/.

4. Independent Oversight and Advisory Committee for the WHO Health Emergencies Programme, "Interim Report on WHO's Response to COVID-19 January–April 2020."

5. Milan Brahmbhatt and Arindam Dutta, *On SARS-Type Economic Effects during Infectious Disease Outbreaks* (Washington, DC: World Bank, 2008).

6. World Health Organization, "WHO Event Management for International Public Health Security Operational Procedures," 7, web.archive.org/web/20220119091107/http://www.who.int/csr/resources/publications/WHO_HSE_EPR_ARO_2008_1/en/.

7. World Health Organization, "WHO Event Management," 3.

8. World Health Organization, "WHO Event Management," 9–10.

9. World Health Organization, "International Health Regulations (2005)," https://www.who.int/publications/i/item/9789241580496.

10. World Health Organization, "WHO Event Management," 11.

11. World Health Organization, "International Health Regulations (2005)," 14.

12. Michael Edelstein et al., "Validity of International Health Regulations in Reporting Emerging Infectious Diseases," *Emerging Infectious Diseases* 18, no. 7 (July 2012): 1115–20, https://doi.org/10.3201/eid1807.111608.

13. Edelstein et al., "Validity of International Health Regulations," 116.

14. Edelstein et al., "Validity of International Health Regulations."

15. Daniel Lucey and Lawrence O. Gostin, "A Yellow Fever Epidemic: A New Global Health Emergency?," *JAMA* 315, no. 24 (June 28, 2016): 2661–62, https://doi.org/10.1001/jama.2016.6606; Lawrence O. Gostin, Daniel Lucey, and Alexandra Phelan, "The Ebola Epidemic: A Global Health Emergency," *JAMA* 312, no. 11 (September 17, 2014): 1095–96, https://doi.org/10.1001/jama.2014.11176.

16. This research was facilitated under an ethics review from the Boston University Internal Review Board. As part of its ethical criteria, I am not permitted to interview elected officials for whom their comments may have proved potentially detrimental to their careers.

17. Sampling therefore prioritized representation of a distribution across emergency committees rather than a significant, clustered interview population. These data collected from interviews were supplemented by archival research conducted on official WHO correspondence and documents collected at the WHO archives in Geneva as well as through their online archive IRIS. All names and affiliations of interview subjects have been anonymized to protect the identities of interview subjects as per the conditions of the Boston University Internal Review Board.

In conducting interviews, particular attention was paid to the considerations that were brought to bear on the deliberations, including any disputes that may have arisen within the emergency committees. A focus of these interviews was also the materiality of the meetings itself: how epidemiological data was conveyed to the committee members and how meetings were organized, coordinated, and run. The reason for these foci is theoretically driven. In attempting to claim a level of scientific validity for this designation, emergency committee members are tasked with sifting the available disease surveillance information to explore the possibilities for international disease spread in the context of global trade and travel. Scholarship in science and technology studies has often found that the localized practice of building scientific consensus is often obscured in the final presentation of findings. An attention to these details aimed to uncover these processes that may go underexamined in the final documents justifying the declaration or nondeclaration of a PHEIC.

18. Donald G. Mcneil Jr, "W.H.O. Calls Yellow Fever in Africa 'Serious Concern,'" *New York Times*, May 19, 2016, http://www.nytimes.com/2016/05/20/health/who-yellow -fever-africa.html; World Health Organization, "Mass Vaccination Campaign to Protect Millions against Yellow Fever in Angola and Democratic Republic of the Congo," August 16, 2016, https://www.who.int/news-room/feature-stories/detail/mass-vaccination -campaign-to-protect-millions-against-yellow-fever-in-angola-and-democratic-repub lic-of-the-congo.

19. Catherine Z. Worsnop, "Provoking Barriers: The 2014 Ebola Outbreak and Unintended Consequences of WHO's Power to Declare a Public Health Emergency," *Journal of Global Health Governance* 11, no. 1 (2017).

20. Mark Harrison, *Contagion: How Commerce Has Spread Disease* (New Haven, CT: Yale University Press, 2013); Worsnop, "Provoking Barriers."

21. Worsnop, "Provoking Barriers."

22. Lucey and Gostin, "A Yellow Fever Epidemic."

23. Stephen J. Collier and Andrew Lakoff, eds., *Biosecurity Interventions: Global Health and Security in Question* (New York; Columbia University Press, 2013); Randall M. Packard, *The Making of a Tropical Disease: A Short History of Malaria* (Baltimore, MD: Johns Hopkins University Press, 2011); Harrison, *Contagion*.

24. "Health Authorities Seek to Identify Cause of Pneumonia Outbreak in China as Cases Rise – The Globe and Mail," *Globe and Mail*, January 3, 2020, https://www.the globeandmail.com/world/article-health-authorities-seek-to-identify-cause-of-pneumo nia-outbreak-in/.

25. World Health Organization, "Statement on the Meeting of the International Health Regulations (2005) Emergency Committee Regarding the Outbreak of Novel Coronavirus (2019-n-CoV)," January 23, 2020, https://www.who.int/news/item/23 -01-2020-statement-on-the-meeting-of-the-international-health-regulations-(2005) -emergency-committee-regarding-the-outbreak-of-novel-coronavirus-(2019-ncov).

26. World Health Organization, "Statement on the Meeting of the International Health Regulations (2005) Emergency Committee Regarding the Outbreak of Novel Coronavirus 2019 (n-CoV) on 23 January 2020."

27. World Health Organization, "Statement on the Meeting of the International Health Regulations (2005) Emergency Committee Regarding the Outbreak of Novel Coronavirus 2019 (n-CoV) on 23 January 2020."

28. World Health Organization, "Statement on the Second Meeting of the International Health Regulations (2005) Emergency Committee Regarding the Outbreak of Novel Coronavirus (2019-NCoV)," January 30, 2020, https://www.who.int/news/ item/30-01-2020-statement-on-the-second-meeting-of-the-international-health-reg ulations-(2005)-emergency-committee-regarding-the-outbreak-of-novel-corona virus-(2019-ncov).

29. World Health Organization, "Statement on the Second Meeting of the International Health Regulations (2005) Emergency Committee Regarding the Outbreak of Novel Coronavirus (2019-NCoV)." https://www.who.int/news/item/30-01-2020-statement-on-the-second-meeting-of-the-international-health-regulations-(2005)-emergency-committee-regarding-the-outbreak-of-novel-coronavirus-(2019-ncov).

30. Kansas City Star Editorial Board, "No Chinese People Means No COVID-19 in Kansas Town," *Kansas City Star*, March 19, 2020, https://www.kansascity.com/opinion/editorials/article241353836.html.

31. Nitsan Chorev, *The World Health Organization between North and South* (Ithaca, NY: Cornell University Press, 2012).

32. Srinivas Mazumdaru, "What Influence Does China Have over the WHO?," *Deutsche Welle*, April 17, 2020, https://www.dw.com/en/what-influence-does-china-have-over-the-who/a-53161220.

33. Yulin Hswen et al., "Association of '#covid19' Versus '#chinesevirus' with Anti-Asian Sentiments on Twitter: March 9–23, 2020," *American Journal of Public Health* 111, no. 5 (2021): 956–64, https://doi.org/10.2105/AJPH.2021.306154.

34. Lawrence O. Gostin et al., "US Withdrawal from WHO Is Unlawful and Threatens Global and US Health and Security," *The Lancet* 396, no. 10247 (August 1, 2020): 293–95, https://doi.org/10.1016/S0140-6736(20)31527-0.

35. Betsy Klein and Jennifer Hansler, "Trump Halts WHO Funding over Handling of Coronavirus Outbreak," *CNN*, April 15, 2020, https://www.cnn.com/2020/04/14/politics/donald-trump-world-health-organization-funding-coronavirus/index.html.

36. Karen Weintraub, "Experts Worry That a COVID-19 Vaccine Won't Help If Not Enough People Are Willing to Get One," *USA Today*, August 13, 2020, https://www.usatoday.com/story/news/health/2020/08/13/covid-vaccine-hesitancy-ending-coronavirus-pandemic/5529638002/.

37. Independent Oversight and Advisory Committee for the WHO Health Emergencies Programme, "IOAC Group Statement at the Seventy-Fourth World Health Assembly" (World Health Assembly, May 25, 2021), 2.

38. World Health Organization, "COVAX," https://www.who.int/initiatives/act-accelerator/covax.

39. World Health Assembly, "World Health Assembly Resolution WHA73.1," Pub. L. No. WHA73.1 (2020), https://apps.who.int/gb/ebwha/pdf_files/WHA73/A73_R1-en.pdf, 1.

40. Independent Oversight and Advisory Committee for the WHO Health Emergencies Programme, *Interim Report on WHO's Response to COVID-19 January-April 2020*, https://www.who.int/publications/m/item/interim-report-on-who-s-response-to-covid---january---april-2020, 4.

41. Review Committee on the Functioning of the International Health Regulations (2005) during the COVID-19 response, "A74/9 Add.1 WHO's Work in Health Emergencies Strengthening Preparedness for Health Emergencies: Implementation of the International Health Regulations (2005)" (75th World Health Assembly, May 5, 2021),

https://www.who.int/publications/m/item/A75-16-Independent-Oversight-and-Advisory-Committee-for-the-WHO-Health-Emergencies-Programme, 9.

Chapter 6

1. Médecins Sans Frontières International, "Ebola: Pushed to the Limit and Beyond," March 23, 2015, http://www.msf.org/en/article/ebola-pushed-limit-and-beyond; World Health Organization, *Report of the Ebola Interim Assessment Panel—May 2015*, https://cdn.who.int/media/docs/default-source/documents/evaluation/report-ebola-interim-assessment-panel.pdf.

2. Rachel Estrada et al., "Pandemics in a Changing Climate—Evolving Risk and the Global Response," Johns Hopkins University Paul H. Nitze School of Advanced International Studies and Swiss Re, 2016, 7. https://www.swissre.com/dam/jcr:552d59b2-76c6-4626-a91a-75b0ed58927e/Pandemics_in_a_changing_climate_Full_report_FINAL.pdf.

3. World Health Organization, *Report of the Ebola Interim Assessment Panel—May 2015*.

4. World Health Organization, *Report of the Ebola Interim Assessment Panel—May 2015*,16.

5. Karen A. Grépin, "International Donations to the Ebola Virus Outbreak: Too Little, Too Late?," *BMJ* 350 (February 3, 2015): h376, https://doi.org/10.1136/bmj.h376.

6. Office of the United Nations Special Envoy on Ebola, *Resources for Results V: 1 September 2014 to 31 October 2015*, 2015, 5. https://ebolaresponse.un.org/sites/default/files/resources_for_results_v.pdf.

7. World Health Organization, *Report of the Ebola Interim Assessment Panel—May 2015*.

8. World Bank, "World Bank Group President Calls for New Global Pandemic Emergency Facility," October 2014, https://www.worldbank.org/en/news/press-release/2014/10/10/world-bank-group-president-calls-new-global-pandemic-emergency-facility.

9. Press and Information Office of the Federal Government, Germany, *G7 Presidency 2015: Final Report by the Federal Government on the G7 Presidency 2015*, December 15, 2015, https://www.g7germany.de/resource/blob/998440/456776/55d315d9e1983d38459 09c588331e03f/2016-01-20-g7-abschluss-eng-en-data.pdf.

10. World Bank, "World Bank Launches First-Ever Pandemic Bonds to Support $500 Million Pandemic Emergency Financing Facility," June 28, 2017, http://www.worldbank.org/en/news/press-release/2017/06/28/world-bank-launches-first-ever-pandemic-bonds-to-support-500-million-pandemic-emergency-financing-facility.

11. Currently available only to the International Development Association (IDA) borrower nations.

12. Reuters, "World Bank Launches 'Pandemic Bond' to Tackle Major Outbreaks," June 28, 2017, https://www.reuters.com/article/us-global-pandemic-insurance/world-bank-launches-pandemic-bond-to-tackle-major-outbreaks-idUSKBN19J2JJ.

13. World Bank, "Fact Sheet: The World Bank Support to the 10th Ebola Outbreak in Democratic Republic of Congo," July 24, 2019, https://www.worldbank.org/en/topic/pandemics/brief/fact-sheet-world-bank-support-to-10th-ebola-outbreak-in-demo cratic-republic-of-congo; Steven Evans, "World Bank Pandemic Facility Sends Another $30m for Ebola Response," Artemis, August 27, 2019, https://www.artemis.bm/news/world-bank-pandemic-facility-sends-another-30m-for-ebola-response/.

14. Lynne McChristian, *Hurricane Andrew and Insurance: The Enduring Impact of an Historic Storm*, Insurance Information Institute, August 2012, 2, 4. https://www.iii.org/sites/default/files/paper_HurricaneAndrew_final.pdf.

15. Neil A. Doherty, "Innovations in Managing Catastrophe Risk," *Journal of Risk and Insurance* 64, no. 4 (1997): 713–18, https://doi.org/10.2307/253893.

16. Man Institute, "Catastrophe Bonds: Investing with Impact," https://www.man.com/maninstitute/catastrophe-bonds-investing-with-impact.

17. Doherty, "Innovations in Managing Catastrophe Risk," 715.

18. Steve Evans, "Q2 2019 Catastrophe Bond & ILS Market Report: Repeat Sponsors and Risks Underpin Issuance." Artemis, 2019. https://www.artemis.bm/wp-content/up loads/2019/06/q2-2019-cat-bond-ils-market-report.pdf.

19. Doherty, "Innovations in Managing Catastrophe Risk," 715.

20. The World Bank Group or World Bank is the combination of two institutions: the International Bank for Reconstruction and the Development and the International Development Association.

21. Pandemic Emergency Financing Facility Steering Body, *Pandemic Emergency Financing Facility Operations Manual*, October 15, 2018, 8. https://pubdocs.worldbank.org/en/842101571243529089/PEF-Operations-Manual-approved-10-15-18.pdf.

22. Pandemic Emergency Financing Facility Steering Body, *Pandemic Emergency Financing Facility Operations Manual*, 4.

23. Steven Evans, "Swiss Re in Vita Capital V Mortality Cat Bond Early Redemption," Artemis, March 22, 2016, https://www.artemis.bm/news/swiss-re-in-vita-capital -v-mortality-cat-bond-early-redemption/; Andrew Hunt and David Blake, "Modelling Longevity Bonds: Analysing the Swiss Re Kortis Bond," in "Longevity Nine—the Ninth International Longevity Risk and Capital Markets Solutions Conference," special issue, *Insurance: Mathematics and Economics* 63 (July 1, 2015): 12–29, https://doi.org/10.1016/j.insmatheco.2015.03.017; "Swiss Re Issues New Mortality Catastrophe Bond," *Reuters*, June 10, 2010, https://uk.reuters.com/article/swiss-re-catbond-idUKLDE6591HD20100610.

24. Evans, "Swiss Re in Vita Capital V Mortality Cat Bond Early Redemption."

25. Doug Fullam and Nita Madhav, "Quantifying Pandemic Risk," *Actuary Magazine*, March 2015.

26. International Bank for Reconstruction and Development, *Pandemic Emergency Financing Facility Prospectus Supplement*, June 28, 2017, I–1, http://pubdocs.worldbank.org/en/882831509568634367/PEF-Final-Prospectus-PEF.pdf.

27. International Bank for Reconstruction and Development, *Pandemic Emergency Financing Facility Prospectus Supplement*, I–1.

28. Pandemic Emergency Financing Facility Steering Body, *Pandemic Emergency Financing Facility Operations Manual*, 5.

29. Pandemic Emergency Financing Facility Steering Body, *Pandemic Emergency Financing Facility Operations Manual*, 6.

30. Pandemic Emergency Financing Facility Steering Body, *Pandemic Emergency Financing Facility Operations Manual*, 6.

31. Pandemic Emergency Financing Facility Steering Body, *Pandemic Emergency Financing Facility Operations Manual*, 6.

32. The London Interbank Offering Rate (LIBOR) is the interest rate at which major global financial institutions lend to one another. The six-month US LIBOR is the interest rate that banks lend at for a six-month loan.

33. Kate Allen, "World Bank Issues First Bond to Tackle Pandemic Disease," *Financial Times*, June 28, 2017, https://www.ft.com/content/f919ec59-0a0c-3229-9e76-f1c08689fd02; Nikou Asgari, "Ebola Escalation Keeps World Bank's 'Pandemic Bonds' in Spotlight," *Financial Times*, June 13, 2019, https://www.ft.com/content/30dc1a0c-8da4-11e9-a24d-b42f641eca37.

34. World Bank, "World Bank Launches First-Ever Pandemic."

35. Bangin Brim and Clare Wenham, "Pandemic Emergency Financing Facility: Struggling to Deliver on Its Innovative Promise," *BMJ* 367 (October 9, 2019): l5719, https://doi.org/10.1136/bmj.l5719.

36. Brim and Wenham, "Pandemic Emergency Financing Facility."

37. Asgari, "Ebola Escalation Keeps World Bank's 'Pandemic Bonds' in Spotlight"; Allen, "World Bank Issues First Bond to Tackle Pandemic Disease"; Kate Allen, "World Bank's 'Pandemic Bonds' under Scrutiny After Failing to Pay Out on Ebola," *Financial Times*, February 21, 2019, https://www.ft.com/content/c3a805de-3058-11e9-ba00-0251022932c8.

38. Estrada et al., "Pandemics in a Changing Climate," 9.

39. Estrada et al., "Pandemics in a Changing Climate," 20.

40. J.-A. Mbembe, "Necropolitics," trans. Libby Meintjes, *Public Culture* 15, no. 1 (2003): 39.

41. Mbembe, "Necropolitics," 40.

42. Mbembe, "Necropolitics," 27.

43. Mbembe, "Necropolitics," 39–40.

44. James Lorand Matory, *The Fetish Revisited: Marx, Freud, and the Gods Black People Make* (Durham, NC: Duke University Press, 2018); C. L. R James, *The Black Jacobins: Toussaint L'Ouverture and the San Domingo Revolution* (New York: Vintage, 1989); Cedric J. Robinson, *Black Marxism: The Making of the Black Radical Tradition* (Chapel Hill: University of North Carolina Press, 2000); Paul Gilroy, *The Black Atlantic: Modernity and Double-Consciousness* (Cambridge, MA: Harvard University Press, 1995).

45. Jean Baudrillard, *For a Critique of the Political Economy of the Sign* (St. Louis, MO: Telos, 1981), 88.

46. Baudrillard, *For a Critique of the Political Economy of the Sign*, 93.

47. Nicholas Radburn, "Keeping 'the Wheel in Motion': Trans-Atlantic Credit Terms, Slave Prices, and the Geography of Slavery in the British Americas, 1755–1807," *Journal of Economic History* 75, no. 3 (September 2015): 660–89, https://doi.org/10.1017/S0022050715001084; Robin Pearson and David Richardson, "Insuring the Transatlantic Slave Trade," *Journal of Economic History* 79, no. 2 (June 2019): 417–46, https://doi.org/10.1017/S0022050719000068; Robin Pearson and David Richardson, "Social Capital, Institutional Innovation and Atlantic Trade before 1800," *Business History* 50, no. 6 (November 2008): 765–80, https://doi.org/10.1080/00076790802420336.

48. Sowande' M. Mustakeem, *Slavery at Sea: Terror, Sex, and Sickness in the Middle Passage* (Urbana: University of Illinois Press, 2016); Stephanie E. Smallwood, *Saltwater Slavery: A Middle Passage from Africa to American Diaspora* (Cambridge, MA: Harvard University Press, 2008). This process was also resisted at every step of the way by the enslaved. "At every point along the passage from African to New World markets, we find a stark contest between slave traders and slaves, between the traders' will to commodify people and the captives' will to remain fully recognizable as human subjects" (Smallwood, *Saltwater Slavery*, 5).

49. Viviana A. Rotman Zelizer and Kieran Joseph Healy, *Morals and Markets: The Development of Life Insurance in the United States* (New York: Columbia University Press, 2017), 69.

50. Sarah Quinn, "The Transformation of Morals in Markets: Death, Benefits, and the Exchange of Life Insurance Policies," *American Journal of Sociology* 114, no. 3 (2008): 738–80, https://doi.org/10.1086/592861.

51. Karl Marx, *Capital: A Critique of Political Economy*, ed. David Fernbach, trans. Ben Fowkes, vol. 1 (London: Penguin Books in association with New Left Review, 1867); Baudrillard, *For a Critique of the Political Economy of the Signs*.

52. Moldova has now been removed from the list of IDA borrower nations.

Conclusion

1. *Proceedings of the International Sanitary Conference Opened at Constantinople on the 13th February 1866* (Calcutta: Office of Superintendent of Government Printing, 1868), 155, http://hdl.handle.net/10973/23485.

2. Andrew Lakoff, *Unprepared: Global Health in a Time of Emergency* (Oakland: University of California Press, 2017); Stephen J. Collier, Andrew Lakoff, and Paul Rabinow, "Biosecurity: Towards an Anthropology of the Contemporary," *Anthropology Today* 20, no. 5 (October 1, 2004): 3–7, https://doi.org/10.1111/j.0268-540X.2004.00292.x; Lawrence O. Gostin, "Ethical Allocation of Drugs and Vaccines in the West African Ebola Epidemic," *Milbank Quarterly* 92, no. 4 (December 2014): 662–66, https://doi.org/10.1111/1468-0009.12089; Nitsan Chorev, "Changing Global Norms through Reactive Diffusion: The Case of Intellectual Property Protection of AIDS Drugs," *American Sociological Review* 77, no. 5 (October 2012): 831–53, https://doi.org/10.1177/0003122412457156.

INDEX

Note: Page numbers in *italics* denote figures.

Africa: LNHO conferences for social medicine, 144–45; as non-Western threat, 83–84; sanitation protocols, North Africa, 100–101. *See also* Cape Town, South Africa; Ebola virus
Ahuja, Neel, 13–14, 26
AIR Pandemic Model, 236–40, *240*
Ali Begh, Mirza Irfan, 53–54
Alma-Ata Declaration (1978), 177–78
American Journal of Public Health, 149
American Public Health Association, 155
Améry, Jean, 46
Anderson, Warwick, 26, 135
Arnold, David, 26
Asia: 19th-century cholera outbreaks, 69; anti-Asian racism, 98, *99*, 137–41, *138, 139, 140,* 222–23, 250; as incapable of disease management, 80; LNHO conference for social medicine, 145–47. *See also* China; India
Australia, 96, 166, 185
Austria, 69–70, 73–74

Baldwin, Peter, 57, 76
Bandoeng Health Conference (1937), 135, 145–47
Bashford, Alison, 26
Baudrillard, Jean, 244

Bauman, Zygmunt, 95
Beck, Ulrich, 13–14
Bennett, Michael, 230
Bhabha, Homi, 22
Biden, Joseph, 224
biopolitics: epidemic Orientalism and, 26–29; necrofinance, 243–48; necropower, 27–28, 242–43. *See also* geopolitics
biosecurity, emergence of, 13–14
Biraud, Yves, 152, 153–54, 155
blocks away disinsection, 184–86, 189
Blue, Rupert, 142
Bombay, India, 1901 plague outbreak, 112, *113,* 119, 120
Borowy, Iris, 129
Brazil, support for WHO, 152, 155
Britain: 19th-century cholera outbreaks, 69; disinsection practices affecting, 185; quarantine measures for plague, 66, 94; racial quarantine, Cape Town, 114–18; relations with WHO, 156, 178; sanitary controls for cholera, 73, 74, 76, 81–82, 84, 85; Venice International Sanitary Convention and, 94. *See also* colonialism
British India. *See* India
British Indian Native Passengers' Act (1858), 81

Brundtland, Gro Harlem, 179
bubonic plague: in China, 91, 94, 112, *113*; in India, 91, 101–3, 112–14, *113*, 119, 120; responses to, Cape Town, *11*, 106–12; and smallpox, Cape Town, 103–6

Canada, 182, 183
Canadian Advisory Committee on Epidemiology, 182
Canadian Quarantine Health Services, 191
Cape Plague Advisory Council, 106, 126
Cape Slave Codes, 125
Cape Town, South Africa: bubonic plague and smallpox, 103–6; contrasting epidemic responses in, 106–12, *111*; LNHO conference for social medicine, 144–45; racial mixing, threat of, 118–24; racial quarantine, 114–18
Capital (Marx), 244
capitalism, 244
Casimir-Perier, Jean, 85
catastrophe bonds, 231–34, *233*, 235–36
Centers for Disease Control (CDC), 185, 195
Ceylon, 96–97, 165–66
Chadwick, Edwin, 67
Chagas, Carlos, 148–49
Chatterjee, Partha, 39
chikungunya virus, 184
China: anti-Chinese racism, 98, *99*, 137–41, *139*, *140*, 222–23, 250; bubonic plague, 91, 94, 112, *113*; COVID-19 pandemic, 220–26, 250; as incapable of disease management, 80; Mukden International Plague Conference (1911), 135, 147, 279n47; support for WHO, 153, 155
Chinese Exclusion Act (1882), 137
Chisholm, Brock, 156
cholera: 19th-century quarantine efforts, 67–71; contagionist-anticontagionist debate, 67–68, 74–75, 83–84; as economic threat, 77–78; final

International Sanitary Convention, 148–51; first International Sanitary Conference, 73; and the Muslim other, 75–78; as non-Western threat, 30, 61, 83–88; primacy as quarantinable disease, 4–6, *5*, 61, 135, 157, 166–67, 172; sanitary policing for, 78–82
Chorev, Nitsan, 177
Class A/B Notes (pandemic bonds), 237–40, *240*, 241, 247
Cold War era and emergence of biosecurity, 13–14
colonialism: biosecurity and, 14; decolonization as perceived threat, 164–65, 168, 177; disease control and, 15–17, 41–45, 94–96, 154–55; epidemic Orientalism and, 18, 21–26, 83–88; in global health research, 9–11; myth of modernity and, 38–41, 262n86; necropower and, 27–28; plague as threat to, 125–27; racialized geographies, 96–101, *99*; racial quarantine, 114–18; rule of colonial difference, 60–62, 91; shift in colony-metropole relations, 61–62, 91–94; US sanitation practices, 136–41, *138*, *139*, *140* 169. *See also* epidemic Orientalism; racism
commodity fetishism, 244–48, 266n25
Constantinople International Sanitary Conference (1866), 75
Corfu, quarantine measures in, 69–70
COVID-19 (coronavirus disease 2019): within discursive framework, 2–3, 17; epidemic Orientalism and, 249–50; impact in United States, xii–xiii, 250; pandemic bond deployment, 240, 247; PHEIC designation, 199, *202*, 220–26
Cuba, 136
Cueto, Marcus, 135
Cumming, Hugh S., 143, 149–50, 152

decolonization, threat of, 164–65, 168, 177
Decoteau, Claire, 39

DeFazio, Peter, 185–86
The Defense of Europe Against Cholera
    (Proust), 83
Democratic Republic of the Congo. *See*
    Ebola virus
dengue fever, 184
Department of Epidemic and Pandemic
    Alert and Response, 206
Description de l'Egypte (Napoleon), 58
difference, signification of, 19–20, 24–26,
    29–33, 76–78
diphtheria, 62
disinsection, 184–86, 189
Dresden Sanitary Conference (1893), 84
Drummond Castle steam ship, 108
Dussel, Enrique, 40–41

Ebola virus: economic response, 228–31,
    240, 242, 247; emergence of biosecu-
    rity and, 13–14; IHR reform and, 173,
    174, 187; PHEIC designation, 199, *201,*
    204, 212–13, 215–16, 217–18; WHO
    management of, 8, 174, 187, 228–29
economics: cholera containment and,
    77–78, 85, 88–89; commodity fetish-
    ism, 244–48, 266n25; disinsection
    practices, 185; economic and sanitary
    protectionism, 166; International
    Sanitary Conferences formation,
    71–75; International Sanitary Regula-
    tions mandate, 157; PHEIC designa-
    tions, 204, 213–16; plague as economic
    issue, 125–27; quarantine measures
    and, 61–62, 66–67, 69–70; resistance
    to WHO funding, 178–79; sanitary
    protocols for plague, 96–101; support
    for world health initiative, 154–55; sur-
    veillance for trade and travel, 159–61,
    168–70. *See also* necrofinance
Effendi, Salih, 80–81, 251
Egypt, 58, 64, 77, 156, 158, 161–62
Emerging Infections (US Institute of
    Medicine), 182

Environmental Protection Agency, 185
Epidemic Diseases Act (1897), 101
epidemic Orientalism: characterized,
    18–26; biopolitics and, 26–29; cholera,
    the Muslim other and, 75–78, 84, 85–
    86; COVID-19 and, 249–50; European
    visions of disease threat, 53–58, 251;
    International Sanitary Conferences,
    71–75; medical knowledge and, 67–71;
    necrofinance and, 248; Orientalism,
    18, 21–24, 58–60; PHEIC designations
    and, 209–10, *210,* 212, 213–16, 222–23;
    producing a "vision of division," 24–
    25; racial perspectivism of, 34–38; rise
    and consolidation of, 62–67, 83–88;
    rule of colonial difference, 60–62, 91;
    sanitation, sovereignty and, 78–82; in
    WHO reform strategies, 195–97. *See
    also* colonialism; International Health
    Regulations (IHR); International
    Sanitary Conventions; necrofinance;
    Public Health Emergency of Inter-
    national Concern (PHEIC); World
    Health Organization (WHO)
epidemics in discourse, 11–12, 17, 254n4
exceptionalism, European and Western:
    in disease security, 14, 76–78, 83–88;
    epidemic Orientalism discourse, 18–
    20, 28; modernity and, 29–33, 34–38

Fanon, Frantz, 23
Fauci, Anthony, 179
financial speculation and HIV/AIDS,
    245–46. *See also* necrofinance
Florence, Italy, quarantine measures, 62
Forel, Oscar, 153
Foucault, Michel, 18, 26–27, 243
France, 66, 70–71, 73–74, 82, 156

Ganges River, as cholera source, 75, 76
Gates, Henry Louis, 22
Gautier, Raymond, 152, 155
Gear, Dr., 158

geopolitics: within global health research, 12–15; managing global epidemic response, 210–13; PHEIC as global signal, 216–20. *See also* biopolitics

Germany, PEF contributions, 234, 241

Gilroy, Paul, 38, 40

Global Fund, 8

global health research, 9–11, 12–15

Global Outbreak Alert and Response Network, 194, 206

Global Program on AIDS (GPA), 181

Gorgas, William, 136–37

Gostin, Lawrence O., 175, 176

Great Bukharia, 80

Gregory, John, 106, 115, 121–22, 123

Gunn, Selskar, 137, 152

Gushulak, Brian, 189, 191

H1N1 (swine flu), PHEIC designation, 199, *201*

Haffkine, Dr., 114–15

Hajj. *See* pilgrimage to Mecca, sanitary policing of

Hall, Stuart, 18

Harrison, Mark, 81

Hartman, Saidiya, *Scenes of Subjection,* 46

Hawaii, quarantine measures, 98, *99*

Haynes, A. S., 145

Hazeman, R. H., 152

HIV/AIDS: biosecurity approach, 13–14; emergence, 179–81; failure of IHR to address, 8, 181, 253n2; financial speculation markets, 245–46; in global health research, 9; IHR reform and, 174, 195; tradition vs. modernity debate, 39–40

Hong Kong, China, 94, 96, 112, *113*, 116

Honolulu, Hawaii, 98, *99*

Hougendobler, D., 175, 176

Huber, Valeska, 26, 75

immigration: as cause of plague-spread, 119; US sanitation practices and, 137–41, *138*, *139*, *140*

imperialism: disease control, modernity and, 41–45; knowledge acquisition for, 58–59, 62–63; rule of colonial difference, 60–62, 91; sanitary policing and, 78–83

Independent Oversight and Advisory Committee (IOAC), 224–25

India: 1817-1821 cholera epidemic, 68–69; 1994 pneumonic plague, 174, 192, 204; bubonic plague, 91, 101–3, 112–14, *113*, 119, 120; sanitary policing in, 81–82; as source of cholera epidemic, 74, 75–76

influenza pandemic (1918-1920), 129

International Bank for Reconstruction and Development (IBRD), 234

International Civil Aviation Organization (ICAO), 156, 157, 185

International Conference of American States (1906), 142

International Development Association (IDA), 238, 241, 247

international disease control: colonial foundations of, 9–11; early forms of, 62–67; embedded in Western exceptionalism, 15–17; epidemic Orientalism discourse and, 20–21; within global health research, 12–15; imperialism, modernity and, 41–45; signification of racial difference, 19–20, 24–26, 29–33, 76–78. *See also* International Health Regulations (IHR); International Sanitary Conventions; quarantine; surveillance; World Health Organization (WHO)

International Health Regulations (IHR): challenges to efficacy and authority, 8, 181–88, 228; embedded in Western exceptionalism, 15–17; emergence of HIV/AIDS, 180–81; global politics, 176–79; inception and mandate, 5, 6–8; persistent colonial ideologies in, 14–15; PHEIC designation structure, 220–26; reform under WHO, 171–75, 188–97;

role within WHO, 175–76; signification of difference and, 24–26, 29–33, 35–36. *See also* Public Health Emergency of International Concern (PHEIC); World Health Organization (WHO)

International Office of Public Hygiene (OIHP): International Sanitary Conventions and, 4, 148, 156; LNHO conferences for social medicine, 145; postwar international health, 152, 155

International Sanitary Bureau, 128, 136, 141–43

International Sanitary Conferences: addressing threat of cholera (1866), 75–78, 81; first conference in Paris (1851), 73–75; inception of, 4, 56–57; objectives emerging from, 71–72; producing vision of difference, 24–26, 34–35

International Sanitary Conventions, *132*; adoption and mandate of, 4, *5*, 55–57, 130, 132–35; colonial ideologies in, 14–15, 129, 196; divergent epidemic responses, 53–55, 106–12, *111*; economics and colonial legitimacy, 125–27; embedded in Western exceptionalism, 15–17; final convention (1944), 148–51; imperial expansion and, 85, 88–89; metropole-colony relations, 91–94; plague in India, 101–3, 112–14; policies on plague and yellow fever, 84, 88; policies toward Muslim pilgrims, 162; producing racial difference, 25; racialized disease control, 94–101, *99*, 103–6, 108–9, 114–18, 273n32; racial mixing, threat of, 118–24; transition to International Health Regulations, 6, 155–61; US sanitation practices and, 135–36, 137, 141–43

International Sanitary Regulations: drafting of, 155–61; post-ratification, 164–67; role of, 131, 132–35, 195; surveillance for trade and travel, 168–70. *See also* International Health Regulations (IHR)

Islam, as threat to Europe, 149–51. *See also* Muslim populations

Istanbul Supreme Council of Sanitation, 71

Italy, 62, 66

JanMohamed, Abdul, 22, 23

Japan, PEF contributions, 234, 241

Jasanoff, Sheilah, 134

Johannesburg, South Africa, 144–45

Jyllands-Posten newspaper, 222–23

Kendal, Julia, 184

KhoeKhoe people, 107

knowledge: colonialism in global health research, 9–11; contagionist vs. sanitationist approaches, 67–71; first International Sanitation Conferences and, 73; imperial knowledge and disease control, 41–45, 262n94; knowledge acquisition for conquest, 58–59; media role in dissemination, 192–93, 216–17; myth of modernity and, 38–41, 262n86. *See also* Public Health Emergency of International Concern (PHEIC)

Koch, Robert, 83

Kosovo, as IDA borrower, 247

Kuefstein, Count, 87–88

Langen, C. D. de, 145

The Last Man (Shelley), 1–2

League of Nations Health Organization (LNHO): within final International Sanitary Convention, 148, 151; postwar disease control, 152, 154, 155; social medicine and, 135, 143–47

Leahy, Patrick, 185–86

Lederberg, Joshua, 31, 32, 180, 190

leprosy, 63–64

Levant region, 66, 70

Levet, Henry Jean-Marie, 53–54

Liberia, Ebola epidemic in, 229
Licéaga, Eduardo, 141
Lindsay-Poland, John, 135
Livingstone, Julie, 26

Mahler, Halfdan, 177
malaria: designation as notifiable disease, 167; disinsection for, 184; early management efforts, 62, 126; LNHO conference for social medicine, 144–45; US sanitary practices for, 136, 137
Malaria Eradication Division (WHO), 167
Malay people, 109, 274n51
Marx, Karl, *Capital,* 244
Matory, James Lorand, 244
Mazumdar, Sucheta, 138
Mbeki, Thabo, 39
Mbembe, Achille, 27–28, 242–43
measles, 62
"Memorandum on the Influence of Rats in the Dissemination of Plague" (Simpson), 115
MERS coronavirus, 199, 200, *201,* 237
Mexico, yellow fever eradication campaigns, 141
Ministry of Health of the People's Republic of China, 221
modernity: colonialism and Western, 16–17; imperialism, disease control and, 10–11, 41–45; myth of, 38–41, 262n86; racial perspectivism, 34–38; signification of difference and, 29–33; tradition vs. modernity and HIV/AIDS, 39–40
Moldova, as IDA borrower, 247
Montesquieu, Charles de Secondat, *The Spirit of the Laws,* 63–64
Mudimbe, V. Y., 42
Mukden International Plague Conference (1911), 135, 147, 279n47
Munich Re (insurance company), 236, 237

Muslim populations: 14th-century disease controls and, 62; sanitary policing of, 53–54, 75–78, 80–82, 84–88, 149–51, 161–64; smallpox contagion, Cape Town, 109
Mustakeem, Sowande' M., 245

Nakajima, Hiroshi, 190
Napoleon I, Emperor of the French, 58
National IHR Focal Points, 194
Ndabeni, Cape Town, 104, 125, 127
necrofinance: characterized, 227, 242–48; calculating pandemic risk, 236–40, *240*; catastrophe bonds, 231–34, *233,* 235–36; Ebola epidemic response, 228–31, 240, 242, 247; epidemic Orientalism and, 248; logics of response, 242; Pandemic Emergency Financing Facility, 230, 234–36, *235,* 237, 240–42, 243–48. *See also* economics
necropower, 27–28, 242–43
neoliberalism, 178–79
New Orleans, Louisiana, 142
Nikolaus II, Prince Esterházy, 69–70
North Africa, sanitation protocols, 100–101
Norway, 156
Nymadawa, D. P., 190

Orientalism, 18, 21–24, 58–60, 168–69
Orientalism (Said), 58
Ottoman Empire: first International Sanitary Conference, 73, 74; regulations for plague control, 71; threat of cholera and, 75, 77, 78–79, 82, 85
Ottoman Supreme Council of Health, 71

Packard, Randall, 13, 129, 135, 136
Page Act (1875), 137, 138
Pampana, E. J., 145
Pan-African Health Conferences (1932), 135
Panama Canal sanitary responses, 136–37, 169

Pan American Health Organization
(PASB/PAHO): establishment of, 141,
142–43; within final International Sani-
tation Convention, 148; International
Sanitary Conventions reform, 156, 157;
LNHO conferences for social medicine, 145, 147; postwar international
health initiatives, 152, 155; US responses to disease management, 137
Pan American Sanitary Bureau, 128
Pan American Sanitary Code (1924), 142,
143, 151
Pan-American Sanitary Conventions,
134
Pan American Sanitary Conventions on
Aerial Navigation, 143
pandemic bonds, 231, 235–40, *240*, 241,
247
Pandemic Emergency Financing
Facility (PEF): development, 8, 228,
229–30; future possibilities, 240–42;
as necrofinancing, 243–44, 246–48;
pandemic bonds, 231, 234–36, *235*,
236–40, *240*
Parry, Benita, 22
PEPVFAR (President's Emergency Plan
For AIDS Relief), 8
Persian Empire, 77, 78–80, 114
pertussis, 62
Philippines, US disease eradication in,
136
pilgrimage to Mecca, sanitary policing
of, 53–54, 75–78, 80–82, 84–88, 149–51,
161–64
plague: 1901 outbreak, 112–14, *113*;
as anticolonial disease, 125–27; as
consequence of racial mixing, 118–24;
disease control at colonial sites,
91–94; early management efforts, 62,
66–67, 70; final International Sanitary
Convention, 148–51; focus of first
International Sanitary Conference, 73;
in India, 91, 101–3, 112–14, *113*, 119, 120;

LNHO conference for social medicine, 145; as non-Western threat, 61;
primacy as quarantinable disease, 4–6,
5, 61, 88, 135, 157, 166–67, 172; racial
quarantine, 114–18; and smallpox,
Cape Town, 103–6; and smallpox,
divergent responses, 64–65, 106–12,
111; Venice Sanitary Conventions and,
96–98
Plague Advisory Council, 107, 115, 122,
123, 124
poliovirus (2014), 199, *201*
Portugal, early quarantine measures, 66
Program for Monitoring Emerging Diseases (ProMED), 187, 188, 285n47
Proust, Adrien, 30, 32, 83–84
Public Health Acts (1883; 1897), 110
Public Health Emergency of International Concern (PHEIC): COVID-19,
220–26; designation criteria, 6–7,
199–203, *201–2*, 204–8, *205*; economic
effects, 204, 213–16; emergency committee interviews, 208, 287n17; epidemic Orientalism and, 209–10, *210*,
212, 213–16, 222–23; as global signal,
216–20; IHR reform and, 172, 173, 194;
limitations of, 242; managing global
response, 210–13

quarantine: 1901 plague outbreak,
112–14; contagionist-anticontagionist
debate, 67–71, 74–75, 83–84; divergent
responses, smallpox vs. plague, 109–12,
111; in Honolulu, 98, *99*; onus placed
on colonies, 91–94; plague and cholera, 19th-century, 67–71, 98; pre-19th
century, 62, 64–67; racialized, Cape
Town, 104–6, 108–9, 114–18, 273n32;
shift to surveillance from, 148–51,
159–61. *See also* surveillance

racial capitalism, 18
racial perspectivism, 34–38

racism: anti-Asian, 98, 99, 137–41, 138, 139, 140, 222–23, 250; biosecurity and, 14; disease control and colonial rule, 94–96; in epidemic responses, Cape Town, 109–12, 111; in global health research, 9–11; racial difference, signification of, 19–20, 24–26, 29–33, 76–78; racialized segregation, Cape Town, 104–6, 108–9, 114–18, 273n32; racializing geographies, 96–101, 99; racial mixing, threat of, 118–24, 125–27; racial surveillance, 91–94, 106–7, 124; in US sanitation practices, 136–41, 138, 139, 140. See also colonialism
Rajchman, Ludwick, 154, 155
Raška, K., 168
Reagan administration, 178, 223
relapsing fever, 157, 166–67
Rockefeller Foundation, 136, 137, 145, 182
Rodney, Walter, 41
rural hygiene, 135, 143–47
Russia, 73, 80, 150

Said, Edward, 18, 21–24, 58–60
San Francisco, California, 142
sanitation: contagionist approach vs., 67–71, 74–75, 83–84; sovereignty and, 78–82; US disease management, 135–41, 138, 139, 140
Sanitation in Panama (Gorgas), 136–37
The Sanitation Syndrome (Swanson), 109
San people, 107
SARS-CoV-2. See COVID-19 (coronavirus disease 2019)
Scenes of Subjection (Hartman), 46
Second International Conference of American States, 141
Shelley, Mary Wollstonecraft, The Last Man, 1–2
Siddiqi, Javed, 74
Simpson, William John Ritchie, 106, 112, 114–18, 120, 122–23, 124
slavery and commodity fetishism, 245, 266n25

sleeping sickness, 144
smallpox: and bubonic plague Cape Town, 103–6; distribution by race, 120–21, 121; divergent epidemic responses, 64–65, 106–12, 111; early efforts at disease governance, 62; final International Sanitary Convention, 148–51; as quarantinable disease, 157, 166–67
Smallwood, Stephanie, 245
Smith, Stephen, 85–86
social medicine, 135, 143–47, 177–78
South African League, 119
sovereignty, European sanitary policing and, 78–82
Spanish flu, 129
The Spirit of the Laws (Montesquieu), 63
Sridhar, D., 175, 176
Stepan, Nancy, 129
Stewart, Balfour, 114–15
Stoler, Ann, 14–15
Suez Canal, 76, 78–79, 149–50
Superior Council of Health of Mexico, 141
surveillance: at colonial outbreak sites, 91–94, 106–7, 124; decolonization, threat of, 164–65; emergence of HIV/AIDS and, 180; IHR reform and, 174–75, 190–94; of Muslims, 53–54, 75–78, 80–82, 84–88, 149–51, 161–64; post-World War I, 153; shift from quarantine to, 148–49, 159–61; for trade and travel, 168–70; WHO authority and, 181–83, 194–97. See also quarantine
Swanson, Maynard, The Sanitation Syndrome, 109
swine flu (2009), 199, 201
Swiss Re (insurance company), 236, 237, 241–42
syndromic surveillance, 190–94
syphilis, 63, 138

telegraph systems, emergence of, 92, 97–98

Third Plague pandemic, 91–94

trade: cholera containment and, 77–78, 85, 88–89; disease surveillance and, 159–61. 168–170; International Sanitary Conferences formation, 71–75; International Sanitary Regulations mandate and, 157; quarantine measures and, 61–62, 66–67, 69–70; sanitary protocols for plague, 96–101; support for world health initiative and, 154–55. *See also* economics

tradition vs. modernity, 39–40

travelling theory, 24

Trump administration, COVID-19 response, xii–xiii, 223–24

tuberculosis, 144

Turkey, 73, 80, 150

Tuskegee Study of Untreated Syphilis in the Negro Male, 152

typhus, 145, 148–51, 157, 166–67

Uitvlugt, South Africa, 104, 107

UNAIDS (Joint United Nations Programme on HIV and AIDS), 8, 181

United States: Hawaii, quarantine measures, 98, 99; IHR disinsection policies, 184–86; impact of COVID-19, xii–xiii, 250; International Sanitary Bureau, 141–43; relations with WHO, 178–79, 223–24; responses to disease management, 134–41, *138, 139, 140,* 169; sanitary policing of pilgrims, 86–87; shift to disease surveillance, 159–60; support for world health initiative, 154–55

University College Liverpool, 114–15

US National Institutes of Health, 182

vaccine nationalism, 211–12, 251

Vaughn, Meghan, 26

Venice International Sanitary Conference (1892), 83, 112–14

Venice International Sanitary Convention (1897), 93, 94, 96–98, 105, *113,* 122

Washington Sanitary Convention (1905), 141

Winslow, Charles-Edward, 155

women, racism toward, 137–38

World Bank, catastrophe bonds and, 231–34, *233,* 235–36. *See also* Pandemic Emergency Financing Facility (PEF)

World Health Assembly, 6, 49, 131, 164, 176, 177, 224–25, 228

World Health Organization (WHO): challenges to authority and legitimacy, 8, 174, 181–88, 214–16, 228–29; from conventions to regulations, 155–61; COVID-19, 220–26; as dominant surveillance authority, 194–97, 198–200; Ebola epidemic response, 8, 174, 187, 228–31; emergence of HIV/AIDS, 179–81; establishment of, 4; final International Sanitary Convention, 148–51; global politics and, 176–79; IHR reform under, 171–76; international sanitary authority under, 132–35; International Sanitary Bureau, 141–43; International Sanitary Regulations, effects of, 164–67; Muslims, sanitary policing of, 161–64; PHEIC designation, 6–8, 194, 199–203, *201–2,* 204–8, *205;* postwar disease control and, 152–55; precursors to, 128–31; reform strategies, 171–75, 188–97; social medicine, 135, 143–47; surveillance for trade and travel, 168–70; US responses to disease management, 134–41, *138, 139, 140. See also* Public Health Emergency of International Concern (PHEIC)

World War I, 129, 153, 168

World War II: as distinct era, 12–13, 37–38; postwar international disease control, 129, 152–55, 168

Wyman, Walter, 141
Wynter, Sylvia, 18, 39, 42

xenophobia: in COVID-19 responses, 250; disease surveillance systems, 10; early quarantine measures and, 66–67, 68; signification of difference, 19–20, 24–26, 29–33, 76–78; US sanitation practices, 136–41, *138, 139, 140. See also* exceptionalism, European and Western; racism

yellow fever: differences in epidemic response, 64–65, 135–36; early efforts at disease governance, 62; epidemic Orientalism in regulation of, 30, 32; eradication campaigns, 137, 141–42; exclusion from PHEIC designation, 199, 211–12; final International Sanitary Convention, 148–51; focus of first International Sanitary Conference, 73; in global health research, 9; LNHO conference for social medicine, 144; non-Western disease risk, 61; pesticide spraying for, 184; primacy as quarantinable disease, 4–6, *5,* 61, 157, 166–67, 172

Zelizer, Viviana, 245
Zika virus: in global health research, 9; under IHR (2005), 173; pesticide spraying for, 184; PHEIC designation, 199, *201,* 217; WHO management of, 203
Zuid Afrikaan newspaper, 125

CPSIA information can be obtained
at www.ICGtesting.com
Printed in the USA
JSHW051343231122
33639JS00002B/2

9 781503 634121